# Research Developments in World Englishes

# BLOOMSBURY ADVANCES IN WORLD ENGLISHES

**Series Editor:**
Alexander Onysko, University of Klagenfurt, Austria

**Advisory Board:**
Umberto Ansaldo (Curtin University, Australia)
Suzanne Hilgendorf (Simon Fraser University, Canada)
Allan James (University of Klagenfurt, Austria)
Andrew Kirkpatrick (Griffith University, Australia)
Lisa Lim (Curtin University, Australia)
Christiane Meierkord (University of Bochum, Germany)
Salikoko Mufwene (University of Chicago, USA)
Alastair Pennycook (University of Technology Sydney, Australia)
Mario Saraceni (University of Portsmouth, UK)
Philip Seargeant (The Open University, UK)
Peter Siemund (University of Hamburg, Germany)
Bertus Van Rooy (University of Amsterdam, The Netherlands)
Lionel Wee (National University of Singapore)

Capturing the intense interest in research on Englishes worldwide, *Bloomsbury Advances in World Englishes* promotes approaches to the complexities of world Englishes from a multitude of linguistic perspectives. Responding to recent trends in socio-cognitive, critical sociolinguistic, contact linguistic and communication-based research, books in this series investigate the interactions of Englishes with other languages and add new theoretical, methodological and applied perspectives to the field.

*Bloomsbury Advances in World Englishes* adopts an inclusive understanding of world Englishes and their interactions, which considers all dialects of English, Englishes in multilingual constellations, English-based pidgins and creoles, learner Englishes and the global spread of English as significant manifestations of Englishes in the world. Encouraging methodological and theoretical pluralism, encompassing sociolinguistics, cognitive and psycholinguistics, anthropological linguistics, historical linguistics, pragmatics, literary-linguistics and discourse analysis, this series offers an innovative insight into the manifold instantiations and usages of Englishes in the world.

**Forthcoming Titles in the Series:**
*Research Developments in World Englishes* (inaugural volume),
edited by Alexander Onysko
*Metaphor in Language and Culture across World Englishes*,
edited by Marcus Callies and Marta Degani
*The Societal Codification of Korean English*, Alex Baratta

# Research Developments in World Englishes

Edited by Alexander Onysko

BLOOMSBURY ACADEMIC
LONDON • NEW YORK • OXFORD • NEW DELHI • SYDNEY

BLOOMSBURY ACADEMIC
Bloomsbury Publishing Plc
50 Bedford Square, London, WC1B 3DP, UK
1385 Broadway, New York, NY 10018, USA
29 Earlsfort Terrace, Dublin 2, Ireland

BLOOMSBURY, BLOOMSBURY ACADEMIC and the Diana logo are trademarks of
Bloomsbury Publishing Plc

First published in Great Britain 2021
Paperback edition published in 2023

Copyright © Alexander Onysko and Contributors, 2021

Alexander Onysko has asserted his right under the Copyright, Designs and Patents Act, 1988, to be identified as Editor of this work.

For legal purposes the Acknowledgments on p. xiv constitute an extension of this copyright page.

Series design by Rebecca Heselton

This work is published open access subject to a Creative Commons Attribution-NonCommercial-NoDerivatives 3.0 licence (CC BY-NC-ND 3.0, https://creativecommons.org/licenses/by-nc-nd/3.0/). You may re-use, distribute, and reproduce this work in any medium for non-commercial purposes, provided you give attribution to the copyright holder and the publisher and provide a link to the Creative Commons licence.

Bloomsbury Publishing Plc does not have any control over, or responsibility for, any third-party websites referred to or in this book. All internet addresses given in this book were correct at the time of going to press. The author and publisher regret any inconvenience caused if addresses have changed or sites have ceased to exist, but can accept no responsibility for any such changes.

A catalog record for this book is available from the British Library.

Library of Congress Cataloging-in-Publication Data

Names: Onysko, Alexander, editor.
Title: Research developments in world Englishes / edited by Alexander Onysko.
Description: London ; New York : Bloomsbury Academic, 2021. | Series: Bloomsbury advances in world Englishes | Includes bibliographical references and index. |
Identifiers: LCCN 2021000363 (print) | LCCN 2021000364 (ebook) |
ISBN 9781350167056 (hardback) | ISBN 9781350167063 (ebook) |
ISBN 9781350167070 (epub)
Subjects: LCSH: English language–Foreign countries. | English language–English speaking countries. | English language–Variation–Foreign countries. | English language–Globalization–Foreign countries. | English language–Social aspects–Foreign countries. | English language–Study and teaching–Foreign countries.
Classification: LCC PE2751 .R45 2021  (print) | LCC PE2751  (ebook) | DDC 428.0071—dc23
LC record available at https://lccn.loc.gov/2021000363
LC ebook record available at https://lccn.loc.gov/2021000364

ISBN:  HB:   978-1-3501-6705-6
       PB:   978-1-3502-4959-2
       ePDF: 978-1-3501-6706-3
       eBook: 978-1-3501-6707-0

Series: Bloomsbury Advances in World Englishes

Typeset by RefineCatch Limited, Bungay, Suffolk

To find out more about our authors and books visit www.bloomsbury.com
and sign up for our newsletters.

# Contents

List of Figures — vii
List of Tables — ix
List of Contributors — x
Acknowledgments — xiv

1  Where are WEs Heading to? An Introduction to the Inaugural Volume of *Bloomsbury Advances in World Englishes*
   Alexander Onysko — 1

2  Decolonizing (World) Englishes
   Mario Saraceni and Camille Jacob — 11

3  "The Communicative Event" in International English(es) as Social Practice: Adducing a Tricodal/Trimodal Theory of the Linguistic Structuring of Social Meaning
   Allan James — 29

4  Extending the Scope of World Englishes: Interactions across Englishes in Post-Protectorates and at the Grassroots
   Christiane Meierkord — 47

5  Contact, Asia, and the Rethinking of Englishes in Multilingual Ecologies
   Lisa Lim and Umberto Ansaldo — 73

6  Multilingualism and the Role of English in the United Arab Emirates, with views from Singapore and Hong Kong
   Peter Siemund, Ahmad Al-Issa, Sharareh Rahbari and Jakob R. E. Leimgruber — 95

7  The History of English Language Attitudes within the Multilingual Ecology of South Africa
   Susan Coetzee-Van Rooy and Bertus Van Rooy — 121

8  Transnational Dialect Contact and Language Variation and Change in World Englishes
   Rebecca Lurie Starr — 149

9  "I Don't Get It": Researching the Cultural Lexicon of Global Englishes
   David Crystal — 173

10 Colonial Cultural Conceptualizations and World Englishes
   Frank Polzenhagen, Anna Finzel and Hans-Georg Wolf — 199

11　Individual Lives in Collectivist Faces: On Social Norms in a Radio Show
　　*Eric A. Anchimbe* 231
12　Teaching (About) World Englishes and English as a Lingua Franca
　　*Andy Kirkpatrick* 251
13　Documenting World Englishes in the *Oxford English Dictionary*: Past Perspectives, Present Developments, and Future Directions
　　*Danica Salazar* 271

Index 295

# Figures

| | | |
|---|---|---|
| 6.1 | Number of languages declared, by citizenship | 101 |
| 6.2 | Languages used by citizenship | 102 |
| 6.3 | Mean proficiency rating for English and Arabic | 102 |
| 6.4 | Self-reported proficiency in English and Arabic, by citizenship | 103 |
| 6.5 | Most frequent language combinations, by citizenship | 104 |
| 6.6 | Selected attitudes towards Arabic | 105 |
| 6.7 | Selected attitudes towards English | 106 |
| 6.8 | Home language use in Singapore (data from Wong 2011; Siemund et al. 2014; Leimgruber et al. 2018; Cavallaro and Ng 2021; Singapore Department of Statistics) | 112 |
| 6.9 | Usual spoken language, percent (population aged 5 or older), without Cantonese (Census and Statistics Department: Items A107, censuses and by-censuses 1991–2016; reproduced and adapted from Fuchs 2021: 297) | 113 |
| 6.10 | Differences in home language use according to age in thousand (Singapore Department of Statistics, General Household Survey 2015) | 113 |
| 6.11 | Language combinations among university, polytechnic, and vocational training (ITE) students that occur at least five times (Leimgruber, Siemund and Terassa 2018: 293) | 114 |
| 6.12 | Differences in home language use (own data, total in percent) | 115 |
| 13.1 | Murray's model of the English lexicon (1884) | 273 |
| 13.2 | Entry for *abaca*, n. in the *First Fascicle of A New English Dictionary on Historical Principles* (1884, 5) | 274 |
| 13.3 | *Oxford English Dictionary (OED)* 3 definition for *calamansi*, n., first published in 2018 | 281 |
| 13.4 | OED3 definition for *HDB*, n., first published in 2016 | 281 |
| 13.5 | IPA transcriptions and audio pronunciations for the South African entry *skedonk*, n., in British English, American English, and South African English | 282 |

| | | |
|---|---|---|
| 13.6 | OED entry for *buka*, n. | 282 |
| 13.7 | Extract from *OED* entry for *kilig*, adj. and n. | 283 |
| 13.8 | *OED* entry for *jeepney*, n. | 284 |
| 13.9 | Extract from *OED* entry for *sisig*, n. | 284 |
| 13.10 | Extract from *OED* entry for *pulutan*, n. | 285 |
| 13.11 a/b | Advanced Search results for words from Indian subcontinent languages in the *OED* (11a) / Advanced Search results for words from Indian subcontinent languages in the *OED*, limited to the subject category religion and belief | 286 |
| 13.12 a/b | Advanced Search results for words from African languages in the *OED* (12a) / Advanced Search results for words from the Caribbean in the *OED* (12b) | 287 |
| 13.13 | *OED* Timeline graph for words originating in Niger-Congo languages | 288 |
| 13.14 | *OED* entry for *comfort room*, n. | 289 |
| 13.15 | Extract from *OED* entry for *chaudhuri*, n. | 290 |
| 13.16 | *OED* Text Visualizer graph for an excerpt from Sarong Party Girls (Tan 2016) | 290 |

# Tables

| | | |
|---|---|---|
| 3.1 | Categories of Analysis | 33 |
| 3.2 | Corollaries of the Categories of Analysis | 34 |
| 3.3 | Codes/Modes and Contact Phenotypes | 37 |
| 4.1 | Uses of English in Former Protectorates, Protected States, League of Nations (LoN) Mandates and United Nations (UN) Trust Territories under Inner Circle Countries' Rule | 63 |
| 6.1 | Citizenship and Gender | 100 |
| 7.1 | Codebook for the Analysis of Attitudes towards English People and the English Language in the Historic Black South African English Corpus | 140 |
| 9.1 | The Domain of EARTH SCIENCE Exemplified | 180 |
| 9.2 | US-specific Cultural Symbols in the Domain of NATURAL HISTORY | 181 |
| 12.1 | Knowledge of English in Expanding Circle Asian Societies | 263 |
| 12.2 | Knowledge of English in Outer Circle Asian societies | 263 |
| 13.1 | Examples of World Englishes words recently added to the *OED*, created using different processes of word formation | 278 |
| 13.2 | Examples of World Englishes words recently added to the *OED* from different culturally specific semantic fields | 279 |
| 13.3 | List of Varieties of English for which the *OED* has a Pronunciation Model (as of July 2020) | 281 |

# Contributors

**Ahmad Al-Issa** is a Professor of English Linguistics at the American University of Sharjah in the United Arab Emirates. He is also an Associate Dean of the College of Arts and Sciences. His research interests are in the areas of sociolinguistics, intercultural communication, language and identity, global English, pragmatics, language planning and language policy. He is a member of many international organizations and a recipient of several international research grants. He has published many articles and book chapters, and presented papers and workshops in many parts of the world.

**Eric A. Anchimbe** is an Associate Professor of English Linguistics at the University of Bayreuth, Germany. His main research interests are in pragmatics (with a focus on postcolonial pragmatics), sociolinguistics, World Englishes, and political discourse. Among his publications are the monographs, *Offers and Offer Refusals: A Postcolonial Pragmatics Perspective on World Englishes* (2018) and *Language Policy and Identity Construction* (2013). He is the editor of *Structural and Sociolinguistic Perspectives on Indigenisation* (2015), *Language Contact in a Postcolonial Setting* (2012), and *Postcolonial Linguistic Voices* (2011, with Stephen A. Mforteh).

**Umberto Ansaldo** is Head of the School of Media, Creative Arts, and Social Inquiry at Curtin University. His research interests include language contact—in particular pidgin and creole studies, and linguistic typology of East, South, and Southeast Asia. Before going to Perth, Umberto held positions in Singapore, Amsterdam, Hong Kong, and Sydney.

**Susan Coetzee-Van Rooy** After twenty-one years in academic management Susan returned to her position as research professor in UPSET from January 1, 2019. UPSET is a linguistic research group at the NWU that is interested in the *Understanding and Processing of Language in Complex Settings*. In UPSET, Susan specializes in macro-sociolinguistics and the sociology of language, and she currently focuses on issues related to the multilingual repertoires of people and how these link to language learning, language in education policies, language and identity, and language and social cohesion. She uses larger scale language surveys, language history interviews, language portraits, and social networks in her mostly mixed methods studies.

**David Crystal** is Honorary Professor of Linguistics at the University of Bangor and works from his home in Holyhead, North Wales, as a writer, editor, lecturer, and broadcaster. He has authored and edited more than a hundred books and much of his work deals with the English language and its varieties. Among his publications are *The Cambridge Encyclopedia of the English Language* (3rd edn., 2018), *English as a Global Language* (1997), *The English Language* (2nd edn., 2002), *The Stories of English* (2004),

*Internet Linguistics* (2011), and, most recently, *Let's Talk: How English Conversation Works* (2020).

**Anna Finzel** holds a teaching and research position at the Department of English and American Studies at the University of Potsdam, Germany. Her research interests include the study of World Englishes, cognitive sociolinguistics, cultural linguistics, corpus linguistics, multimodality, and questions circling around gender and language.

**Camille Jacob** is a Postdoctoral Fellow at the University of Portsmouth working on discourses and practices of English in Northwest Africa. She is particularly interested in how the politics of language at the global level interact with local and national understandings of decolonization, identities, security, and "development" in countries historically considered as "French-speaking."

**Allan James** is Emeritus Professor of English Linguistics at the University of Klagenfurt, having held previous positions at the Universities of Tübingen, Nairobi and Amsterdam. His main research interests are in the sociolinguistics of international Englishes, literary linguistics, Celtic and English in contact (especially with reference to Welsh Studies), English prosody, second language phonology and pronunciation teaching, and has published widely on these areas. He serves on the editorial board of a number of international journals and book series in linguistics and English Studies and is a Fellow of the Netherlands Institute for Advanced Study, Royal Netherlands Academy of Sciences.

**Andy Kirkpatrick** is Professor in Linguistics at Griffith University and a Fellow of the Australian Academy of the Humanities. He has lived and worked in many countries in East and Southeast Asia, including China, Hong Kong, Malaysia, Myanmar, and Singapore. His research interests include the development of new varieties of English in Asia and the roles of English as a lingua franca in the region, language education policy in Asia and Chinese Rhetoric. The second edition of the *Routledge Handbook of World Englishes* which he edited will be published in 2021. His most recent book is *Is English an Asian Language?* (2021).

**Jakob R. E. Leimgruber** is currently Lecturer at the University of Basel (Switzerland) and Substitute Professor at the University of Freiburg (Germany). His research focuses on world Englishes, sociolinguistics (including language planning and policy, globalization, indexicality), and English in multilingual contexts. He is the author of *Singapore English: Structure, Variation, and Usage* (2013), *Language Planning and Policy in Quebec: A Comparative Perspective* (2019), and, with Peter Siemund, is editor of *Multilingual Global Cities: Singapore, Hong Kong, Dubai* (2021).

**Lisa Lim** is Associate Professor in the School of Education at Curtin University in Perth, having held positions in Singapore, Amsterdam, Hong Kong, and Sydney. Her interests center around New Englishes, especially Asian contact varieties in multilingual, postcolonial ecologies; issues of language shift, endangerment, and postvernacular vitality in minority and endangered language communities, such as the Peranakans of

Singapore and the Malays of Sri Lanka; and the sociolinguistics of globalization, with attention to mobility, computer-mediated communication, and urban linguistic diversity, and their impact on contact dynamics. She writes a fortnightly "Language Matters" column for Hong Kong's *South China Morning Post*'s *Sunday Post Magazine* https://www.scmp.com/author/lisa-lim.

**Christiane Meierkord** holds the Chair of English Linguistics at the Ruhr-University of Bochum. She is author of *Interactions across Englishes: Linguistic Choices in Local and International Contact Situations* (2012) and has published extensively on the use of English as a lingua franca. She has also edited *Ugandan English. Its Sociolinguistics, Structure and Uses in a Globalising Post-Protectorate* (2016), with Bebwa Isingoma and Saudah Namyalo, and *World Englishes at the Grassroots* (2021), with Edgar Schneider. Her recent research focuses on the forms and functions of English in post-protectorates and on the current spread of English at the grassroots of societies.

**Alexander Onysko** is Professor in English Linguistics at the University of Klagenfurt. His main research interests and publications are in the areas of World Englishes, Language Contact, Bi/Multilingualism, and Cognitive Linguistics. He is the editor of the series *Bloomsbury Advances in World Englishes* and some of his recent publications include *Language Contact and World Englishes* (2016), *Metaphor Variation in Englishes Around the World* (2017, with Marcus Callies), "Processes of language contact in English influence on German" (2019), and "Reconceptualizing language contact phenomena as cognitive processes" (2019).

**Frank Polzenhagen** is Chair Professor for English Linguistics at the University of Koblenz-Landau (Campus Landau), Germany. He received his PhD from Humboldt-University Berlin (2005) and his *habilitation* from Heidelberg University (2014). Much of his work has been devoted to the study of second-language varieties of English from a cognitive-sociolinguistic and cultural-linguistic perspective. His publications in this field include *Cultural Conceptualisations in West African English* (2007) and *World Englishes: A Cognitive Sociolinguistic Approach* (2009, with Hans-Georg Wolf). Closely related is his work on the lexicographic description of these varieties. He is co-editor of *A Dictionary of Indian English* (2017), and a comprehensive dictionary of West African English is in preparation (with Hans-Georg Wolf and Lothar Peter).

**Sharareh Rahbari** is a PhD student in English Linguistics at the University of Hamburg. She completed her undergraduate studies "Language, Culture & Translation" at the Johannes Gutenberg University Mainz and attained her master's degree in English and American Studies at the University of Hamburg. Her research interests lie in the area of second and third language acquisition, multilingualism, English as a foreign language, language contact, and cross-linguistic influence.

**Bertus Van Rooy** is Professor of English at the University of Amsterdam, and Extraordinary Professor at North-West University, South Africa. His interests in World Englishes include grammatical variation, language change, and the development and acceptance of new grammatical features in varieties of English. He is a past president of the International Association of World Englishes.

**Danica Salazar** is World English Editor for Oxford Languages, where she oversees policy, procedures, and strategy for world varieties of English, as well as researches and writes entries for the *Oxford English Dictionary*. She publishes and lectures regularly on lexicography, phraseology, World Englishes, and Spanish- and English-language teaching. Dr Salazar is the author of *Lexical Bundles in Native and Non-native Scientific Writing* (2014), co-editor of *Biomedical English: A Corpus-based Approach* (2013), and co-author of several language textbooks for learners of Spanish.

**Mario Saraceni** is Reader in English Language and Linguistics in the School of Languages and Applied Linguistics at the University of Portsmouth. His main research interests revolve around political and ideological understandings of English, particularly in contexts where it coexists and blends with other languages. In recent years he has become interested in the ways in which the English language is caught up within the process of decolonization in former British colonies. Mario has published extensively in these areas.

**Peter Siemund** is Professor and Chair of English Linguistics at the University of Hamburg. His areas of interest include World Englishes, the use of English as an additional language, and multilingual development. His publications include, as author, *Pronominal Gender in English: A Study of English Varieties from a Cross-Linguistic Perspective* (2008), *The Amazing World of Englishes: A Practical Introduction* (with Julia Davydova and Georg Maier, 2012), *Varieties of English: A Typological Approach* (2013), and *Speech Acts and Clause Types: English in a Cross-Linguistic Context* (2018), and, as editor, *Language Contact and Contact Languages* (with Noemi Kintana, 2008), *Linguistic Universals and Language Variation* (2011), *Foreign Language Education in Multilingual Classrooms* (with Andreas Bonnet, 2018), and *Multilingual Global Cities: Singapore, Hong Kong, Dubai* (with Jakob Leimgruber, 2021).

**Rebecca Lurie Starr** is an Associate Professor in the Department of English Language and Literature at the National University of Singapore. She received her PhD in Linguistics with a designation in Cognitive Science in 2012 from Stanford University. Her research focuses on language variation and change in multilingual and multidialectal settings, children's sociolinguistic development, and the sociolinguistic construction of style. Her work has been published in *Language in Society, Journal of Sociolinguistics, Language Variation and Change,* and *World Englishes,* among others. Her book, *Sociolinguistic Variation and Acquisition in Two-Way Language Immersion: Negotiating the Standard*, was published in 2017.

**Hans-Georg Wolf** is Chair Professor of The Development and Variation of the English Language at the University of Potsdam, Germany. His research interests include Cognitive Sociolinguistics (in particular World Englishes), Cultural Linguistics, lexicography, and intercultural pragmatics.

# Acknowledgments

The open access publication of this volume is financed by three different funding bodies at the University of Klagenfurt, Austria: the Open Access Fund, the Research Council and the Faculty of Humanities. All the support is gratefully acknowledged.

1

# Where are WEs Heading to?

## An Introduction to the Inaugural Volume of *Bloomsbury Advances in World Englishes*

Alexander Onysko

## 1. World Englishes and Varieties of English

Research in World Englishes[1] (WEs) has come a long way since its beginnings in the 1980s when the conceptual ground was laid for addressing the plurality of Englishes, with the aim of moving away from a monolithic conception of English and its ideological and attitudinal implications expressed in terms such as Standard vs. Non-Standard Englishes. Early work in the field (e.g., Strevens 1978) emphasized a common source English that diversified across the world into different varieties as part of the British Empire's colonial extensions and trade. This "varieties of the same language" point of view is also upheld in other early models of Englishes such as Görlach's (1988) Circle Model of English and McArthur's (1987) Circle of World English (note the singular in each of the names).

At the same time, Braj Kachru, who was the major founding figure of the World Englishes paradigm, introduced the conceptual leap of pluralizing English to emphasize an egalitarian approach towards Englishes as fully emancipated and appropriated codes in their diverse social and geographical localities around the world. He modelled this plurality in the Three Circles Model (1985), which, despite relevant criticism (e.g., Bruthiaux 2003; also cf., Deshors 2018 for a recent overview), still remains a firm reference point for many studies in the field today.

In line with these two conceptualizations of English/es as plurality within (i.e., varieties of English) vs. plurality among separate entities (i.e., world Englishes), a rich body of research developed supported by findings in both strands. The two-tiered perspective is also evident in the names of the two leading journals in the field, *English World-Wide* (Benjamins) and *World Englishes* (Wiley-Blackwell), which published their first issues in 1980 and 1981, respectively. Despite this conceptually different approach to the notion of English/es, work on varieties of English and Englishes has often been driven by similar concerns and some scholars in the field have been operating on both tiers as a look at the editorial and advisory boards of both journals and at the editorships of major handbooks in the field shows. Yet a slight tendency can be discerned in that research on varieties of English has tended to focus on feature-based analyses of Englishes, which is grounded in traditions of dialectology, language typology, and variationist sociolinguistics. This is exemplified in major works such as the *Handbook of Varieties of English* (vol.1/2, Kortmann and Schneider 2004) and in the two volumes on "Lesser-Known Varieties of English" (Schreier et al. 2010; Williams et al. 2015). By contrast, research in the framework of World Englishes has traditionally been concerned more with the larger socio-political and ideological implications of Englishes co-existing and influencing other languages, as well as with the application of diverse linguistic frameworks in the analysis of Englishes as exemplified in the *Handbook of World Englishes* (B. B. Kachru, Y. Kachru, Nelson 2006). In one of his contributions to this handbook, Bolton (2006) highlights the various sub-disciplines within linguistics that inform research into world Englishes such as applied linguistics, sociolinguistics, English studies, lexicography, and critical linguistics.

When considering more recent major publications in the field, there are signs that the Varieties of English and World Englishes strands have been converging more strongly and that the pluralized conception of Englishes has become foregrounded, at least as a label for research in the field. Thus, the *Routledge Handbook of World Englishes* (Kirkpatrick 2010, second edition fthc. in 2021), the *Oxford Handbook of World Englishes* (Filppula, Klemola and Sharma 2017), and the *Cambridge Handbook of World Englishes* (Schreier, Hundt and Schneider 2020), all adopt "World Englishes" as a name while altogether providing a mixture of articles that address historical issues, reflect on the relation of linguistic approaches to the study of world Englishes and provide areal overviews and case studies of individual Englishes. The three-volume set on *World Englishes* by Hopkins, Decker and McKenny (2017) is the most pronounced example of a handbook type of publication that provides close descriptions of varieties of English using the label of World Englishes. The forthcoming three volumes on *World Englishes* (Saraceni et al.) entitled *Paradigms* (vol. 1), *Ideologies* (vol. 2) and *Pedagogies* (vol. 3), on the other hand, tackle current issues in the use of Englishes around the world by means of exploring recent linguistic approaches to world Englishes such as translanguaging, by reflecting on various ideological ramifications, and by critically discussing the roles of Englishes in educational contexts.

Further signs of convergence between World Englishes and Varieties of English can be gleaned from the titles of the longstanding book series *Varieties of English Around the World* (Benjamins). While the series started publishing in 1979, the term "World Englishes" appeared for the first time in the title of an edited volume in 2009, but now four among the seven most recent books of the series state "World Englishes" in their titles.

Other book series that provide focused outlets for studies on Englishes are *Dialects of English* (De Gruyter), which specializes in giving accessible descriptions of varieties of English following the tradition of feature-based phonological, morphosyntactic and lexical characterizations of individual Englishes in their socio-historical contexts, and the fairly recent *Routledge Studies in World Englishes*. With the first volume published in 2015, this series has so far exhibited a focus on Englishes in Asia and is more strongly couched in the World Englishes tradition (cf., the volume by Low and Pakir 2017) even though one of the latest titles, *The Shetland Dialect*, falls in line with a varieties of English approach to the documentation of Englishes (Sundkvist 2020).

Judging from the publications and major outlets of research on Englishes discussed here, which merely scratches the surface of a rich, vibrant, and evolving field of study (cf., e.g., *English Today* and *Asian Englishes* as further dedicated journals), it appears that the terminological and by extension conceptual pendulum is moving towards the World Englishes end, also in the sense that research which is situated in a Varieties of English framework tends to become labelled as World Englishes. The same holds true for studies on English as an international language or lingua franca. While investigating the use of English as an international medium of communication has given rise to an English as a Lingua Franca (ELF) strand which is manifest in a separate journal and book series, outlets on World Englishes have also continued to incorporate studies on the function of English as a lingua franca (cf., Meierkord 2012 and see contributions in the *Oxford* and *Routledge Handbook of World Englishes* as well as Saraceni et al., fthc., vol. 3 to name just a few). The inclusion of ELF among the uses and instantiations of Englishes across the world also follows from a theoretical perspective when adopting language contact as an underlying criterion of describing world Englishes (Onysko 2016).

Besides some more recent convergence between the two rooted perspectives on the plurality of Englishes, the field of World Englishes (in an inclusive sense as being concerned with all uses and manifestations of English around the world), has been shaped by the world's social, political, economic, and technological developments, in particular from the beginning of the new millennium onwards. Captured in keywords such as globalization, superdiversity, and digitalization, researchers have started to highlight the role of increasing mobility and interconnectedness, leading to changing communicative habits, and moving away from geolinguistic conceptions of languages towards codes based on fluid and truncated, often multilingual repertoires (e.g., Blommaert 2010). Similarly, Pennycook's (2007) observation on global Englishes, i.e., the use of English as part of globalization processes, critically contests the idea of Englishes as nation states or geographically confined entities:

> Thus, while drawing on the useful pluralization strategy of world Englishes, I prefer to locate these Englishes within a more complex vision of globalization. This view seeks to understand the role of English both critically—in terms of new forms of power, control and destruction—and in its complexity—in terms of new forms of resistance, change, appropriation and identity. It suggests that we need to move beyond arguments about homogeneity or heterogeneity, or imperialism and nation states, and instead focus on translocal and transcultural flows. English is a translocal language, a language of fluidity and fixity that moves across, while becoming embedded in, the materiality of localities and social relations. English is bound up with transcultural flows, a language of imagined communities and refashioning identities.
>
> Pennycook 2007: 5–6

In line with that and similar views, the relation between Englishes and globalization has raised continued interest (e.g., Saxena and Omoniyi 2010) and has fostered the emergence of studies focusing on phenomena such as translanguaging (e.g., J. W. Lee 2018; contributions in Jenks and J. W. Lee 2020), metrolingualism (Pennycook and Otsuji 2015) and a concern with studying the use of English in digital spaces (e.g., contributions in J. S. Lee 2020; Mair 2020) as well as in linguistic landscapes (e.g., contributions in Bolton 2012). Apart from Pennycook's and Blommaert's paradigm shifts in sociolinguistics, Benor's notion of the ethnolinguistic repertoire as a "fluid set of resources that members of an ethnic group may use variably to index their ethnic identities" (2010: 160), is a sign that the domain of variationist sociolinguistics is also drifting away from essentialist categorizations of speaker groups by variety type (cf., D'Arcy 2020 for recent discussion).

Considering the historically rooted approaches to researching world Englishes in contrast to the more recent developments that defy the reification of codes as Englishes, one can arrive at the conclusion that research on Englishes around the world has reached an "impasse" as Saraceni (2015: 3) aptly observes. Ultimately grounded in our human conceptual system and the ability to shift our perceptual attention, this impasse or dilemma can actually be conceived as being two-fold. On the one hand, if we zoom in on individual uses of Englishes, we can gain a detailed view of the complex interactions of codes in a speaker's repertoire and the multiple external and internal factors that influence linguistic output in context. However, this kind of zooming in limits the ability to generate knowledge via categorizing perceived similarities and patterns across speaker communities. On the other hand, if we zoom out, i.e., if we abstract away from individual language use towards the level of communities, we are able to establish similarities and patterns shared across speakers. At the same time, however, this makes us prone to run into the essentialist trap of reifying codes according to external criteria (e.g., ethnicity, social class, gender, geographical areas or socio-political entities such as nation states). Reflecting this back onto research on Englishes in the world, the dilemma can be portrayed as a tug of war between our cognitive capacities of focusing our attention on details at a moment in time (i.e., processing rich perceptual input) and of categorizing our perceptual input via the conception of similarities over repeated input. While the latter bears the danger of overgeneralization and the construction of essentialist categories of Englishes that do not (or only to a very limited extent) portray realities of English use, the former is not sufficient to build up knowledge (i.e., categories) that persist and generate larger insight in the field. If researchers are aware of that, the dilemma can actually turn into a strength and a way forward for research on world Englishes (in the inclusive sense). Thus, it will be the task of future research to strike the right balance between the two forces and, being conscious of the inherent limitations and strengths of each capacity, generate informed insights into the complexities of Englishes in their different contexts of use and on their diverse instantiations in (groups of) speakers and localities (be they areal or virtual).

## 2. Ways Forward for WEs

If investigations are conducted coherent with these different perspectival affordances, there are many ways in which research on world Englishes can move forward in the future. The question then is not so much which approach, paradigm, or model to follow or to discover, but rather how to use or develop ideas so that novel insights can be generated which are cogent with the situation that is studied. For that, it is also crucial that researchers remain critically conscious about the scope of their findings and interpretations. Just as the uses of Englishes in the world are highly versatile, diverse approaches to this complex subject area will lead to more insights and synergic knowledge in the field.

When looking at the plethora of research dealing with Englishes in some form or other, certain areas of concern can be identified that have been driving world Englishes research forward, drawing on methods and approaches of diverse linguistic disciplines. These concerns can be captured in a range of questions that address different aspects of the role, status and uses of Englishes in the world:

- How can the complexities of Englishes in the world be understood and theoretically modelled?
- By which means can the existence of Englishes be determined in relation to their users and what are the limits of approaches that try to label Englishes according to shared features across user groups?
- What are the social and psychological effects that Englishes have on speakers that also master other, particularly smaller languages?
- How do Englishes influence other codes and how do they interact with other codes in the multilingual repertoires of their speakers?
- What is the role of Englishes in globalizing processes?
- In which ways do Englishes function as purveyors of culturally grounded ideas, interactional modes and knowledge in different cultural contexts?
- How can the diversity of ideas and concepts in the word stocks of Englishes be documented?
- Why do we continue to teach certain standard varieties of English when the world is speaking and using Englishes differently?
- How do Englishes function in international communication?
- In which ways are the representations of Englishes shaped by different modes and media?

These questions address both some of the ongoing but longstanding and some of the more recent concerns in the field such as finding adequate theoretical models of Englishes, the feature-based, sociolinguistic description and labelling of Englishes, the relation of Englishes to speaker attitudes and identities, the relationship of Englishes and local cultures, Englishes in the new media, standard varieties and the teaching of Englishes, language policy and planning involving Englishes, the lexicographical description of Englishes, and Englishes in relation to globalization, multilingualism, translingualism and language contact.

It is the intention of the book series to provide a platform for innovative research in all these areas. Adopting an inclusive understanding of Englishes as all manifestations and uses of (forms of) Englishes around the world and in line with the belief that new knowledge can be generated from theoretical pluralism and cross-disciplinary perspectives, the series encourages research that breaks new ground and pushes knowledge in the field forward.

## 3. Research Developments in World Englishes

The inaugural volume offers a first contribution to this endeavor by showcasing twelve chapters that explore various issues in line with the central questions posed above. Written by renowned and up and coming scholars in the field, the chapters provide a critical reflection on the research paradigm of World Englishes, postulate a novel and comprehensive model of understanding Englishes, investigate so far neglected localities of Englishes, delve into various multilingual ecologies where Englishes play an important part, take a close look at variation and contact between Englishes, give insight into the impact of English cultural conceptualizations on other cultures and the expression of cultural frames in the use of English, provide a perspective on how to avoid the stalemate of teaching world Englishes and English as a lingua franca, and propose ways of documenting the cultural meanings that characterize different Englishes across the globe.

In detail, the volume starts with a wake-up call for scholars working in the research paradigm of World Englishes. In "Decolonizing (World) Englishes," Mario Saraceni and Camille Jacob highlight the fact that while the World Englishes paradigm was from its very beginnings propelled by the notion of decolonization in the sense of approaching all Englishes as equal, that kind of equality has been reserved for an elite of intellectuals, writers and professionals using English but not for the diverse users of Englishes in their different cultural and social circumstances. To be true to the aspiration of equality, the authors outline a strategic framework of decolonization for future research on world Englishes, which aims at de-mythologizing, de-silencing, and de-colonizing Englishes.

An appropriate and comprehensive way of theorizing Englishes from a functional linguistic perspective, which—even if not explicitly intended—would work in a truly egalitarian framework as it steers clear of contextual factors, is proposed by Allan James in the next chapter. His tricodal/trimodal model of Englishes as social practice zooms in on the usage events of Englishes and provides a convincing matrix that captures the social events (in the sense of Fairclough 2006) of English in a threefold typology of social meaning ("identification," "representation," and "action" as modes) which is mapped onto three layers of linguistic substance (the lexicophonological, the lexicosemantic and the lexicogrammatical as codes). This model is a considerable step forward in the field as its focus on Englishes as social practice and events does not rely on notions of reified Englishes.

In chapter 4, "Extending the Scope of World Englishes: Interactions across Englishes in Post-Protectorates and at the Grassroots," Christiane Meierkord emphasizes that, nowadays, Englishes are to a large extent used in communication among speakers for whom English is one language among others. While this interactional perspective has been investigated to a good extent in research on English as lingua franca, Meierkord breaks new ground as she explores new interactional contexts in former protectorates, League of Nations mandates and United Nations trust territories. Taking the examples of the Maldives and Uganda, she discusses the status of English in these territories with a particular focus on Englishes at the grassroots, i.e., non-elitist uses and forms of Englishes. This is an important pathway for future research.

The interaction of Englishes with other languages in speaker's multilingual repertoires and in multilingual societies is at the center of the next three chapters. In "Contact, Asia, and the Rethinking of Englishes in Multilingual Ecologies" Lisa Lim and Umberto Ansaldo offer a rich and detailed account that traces the contact history of Englishes in several Asian non-settler exploitation colonies. The authors unveil new historical dynamics in the shaping of these Englishes, and they illustrate the important role of language typology in explaining substratal influences in Asian Englishes. This is convincingly discussed with the examples of the Sinitic language features of tone and particle use.

Peter Siemund, Ahmad Al-Issa, Sharareh Rahbari, and Jakob R. E. Leimgruber investigate the role of English in the United Arab Emirates (UAE) from a macro-sociolinguistic perspective and compare that to the situation of Englishes in Singapore and Hong Kong. Their contribution creates an insightful picture of the societal status of English in the UAE, which is supported by a large survey on speakers' multilingual repertoires and language attitudes. Comparable data on Singapore and Hong Kong allow the authors to carve out similarities and differences between the three multilingual localities where Englishes are widely used.

Language attitudes in a multilingual ecology are also at the core of Bertus Van Rooy and Susan Coetzee-Van Rooy's contribution. In contrast to the previous chapter, the authors take a look back into the history of language attitudes towards English, Afrikaans and other languages in South Africa. A fine analysis of historical documents in the corpus of Black South African English uncovers that the factors of political freedom, economic success and access to quality education outweigh the relevance of language attitudes in nineteenth-century South Africa.

The article by Rebecca Lurie Starr adds a crucial variationist sociolinguistic view for understanding internal variation within Englishes and dialect contact among Englishes, which bears the potential of triggering change in the use of Englishes. With the support of many examples, she makes the convincing case for how specific language features can index diverse social meanings. In addition, she discusses institutional exonormativity, transnational mobility, and media consumption as important sources of dialect contact.

In "'I Don't Get It': Researching the Cultural Lexicon of Global Englishes," David Crystal provides a refreshing take on the question of how we can understand and document the ever-more diversifying vocabularies of Englishes around the world. He puts forward an encyclopedic taxonomical approach which would result in a comprehensive and comparative record of culturally grounded terms across different Englishes. Recognizing the problem of metaphors for the taxonomical structuring of English lexica, David Crystal discusses the issue of metaphorical adaptations that occur as part of the evolving idiomatic use of Englishes in their diverse cultural contexts.

Metaphors and cultural conceptualizations are also central to Frank Polzenhagen, Anna Finzel, and Hans-Georg Wolf's study, which is an example of the still emerging strand of research in world Englishes that applies cognitive sociolinguistics, conceptual metaphor theory and cultural conceptualizations. The authors conduct a thorough investigation into how the British colonizers made sense of the socio-cultural realities in the colonies through their western conceptual lenses. Focusing on texts of the colonial history in India and Sub-Saharan Africa, the authors show the way in which "disturbing" social practices in the colonies were conceptualized by the colonizers and how their western interpretations led to interference in the colonial societies which has left lasting marks up to the present day.

The function of Englishes to express local cultural conventions is lucidly described in the chapter "Individual Lives in Collectivist Faces: On Social Norms in a Radio Show." Taking the case of Cameroon English, Eric Anchimbe applies the framework of postcolonial pragmatics to analyze exchanges between a radio host and young mothers which are put on air in a weekend prime time broadcast. His findings show how the collectivist cultural framing prevalent in Cameroonian society is instantiated on the discourse level and used to evaluate the different situations of the young mothers.

The chapter by Andy Kirkpatrick shifts the focus on another nagging question in the field of world Englishes: how can the prevalent practice of adhering to just a few standard varieties in the teaching of English world-wide be turned around and become aligned with the global reality of Englishes and the diverse needs for local and international communication across different Englishes-speaking communities? Starting with a reconsideration of Kachru's six fallacies in this regard, Andy Kirkpatrick provides a succinct account of the academic discourse that developed on this topic up to the present day, culminating in a compelling conclusion that provides a way forward for future efforts to put into practice the teaching of world Englishes and English as a lingua franca.

The volume closes with a detailed look at the most recent lexicographical developments concerning the major reference work of the English lexicon (note the singular conception here): the *Oxford English Dictionary*. Danica Salazar offers engaging insight into the latest developments of this dynamically evolving dictionary project, which, crucially, has recently set out to focus much more extensively on recording words from Englishes around the world. From a world Englishes point of view, this is certainly a much-needed evolution in line with the reality of Englishes used around the world. If this lexicographical acknowledgment of plurality is based on a true conceptual shift, we will in a few years' time perhaps speak of the *Oxford Dictionary of Englishes*.

As a whole, the different topics and perspectives covered in the inaugural volume of *Bloomsbury Advances in World Englishes* intend to hint at the manifold concerns and the diverse current developments in the field. This will hopefully be inspiring for future research on the complexities of Englishes around the world and bring to the fore many more informed voices that will propel our critical understanding and offer insights couched in a spirit of plurality and diversity.

## Notes

1  Please note that the volume adopts the spelling convention of capitalizing "World Englishes" when reference is made to the academic discipline and field of research. The spelling "world Englishes" refers to individual Englishes as such.

## References

Benor, S. B. (2010), "Ethnolinguistic repertoire: Shifting the analytic focus in language and ethnicity," *Journal of Sociolinguistics*, 14 (2): 159–83.

Blommaert, J. (2010), *The Sociolinguistics of Globalization*, Cambridge: Cambridge University Press.

Bolton, K. (2006), "World Englishes today," in B. B. Kachru, Y. Kachru and C. L. Nelson (eds.), *The Handbook of World Englishes*, 240–70, Malden, MA: Wiley-Blackwell.

Bolton, K., ed. (2012), "Symposium on world Englishes and linguistic landscapes: Five perspectives," *World Englishes*, 31 (1).

Bruthiaux, P. (2003), "Squaring the Circles: Issues in modeling English worldwide," *International Journal of Applied Linguistics*, 13 (2): 159–78.

D'Arcy, A. (2020), "The relevance of World Englishes for Variationist Sociolinguistics," in D. Schreier, M. Hundt and E. W. Schneider (eds.), *The Cambridge Handbook of World Englishes*, 436–58, Cambridge: Cambridge University Press.

Deshors, S. C. (2018), "Modeling World Englishes in the 21st century: A thematic introduction," in S. C. Deshors (ed.), *Modeling World Englishes: Assessing the Interplay of Emancipation and Globalization of ESL Varieties*, 1–14, Amsterdam: John Benjamins.

Fairclough, N. (2006), *Language and Globalization*, London: Routledge.

Filppula, M., J. Klemola and D. Sharma, eds. (2017), *The Oxford Handbook of World Englishes*, Oxford: Oxford University Press.

Görlach, M. (1988), "Sprachliche Standardisierungsprozesse im englischsprachigen Bereich," *Soziolinguistica* 2 (1): 131–85.

Hopkins, T., K. Decker and J. McKenny, eds. (2017), *World Englishes Volumes I-III Set Volume I: The British Isles Volume II: North America Volume III: Central America*, London: Bloomsbury.

Jenks, C. and J. W. Lee (2020), "Special Issue: World Englishes and Translanguaging," *World Englishes*, 39 (2).

Kachru, B. B. (1985), "Standards, codification and sociolinguistic realism: The English language in the Outer Circle," in R. Quirk and H. G. Widdowson (eds.), *English in the World: Teaching and Learning the Language and Literatures*, 11–30, Cambridge: Cambridge University Press.

Kachru, B. B., Y. Kachru and C. L. Nelson, eds. (2006), *The Handbook of World Englishes*, Malden, MA: Wiley-Blackwell.

Kirkpatrick, A., ed. (2010), *The Routledge Handbook of World Englishes*, first edition, London: Routledge.

Kirkpatrick, A., ed. (2021), *The Routledge Handbook of World Englishes*, second edition, London: Routledge.

Kortmann, B. and E. W. Schneider, eds., in collaboration with K. Burridge, R. Mesthrie and C. Upton (2004), *A Handbook of Varieties of English – A Multimedia Reference Tool, vol. 1: Phonology, vol. 2: Morphology and Syntax*, Berlin: De Gruyter.

Lee, J. S., ed. (2020), "Special Issue: World Englishes and Digital Media," *World Englishes*, 39 (1).

Lee, J. W. (2018), *The Politics of Translingualism: After Englishes*, New York: Routledge.

Low, E. L. and A. Pakir, eds. (2017), *World Englishes: Rethinking Paradigms*, London: Routledge.

Mair, C. (2020), "World Englishes in cyberspace," in D. Schreier, M. Hundt and E. W. Schneider (eds.), *The Cambridge Handbook of World Englishes*, 360–83, Cambridge: Cambridge University Press.

McArthur, T. (1987), "The English languages?," *English Today*, 3 (3): 9–13.

Meierkord, C. (2012), *Interactions Across Englishes: Linguistic Choices in Local and International Contact Situations*, Cambridge: Cambridge University Press.

Onysko, A. (2016), "Modeling world Englishes from the perspective of language contact," *World Englishes*, 35 (2): 196–220.

Pennycook, A. (2007), *Global Englishes and Transcultural Flows*, London: Routledge.

Pennycook, A. and E. Otsuji (2015), *Metrolingualism: Language in the City*, London: Routledge.

Saraceni, M. (2015), *World Englishes: A Critical Analysis*, London: Bloomsbury.

Saraceni, M., ed. (fthc.), *Bloomsbury World Englishes, vol. 1 Paradigms, vol. 2 Ideologies, vol. 3 Pedagogies*, London: Bloomsbury.

Saxena, M. and T. Omoniyi, eds. (2010), *Contending with Globalization in World Englishes*, Bristol: Multilingual Matters.

Schreier, D., P. Trudgill, E. W. Schneider and J. P. Williams, eds. (2010), *The Lesser-Known Varieties of English*, Cambridge: Cambridge University Press.

Schreier, D., M. Hundt and E. W. Schneider, eds. (2020), *The Cambridge Handbook of World Englishes*, Cambridge: Cambridge University Press.

Strevens, P. (1978), "English as an international language – When is a local form of English a suitable target or ELT purposes?," in The British Council (ed.), *English as an International Language*, 25–33. London: The British Council.

Sundkvist, P. (2020), *The Shetland Dialect*, London: Routledge.

Williams, J. P., E. W. Schneider, P. Trudgill and D. Schreier, eds. (2015), *Further Studies in the Lesser-Known Varieties of English*, Cambridge: Cambridge University Press.

# 2

# Decolonizing (World) Englishes

Mario Saraceni and Camille Jacob

## 1. Introduction

Even though decolonization was rarely mentioned explicitly, the academic field of World Englishes can be said to have been animated by a decolonizing "spirit," especially in its early stages decades ago. In the 1980s the work of Braj Kachru, S. N. and Kamal Sridhar, Edwin Thumboo, Ayo Bamgbose, Larry Smith, Peter Strevens, Peter Lowenberg, and many others had the goal of redressing the inherent inequality that existed between varieties of English in the Inner Circle and those in the Outer Circle. Such inequality had its roots in empire and colonization, and so the ambition to achieve equal Englishes was also the ambition to decolonize the language and its varieties. Key to this was the recognition of the plurality and validity of the forms and functions of English in such postcolonial countries as India, Singapore, Nigeria, Kenya and so on, and the consequent claims of "ownership" that people in those settings could make over the language. English, in all its localized forms, rightfully belonged to anybody who used it. This project, however, has received significant criticism over the years. On the one hand, those who see the expansion of English as a cause of linguistic imperialism have accused World Englishes scholars of providing a justification for the continuing dominance of English over other languages. On the other hand, a more recent critique has pointed out how the World Englishes egalitarian ethos actually reflects and is based on the aspirations of a rather restricted elite of creative writers and intellectuals who enjoyed the privilege not only of possessing a sophisticated mastery of the English language, but also of using that very mastery as the core of their profession. Consequently, the idea of World Englishes ends up being an illusion masking the reality that sees English very much entangled with severe forms of inequality that still exist in postcolonial societies. "Equal Englishes" is then a mere beautiful facade of what is, in effect, "unequal Englishes" (Tupas 2015). In this chapter we argue that World Englishes needs to engage with decolonization more in depth and in more complex ways and examine its subject matter and its research paradigms by adopting a "decolonial strategic framework" (Rutazibwa 2019) consisting of three aims: to de-mythologize (what is "English"?), to de-silence (which aspirations, struggles, lives are entangled with "English"?) and to de-colonize (how do we de-centralize the development of knowledge about "English"?).

## 2. The Meaning of Decolonization

In a panel discussion entitled "Understanding Decolonization in the 21st Century," organized by Chatham House on February 14, 2020, Tristram Hunt noted that "the origins of the Victoria and Albert Museum are embedded in the British imperial and colonial stories, and this is why I think to decolonize the V&A in many ways doesn't make sense because you can't" (Hunt 2020). Hunt, who is the director of the Victoria and Albert Museum (V&A), also remarked elsewhere that "for a museum like the V&A, to decolonize is to decontextualise: the history of empire is embedded in its meaning and collections" (Hunt 2019). He therefore rejects the notion of decolonizing the museum on the grounds that colonial history is too much an intrinsic part of it and cannot be dislodged from it. In response to Hunt's argument, Sumaya Kassim contends that this line of reasoning consists in sticking to "a script that continues to be rehearsed despite being resisted, debunked and complicated even as it is first documented" (Kassim 2019), and that perpetuates "a one-sided story" serving the interests of "colonial apologists."

The script that Kassim refers to is evident, too, in debates surrounding monuments of imperialists in public spaces. In 2015, the "Rhodes Must Fall" movement in South Africa advocated the removal of a statue of British imperialist and white supremacist Cecil Rhodes from the University of Cape Town, on the grounds that the values that Rhodes represented were completely incompatible with those of an educational setting and, in general, of post-Apartheid South Africa. The principles of the movement quickly expanded to other university campuses and other countries, including Britain, where a statue of Rhodes adorned Oriel College at Oxford University (Ahmed 2020). The controversy that ensued was similar to that about the decolonization of museums. Those who opposed the removal of the statue argued that "Rhodes cannot be expunged from the history of Oxford, Britain and South Africa" (Hutton 2015). Recent renewed calls for the removal of statues of slave traders from British towns in June 2020 have been met with the same argument. British Prime Minister Boris Johnson posted a comment on Twitter in which he said that "We cannot now try to edit or censor our past. We cannot pretend to have a different history" (June 12, 2020).

Those who maintain that history cannot be re-written tend to believe, more or less innocently, that it is simply a fixed sequence of events, and forget that how those events are (or not!) talked about in history books varies depending on who writes those books, from which perspective, what is emphasized and what is left out. The historiography of the British Empire offers perhaps one of the most striking pieces of evidence of the importance of history as narrative. While some scholars still tenaciously cling on to a romantic view of the empire as a benign force that helped spread civilization, democracy, and liberty around the world (see, for example, Ferguson 2003), others, less influenced by patriotic feelings, have not refrained from revealing the atrocities perpetuated by British imperialists. When the empire was coming to an end, the systematic destruction of archival documents relating to such atrocities is a very clear illustration of how history is manipulated for specific reasons (Elkins 2015). And, in fact, "interpretations of the past are shaped by the political demands of the present" (Vince, forthcoming), and the political demands of post-imperial and post-war Britain have produced a vignette in which the British empire civilized the world and, eventually, also saved it from the threat of the Third Reich.

Decolonization, then, is not about attempting to remove segments of history. On the contrary, it is about engaging with colonial history seriously, understanding how it determines many aspects of the present, and changing practices accordingly. So the removal of statues of dubious figures, like Cecil Rhodes or Edward Colston, a slave trader commemorated in the iconography and toponymy of Bristol should be regarded as something that "begins a conversation about how we are shaped by our past and that we are accountable for how it configures the present" (Bhambra 2020). From this perspective, decolonization is only a means, not a goal, towards a different system of relationships to others, to land, to knowledge (Cairns 2020).

These debates point to (1) the concept of decolonization as both event and process (Jansen and Osterhammel 2017), and (2) the continuation of uneven political, economic, epistemic, cultural, and social power relations that are the legacies of imperialism and colonialism. The former includes the acknowledgement that "the colonizers did not simply turn off the light and vanish into the night" (Jansen and Osterhammel 2017: 15) and that political, economic, cultural, and social relations between former colonies and the metropoles remained closely entangled even after the formal advent of independence. Decolonization is also the process of disentangling some of these relations, or at least questioning and reshaping them from the perspective of the former colonies. The second aspect is an extension of the first, the recognition of the coloniality of present modes of learning, using language, organizing a state, defining citizenship, and "continuity of colonial forms of domination after the end of colonial administrations, produced by colonial cultures and structures in the modern/colonial capitalist/patriarchal world-system" (Grosfoguel 2007: 219–20). Taking a decolonial approach thus means recognizing the entanglement, or intersectionality (after Crenshaw 1989) of multiple global and localized linguistic, racial, epistemic, political, economic, spiritual, and sexual hierarchies (Grosfoguel 2007: 217).

In conclusion, decolonization

> has two key referents. First, it is a way of thinking about the world which takes colonialism, empire and racism as its empirical and discursive objects of study; it re-situates these phenomena as key shaping forces of the contemporary world, in a context where their role has been systematically effaced from view. Second, it purports to offer alternative ways of thinking about the world and alternative forms of political praxis.
>
> Bhambra et al. 2018: 2

Having outlined our theoretical backdrop, in the rest of this chapter we discuss how the principle of decolonization applies to discourses about English and to the World Englishes academic field.

## 3. Decolonization and World Englishes

Paraphrasing Tristram Hunt's words above, the origins of English in the world are embedded in British imperial history. The so-called "spread" of English (see below for a critique of this term) was a direct result of the expansion of the British empire. "Expansion of the British empire" is of course an expression that, if left unpacked, may hide the actual human activities that went on during imperialism: land grabbing, mass murder, slavery, concentration camps, looting, buccaneering, subjugation, and exploitation of entire societies. It is these activities, nominalized into the less offensive "British empire," that are the primary historical reasons why people in New York, Kingston, Lagos or New Delhi use English in their daily lives. The origins of the World Englishes academic field can be said to stem, at least in part, from the awareness of the imperial matrix of English in the world. Braj Kachru's critical reflections in the late 1960s and 1970s, which would later develop into the World Englishes paradigm, focused very much on the decolonization[1] of English. "What is 'colonial' about English?," and "How can the process of 'decolonization' of the language be initiated?" he asks (Kachru 1987: 255).

Kachru's answer to those questions, throughout his academic career, and which indeed formed the core of the World Englishes ethos, centered on the need for "Third World" varieties of English to be recognized and for attitudes towards them to change:

> It will [...] be appropriate that the native speakers of English abandon the attitude of linguistic chauvinism and replace it with an attitude of linguistic tolerance. The strength of the English language is in presenting the *Americanness* in its American variety, and the *Englishness* in its British variety. Let us, therefore, appreciate and encourage the Third World varieties of English too. The individuality of the Third World varieties, such as the *Indianness* of its Indian variety, is contributing to the linguistic mosaic which the speakers of the English language have created in the English speaking world. The attitude toward these varieties ought to be one of appreciation and understanding.
>
> Kachru 1976: 236

Kachru's plea was about a radical change of mindset with regard to the forms and functions of English beyond the inner circle and, consequently, with regard to the cultures in which English had been absorbed and nativized. His sentiments were inspired by those expressed by creative writers in postcolonial settings, such as Raja Rao in India and Chinua Achebe in Nigeria, who had made claims of "ownership" of the English language. These writers felt that although it had arrived within very dubious circumstances, English had become integral to the social fabric of postcolonial societies and their creative efforts were testimony to the extent to which the language had set new roots and regrown in the new lands. In one of his most frequently cited essays, Achebe stated: "I feel that the English language will be able to carry the weight of my African experience. But it will have to be a new English [...], altered to suit its new African surroundings" (Achebe 1965: 30). The deliberate alteration of the English language, of its lexis, grammar and rhythm, was key to the process whereby the language would simultaneously lose its colonial baggage and become capable of expressing Caribbean, African and Asian cultures. Speaking about Raja Rao's novel *Kanthapura* (1938), Srivastava (2010: 316) notes: "In translating Gandhian notions into English, Rao forces the erstwhile colonial language to adapt to Kannada rhythms and structures of speech. He is transforming it into a tool for the Indian bilingual patriotic intelligentsia to identify themselves as 'Indians.'" In this way, English "becomes the vehicle for radically anti-colonial notions." Turning English into an instrument of decolonization is the central idea here: "What writers like Desani, Rao, and Rushdie are trying to do is to decolonize the English language so as to recover the deeper springs of Indian consciousness which lie hidden beneath the crusts of language" (Dissanayake 1985: 241).

This subversion of the English language has been described in terms of two distinct processes by Ashcroft et al. (1989): *abrogation* and *appropriation*. The former, defined as "a vital moment in the de-colonizing of the language" (38), involves rejecting all the parameters of correctness – in terms of values, behaviour as well as language – emanating from the former colonizers" cultural base, while the latter is the re-forging of the language to make it capable of expressing local values and ideas. In this way, English ceases to be somebody else's language and becomes one's own. Kamal Das (1973: 26) expresses this notion in "An Introduction" particularly cogently:

The language I speak,
Becomes mine, its distortions, its queernesses.
All mine, mine alone
It is half English, half Indian

Crucially, a localized form of English can be used to "write back" to the center of the former empire, that is to respond to centuries of representations of the colonies from a British imperial perspective—as *Orientalism* was deconstructed by Edward Said in the case of the "Middle East" and North Africa (1978). The idea of "writing back" originally came from Salman Rushdie's article "The Empire writes back with a vengeance" (1982). In it, the writer states that the English language, "tainted by history," "needs to be decolonized," and this can be done if writers are willing and able to "infuse English with new rhythms, new histories, new angles on the world." He uses the expressions "assaults on the classical frontiers of the language" to refer to this kind of alteration of English, giving metaphorically violent undertones to such literary efforts. Interestingly, the Caribbean/British poet John Agard (1985) encapsulates this sentiment in his "Listen Mr Oxford Don" poem, where he declares "mugging de Queen's English is the story of my life" and "I making de Queen's English accessory/to my offence." Language becomes a weapon of resistance as well as attack.

Rushdie then refers explicitly to the transplantation of English in new places, a key concept in World Englishes: "English, no longer an English language, now grows from many roots; and those whom it once colonized are carving out large territories within the language for themselves" (Rushdie 1982). These notions constitute the very core of the World Englishes ethos: British imperialism transplanted and, to some extent, imposed English in new sociocultural milieus, but the language subsequently went through a process of nativization and acculturation and was re-shaped, appropriated and ultimately freed of its colonial heritage. In the next section we discuss the limitations of this analysis.

## 4. The Limitations of the Decolonization Spirit in WE

Our critique in this section is articulated along two main lines of reasoning. First, we question the casual and often uncritical way in which the notion of language appropriation in former British colonies is talked about and, secondly, we argue that the primacy of the formal aspects of language such as syntax, vocabulary or accent, is ill conceived when discussing decolonization and the place of language within it.

### 4.1 The Grammar of World Englishes

The following sentence by Salikoko Mufwene, in his series editor's foreword to Edgar Schneider's *Postcolonial English: Varieties Around the World* (2007), encapsulates the premise of World Englishes: "Having been appropriated by new speakers in diverse contact ecologies, English has been adapted to different communicative practices and indigenized to express local and novel cultures" (xi). Mufwene's succinct description is representative of the prevalent manner in which this core concept is talked about in the literature, from a syntactic point of view. Namely, the use of the passive voice not only allows for a more agile prose, but it also has the advantage of foregrounding "English" by placing it in the subject position. In fact, on the surface, there is nothing particularly remarkable about this syntactic choice, which can be easily explained by the fact that, after all, the topic of Schneider's book, and indeed of the vast majority of WE literature, is indeed the English language and its distinct worldwide varieties. However, one potential problem with such constructions is that they hide agency or relegate it to a secondary position. In this particular case, "new speakers" are mentioned, but the focus is very much on "English" and on the verbs "appropriated," "adapted" and "indigenized." We argue that this kind of syntax is not just a matter of style but it encodes a general and rather problematic orientation towards the role of English(es) in decolonization. The erasure or de-emphasizing of human agency produces discourse where English is elected as the primary subject but is also somewhat detached from the social fabric within which it is in reality intricately embedded. In turn, this causes both over-simplified representations of the relationship between language and society and an exaggeration of the role of language in complex societal issues, mechanisms, processes, such as decolonization or the unequal distribution of wealth.

#### 4.1.1 Who Owns What?

The topic of appropriation and ownership of English can serve as a good illustration of the issue of over-simplification of society. Just as an example, Rose et al.'s assertion (2020: 50) that "English has been appropriated first by the Outer Circle countries where English is used locally as a second language, such as India and Nigeria" is both a cliché in the literature and an instance of extreme simplification of the role of people and societies. Here, human agency is rendered metonymically with reference to whole countries and hence obfuscated. Discounting a literal interpretation, i.e., that countries such as India and Nigeria have somehow appropriated the English language, the meaning of this sentence is that *people* in India and Nigeria have gained ownership of the language (e.g., by altering it to make it suitable to their respective sociocultural environments). Even so, this is still a huge generalization, which describes a complex phenomenon in very broad brushstrokes. For a start, statements of this kind depict English as uniformly present among very large populations, even if in reality this is far from being the case. In India, for example, "There is a wide range of estimates on the circulation of English," but "Ultimately, the only real consensus is that it is spoken by an elite minority" (Bhattacharya and Mohanty, forthcoming). Even if quantifying the use of English in a country is a futile exercise, the significant point here is "the colonially induced élitist nature of English-language use" (Tupas 2016: 57). And the nativization of the language, intended as its deliberate moulding according to local sociocultural environments, is a privilege of precisely the intellectual elite.

English is not only a language of the elite, but is also a language that "benefits the already English-rich … more than the English-poor and the gap between them increases progressively" (Mohanty 2017: 275). Mohanty's words echo Rao's:

> English has certainly benefited the already privileged—those economically well off and those with a tradition of formal education in the family.... In a country with increasing inequalities, English has become a source of social division and exclusion, thereby undermining the social justice agenda of education in a democracy.
>
> Rao 2016: 205–6

But even this view might not necessarily tell the whole story. For example, Vaish (2005: 203) claims that in India "English is a tool of decolonization in the hands of subaltern communities and can help them access the global economy." The ways in which English is entangled with economy, identity, nationalism, power and so on certainly should not be reduced to a single monochrome portrayal: the English language is "a site of competing (and contradictory) ideologies" (Canagarajah 2000: 130). And, still with reference to South Asia, Mahapatra and Mishra (2019) remind us:

> Sometimes, [English education] is the means through which identity is constructed and at times, resisting English becomes a way of affirming an identity. If English was the chief means of constructing colonial modernity and structuring a nationalist identity among the elite, rejecting it in favour of the vernaculars and identifying with common masses was a means of expressing anti-colonial sentiment and structuring an alternative identity. With the growing importance of English globally, and the opening up of India to the global economy, English education is also seen as a means of acquiring a new identity, an identity of resistance to the traditional upper-class, upper-caste hegemony in India.
>
> Mahapatra and Mishra 2019: 352

So, the obfuscation or over-simplification of human agency in the ways in which the appropriation of English in former British colonies is talked about has, as a corollary, the exaggeration of the role that the language itself plays in the complex and tortuous dynamics of decolonization.

### 4.1.2 *The Place of Language*

The syntactic centrality of English we mentioned earlier often goes beyond the use of the passive voice. English, that is, is not just the subject of clauses but also the doer of actions. Indeed, the primacy of language in World Englishes and, more in general, in much scholarship in sociolinguistics, causes inevitable overreliance on metaphorical representations of English (Saraceni 2015) as an entity capable of performing actions, independently of the people who use it. David Crystal's statement explaining the global expansion of English thanks to its being "a language which has repeatedly found itself in the right place at the right time" (2003: 120) is one of the best-known examples of this particular depiction of English. The ENGLISH IS A TRAVELLER metaphor underpins many historical-geographical accounts of English as a global language. The idea of English having "travelled around the world" (Halliday 2016: 115) is often utilized as a convenient shortcut to describe the ways in which British imperialists brought their language with them as they went about seizing land and exploiting local communities, at times imposing their language, at other times deliberately limiting access to it, and the ways in which local communities, on their part, began to use the language for various purposes, such as education, legislation, creative writing, or indeed to affirm anti-colonial stances.

Once again, the economy of syntax and agility of prose may be part of the reason why such expressions are utilized. Still, metaphors like ENGLISH IS A TRAVELLER are particularly insidious, especially if they are used repeatedly enough to become sedimented in academic discourse, since they produce a systematic erasure of the actual social actors involved and their actions in the so-called "spread of English" and, consequently, a sanitization of it by removing its imperialistic dimension. In fact, the very phrase "spread of English" is itself problematic for precisely these reasons. In his critique of what he calls the "conspiracy theory," Spolsky (2004: 79) rhetorically asks if the spread of English in the world happened or it was caused, but the point we wish to make here is that the very possibility of that question is given by the de-contextualized nature of the phrase "spread of English."

One of the harshest critics of this type of aseptic descriptions of the history and geography of English in the world has been Robert Phillipson. With the publication of his *Linguistic Imperialism* in 1992, "the discourse on world English(es) changed gear dramatically" (Bolton 2006: 203). More than anyone before him, Phillipson emphasized the importance of structural inequalities between the West—and in particular the Anglophone countries—and developing countries and, in his view, the fundamental role that the English language had in perpetuating the hegemony of the West. His argument was that Anglophone countries, mainly Britain and the USA, had a vested interest in promoting the English language globally and then this created a situation in which "the dominance of English is asserted and maintained by the establishment and continuous reconstitution of structural and cultural inequalities between English and other languages" (Phillipson 1992: 47). From this perspective, the dominant position of English is a vehicle of the hegemonic position of Anglophone countries in the world in what can be described as neo-colonialism. Yet, even in Phillipson's analysis, it is language that takes center stage. Linguistic imperialism is, according to him, a form of *linguicism*, which "involves representations of the dominant language, to which desirable characteristics are attributed, for purposes of inclusion, and the opposite for dominated languages, for purposes of exclusion" (Phillipson 1992: 55).

Bernard Spolsky, one of Phillipson's critics, pointed out that

> [Phillipson's] linguicentric approach distracts attention from the central problem. It was not colonial language policy, whether to use the metropolitan or the local vernacular language as a medium in schools, that was the core issue; ... Rather, it was the colonial situation, whereby one nation came to rule another, that produced the underlying inequality that turned out to be virtually impossible to overcome. In other words, imperialism and not linguistic imperialism is the real issue.
> 
> Spolsky 2004: 84–5

Consequently, for Spolsky, "Rather than gross generalizations suggesting that English is always dominant, we need more detailed studies of how it enters into the complex set of language choices made in a specific community" (Spolsky 2004: 86). Similarly, Rubdy (2015: 58) notes how "The real issue for former colonial countries is not of opposing either globalization or English, but rather of bringing about a more equitable distribution of globalization's benefits." Taking this point seriously into account, one could question whether language plays any part at all in mechanisms of imperialism and, especially, decolonization. For Ngũgĩ wa Thiong'o, language and (de-)colonization are inseparable: "In my view language was the most important vehicle through which that power fascinated and held the soul prisoner. The bullet was the means of the physical subjugation. Language was the means of the spiritual subjugation" (Ngũgĩ wa Thiong'o 1986: 9). Ngũgĩ's statement is part of his discussion about "decolonizing the mind," which can be much more arduous than the process whereby a country gains its political independence. But, again, the distinction that must be made is between language as code, i.e., its grammar, lexis, phonology, and the ways in which language is part of a wider discourse of systemic inequality: "it is not English—if by that, we mean a certain grammar and lexicon—that is the problem. It is the *discourses* of English that are the problem" (Pennycook 2012: 26, our emphasis).

The place of English in the colonial and neo-colonial word order is described particularly compellingly by Kabel (forthcoming): "English is encrusted in the coloniality of knowledge" and "[t]his lodges knowledge and English at the center of a new planetary cartography of accumulation by dispossession wherein the Global South is locked into a lopsided post-Fordist architecture resolutely beholden to the interests of the North." What all of this means is that a narrow and superficial linguistic focus is clearly not sufficient if we want to engage with and begin to understand how English is "encrusted" in persistent forms of colonialism and what parts it may play in the decolonization of the mind as well as of the world economy. To return to the idea that the nativization and appropriation of English have taken place and are instruments of decolonization, it is fair to say that it is a rather optimistic or perhaps even naive concept. Nativization

> is a relatively simple process of indiginizing the phonological, syntactic and pragmatic aspects of the linguistic system of the English language—a target that has been largely achieved. Decolonization is a fairly complex process of taking control of the principles and practices of planning, learning, and teaching English—a task that has not been fully accomplished.
>
> Kumaravadivelu 2003: 540

So, even if the nativization of the English code has taken place and even if we accept that this may mean decolonizing the language, we must not lose sight of the fact that "Having colonized the English language ... does not mean its speakers have been freed from conditions of coloniality." (Tupas 2019: 7) We must not forget that coloniality

> can be read as a matrix of power ... resulting in, allowing for and sustaining a triple system of violence and destruction: (1) *genocide* as in the physical killing, destruction and disposability of certain peoples ... (2) *epistemicide* as in the destruction of certain (peoples') knowledges and ways of knowing ... (3) *ecocide* as in the destruction of life environments and ecosystems.
>
> Rutazibwa 2020: 224

Decolonizing therefore cannot only be about recognizing that "English" is not the "property" of the Inner Circle, or that it has been appropriated, nativized in postcolonial contexts, but rather must take into account the matrix of power and the very real system of violence and destruction on which the learning, teaching and using of this language is based and within which they are still taking place. The question of who benefits from the promotion of pluralist perspectives of English remains unspoken, especially in terms of career gains for researchers themselves as well as for the wider ELT industry (Kubota 2015: 36). In practice, this means that appropriated forms of Englishes are extolled in academic spaces where Inner Circle norms are firmly policed (Rambukwella 2019: 129).

Finally, Tuck and Yang draw our attention to the pitfalls of the use of the word "decolonizing" as a generic referent to social justice or an empty signifier of any attempts at "inclusivity" (Tuck and Yang 2012). They underline the situatedness of the colonial experience and the coloniality of power relations: in settler states such as the USA, Canada, Australia, and New Zealand, decolonizing cannot just mean a change in the curriculum, but entails a fundamental unsettling of wealth, land, and ownership. "Decolonizing" Englishes in India therefore means something different than decolonizing Englishes in South Africa, where settlers continue to own the majority of the land and wealth, and English-speakers have reinvented / re-labelled the language as "neutral," "innocent" of the continued damages of colonization and apartheid, and supposedly allowing for greater political, economic and social participation.

# 5. What does Decolonizing World Englishes Mean?

## 5.1 De-mythologize

In World Englishes we need to be more humble and recognize the limitations imposed by disciplinary boundaries that are like fortified walls encircling academic citadels, unwillingly but nearly inevitably erected and reinforced by university courses, academic publications (including this one), conferences, seminars etc. We need to be more humble about the subject of our enquiry and, as Tupas (2019: 1) says, "in our desire to study language in society, we must not assume that language is central to speakers" lives as is usually the case when we study the role of language in society." In fact, Braj Kachru himself noted how "questions about language and power need not necessarily involve linguistic issues. The issues go beyond linguistics into the realms of history, sociology, attitude studies, politics, and into very mundane economic considerations" (Kachru 1986: 122). The problem, Tupas continues, is that "studies on World Englishes have broadly been about the 'Englishes' and much less about the 'world'" (2019: 2), and so we need to "make as our central object of investigation the cultural, economic and sociopolitical constitution of 'the world' in which the Englishes are produced and embedded" (2019: 3–4). And, once again, we need to abandon the familiar and protective comfort produced by self-reference, and we need to transcend disciplinary boundaries and establish meaningful dialogues with historians, political scientists, sociologists, and scholars in international relations, development studies, etc.

We must be more alert to how we talk about English, too. Conceptual shortcuts afforded by the use of metaphors that represent English as an autonomous being, capable of performing actions such as travelling, spreading, bringing riches, adapting, influencing, dominating and so on have the detrimental effects of erasing human agency and magnifying the role of language per se, as if it could be separated from the linguists and researchers who played a role in elaborating "English" as a subject of study. We have to be prepared to talk about people and society far more than we currently do. De-mythologizing English is thus a first step towards de-silencing, the second principle of decolonizing World Englishes.

## 5.2 De-silence

In trying to understand what "English" is and how it is used, we must contend with the contradictions and complexities of people's responses rather than simply stake out our beliefs in transformative conceptual frameworks such as World Englishes or translanguaging. Therefore decolonizing World Englishes might mean decolonizing its speakers, but most importantly also entails decolonizing the practices (including research practices) of its proponents. While other disciplines have reckoned with their role as "handmaiden of colonialism" (Gough 1968), debates over the historical development of sociolinguistics in conjunction with the colonial project have remained largely contained within studies of African languages (Irvine and Gal 2000; Lüpke 2017; van den Avenne 2017).

In addition, social sciences and humanities disciplines as a whole have so far engaged with their participants largely as sources of evidence and anecdotes, despite attempts to move away from seeing them as data-producing machines (Oakley 1981: 36–40). Within this approach to research, the capacity of participants (informants, interviewees, respondents …) to theorize and make sense of their own societies are sidelined, erased or discounted, to make more space for the researcher's voice. As Yarimar Bonilla argues,

> ethnographers rarely demonstrate their interlocutors' ability to speak with analytic value about their own society—much less the society of others. The voices of informants might be rallied as evidence within a scholar's argument, but the position of those informants within that argument—and their assessment of its stakes—are rarely explored.
>
> Bonilla 2015: xv

Although World Englishes research relies heavily on qualitative or even ethnographic approaches, methodological and ethical questions of the hierarchical relations between the researcher and the subject-turned-object of study have not been prevalent, and in practice, "scholars rarely engage the objects of their research as full citizens of the world capable of thinking, writing, and answering back" (Muppidi 2013: 300). This is particularly problematic within the context of wanting to conduct research *and* write about research findings while challenging the supremacy of Inner Circle norms. It tends to reproduce not only knowledge production mechanisms inherited from the colonial era, but also monolithic views of language and languaging, by seeking a "truer" narrative and single explanatory framework to account for the contradictions and messiness of participants' voices. In contrast, Bonilla proposes to take participants' explanatory frameworks seriously, rather than relegating them to "naive informants" status. As she explains in the preface to *Non-Sovereign Futures: French Caribbean Politics in the Wake of Disenchantment*:

> I purposefully engage with my informants as theorists—that is, as reflective actors who seek to make sense of their experiences in relation to the ideas and experiences of others. In deciding when to cite, quote, or paraphrase, I treat their reflections and arguments as I do those of other theorists: I cite when I wish to rally their authority; I quote when I think they have found *le mot juste* to describe a particular phenomena [sic], and I paraphrase when I feel like I can articulate their vision more succinctly, or more accessibly, to my presumed audience. Moreover, I engage with my informants as a literary critic might engage with an author's reflections about their oeuvre: that is, I grant them analytic competency over their own acts and forms of cultural production.
>
> 2015: xvi

The questions raised by the ethical and methodological issues related to languages other than English can be helpful here. For instance, in relying on "native speakers" with no linguistics credentials to ascertain the applicant's region of origin from a brief interview (Patrick 2019), current asylum procedures of the British Home Office reproduce colonial relations of the "native informant," allowed to speak only within a narrow remit. The way recognition of and knowledge about natural language variation is used is not inherently transformative. In this scenario, the recognition of expertise is embedded within deeply unequal structures of power which pre-determine the questions and the answers. The question of finding categories and discourses relevant to participants rather than the researcher have given rise to "folk linguistics" approaches, which have been held as an important element of critical sociolinguistics (Albury 2017). However, in the literature these are often used to show "uninformed" locals unaware of more transformative frameworks of understanding language, holding on to beliefs in "proper" language vs. slang, and in the existence of language as a "thing." The discussion is one between the expert and laypeople who have to be corrected, rather than between different analytical interpretations. An alternative approach towards de-silencing voices (and bodies) historically marginalised by research on Englishes has included citizen sociolinguistics (Rymes and Leone 2014, see also the Citizen Sociolinguistics blog), taking its cues from citizen science (Irwin 1995) in order to foreground non-academic expertise.

Scholars have also pointed to many academic practices which lead to silencing, from disqualifying local voices (Trouillot 2003: 132) and strategic appropriation (Cusicanqui 2012) to the erasure of issues of race and the upholding of whiteness as the "neutral" standard, whether in TESOL (Flores and Rosa 2015) or in World Englishes more specifically (Kubota 2018). All are mechanisms which maintain practitioners and researchers of colour and/or based in the Global South as "subaltern intellectuals" (Kumaravadivelu 2016: 76), as well as hide hierarchies of power and the violence of colonial legacies through "the power to define what is and what is not a serious object of research and, therefore, of mention" (Fernando 2014: 99). De-silencing Englishes users within World Englishes thus requires the rethinking of research, collaboration and dissemination practices through a profound unsettling of existing norms and hierarchies at the local and global levels.

## 5.3 De-colonize

In Section 3, we pointed out to the gap between the promotion of equal varieties within a World Englishes framework at the academic level and the reinforcement of Inner Circle norms in practice. Suggestions on how to de-center English and re-center Englishes abound, from reforming teacher training to creating new textbooks. Already in 2002, Lin et al. had suggested a glocalized form of learning, "where the global and the local dissolve in the situated appropriation of a global means by local social actors for local purposes" (Lin et al. 2002: 313) alongside a de-centering of authority in the production of pedagogical knowledge. Changes in the classroom cannot occur without wider social changes and therefore "collectively disclose and act upon the core of social inequality produced through language" (Martín Rojo 2020: 154).

Unsettling authority is a necessary step in decolonizing World Englishes as a discipline and as a set of language practices. Who gets to be heard, who acts as gatekeeper, who is recognized as an expert, who is rewarded for praising decolonized Englishes, and who is rewarded for continuing to use Inner Circle norms? This unsettling must take several forms, as decolonizing entails adapting to the local conditions of coloniality. Moving from knowledge production (an accumulation of knowledge for knowledge's sake) to knowledge cultivation ("to till, to turn matter around and fold back on itself so as to encourage growth," Shilliam 2013) would enable the inclusion of local histories and knowledge to more effectively question power hierarchies. De-silencing and de-centering are therefore key in this process. De-centering analytical authority (Higgins 2009: 17) is well developed in feminist methodologies and further emphasized in Yarimar Bonilla's approach to recognizing the knowledge, experience and expertise of participants/respondents/interviewees beyond falling into "folk" conceptions of research. In addition, paraphrasing Chakrabarty, we need to provincialize Inner Circle Englishes, in other words, cut them down to size by acknowledging our use of particular varieties rather than a neutral standard. Decolonizing World Englishes cannot happen without Inner Circle speakers decolonizing themselves and recognizing their variety as just one variety amongst others.

## 6. Conclusion

In this chapter we have discussed the principle of decolonization as it applies to discourses about English with specific references to World Englishes as a research area. As we have shown, the focus on the nativization and appropriation within World Englishes does not question and sometimes may even encourage the sanitizing of history and the erasure of social actors, for example through the employment of insidious metaphors such as ENGLISH IS A TRAVELLER or the "spread" of English. We made the point that colonialism, empire, inequality and power should be brought firmly to the fore when discussing the roles of English(es) in the world and avoid superficial and casual references to notions such as the "neutrality" or "ownership" of the language. Finally, borrowing Rutazibwa's paradigm, we have drawn out a blueprint for a bolder approach to producing alternative ways in which we discuss and research the roles of English(es) in the world.

## Notes

1  Kachru, however, made rare explicit references to this specific term.

## References

Achebe, C. (1965), "English and the African Writer," *Transition*, 18: 27–30.

Agard, J. (1985), *Mangoes and Bullets: Selected and New Poems 1972–1984*, London: Pluto Press.

Ahmed, A. K. (2020), "#RhodesMustFall: How a decolonial student movement in the Global South inspired epistemic disobedience at the University of Oxford," *African Studies Review*, 63 (2): 281–303.

Albury, N. J. (2017), "How folk linguistic methods can support critical sociolinguistics," *Lingua*, 199: 36–49.

Ashcroft, B., G. Griffiths, F. M. Ashcroft and H. Tiffin (1989), *The Empire Writes Back: Theory and Practice in Post-colonial Literatures*, London: Routledge.

Bhambra, G. K. (2020), "A Statue was Toppled. Can We Finally Talk about the British Empire?," *The New York Times*, June 12. Available online: https://www.nytimes.com/2020/06/12/opinion/edward-colston-statueracism.html

Bhambra, G. K., D. Gebrial and K. Nişancıolu (2018), "Introduction: Decolonising the University?," in G. K. Bhambra, D. Gebrial and K. Nişancıolu (eds.), *Decolonising the University*, 1–17, London: Pluto Press.

Bhattacharya, U. and A. K. Mohanty (fthc.), "Ideological plurality: English in policy and practice in India," in R. Rubdy and R. Tupas (eds.), *Bloomsbury World Englishes, Vol. III: Ideologies*, London: Bloomsbury.

Bolton, K. (2006), "World Englishes," in K. Bolton and B. B. Kachru (eds.), *World Englishes: Critical Concepts in Linguistics*, 186–216, London: Routledge.

Bonilla, Y. (2015), *Non-Sovereign Futures: French Caribbean Politics in the Wake of Disenchantment*, Chicago: University of Chicago Press.

Cairns, P. (2020, February 10), "Decolonise or indigenise: Moving towards sovereign spaces and the Māorification of New Zealand museology," blog entry, retrieved June 5, 2020, from https://blog.tepapa.govt.nz/2020/02/10/decolonise-orindigenise-moving-towards-sovereign-spaces-and-the-maorificationof-new-zealand-museology/

Canagarajah, S. A. (2000), "Negotiating ideologies through English: Strategies from the periphery," in T. Ricento (ed.), *Ideology, Politics and Language Policies: Focus on English*, 121–31, Amsterdam: John Benjamins.

Chakrabarty, D. (2000), *Provincializing Europe: Postcolonial Thought and Historical Difference*, Princeton: Princeton University Press.

Crenshaw, K. (1989), "Demarginalizing the intersection of race and sex: A black feminist critique of antidiscrimination doctrine, feminist theory and antiracist politics," *University of Chicago Legal Forum*, 1989 (1): 139–67. Available online: https://heinonline.org/HOL/Page?handle=hein.journals/uchclf1989&id= 143&div=&collection=

Crystal, D. (2003), *English as a Global Language*, 2nd Edition, Cambridge: Cambridge University Press.

Cusicanqui, S. R. (2012), "Ch'ixinakax utxiwa: A reflection on the practices and discourses of decolonization," *South Atlantic Quarterly*, 111 (1): 95–109.

Das, K. (1973), *The Old Playhouse And Other Poems*, Hyderabad: Orient Longman.

Dissanayake, W. (1985), "Towards a decolonized English: South Asian creativity in fiction," *World Englishes*, 4 (2): 233–42.

Elkins, C. (2015), "Looking beyond Mau Mau: Archiving violence in the era of decolonization," *American Historical Review*, 120 (3): 852–68.

Ferguson, N. (2003), *Empire: How Britain made the modern world*, London: Allen Lane.

Fernando, M. L. (2014), "Ethnography and the politics of silence," *Cultural Dynamics*, 26 (2): 235–44.

Flores, N. and J. Rosa (2015), "Undoing appropriateness: Raciolinguistic ideologies and language diversity in education," *Harvard Educational Review*, 85 (2): 149–71.

Gough, K. (1968), "Anthropology and Imperialism," *Monthly Review*, 19 (11): 12–27.

Grosfoguel, R. (2007), "The epistemic decolonial turn," *Cultural Studies*, 21 (2–3): 211–23.

Halliday, M. A. K. (2016), *Aspects of Language and Learning*, (J. Webster, ed.), Heidelberg: Springer.

Higgins, C. (2009), *English as a Local Language: Post-Colonial Identities and Multilingual Practices*, Bristol: Multilingual Matters.

Hunt, T. (2019), "Should museums return their colonial artefacts?," *The Guardian*, June 29. Available online: https://www.theguardian.com/culture/2019/jun/29/should-museumsreturn-their-colonial-artefacts?

Hunt, T. (2020, February 14), "Understanding decolonization in the 21st Century," panel discussion at Chatham House, London.

Hutton, W. (2015), "Cecil Rhodes was a racist, but you can't readily expunge him from history," *The Observer*, December 20, 2015.

Irvine, J. T. and S. Gal (2000), "Language ideology and linguistic differentiation," in P. V. Kroskrity (ed.), *Regimes of Language: Ideologies, Polities, and Identities*, 35–83, Santa Fe, NM: School of American Research Press.

Jansen, J. C. and J. Osterhammel (2017), *Decolonization: A Short History*, (J. Riemer, Trans.), Princeton: Princeton University Press.

Kabel, A. (fthc), "'The tide is coming in fast'": Ideologies of English, global linguistic coloniality and decolonial pluriversalingualism," in R. Rubdy and R. Tupas (eds.), *Bloomsbury World Englishes, Vol. III: Ideologies*. London: Bloomsbury.

Kachru, B. B. (1976), Models of English for the third world: White man's linguistic burden or language pragmatics?," *TESOL Quarterly*, 10 (2): 221–39.

Kachru, B. B. (1986), "The power and politics of English," *World Englishes*, 5 (2–3): 121–40.

Kachru, B. B. (1987), "The past and prejudice: Toward de-mythologizing the English canon," in R. Steele and T. Threadgold (eds.), *Language Topics: Essays in honour of Michael Halliday*, 245–56, Amsterdam: John Benjamins.

Kassim, S. (2019), "The museum is the master's house: An open letter to Tristram Hunt," *Medium*, retrieved May 10, 2020, from https://medium.com/@sumayakassim/the-museum-is-the-mastershouse-an-open-letter-to-tristram-hunt-e72d75a891c8

Kubota, R. (2015), "Inequalities of Englishes, English speakers, and languages: A critical perspective on pluralist approaches to English," In R. Tupas (ed.), *Unequal Englishes: The Politics of Englishes Today*, 21–42, Basingstoke: Palgrave.

Kubota, R. (2018), "Unpacking research and practice in world Englishes and Second Language Acquisition," *World Englishes*, 37 (1): 93–105.

Kumaravadivelu, B. (2003), "A postmethod perspective on English language teaching," *World Englishes*, 22 (4): 539–50.

Kumaravadivelu, B. (2016), "The decolonial option in English teaching: Can the subaltern act?," *TESOL Quarterly*, 50 (1): 66–85.

Lin, A., W. Wang, N. Akamatsu and A. M. Riazi (2002), "Appropriating English, expanding identities, and re-visioning the field: From TESOL to teaching English for glocalized communication (TEGCOM)," *Journal of Language, Identity & Education*, 1 (4): 295–316.

Lüpke, F. (2017), "African(ist) perspectives on vitality: Fluidity, small speaker numbers, and adaptive multilingualism make vibrant ecologies (Response to Mufwene)," *Language*, 93 (4): e275–e279.

Mahapatra, S. and S. Mishra (2019), "Articulating identities: the role of English language education in Indian universities," *Teaching in Higher Education*, 24 (3): 346–60.

Martín Rojo, L. (2020), "Blog: Citizen Sociolinguistics," *Journal of Sociolinguistics*, 24 (1): 151–55.

Mohanty, A. (2017), "Multilingualism, education, English and development: Whose development?," in H. Coleman (ed.), *Multilingualisms and Development*, 261–80, London: British Council.

Muppidi, H. (2013), "On the politics of exile," *Security Dialogue*, 44 (4): 299–313.
Ngũgĩ wa Thiong'o. (1986), *Decolonising the Mind: The Politics of Language in African Literature*, Portsmouth, NH: Heinemann.
Oakley, A. (1981), "Interviewing women: A contradiction in terms," in H. Roberts (ed.), *Doing Feminist Research*, 30–61, London: Routledge.
Patrick, P. (2019), "Linguistic justice: Evaluating the speech of asylum claimants," in R. Blake and I. Buchstaller (eds.), *The Routledge Companion to the Work of John R. Rickford*, 251–58, London: Routledge.
Pennycook, A. (2012), "Afterword: Could Heracles have gone about things differently?," in V. Rapatahana and P. Bunce (eds.), *English Language as Hydra: Its Impacts on Non-English Language Cultures*, 255–62, Bristol: Multilingual Matters.
Phillipson, R. (1992), *Linguistic Imperialism*, Oxford: Oxford University Press.
Rambukwella, H. (2019), "On hybridity, the politics of knowledge production and critical language studies," *Language, Culture and Society*, 1 (1): 126–31.
Rao, G. (2016), "The (illusory) promise of English in India," in P. Bunce, R. Phillipson, V. Rapatahana and R. Tupas (eds.), *Why English?: Confronting the Hydra*, 197–210, Bristol: Multilingual Matters.
Rose, H., M. Syrbe, A. Montakantiwong and N. Funada (2020), *Global TESOL for the 21st Century: Teaching English in a Changing World*, Bristol: Multilingual Matters.
Rubdy, R. (2015), "Unequal Englishes, the native speaker, and decolonization in TESOL," in R. Tupas (ed.), *Unequal Englishes: The Politics of Englishes Today*, 42–58, Basingstoke: Palgrave Macmillan.
Rushdie, S. (1982), "The Empire writes back with a vengeance," *The Times*, July 3, 1982.
Rutazibwa, O. U. (2019), "On babies and bathwater: Decolonizing International Development Studies," in S. De Jong, R. Icaza and O. U. Rutazibwa (eds.), *Decolonization and Feminisms in Global Teaching and Learning*, 158–80, London: Routledge.
Rutazibwa, O. U. (2020), "Hidden in plain sight: Coloniality, capitalism and race/ism as far as the eye can see," *Millennium: Journal of International Studies*, 48 (2), 221–41.
Rymes, B. and A. R. Leone (2014), "Citizen Sociolinguistics: A new media methodology for understanding language and social life," *Working Papers in Educational Linguistics*, 29 (2), 24–43.
Said, E. (1978), *Orientalism*, London: Routledge and Kegan Paul.
Saraceni, M. (2015), *World Englishes: A Critical Analysis*, London: Bloomsbury.
Schneider, E. (2007), *Postcolonial English: Varieties Around the World*, Cambridge: Cambridge University Press.
Shilliam, R. (2013, December 1), "Living knowledge traditions and the priestly caste of the Western Academy," retrieved July 3, 2019, from https://thedisorderofthings.com/2013/12/01/living-knowledgetraditions-and-the-priestly-caste-of-the-western-academy/
Spolsky, B. (2004), *Language Policy*, Cambridge: Cambridge University Press.
Srivastava, N. (2010), "Towards a critique of colonial violence: Fanon, Gandhi and the restoration of agency," *Journal of Postcolonial Writing*, 46 (3–4): 303–19.
Trouillot, M.-R. (2003), *Global Transformations: Anthropology and the Modern World*, New York: Palgrave Macmillan.
Tuck, E. and K. W. Yang (2012), "Decolonization is not a metaphor," *Decolonization: Indigeneity, Education and Society*, 1 (1): 1–40.
Tupas, R., ed. (2015), *Unequal Englishes: The Politics of Englishes Today*, Basingstoke, Palgrave.

Tupas, R. (2016), *English, Neocolonialism and Forgetting*, in P. Bunce, R. Phillipson, V. Rapatahana and R. Tupas (eds.), *Why English?: Confronting the Hydra*, 47–58, Bristol: Multilingual Matters.

Tupas, R. (2019), "Decentering language: Displacing Englishes from the study of Englishes," *Critical Inquiry in Language Studies*, 1–18.

Vaish, V. (2005). "A peripherist view of English as a language of decolonization in post-colonial India," *Language Policy*, 4 (2), 187–206.

van den Avenne, C. (2017), *De la Bouche Même des Indigènes: Echanges Linguistiques en Afrique Coloniale*, Paris: Vendémiaire.

Vince, N. (fthc.), *The Algerian War/The Algerian Revolution*, Basingstoke: Palgrave Macmillan.

# 3

# "The Communicative Event" in International English(es) as Social Practice: Adducing a Tricodal/Trimodal Theory of the Linguistic Structuring of Social Meaning

Allan James

## 1. Introduction

Current research into world Englishes may be said to have effected a communicative turn in that the extensive analysis of anglophone lects around the globe focusing on their development and codification as (postcolonial) "varieties" (e.g., Schneider 2007) has been increasingly supplemented by attention to the communicative significance of anglophony as embedded in diverse types of multilingual discourses worldwide (e.g., Saraceni 2014), most prominently within a "translanguaging" conception of "codemeshing" (see, e.g., Li 2017). Such latter analysis of situated anglophony has been characterized as a "post-varieties approach" to language (Seargeant and Tagg 2011). However, most recently, a readiness has been signalled also within the varieties approach to world Englishes itself to engage with the linguistic realities of the "communicative space" (Mair 2018) or "communicative event" (Deshors and Gilquin 2018) in which English is co-present in new domains, e.g., with German as in pop culture and migrant discourses (Mair 2018) or as "modes of communication" (Deshors and Gilquin 2018), foremostly involving computer-mediated communication. From a more structural perspective, the Englishes manifested in such new "genres of expression" (Deshors and Gilquin 2018: 284) have been identified in particular for their hybridity (Schneider 2016).

In comparison, a post-varieties approach to world Englishes as situated anglophony and as practised in translanguaging research considers itself in the first place as "a practical theory of language" which moves beyond the construct of hybridity itself to see language as a holistic mix, i.e., as "a multilingual, multisemiotic, multisensory, and multimodal resource for sense- and meaning-making" (Li 2017: 14). The analysis of anglophony is then not so much oriented to its linguistic codal properties, but rather to its role as a signalling resource on a par with other semiotic resources present in a verbal exchange.

However, returning to the structural hybridity of English(es) worldwide, inasmuch as this is the product of language contact between such English(es) and other languages locally co-present and in actual verbal exchanges, then this hybridity can be analyzed further as the result of specific language contact phenomena. As Onysko (2019) expands, these in turn are the result of the "socio-pragmatic conditions" of the communication situation itself, which determine whether a mono- or multilingual (or "oscillating") mode of production is activated (2019: 36–8). While the main expectation of the above communicative event-oriented approach to varieties is that it would provide "a window into the development of World Englishes" (Deshors and Gilquin 2018: 288), the aim of language contact research into situationally determined structural hybridity is to establish the cognitive basis of the well-established contact types (such as codeswitching) which characterize such hybridity (Onysko 2019: 38–44).

In sum, the purpose of paying attention to the contexts of world Englishes use in the three approaches considered is to establish the communication frameworks within which a refined typology of varieties (in the first approach), and of contact phenomena (in the third approach) is facilitated, and within which the specification of "translanguaging space" (in the second approach) can be concretized (see Li 2017: 15–16).

By comparison, the aim of the present approach to the analysis of communicatively contextualized international English(es) is to draw together formal and functional, structural and semiotic properties of language as discourse and to show how these are mutually specifying. It will be argued that in any linguistically driven communicative event the structural codes within which social meanings are consistently expressed are not those of language or variety, but rather of structurally and semiotically definable subsets of (a) language which manifest a unity of form and function. Such codes are familiar as "dialects," "registers" and "genres" and have been previously theorized from a sociolinguistic perspective by Ferguson (1994), and from a social semiotic perspective by Fairclough (2003) as "styles," "discourses" and "genres," respectively, which as forms of "social practice" constitute "ways of being," "ways of representing" and "ways of acting" (2003: 31). Developing the argument further, Fairclough proceeds to show that when these styles, discourses and genres are textualized as occurring social events they then express a social semiotics of, respectively, "identification of persons," "representations of the world" and "actions and their social relations" (2003: 26). Given that these social events manifest both a structural linguistic identity (as constituting "dialects," "registers" and "genres," James 2008: 101–2) and a social semiotic identity (as expressing "identification," "representation" and "action," James 2008: 105–6), they may therefore equally be interpreted as codes of language use (the former) and modes of language use (the latter). It is the recognition of these structural-functional linguistic unities which enables the analysis of the formal structure of language to be directly combined with the analysis of its function as a (social) semiotic resource.

The interpretation of these codes as modes and vice-versa in the analysis of contextually embedded international English(es)—either in mono- or multilingual discourses—furthers an understanding of such linguistic practice as the deployment of selective structured anglophony (as codes) for selective social semiotic purposes (as modes) characteristic of a myriad of such actually occurring communicative events as social events worldwide.

This bare outline of a tricodal/trimodal approach to world Englishes in context will now be further substantiated in the following and then applied in the analysis of communicatively situated anglophone data in Section 4 below.

## 2. A Tricodal/Trimodal Approach Elaborated

### 2.1 Basic Categories

An approach which aims to develop a co-specifying relation between linguistic codes as formal entities and social semiotic modes as functional entities in anglophone social events conflates in doing so context of language use as mode with structure of language use as code, obviating in the first instance recourse to situationally determining factors which go beyond the immediately linguistic structural or social semiotic. That is, conditioning factors such the new domains, genres of expression or even socio-pragmatic conditions of above inasmuch the details of these are not tied closely to a particular co-defining typology of linguistic structure, may be nonetheless regarded as constituting a valuable second level of contextual explanation for the communicative events that characterize the deployment of English in the world.

In a statement reflecting on the sociolinguistics of globalization and "super-diverse" contexts of language use commensurate with a translanguaging approach, Blommaert (2010) highlights the "truncated" nature of multilingual repertoires, that "constitute a complex of specific semiotic resources which are concrete accents, language varieties, registers, genres, modalities such as writing," as "ways of using language in particular settings and spheres of life" (2010: 102; original emphasis). This clearly acknowledges the co-presence and co-functionality of both linguistic codes and semiotic modes in such contexts of use – paradigmatic for the communicative events as social events involving anglophony worldwide.

However, further theorization is now required on the co-specifying nature of code and mode, as, e.g., developed in previous research on Lingua Franca English (James 2005, 2008), a typology of International Englishes and globalization theory (James 2009), and anglography in polylingual texts (James 2014). Concerning "identification," "representation" and "action" constituting the social semiotic modes, it might be noted that these closely correspond to Foucault's (1972) threefold "relations with oneself," "relations of control over things" and "relations of action upon others" of social theory. Concerning "dialect," "register" and "genre" constituting the linguistic structural codes, these also link to earlier research of Halliday (1978) on language as social semiotic, where he specifies dialect as "a variety according to user," and register as "a variety according to use" (1978: 35), to which James (2008) adds the "genre" of Fairclough (2003) and of McCarthy (1998) and as the "primary genre" of Bakhtin (1986) as "a variety according to using" (2005: 142). Crucially, Halliday notes that "dialect" is foremostly expressed via lexicophonological structure, and "register" via lexicosemantic structure, to which James (2005) adds "genre" as being expressed via lexicogrammatical structure (2005: 142).

These threefold hybrid layers of linguistic structure are seen as the norm or unmarked realizations as codes of the threefold social semiotic modes, respectively. In other words, this postulation allows a direct and mutually defining functional-structural link to be established between social meaning and linguistic form in social events as texts. At the same time, the modes, and with them the codes, exist in a relation of "interdiscursivity," such that they compete, combine and interact in texts (Fairclough 2003: 218)—hardly any one text in reality exclusively manifesting a single mode/code. They may even in marked cases manifest a "dialectics of discourse" in that, e.g., representational meanings (= register) may be contextually enacted in genres (=actional meanings), identificational meanings (=dialect) in registers (=representational meanings), etc. (Fairclough 2003: 29). However, despite the tight interaction of modes and codes, considerable empirical evidence has been adduced from the close data analysis of various contexts of international English(es) use to suggest that these co-specifying functional-structural, modal-codal dualities can indeed be identified, thereby permitting a potentially robust typology of situational usage (cf., James 2008, 2014, 2016).

## 2.2 Codes and Modes Continued

Dialect as a code expressing identification as a mode is understood as providing the linguistic structure(s) most readily employed to realize social meanings of user specification. In sociolinguistic theory, user identity as such is ultimately emergent in interactive discourses and in the course of a communicative exchange can take on micro (temporary/restricted/local), meso (semi-temporary/-restricted/-local) and macro (non-temporary/-restricted/-local) dimensions of construction and display (cf., "the emergence principle" and "the partialness principle," Bucholtz and Hall 2005). At the same time, as Bucholtz and Hall confirm, the "indexicality principle," as "the mechanism whereby identity is constituted ... involves the creation of semiotic links between linguistic forms and social meanings" (2005: 592). The identity relations that emerge in interaction via indexical processes include "the use of linguistic structures and systems that are ideologically associated with specific persons and groups" (2005: 594), while "entire linguistic systems such as languages and dialects may also be indexically tied to identity categories" (2005: 597). Dialect hence constitutes the structural linguistic baseline of a user in communicative events, which in an individual personal perspective constitutes his or her idiolect. The particular structural resources within the dialect which are activated for identity expression are lexical and phonological in combination, as they indeed characterize dialects in real life, while not denying a residue significance of grammatical structure.

Register as a code expressing representation as a mode is understood as providing the linguistic structure(s) most readily employed to realize social meanings of use specification. Representation is a concept widely used in sociocultural theory, in particular theories of social constructivism, and concerning language in theories of (critical) discourse analysis, intimately bound up with issues of social semiotics (Webb 2008). In a linguistic interpretation, it is tied in with relations of lexical semantics, specifically of how signs signal the meaning of their referents. Connecting social semiotic and linguistic dimensions of meaning-making, representation in the present context expresses the semiotic framework within which a particular social event is to be understood as text. It frames and creates the particular "text-world" (Werth 1999) within which the communicative event is to be interpreted. Register itself denotes the particular use-type of language that signals specific meanings pertaining to a specific field of discourse (commonly seen as a special purpose variety, associated with particular professional fields of activity such as the law, medicine, business, etc. or of fields of leisure activity such as sports, gaming, etc.). In the present context, as conveying the social meaning of representation, register activates the lexical and semantic structures in combination, which signal the text or discourse type as "field of social action" (Halliday 1978) intended, not excluding a secondary influence of grammatical structure.

Genre as a code expressing action as a mode is understood as providing the linguistic structure/s most readily employed to realize social meanings of a using specification. Action constitutes the verbalization of a social relation between interlocutors, the relation itself being formulatable broadly as one of "interaction" or "transaction" (Fairclough 2003: 26–7). In a more detailed taxonomy in his theory of genre, McCarthy (1998: 8–9) postulates that "action" can be categorized in terms of the fivefold "transactional-professional-pedagogical-socializing-intimate" types. Such a framework would at the same time offer a social situational framework for establishing the more specific "ways of acting" that "social practice" allows for (Fairclough 2003: 26), possibly in terms of a speech act typology.

However, returning to the co-defining link between "action" as social semiotics and "genre" as linguistic structure, Thompson and Couper-Kuhlen (2005) state unambiguously that "the routinized patterns that we call grammar exist because speakers need routinized ways to implement actions" (2005: 482, original emphasis). They then proceed to investigate "grammatical formats as interactional practices" (2005: 483), in which they confirm by a detailed analysis of English and Japanese data that there is incontrovertible evidence that the clause functions as the main structural locus of interaction (2005: 489ff.). Hence the present genre as constituting the code via which action as mode is expressed activates grammatical structure(s) for its realization, which together with the accompanying lexical structures effectuates its social semiotic impact, not denying accompanying semantic effects.

Table 3.1 summarizes the categories of analysis established so far:

**Table 3.1** Categories of Analysis

| | | | |
|---|---|---|---|
| **Codes as social practice and linguistic structure** | dialect | register | genre |
| **Modes as social event and social semiotics/text** | identification | representation | action |
| **Linguistic realization** | lexicophonology | lexicosemantics | lexicogrammar |

Table 3.2 Corollaries of the Categories of Analysis

| Variety characterizing | user | use | using |
|---|---|---|---|
| Orientation as social practice | speaker/writer | message | listener/reader |
| Function fulfilled in social event | display | discourse | dialogue |
| Structural linguistic function | contrastive | culminative | concatenative |
| Language realization function | materiality | significance | temporality/linearity |

Further conceptual corollaries may be suggested of the basic analytical categories here presented. Whereas dialect has already been defined as a variety according to user, register according to use and genre according to using, as social practice dialect may equally be said to be speaker/writer-oriented, register as message-oriented and genre as listener/reader-oriented. As social event, identification serves a function of display, register that of discourse, and genre that of dialogue. Finally, from a structural linguistic point of view, lexicophonology may be said to constitute the structural layer availing a contrastive (distinguishing) function of patterning, lexicosemantics the layer availing a culminative (highlighting) function, and lexicogrammar the layer availing a concatenive (linking) function of patterning (after Trubetzkoy 1969). The reification of the varieties of dialect, register and genre in actual linguistic use, i.e., as a dialect, a register and a genre may be termed lects. Ultimately the lexico-phonological/-graphological layer of linguistic structure provides the materiality (i.e., substance) of language in spoken and written form, the lexicosemantic layer its significance, and the lexicogrammatical its temporality (speech) or linearity (writing). Table 3.2 summarizes these further points.

As already stated, this present tricodal/trimodal theory of the linguistic structuring of social meaning will be applied further below to the analysis of co-lingually situated English(es) in a number of representative communicative events worldwide. However, its full relevance for the understanding of globally situated anglophony must first be clarified in the framework of multilingualism/multilectalism, i.e., heteroglossia, in general.

## 3. Heteroglossia

### 3.1 The Social Meanings of Heteroglossic English

As Tagg (2015: 207) observes in a discussion of translanguaging and a superdiverse internet, "most people have resources from more than one language in ways that reflect the repertoires of 'multilinguals'," i.e., "everyone moves between registers, styles and/or dialects." Heteroglossia, she suggests, "encompasses diversity in all its forms, including multilingual, multimodal and multi-authored practices and which therefore best capture the kind of hybrid language practices that take place in many digital contexts" (2015: 208). It is this conception of heteroglossia that is shared here, in the first instance as a superordinate term covering both multilingualism (more than one language) and multilectalism (here, more than one code), reflecting on the one hand the linguistic "glossodiversity" present in the world, and on the other the equally present "semiodiversity" within language(s) globally (Halliday 2007). It might be noted that the term "heteroglossia" or "double-voicing" originally derives from Bakhtin (1981), who with it designates the fact that "our speech, i.e., all our utterances ... is filled with the words of others" (1981: 89). In a general sense with relation to the present model one could concur that our speech is indeed shared, repeated and therefore routinised within the affordances and constraints of codes/modes.

An ever-increasing number of studies—too numerous to list—have in recent years analyzed language-mixing scenarios involving English(es) and co-present other, predominantly local, languages. Such studies employ the various frameworks of code-switching, hybridity and translanguaging and examine situated anglophony/ anglography in various sound and/or visual media (radio, TV, film) and oral conversation, print media (the press, advertising) and digital (social) media such as Facebook in particular, but also fan-fiction and multiplayer online gaming. Dependent on the framework adopted, researchers point to the particular social meanings that the English serves to express in the context of its co-present language(s), as generally in code-switching and hybridity approaches, or, as in a translanguaging perspective, pointing to the sociocultural capacities of users, foremostly of creativity and criticality, that emerge as they "move dynamically between the so-called languages, language varieties, styles, registers, and writing systems, to fulfil a variety of strategic and communicative functions" (Li 2017: 18).

In very broad terms, and increasingly to the extent that English is societally perceived as a foreign as opposed to a second or a (co-)native language, the social meanings that have been ascribed to its use in such informal contexts either by the language participants themselves or by the researchers range variously from affective empathy, "mateyness," group solidarity, a cultivated informality and general conviviality to modernity, enlightenment, cultural sophistication, global connectivity and general "cool"—all most prominently expressed in contexts of digital communication. These positive attributes manifest a well-observed local as well global dimension of sociolinguistic practice. Indeed the English here appears as a valued-added linguistic resource for positive social effect, as "anglographic enhancement" via the verbal and visual impact of its written form (James 2014: 34ff., 2016: 260ff.). Extrapolating further, one could almost conclude that anglophony/anglography in such co-lingual contexts provides an extra affective modality of expression, perhaps even comparable to tone of voice in oral communication, but also to the physical modalities of facial expression, gesture, posture and proximity—all absent in purely verbal digital communication (but available in multimedia communication).

Moving now to a consideration of the contextual conditions furthering or restricting translingual (or intralingual/translectal) alternations in communicative events as social events beyond the kind of sociolinguistic-semiotic (semi-?) intentionality behind the incorporation of English just discussed, an attempt will be made to explore to what extent the situational deployment of one or the other code/mode might itself constitute such a condition and co-determine the linguistic forms produced.

## 3.2 Contextual Conditions on Heteroglossia: Contact Types

Not only by its perceived global presence, but also partly by analogy to intralingual style-shifting, translingual mixing has been increasingly considered as an unmarked mode of communication, as translanguaging approaches assert (cf., e.g., Saraceni 2015), and the linguistic repertoires of language users are not only seen as multilectal but multilingual, whereby the multiple languages involved may only be partially internalized (Blommaert and Backus 2012). However, the actual contextual activation of the languages employed in multilingual discourses has been attributed in research to a wide array of sociocultural, psycholinguistic and discourse-functional factors (cf., e.g., Myslín and Levy 2015: 873–8), while structural linguistic approaches have resulted in extensive models of code-switching (e.g., Muysken 2000; Myers-Scotton 2002). In the latter, points of switch and types of switch correlate with lexicogrammatical properties of the ongoing utterance, and as such accept the structural unity of multilingual strings. Building on these approaches Onysko (2019) develops a cognitive processing model of language contact, specifically of the four phenotypes of borrowing, transfer/interference, code-switching and replication. It is to a consideration of this model in the light of the present tricodal/trimodal approach that the discussion now turns.

Whereas the proposed tricodal/trimodal model attempts a mutually defining synthesis between linguistic structuring as hybrid layers of lexicophonological, lexicosemantic and lexicogrammatical patterning and the social semiotic significances of identification, representation and action, Onysko's model attempts a mutually defining synthesis between linguistic structuring as types of language contact and the cognitive processing of language as unconscious/conscious activation determining the adoption of monolingual/multilingual/oscillating modes of realization. "[A]pproaching the notion of language contact from cognitive linguistics … throws into relief the basic conceptualisation of language as a bounded entity" (Onysko 2019: 31), i.e., he questions the assumption that processing and production is individual language-specific, as does the present co-defining of linguistic codes from a social semiotic perspective, which thus far has been formulated in (specific) language-neutral terms. Indeed, without doing adequate justice to the full complexities of cognitive processing described by Onysko, a closer comparison of the two models nonetheless reveals further compatible points of connection in the form of the proposed contact phenotypes which may permit a complementarity of explanation for heteroglossic linguistic structuring from cognitive and social semiotic perspectives.

The phenotype borrowing, as "the use of form-meaning units of La in Lb," which in the monolingual mode of production "engages selection from the lexical knowledge base" of the recipient code" (2019: 38), i.e., is seen in the first instance as a word-level phenomenon, that in the present approach employs lexicosemantic structure(s) to express the representation of a particular socially relevant meaning in a heteroglossic discourse (see also the culminative (highlighting) function in 2.2 above). Similarly, calquing as "the replication of La meaning in Lb with the help of linguistic forms of Lb," i.e., as the predominant form of the phenotype "replication" (2019: 42), is primarily a lexicosemantic structuring, again, expressing the representation of a socially

Table 3.3 Codes/Modes and Contact Phenotypes

| Contact types | transfer/interference | borrowing+replication | codeswitching |
|---|---|---|---|
| Social semiotic effects | identification | representation | action |
| Structural realization | lexicophonological | lexicosemantic | lexicogrammatical |
| Code types | dialect | register | genre |

relevant meaning in discourse (cf., also the culminative (highlighting) function in 2.2 above).

Codeswitching (with code here designating language code), as a form of borrowing, involves the use of form-units from La in Lb, but where the selection from the knowledge base is not of the recipient language. "As a socio-pragmatically adequate conversational tool in a multilingual mode, CS [codeswitching] occurs spontaneously, coheres with the contextually conditioned discourse strategies, and carries out multiple functions" (2019: 40). In terms of the present model, the phenotype codeswitching is primarily a lexicogrammatical structuring promoting a social semiotics of action (cf., the concatenative (linking) function in 2.2 above).

Finally, the phenotype transfer/interference as "an analogically stimulated activation of language units in code La that influences the production of a formally/semantically related language unit in code Lb" (2019: 40) is predominantly a lexicophonological structuring in spoken language manifesting a social semiotics of identification (cf., the contrastive (distinguishing) function in 2.2. above). In other words, the contact phenotypes of borrowing and replication characterize in the main register code, codeswitching a genre code and transfer/interference a dialect code. At this point it must be stressed however that these are not relations of exclusivity, but of weighted orientation or default setting—for instance, lexicogrammatical structure(s) can also be borrowed or replicated, lexicophonological structure(s) co-codeswitched in speech and lexicosemantic structure(s) transferred. The relations as outlined are summarized in Table 3.3.

Having established these co-occurrences between contact phenotypes and the present triple linguistic codes and semiotic modes in communicative events as social events at a general level of analysis, it will now be shown how these elements of a tricodal/trimodal approach to the linguistic structuring of social meaning can account for the formal-functional regularities that characterize the use of English in locally constituted heteroglossic discourse worldwide.

## 4. Codes/Modes and Contact Types in Co-Present Anglophony/Anglography: Data Analysis

### 4.1 Further Considerations

In subsequent analysis below, attention will also be given to a type of heteroglossic scenario where English functions as an overlay language to another which would otherwise be the unmarked choice for general communication purposes, including the digital, in the contexts investigated. Findings indicate that in such circumstances its ancillary status stands for both a local "ambient affiliation" (Zappavigna 2012) and a global sophistication, in print and web advertising (e.g., Martin 2007, 2014), but particularly as employed in social communication in the digital media (see also 3.1. above). In contrast, the bulk of the substantial literature in both varieties and post-varieties research paradigms has until recently addressed the use of English as a co-language in multilingual contexts where it is one of societally sanctioned languages present such as, e.g., with users from Singapore, Malaysia and Hong Kong (i.e., Outer Circle locations) or the Philippines and Indonesia (Outer Circle-related locations), with only to a limited extent analyzing digital, as opposed to spoken or written communication. In such circumstances, the English is not so much a linguistic overlay, but a co-language providing its own semiotic resources to an ongoing discourse on a par with the other language(s) employed. However, its very material presence—particularly in informal digital communication and much as in its overlay role—can nonetheless achieve a value-added effect by complementing the material presence of the other language(s) and in doing so confirming and thereby intensifying, but, crucially, <u>maintaining</u> the nature of the code in operation and the social semiotics of its mode. Apart from in any case drawing attention to its own materiality, it evokes via homophoric reference and intertextuality its use and meanings in other codally and modally equivalent anglophone contexts (cf., James 2016: 267), i.e., in Bakhtin's terms, reproducing the voices of others. From a language contact perspective, codeswitching, borrowing and "replication" denote the interlingual matching processes involved. In monolingual discourse this would be equivalent to a stylistic shift via <u>intra</u>lingual codeswitching, borrowing or replication making meaning contextually more explicit (e.g., by switching the lexicophonological structure(s) of one dialect into another), while at the same time confirming the social semiotics of the mode present and the code in place in the discourse.

In the following section, data from informal heteroglossic digital communication involving English will be analyzed to illustrate the points being developed.

## 4.2 Three Data Scenario Types

The three scenario types analyzed are:

i) where English is a fully integrated lingual component of a "fused lect" (Auer 1999) and is used as such in a communicative event
ii) where English is one of two (or more) languages used alternatingly on a regular basis, and used as such in a communicative event
iii) where English is used selectively within the frame of another language in a communicative event

All data are taken from published Facebook communications, both commentaries and chat, where in the present discussion particular attention will be drawn to scenario iii), as constituting, arguably, the most widely encountered social use of English globally, but as presently under-researched in comparison to scenarios i) and ii).

Where English has a societally sanctioned local co-presence with other languages, as in postcolonial Singapore, Hong Kong, Malaysia and India and therefore is employed as such in informal digital communication by users from these locations, its use varies mostly between scenarios i) and ii). Whereas in Singapore English as Singlish functions as a local anglophone variety in its own right with influences from Chinese (Hokkien), Malay and Tamil, in Malaysia a local variety of Malaysian English can be distinguished as well as Rojak (Malay for mixture) variously evidenced in use scenarios i) and ii) (Schneider 2016: 346–7). In Hong Kong, English alternates with Cantonese much as in use scenario ii), while in India apart from its co-presence with Hindi and other Indian languages as in scenario ii), English is also seen to be increasingly fusing with Hindi, as Hinglish, i.e., moving towards use scenario i) (Schneider 2016: 344–5). In the meantime, there is sufficient evidence to suggest that these patterns of English are reproduced if not intensified in social media use.

### 4.2.1 *Scenario i)*

Example 1: Rojak (Saraceni 2015: 121, Text 2, lines 1–8)

A. ni yang hari tu korang nak dapat ^^ lol misai is shaved!
B. Haha … sound tu yg aku meniyirap tu aritu. . .nk tdo pon susah
C. Haha shave jugakkk finally ^^
D. hahahahahhaha! made my day
E. with or without the moustache, you look like snoop dog
F. the sound of shaver klakar gile. siapboleh break2 tu last2
G. meniyirap aku denga music background tu. . .
H. hahaha. . .NICE!!

The comments are those of friends reacting to a user's posting that he has shaved his beard off.

Much could be remarked on regarding the—familiar—media-specific abbreviated word spellings (*tu* for too; *yg* for young, *gile* for Gillette), rebuses (*2* for too), letter repetition for prominence (*jugakkk*), representation of emotions, also by syllable repetition (*hahahahahhaha*), capitalisation for volume (*NICE!!*), acronym (*lol*) and laughter emoticon (^^). B and C capitalize their line-initial "Haha." Apart from D's clause-length codeswitch (*with or without. . . .snoop dog*), the English is fully integrated with the Malay at word level (*sound, shave, finally, break, last*), phrase level (*the sound of shaver, music background*) and predicate level (*is shaved, made my day*).

This indeed indicates that the language displayed by the users is a fused lect, in which the combination of Malay and English is re-created in each communication anew. This speech act of declarative commentary manifests in modal terms a strong identification function with its (digital bilingual) formal appearance, strongly projecting Rojak as dialect in codal terms, with its lexicographological uniqueness. The unity of the fused lect is promoted by the employment of the Roman alphabet as script, but still with different orthographies, the differences of which are partly neutralized via the use of conventional as well constructed digital short forms. The incidental codeswitching of E via a well-formed extended lexicogrammatical string in standard English (complete with comma!) can perhaps be seen as actionally motivated in the context.

From a language contact point of view, since transfer/interference has been claimed above to be associated with dialect code and its lexicophonological—here lexicographological—structuring, one could note that fused lects are indeed formed via the massive mutual transfer/interference of the original languages involved.

### 4.2.2 *Scenario ii)*

Example 2: Taglish (Schneider 2016: 345, Text (1), original lines 1–12, English translations in square brackets)

| | |
|---|---|
| E. | i wasn't online last weekend |
| E. | coz i went to batangas for the fiesta |
| L. | oo ng apala [oh yes, now i remember] |
| L. | bong aba uli [was it lavish/extravagant again] |
| E. | yes…mas bongga ngayon than before […it was more lavish/extravagant now than before] |
| L. | boah |
| E. | kasi mas maraming tao [because there were more people], coz it was on a Saturday |
| L. | tamang tama [that was just the right timing] |
| E. | yup…B was asking about u |
| L. | padala naman ng pics [do send me pictures] |

The transcript is of an online chat protocol, where the Taglish evidences considerable codeswitching between Tagalog and English as the language contact phenotype, each represented in their standard spellings apart from English *i, coz, u,* the onomatopoeic spellings of *boah* and *yup* and the use of lower-case for the first letter of line-/turn-initial words—being all minor concessions to social media usage. Certain key words such as Tagalog *batangas* (a placename with initial letter lower-case) and *bong aba—bongga* and English *pics* constitute lexical insertions (i.e., borrowing(s)), reflecting in modal terms a representation function expressed via codal lexicosemantic structure(s). Otherwise the English and the Tagalog are used alternatingly, mainly signalling turn-takes, with E using English more frequently and L Tagalog. The constructions alternating are well-formed, full clauses plus the minimal responses *boah, yes* and *yup* and contribute to a smooth dialogue. As such in codal/modal terms they evidence the lexicogrammatical structure(s) of genre realizing an actional (here, inter-actional) social semiotics.

Example 3: Denglish (Buschfeld, Kautzsch and Schneider 2018: 35, data (3)–(8))

(3) Female, 35: Well, Nirvana halt, just kult!
(4) Female, 35: […] Und das Gitarrensolo-Thema finde ich suuuuper, let's keep that in mind for next week!

(5) Female, 35 [about a posted song]: Ich leg einen nach [I'll add one more], gimme a minute.
(6) Female, 35: Oh yesssss! (More comments later tonight, du hältst mich vom schweren Arbeiten ab [you're keeping me off from hard work]).
(7) Male, 28: Mensch, da kriegt man so viele Geburtstagsgrüsse [Oh man, you get so many nice birthday greetings], but this knocks it out of the park [...]
(8) Male, 47: Congrats, du Wahnsinniger [you crazy guy]!!! WOW!!!

These are again commentaries on a Facebook posting, but particularly noteworthy is the untypical standard spelling and punctuation of both German and English, apart from *gimme* emphatic *suuuuper* and *yesssss* and conventionally shortened *Congrats*. The hybrid label Denglish for *Deutsch + English*, which in common use refers to extensive lexical borrowing from English into German, is adopted here by analogy to the Taglish above.

The users are described as being "highly educated German speakers of English" (2018: 34) and gender and age of the users are included in the data. The education level of the network users is a likely indicator for the use of standard spelling and punctuation, but the style of the commentaries is in fact reminiscent of informal spoken language. However, the language alternations occur regularly at clause (including minor clause) boundaries, also within turns (as in "Well, Nirvana halt"), making prominent the succession of well-formed lexicogrammatical strings. These therefore in the present analysis constitute genre as code expressing the social semiotic action mode. In language contact terms, the data provide clear cases of the codeswitching phenotype. By juxtaposing data from Taglish and Denglish, the intention is also to confirm that it is the users' own deployment of their linguistic resources that defines the heteroglossic nature of the communication event and not the geographical context of their use as such.

### 4.2.3 *Scenario iii)*

Example 4: Serblish/ Anglosrpski

The data for the present section are taken from a study of the Facebook communication of female Serbian users between the ages of 15 and 25 years (Palibrk and Tošić 2012). In the study, a self-assessment task i) required 150 subjects to list the English words and phrases as well English-based abbreviated forms that they used on a daily basis in correspondence with friends; and a data analysis ii) is undertaken of the 24 Facebook profiles (431 comments, 4,158 words) of 80 users, divided into equal-number groups of 15 to 20 year olds and of 20 to 25 year olds, with special attention to the employment of "English words, chunks or abbreviations," English-influenced Serbian orthography and English pattern abbreviations in Serbian (2012: 157). The terms Serblish and Anglosrpski are those in use to designate extensive lexical borrowing from English into Serbian (cf., e.g., Vasić, Prćić and Nejgebauer 2001). Findings from the data analysis ii) provide the basis for the present discussion.

Overall, while the younger group used almost double the percentage (12.58%) of the English and English-related lexical forms in their total vocabulary than the older group

(7.46%), the latter group used significantly more "whole phrases or chunks of language" (37% of all examples of English) than the former (18.4%) (2012: 158), a fact in the light of the present discussion perhaps indicating something more of a lexicogrammatically characterized actional semiotics of the English. However, in language contact terms, lexical borrowings and replications represent the most prominent anglophone/anglographic influences. Examples of lexical borrowings included are *refreshing*, *honey bunny*, *true love* and *teenage films*, whereas of particular prominence are the "arbitrary adaptation" forms constituting replications such as *prajvat parti* ('private parts'), *sou long sakrz* ('solong suckers'), *lajkjues* ('like you's') and *very najs pikcr* ('very nice picture') (2012: 159). Further examples of orthographic creativity are the substitution of Serbian *š*, *č* and *ć* by *sh* and *ch*, and *ks* by *x* (2012: 161), while combinations of a replicated English stem combined with a Serbian inflection, above all with verb forms, are also common (but see also the nominal inflection in *parti* above).

In terms of the present model, English in these data constitutes an overlay language (cf., 4.1. above) and is adduced primarily in its lexicosemantic dimension, i.e., as register, to express a social semiotics of representation—literally, the representation of a Facebook community via a co-constructed group vocabulary. It thereby enhances the desired projection via its valued-added linguistic substance. Apart from the direct borrowing of anglophone lexical items in their original orthography, there are also frequent occurrences of replication, where the items are transliterated into Serbian orthography and in certain cases further truly nativized by adding Serbian inflections, as already pointed out. The substitution of certain letters and digraphs from English for their Serbian phonetic equivalents is, strictly, a case of transfer/interference in contact terms and as such a salient identification marker sociosemiotically as executed by the manipulation of lexicophonological/-graphological structure. The identification involved is one of situational bilingual as signalled via a particularly salient orthographic transfer/interference, indexing bi-graphic competence in the two languages involved. It might be relevant to note at this point that Serbian users are in any case bi-literate with the presence of complementary Roman and Cyrillic alphabets, a situation which might facilitate a certain flexibility in orthographic practice. However, the predominant social semiotics signalled remains that of representation in its lexicosemantic structural form.

## 5. Conclusion

The three scenario types serve to illustrate how English as employed as a co-language in heteroglossic informal digital communication, what social semiotics it expresses and via which general layer(s) of linguistic structure(s) this is achieved. It is argued that English in each scenario type not only contributes to and therefore confirms the dominant linguistic code and social semiotic mode in place at the time but in its very anglographic form and with its homophoric/intertextual associations serves to intensify them (see 4.1 above). As an extension of this structured referencing, the English can be assumed too in each scenario type to connotate further positive meanings of a local and global dimension. Such connotations of, very broadly, local conviviality and global sophistication, respectively, will expectedly increase through scenario types i) to ii) to iii) (see also 3.1 above). At the same time, it will be noticed that the data examined do not include any purely graphic representations such as emojis (which indeed were deliberately omitted in the original presentation of scenario iii)), and it will be a task of future research to further explore their semiotic significance in interplay with that of the linguistic as well as graphic impact of English (but, cf., Danesi 2017; James 2017).

Clearly, the actual four communicative events described are not comparable methodologically in that there are considerable variables involved not least concerning chat vs. commentary, age, education (and gender?) of the language users and in any case the practice of the original data collection. Nevertheless, it has been hoped to show that the analysis of such representative samples of empirical data evidencing English in international use in a globally much-frequented communication medium does seem to offer support for the present tricodal/trimodal theory of language as social practice. As such, it also offers a framework within which perspectives of varieties and post-varieties approaches to English(es) worldwide may be combined.

## References

Auer, P. (1999), "From codeswitching via language mixing to fused lects: Toward a dynamic typology of bilingual speech," *International Journal of Bilingualism*, 5 (4): 309–32.

Bakhtin, M. (1981), *The Dialogic Imagination. Four Essays*, ed. Michael Holquist, Austin: University of Texas Press.

Bakhtin, M. (1986), *Speech Genres and Other Late Essays*, eds. Caryl Emerson and Michael Holquist, Austin: University of Texas Press.

Blommaert, J. (2010), *The Sociolinguistics of Globalization*, Cambridge: Cambridge University Press.

Blommaert, J. and A. Backus (2012), "Superdiverse repertoires and the individual," *Tilburg Papers in Culture Studies*, 24.

Bucholtz, M. and K. Hall (2005), "Identity and interaction: a sociocultural linguistic approach," *Discourse Studies*, 7 (4–5): 585–614.

Buschfeld, S., A. Kautzsch and E. W. Schneider (2018), "From colonial dynamisms to current transnationalism. A unified view on postcolonial and non-postcolonial Englishes," in S. C. Deshors (ed.), *Modeling World Englishes. Assessing the Interplay of Emancipation and Globalization of ESL Varieties*, 15–44, Amsterdam: John Benjamins.

Danesi, M. (2017), *The Semiotics of Emoji. The Rise of Visual Language in the Age of the Internet*, London: Bloomsbury.

Deshors, S. C. and G. Gilquin (2018), "Modeling World Englishes in the 21st century. New reflections on model-making," in S. C. Deshors (ed.), *Modeling World Englishes. Assessing the Interplay of Emancipation and Globalization of ESL Varieties*, 281–94, Amsterdam: John Benjamins.

Fairclough, N. (2003), *Analysing Discourse. Textual Analysis for Social Research*, London: Routledge.

Ferguson, C. A. (1994), "Dialect, register, and genre: Working assumptions about conventionalization," in D. Biber and E. Finnegan (eds.), *Sociolinguistic Perspectives on Register*, 15–30, New York: Oxford University Press.

Foucault, M. (1972), *The Architecture of Knowledge*, New York: Pantheon.
Halliday, M.A.K. (1978), *Language as Social Semiotic. The Social Interpretation of Language*. London: Edward Arnold.
Halliday, M.A.K. (2007), "Applied linguistics as an evolving theme," in James Webster (ed.), *Language and Education: Collected Works of M.A.K. Halliday*, 1–19, London: Continuum.
James, A. (2005), "The challenges of the Lingua Franca: English in the world and types of variety," in C. Gnutzmann and F. Intenmann (eds.), *The Globalisation of English and the English Classroom*, 133–44, Tübingen: Narr.
James, A. (2008), "New Englishes as post-geographic Englishes in lingua franca use. Genre, interdiscursivity and late modernity," *European Journal of English Studies*, 12 (1): 97–112.
James, A. (2009), "Theorising English and globalisation: semiodiversity and linguistic structure in Global English, World Englishes and Lingua Franca English," *Apples—Journal of Applied Language Studies*, 3 (1): 79–92.
James, A. (2014), "English as a visual language: theorising the social semiotics of anglography in polylingual texts," *English Text Construction*, 7 (1): 18–52.
James, A. (2016), "From code-mixing to mode-mixing in the European context," *World Englishes*, 35 (2): 259–75.
James, A. (2017), "Prosody and paralanguage in speech and the social media: The vocal and graphic realisation of affective meaning," *Linguistica*, 57 (1): 137–49.
Li, W. (2017), "Translanguaging as a practical theory of language," *Applied Linguistics*, 39 (1): 1–22.
Mair, C. (2018), "Stabilising domains of English-language use in Germany. Global English in a non-colonial languagescape," in S. C. Deshors (ed.), *Modeling World Englishes. Assessing the Interplay of Emancipation and Globalization of ESL Varieties*, 44–75, Amsterdam: John Benjamins.
Martin, E. (2007), "'Frenglish' for sale: Multilingual discourses for addressing today's global consumer," *World Englishes*, 28 (2): 170–90.
Martin, E. (2014), "Linguistic and cultural hybridity in French web advertising," in R. Rubdy and L. Alsagoff (eds.), *The Global-Local Interface and Hybridity. Exploring Language and Identity*, 133–52, Bristol: Multilingual Matters.
McCarthy, M. (1998), *Spoken Language and Applied Linguistics*, Cambridge: Cambridge University Press.
Muysken, P. (2000), *Bilingual Speech: A Typology of Code-Mixing*, Cambridge: Cambridge University Press.
Myers-Scotton, C. (2002), *Contact Linguistics: Bilingual Encounters and Grammatical Outcomes*, Oxford: Oxford University Press.
Myslín, M. and R. Levy (2015), "Code-switching and predictability of meaning in discourse," *Language*, 91 (4): 871–905.
Onysko, A. (2019), "Reconceptualizing language contact phenomena as cognitive processes," in E. Zenner, A. Backus and E. Winter-Froemel (eds.), *Cognitive Contact Linguistics. Placing Usage, Meaning and Mind at the Core of Contact-Induced Variation and Change*, 23–50, Berlin: De Gruyter.
Palibrk, I. and T. Tošić (2012), "Girl talk: English in modern means of communication," *Nasleđe*, 21: 151–64.
Saraceni, M. (2014), "The language of Malaysian and Indonesian users of social networks: Practice vs system," in R. Rubdy and L. Alsagoff (eds.), *The Global-Local Interface and Hybridity. Exploring Language and Identity*, 191–204, Bristol: Multilingual Matters.

Saraceni, M. (2015), *World Englishes. A Critical Analysis*, London: Bloomsbury.
Schneider, E. W. (2007), *Postcolonial English: Varieties Around the World*, Cambridge: Cambridge University Press.
Schneider, E. W. (2016), "Hybrid Englishes: An exploratory survey," *World Englishes*, 35 (3): 339–54.
Seargeant, P. and C. Tagg (2011), "English in the internet and a "post-varieties" approach to language," *World Englishes*, 30 (4): 496–514.
Tagg, C. (2015), *Exploring Digital Communication: Language in Action*, London: Routledge.
Thompson, S. A. and E. Couper-Kuhlen (2005), "The clause as a locus of grammar and interaction," *Discourse Studies*, 7 (4–5): 481–505.
Trubetzkoy, N. (1969), *Principles of Phonology*, Berkeley: University of California Press.
Vasić, V., T. Prćić and G. Nejgebauer (2001), *Rečnik Novijih Anglicizama. Du Yu Speak Anglosrpski?* Novi Sad: Zmaj.
Webb, J. (2008), *Understanding Representation*, London: Sage.
Werth, P. (1999), *Text Worlds: Representing Conceptual Space in Discourse*, London: Longman.
Zappavigna, M. (2012), *Discourse of Twitter and Social Media*, London: Bloomsbury.

# 4

# Extending the Scope of World Englishes: Interactions across Englishes in Post-Protectorates and at the Grassroots

Christiane Meierkord

## 1. Introduction

As is well known, over the centuries, and particularly in the last few decades, English has come to be increasingly, if not predominantly, used for interactions that involve speakers for whom English is a second (L2) or foreign (FL) language, and who interact across their individual Englishes (Meierkord 2012). However, the majority of research into world Englishes has so far typically focused on post-colonial settings and the spread of English has largely been associated with and analyzed as spoken by the "educated" elites[1] of their respective societies. As Saraceni (2015) pointed out, this has resulted in World Englishes research reaching some sort of an impasse, struggling to catch up and draw level with advances in sociolinguistics, such as Blommaert's (2010) "Sociolinguistics of Globalisation" framework, which puts migration but also the grassroots of societies at its focus.

The latter has largely been ignored, resulting in, as Mesthrie and Bhatt (2008: 36), for example, lament, a lack of an integration of social class, which "is noticeably missing from Schneider's [(2007)] model (and in fact from many of the "circles" models)" despite the existence of "a large gap between the middle-class varieties of New Englishes and their jargon, pidgin or basilectal counterparts." In fact, several studies have demonstrated that elite and grassroots uses of English do differ (e.g., Darvin 2017; Toefy 2017; Myrick 2014; Ofori and Albakry 2012; see Section 4.2). Mesthrie and Bhatt (2008: 9) further notice that post-protectorates have not sufficiently been covered and integrated into theorizing world Englishes despite the fact that they "may well have a status intermediate between ESL and EFL territories" and, thus, offer important input to theories. The same, I propose, is the case with those territories that were protected states, League of Nations mandates and United Nations trust territories (PPSMTs[2]).

In fact, former PPSMTs, for example the post-protectorates Uganda or the Maldives, differ crucially from most post-colonial settings in that, due to restrictions on land purchases, a significant settler strand in the sense of Schneider (2007) was crucially missing. Whilst Uganda, despite having a low settler strand, attracted British administrators and colonial personnel, the Maldives did not have any British personnel until 1941, when a military base was established on the island of Gan. And whereas English was quickly established as a medium of instruction (MOI) in Uganda, this domain has only been occupied by English in Maldives since the 1960s. Contrary to these histories, it seems that today there has been a reversal in that English seems to spread more easily at all levels of society in Maldives. In both countries, speakers of English, both from the societal elites and from the grassroots, typically do not interact with speakers of the same variety of English. Rather, they engage in what Meierkord (2012) models as Interactions across Englishes, either with their fellow country people or with individuals (e.g., migrants, expatriates, or tourists) from abroad.

## 2. Interactions across Englishes

Crucially, the enormous spread of English to every part of the world and increasingly into all spheres of societies involves interactions between individuals who speak different varieties of English. Graddol (1999: 57) argued more than two decades ago that, in the future, English would be "used mainly in multilingual contexts as a second language and for communication between non-native speakers." In fact, over the last decades, interactions between speakers for whom English is not their first language (L1) have come to be the majority of all those interactions that are conducted in English. Meierkord (2012) envisages these as Interactions across Englishes (IaEs). The core assumption of the model is that the Englishes spoken by the individual participants potentially merge in these interactions and that this, also potentially, results in an array of new emergent linguistic systems (cf., Meierkord 2012: 2). Depending on how frequent and regular such interactions occur, these outcomes may be stable linguistic patterns that involve accommodation to each other's ways of using English or more ad-hoc communicative solutions that are characterized by processes of simplification and regularization as well as pragmatic strategies employed to cope with the diversity of and unfamiliarity with participants' patterns and conventions of using English.

Generally, IaEs involve communication between two or more speakers who use English as their L2 or as an FL[3], either in a standardized form or in a pidginized or a more or less stable learner language variety. Examples include speakers of Pakistani English, speakers of Cameroon Pidgin English, Turkish or Chinese users of English who may interact in a local Cameroon market place. Similarly, there are intranational interactions, for example in Uganda, between speakers of Ugandan English, who have a Bantu or Nilotic L1, and speakers of Ugandan Indian English. Finally, a Polish and a Philippina nurse may interact in a London hospital.

The individual speakers of these different varieties of English will, albeit to varying degrees, use forms of pronunciation and grammar as well as lexical items and pragmatic strategies that are characteristic of their variety. More generally speaking, individual speakers thus contribute their various features to a feature pool, in the sense of Mufwene (2001): for example, a speaker of Pakistani English may use articles differently and employ the phrase *Insha-Allah* (God willing) to express a polite refusal or a non-committing promise (Mahboob 2009). Potentially, the other speakers in the interaction notice her behaviors and accommodate to it by copying or appropriating it.

As Meierkord (2012) documents, such IaEs occur both at an *intra*national level as well as at an *inter*national level. At the intranational level IaEs are typically found in post-colonial nations, such as South Africa, where different Englishes are spoken within one country. In South Africa, the unfortunate Apartheid system gave rise to the separate development of White South African English, Black South African English, Colored South African English and South African Indian English. Since the collapse of the Apartheid system in 1989/90, speakers of these different varieties have increasingly interacted across their Englishes. Meierkord (2012: 116–27) shows that colored speakers accommodate to black speakers in their extended uses of progressives and their pronunciation of the GOOSE vowel.

Nowadays, international interactions involve speakers from any country, be they L1, L2 or FL speakers of English. However, mostly, international uses of English have been associated with countries of the expanding circle (see Kachru 1985), where English does not hold and perform a special role as L2 within the country, due to the fact that it does not serve as an official language, nor as an MOI, and is not used in the media. Such international cases are, obviously, extremely heterogeneous, with participants in such interactions typically finding themselves in ever-novel constellations. This results in interactions where participants may not be familiar with the different features that characterize each other's Englishes as regards pronunciation, grammar, vocabulary, and pragmatic conventions. As Meierkord (1996) found, participants then frequently resort to what they believe to be safe modes of communication, such as high frequency formulaic phrases for greetings or requests. At the same time, the learner status of individual participants frequently results in the use of paraphrase, shorter sentences and of coping strategies such as frequent back-channels, cooperative overlap, jointly constructed turns and the negotiation of meaning sequences (see Meierkord 2012: 158–94; compare also Kirkpatrick 2007: 155–70), and Firth (1996) finds that participants employ strategies that he calls *let it pass* and *make it normal* to deal with any idiosyncracies in each other's Englishes.

Seemingly, intranational interactions in outer circle countries and international interactions between individuals from expanding circle countries may be two poles on a continuum, and seeking similarities as do, for example, the papers in Mukherjee and Hundt (2011) or those in Deshors (2018), is one important way of understanding the continuum between the two. At the same time, however, along the continuum there seem to exist nodes, but these have not received sufficient attention yet. One of these, I propose, are those countries that have no history of significant English L1 settler populations, as the colonies do. This seems to be the case with former protectorates and protected states, but also former League of Nations mandates and United Nations trust territories, as well as with Commonwealth members that do not belong to either of the aforementioned.

## 3. Post-Protectorates, Protected States, Mandates and Trust Territories—The In-Between Cases

As has been mentioned in the introduction, Mesthrie and Bhatt (2008: 9) argue that countries that were previous British (or American) protectorates may be "in-between" post-colonial nations (for which Schneider's 2007 Dynamic Model proposes a uniform trajectory of the development of their Englishes) and such nations in which English is typically a foreign language, used for international communication. Traditionally, these two have been discussed as outer circle and expanding circle countries, following Kachru (1985).

Whilst colonies were typically intended to provide land for permanent settlement or natural resources (see Mufwene 2001: 8–9 on settlement versus trade and exploitation colonies) and under full sovereignty of the colonizer, protectorates were, typically, contractual arrangements formalized in a treaty between the protector and the protégé, outlining rights and duties of both.[4] This involved "the transfer of the management of some or all of the international affairs to the protecting State," so that the protectorate can no longer act internationally on its own behalf and does "not qualify as an independent or a sovereign State" (Trilsch 2011, no page numbers).

A protected state, on the other hand, maintained some sovereignty over the conduct of her international affairs. Furthermore, it retained full control over her internal affairs. An example is Tonga from 1900 to 1970.

A League of Nations mandate was a legal status resulting from the Covenant of the League of Nations, signed as part of the 1919 Treaty of Versailles, and applied to territories that, as a consequence of WWI, were no longer ruled by their prior sovereign, Germany and the Ottoman (Turkish) Empire. Crucially, annexation of these territories was excluded, as was the construction of fortifications and the raising of an army, but the precise level of sovereign control was determined for each mandate, individually. This ranged from giving administrative advice and assistance (class A mandates, formerly controlled by the Ottoman Empire) via full administration of the territory (class B mandates, all former German territories in West and Central Africa) to administration under the laws of the mandatory power (class C mandates, e.g., Southwest Africa and South Pacific Islands). In any case, mandates typically involved a considerable degree of control over the territory's external and internal affairs (cf., Gordon 2013, no page numbers).

When after WWII, in 1946, the League of Nations dissolved and was replaced by the United Nations, any remaining mandates turned into United Nations Trust Territories, with the sole exception of South-West Africa, which remained under South African control and gained independence in 1990 as Namibia. This status envisaged the "progressive development towards self-governance or independence" (Melnyk 2013, no page numbers), which inevitably implied involvement of the trustee in the internal affairs for some time, which in turn implied the presence of administrative personnel and other L1 speakers of English.

Finally, there are countries, Rwanda and Mozambique, which do not have any history of British control, but became members of the Commonwealth after they had long been independent nations.

## 3.1 English in the British PPSMTs

Given the fact that land purchases were not possible in PPSMTs, these territories typically did not attract large numbers of settlers. However, as Schneider (2007) explains, a settler population is crucial in the development of a post-colonial variety of English, claiming that "to a considerable extent the histories of PCEs [postcolonial Englishes] can be viewed as processes of convergence between these two groups [the settlers and the indigenous population]" (2007: 31) and by labelling the two *strands*, thereby signalling "that they are interwoven with each other like twisted threads."

Informal acquisition of English through interaction with L1 speakers of English was scarce, and English was typically acquired formally, through the education system and only by a minority. As Section 3.3 documents for the case of Maldives, the teaching of English was not necessarily involved in the activities of the sovereign, depending on the degree of involvement in the administration of the territories. That is, when the role of the sovereign restricted itself to foreign affairs, no English-speaking personnel was required to administer the inner/internal affairs.

From the description of the different PPSMTs, it would now be tempting to assume a cline of L1 English-speaking populations as well as a correlating cline of current uses and statuses of English in the independent states. Seemingly, protectorates would range closer to colonies, protected states closer to expanding circle countries, and mandates as well as trust territories in-between.

Table 4.1 in the Appendix provides a list of those PPSMTs that were controlled by inner circle countries. It reveals that English plays a significant role in almost all of these nations today. Whilst it is not an official language in large numbers of the former protectorates, others have retained it in this function after independence (e.g., Uganda). At the same time, English plays a huge role as an MOI in many of these countries, although this varies as regards the onset of its use as MOI, ranging from primary school (for example Maldives) to tertiary education (for example Egypt).

These uses set the post-protectorates (and similar states) apart from those countries that Kachru (1985) had identified as typical expanding circle countries, e.g., Germany, Turkey, Japan or China, in terms of the scope of *intra*national uses of English. Although English is making inroads in the education sector of these countries, too (particularly in the Scandinavian countries (Bolton and Meierkord 2013) and in the Netherlands (Edwards 2016), most courses are still offered in the local official language. Also, for the vast majority of the populations of these countries, English has not attained the status of a L2, but it remains a FL.

However, what also emerges from Table 4.1 is a very heterogeneous picture across the diverse former PPSMTs as regards the current status and use of English. The differences seem largely dependent on whether there is another transnationally relevant language (a super-central language in the sense of de Swaan 2002, 2010) spoken in the country that is deemed capable of fulfilling the same roles as English, particularly in serving as the official language and MOI at the various levels of education. Thus, countries which are dominantly Muslim and where Arabic is known, have chosen not to have English as MOI except for individual courses at tertiary level, as in Egypt or Iraq. Similarly, territories that are now part of China do not have English as OL or MOI, given the Chinese government's language policy. Tibet is a case in point. Those countries that maintained English as the official language after independence frequently use at least one of the indigenous languages as co-official, as in Tanzania or the Cook Islands. On the other hand, several countries have chosen to rely almost entirely on English for official purposes and in the education sector. Obviously, the proposed cline does not result in a correlating cline of current uses of English. In fact, available studies paint a rather kaleidoscopic picture.

## 3.2 Former PPSMTs in World Englishes Research

Research on former PPSMTs under inner circle control is scarce in comparison to that on typical postcolonial nations such as India, Philippines or Singapore, but has been growing recently.

Countries in the Arab world have received some attention: Schaub (2000) describes the sociolinguistics and history of English in Egypt as well as attitudes towards English. More recently, Abouelhassan and Meyer (2016) discuss the history of English and uses of English in Egypt schools. Hamdan and Abu Hatab (2009) focus on the status of English in Jordan, as reflected in job advertisements, finding that English proficiency has become a crucial requirement in the job market. Both Mustafa (1995), and Khuwaileh and Al-Shoumali (2001) explain uses of English in Jordan's universities, and Alomoush (2019) describes how English is used on shopping bags in the country. Dashti (2015) investigates the role and status of English in Kuwait, whilst Fussell (2011) covers the Gulf states as a whole and briefly reports on their history and socio-political context as well as some features. Randall and Samimi (2010) explain the status of English in Dubai (also see Siemund et al., this volume).

African countries have also received attention: Kamwangamalu (1996) analyzes siSwati-English bilingualism, including a brief sketch of the sociolinguistics of eSwatini. Arua (1998) describes selected syntactic features of Swazi English, and Kamwangamalu and Chisanga (1996) discuss the form and function of English in the country. The very short paper by Richmond (1989) provides a list of Gambian expressions but no account of the history or sociolinguistics of English in the country. Kamwendo (2003) offers a very brief discussion of the use of English in Malawi. Stell (2014) is on uses and functions of English in Namibia, which has also received considerable attention by Buschfeld and Kautzsch (2014), and Schröder and Kautzsch (2016). Both Ochieng (2015), and Mohr and Ochieng (2017) discuss the status of English in Tanzania, the latter with a focus on education. Tripathi (1990) offers a brief description of the features of English in Zambia, i.e., pronunciation, vocabulary, and grammar. McGinley (1987) provides a brief account of the status of English in Zimbabwe, which, however, is now outdated. Bernstein (1994) discusses the functions of English and English-Shona diglossia in the country, and Mlambo (2009) describes uses and some features of English. Schmied (1996) covers English in Zimbabwe, Zambia and Malawi, pointing out the colonial histories, post-independence language policies and individual features of English in the three countries.

Research has furthermore covered the Pacific Islands: Pine and Savage (1989) explain the history and recent issues of English as an MOI in the Marshall Islands, and Buchstaller and Wilson (2018) discuss the sociolinguistics of Marshallese English and provide a first sketch of its features. They also find that use of English at home correlates with a high level of education. Watson-Gegeo (1987) juxtaposes the histories and present-day uses of Pijin and English in the Solomon Islands. Jourdan (1989) points out the Pijin-English situation and holds that adults who "come to Honiara seeking unskilled labor jobs for which the knowledge of Pijin but not of English is important" (1989: 29), indicating that, at the grassroots, Pijin was the target language at the time of her writing. Völkel's (2016) comparison of Tongan and English kinship terminology includes a brief description of the sociolinguistics of the island state of Tonga. Biewer (2015) includes descriptions of Samoan English and Cook Islands English.

A large amount of research has been devoted to the Asian state of Brunei: Cane (1994) includes an account of the present-day uses of English in the sultanate of Brunei Darussalam's education system post-independence up until 1994, and Deterding and Sharbawi (2012) is a monograph focusing on English in Brunei. In 2016, *World Englishes* published a special issue on English in Brunei Darussalam. In this issue, Coluzzi (2016) finds a strong presence of English in street signs, particularly in bottom-up signage, and discusses this against the sociolinguistics of Brunei.

Crucially, the picture that emerges is that former PPSMTs are highly heterogeneous, both in terms of their histories of English usage as well as in their present-day uses of English. Sections 3.3 and 3.4 illustrate this heterogeneity with research that has been conducted for Uganda and Maldives.

## 3.3 English in Uganda

Uganda is a landlocked country in East Africa, bordering South Sudan to the North, Tanzania and Rwanda to the South, Kenya to the East, and the Democratic Republic of Congo to the West. Similar to many other East African areas, it became a sphere of British interest at a comparatively late stage in the history of British colonial expansion. In 1858, British explorers arrived in the area, with the aim of discovering the source of the Nile. Following a visit to King Mutesa I of Buganda in 1875, British missionaries established churches and educational facilities in 1876, and traders soon followed. In 1888, the Imperial British East Africa Company was established to trade with the area but also to administer and develop it. Following a period of civil war caused by conflicting religious interests and territorial claims, the British declared a protectorate over the kingdom of Buganda in 1894.

When the British protectorate was formally effected for the whole of what is now Uganda, in 1990, the language policy promoted the use of Kiswahili throughout East Africa from 1926 (see Ssempuuma 2019: 37 ff. for details) and it was used, together with Luganda and other Ugandan languages, in the lower administrative echelons, particularly in the army and police force. English was the language used at higher administrative levels, in the legislation and higher courts and from 1926 "promoted as a unifying language in East Africa" (Ssentanda 2016: 97). However, the amount of

British administrative personnel up until WWII was very low, amounting to only 521 members of staff in 1939 (see Meierkord 2016 for more details). Also generally, the European population during the times of the protectorate remained low, amounting to only 2,282 at the end of 1938. It was outnumbered by Asian immigrants who arrived initially on indentured labor contracts and later voluntarily, from 1896 onwards (see Meierkord 2016; Rathore-Nigsch and Schreier 2016).

Education was entirely mission based until 1920, but when trained personnel was in demand after WWI, governmental schools and later also colleges were established. It was particularly in the prestigious boarding schools where the offspring of an elite part of the society were taught English modelled on the British system, with a very strong exonormative orientation towards British English. The Baganda as well as missionaries demanded the teaching of English such as to bring Ugandans to a position that would allow them to acquire modern Western knowledge and skills. After WWII, the British abandoned the promotion of Kiswahili and promoted the spread of English instead, investing hugely in the education sector (see Meierkord 2021). Nevertheless, only few Ugandans could speak English at independence, and even ten years after, only 21 percent of the population were able to hold a conversation in English (Ladefoged et al. 1972: 25). Nevertheless, Uganda enshrined English as its sole official language in the constitution, resulting also in its being the sole MOI under the Obote government in 1967. At this time, British expatriates were still involved in the education system, and the numbers of Europeans had increased considerably, to 11,200 in 1962, when Uganda gained her independence. However, when Idi Amin overthrew Obote in 1971, he quickly dispelled the Asian community from the country in 1972, which caused most other nationals to leave Uganda, too. Following his rule, a period of political unrest discouraged British as well as other L1 English speaking individuals from entering the country, let alone getting involved in the education system, until political stability was regained in the 1990s. Since English was upheld as a MOI, teaching was then through L2 speaker teachers, which must have paved the way for nativization to proceed quickly in the country.

Since 2005, English has been co-official with Kiswahili, as per the constitution. However, English has remained the sole *de facto* official language, since an enabling law is required to effect the constitutional change, but this has not been passed so far. As regards the education sector, teaching is in the L1 until year 4, after which a transition to English is meant to take place in year 5, after which English then becomes the sole MOI. English is also the sole medium of communication in Uganda's parliament, although, as Namyalo et al. (2016) and Nakayiza (2016) explain, the local languages are used at lower levels of government.

English further serves as a lingua franca for most of the country's elite, for example at conferences and workshops. Ssempuuma (2019: 47) furthermore explains that in larger supermarkets, such as Shoprite, English is the dominant language for interactions, particularly since many tourists and expatriates do their shopping there, as well as Uganda's elite. Additionally, English is increasingly used in the previously Luganda-dominated music and entertainment industry. The elite also favor English-medium schools, given their high mobility and the likelihood of them having to move their family to another part of the multilingual country, where their offspring would not be able to follow instruction in the local language (cf., Ssempuuma 2019: 45).

Whilst uses of English in Uganda clearly have their roots in the history of the country as a former protectorate and in the practices of missionary education, the situation is considerably different in Maldives.

## 3.4 English in Maldives

Despite having been a protectorate from earlier than Uganda, Maldives' history as a British protectorate did not involve any English L1 speakers until 1941. Maldives is an islands state located in the Indian Ocean, south of India. It consists of 1,192 islands which form 26 natural atolls and 21 administrative units.

The language spoken by Maldivians is Dhivehi (see Gnanadesikan 2017 for a concise description of this language), and the nation used to be largely monolingual until the twentieth century, despite the fact that it became a British protectorate in 1887. Before that it had been a British protected area since 1796, following a brutal rule of the Portuguese from 1558 to 1573 and subsequently having been a Dutch protectorate. Britain took a very low-key approach to the Maldives, offering protection in terms of foreign affairs. However, this was administered from what at the time was Ceylon (today Sri Lanka), and no personnel was posted to Maldives. As a result, English speakers did not contribute to the linguistic ecology of the country.

Since Britain did not interfere with the internal affairs (with the exception of giving consent to the throne of the sultan) of Maldives and English was not used as a language of administration, there was no need to raise a group of Maldivians who would be able to serve as clerks in the administration.

The situation changed during WWII, when the British established a military base for the Royal Navy and the Royal Air Force in the southern atoll of Gan in 1941 and 1942. Here, around 600 permanent British personnel interacted regularly with approximately 900 Maldivian and 100 Pakistani members of staff who came from the neighboring islands (The Guardian, 1975). As Masters (2009: 164) explains, the Maldivians in the atoll "spoke good English and had experience working for Westerners." However, this was a regionally restricted phenomenon, which obviously had no impact on the other atolls.

The eventual spread of English resulted from a decision taken in 1960 by the then Prime Minister to introduce a modern state-run education system, modelled on Western systems and with English as the sole MOI. Traditionally, education had been through Madrassas and included teaching of literacy in Divehi, reading the Qur'an and arithmancy. Initially introduced in the capital island Malé, the education reform eventually resulted in a national curriculum in 1984. Almost simultaneously, in 1961, schools in Malé made English the MOI. It took four decades, but by the end of the 1990s all schools throughout Maldives had completed the transition to English as the MOI (UNESCO-IBE, 2012). It is currently introduced at pre-primary level, in a playful way, to prepare children for primary school where English is the MOI for all subjects except Divehi, Qur'an and Islam. Given this policy, English is learned by individuals of all social backgrounds (cf., Meierkord 2018). Given the fact that almost all Maldivian children attend school, which is free at primary and secondary levels, they attain a good command of English, and the younger generations are those with highest proficiency levels. However, "English is spoken widely at rudimentary level, a tribute to the tourist boom in the last decade and local schooling" (Yadav 2014: 104).

Today, Maldives is home to numerous languages, resulting from the high amount of work migration into Maldives, particularly since the advent of tourism in the country in 1972, and English serves as the lingua franca for a now multilingual society. The 2014 census reports 15.83 percent foreigners among the resident population, most of which originate from Bangladesh, India and Sri Lanka. However, the fact that tourism is the country's main economic sector has resulted in a vast number of languages being spoken by staff on the resort islands and, of course, by tourists.

Besides exposure to English via formal instruction, informal acquisition is also taking place via the Internet. Maldives has high speed Internet offered though Dhiraagu and Ooredoo telecommunication systems, which is used by 370,000 Maldivians, that is by 81.9 percent of the population. English is widely used for email communication and text messages and on social media, and "code-mixing between English and Divehi has become increasingly evident, especially among the younger generation" (Mohamed 2013: 188).

As this section has revealed, uses of English in Uganda and Maldives, despite the differences in their histories, were initially restricted to the elites of both countries. However Isingoma (2021) as well as Meierkord (2018, 2020a and 2020b) show that, in both nations, English has spread to the grassroots. Such spread has taken place throughout the world, albeit to much varying extents in the individual countries (see Meierkord 2020a). It is therefore just as timely to also integrate the grassroots in theorizing world Englishes.

## 4. Integrating the Grassroots

### 4.1 English(es) at the Grassroots and Grassroots Englishes

The grassroots of societies have only recently become a focus of attention. The online *Oxford English Dictionary* records its first use in a figurative sense in 1899, when, in the U.S., it referred to "[o]rdinary people considered as the foundation or main body of an organization, industry, etc., or of society more generally." With reference to uses of English, the term has been used in two different meanings.

Khubchandani and Hosali (1999: 254) use the term *grassroots English* with reference to mixed codes used "among those who spontaneously acquire certain rudimentary characteristics of the language in plurilingual settings (and not through formal education)" in such a way that they "are in a position to handle rudimentary tasks in English" (1999: 255). In their paper, this refers to Hinglish and Tamlish, two mixed codes, in which speakers mix English with Hindi and Tamil, respectively. The emphasis on informal acquisition and limited proficiency is also at the center of Schneider's (2016: 3) narrower definition of *grassroots Englishes*. To him, these have typically been learned "in direct interactions rather than through formal education" by individuals of poor backgrounds and with little or no access to formal education.

Somewhat different, Meierkord (2012) prefers to talk of *English(es) at the grassroots* to refer to uses of English that take place outside the contexts of international organizations, education, academia, and the business world, adopting Blommaert's (2008: 7) use of the term for "a wide variety of 'non-elite' forms." A more concise discussion of the term is offered in Meierkord 2020a and 2020b. Crucially, her use of *English(es) at the grassroots* implies that acquisition may be through formal or informal routes, or a combination of both. Furthermore, the Englishes used at the grassroots may be standardized and reflect a range of proficiency levels, and their uses may go much beyond just rudimentary tasks.

What all discussions of the grassroots in relation to the spread of English have in common is the emphasis on a "non-elite", i.e., members of the lower classes of societies. To these, English has spread in different ways, typically depending on whether acquisition was via formal instruction (and whether this was or is available to the masses, cf., Meierkord 2021) or through interaction with L1 speakers of English. Typically, outer circle countries are former British colonies, either trade or exploitation colonies, as distinguished by Mufwene (2001). Exploitation colonies served the purpose of being exploited for their natural resources. As knowledge of English was not necessary for the majority of the colonized people, it was taught only to a local elite. However, Schneider (2011: 46) argues that, at the grassroots, less educated colonial personnel, such as soldiers and traders and farmers used nonstandard forms of English in regular contact with indigenous speakers of similar lower ranks. In trade colonies, contact between the traders and the local population was typically sporadic only, due to the non-permanent nature of these colonies. As Mufwene explains, in the West African coastal regions such interaction was restricted during the times of the slave trade, and resulted in the formation of pidginized varieties of English. Whilst individual locals from these areas were trained as interpreters in Europe and became an ESL-speaking middle class (cf., Mesthrie and Bhatt 2008: 17–18), the majority acquired English in the form of a jargon, pidgin or a basilectal form, with a large gap existing between these two poles (cf., Mesthrie and Bhatt 2008: 36).

More recently, typically after independence, acquisition of English in the outer circle countries has often been through the education system, too, particularly when English serves as the MOI. As Table 4.1, discussed in Section 4.1, shows, however, the spread of English via its use as MOI does not take place in all former PPSMTs of the inner circle. Also, as Meierkord (2020b, 2021) documents, quality English-medium education is not accessible to all citizens in all of these nations.

By stark contrast, in most expanding circle countries, English was normally acquired in schools, (see Meierkord 2020a for details), initially by the offspring of traders and in private schools, later by the masses, when it gradually became part of the curricula of public schools. Informal acquisition in most of these countries has been a recent phenomenon, following increased migration and access to English via the Internet.

## 4.2 Research on English at the Grassroots

Studies of grassroots uses of English are generally scarce (for an account of existing studies see Meierkord 2020a; Meierkord and Schneider 2021b), and studies investigating lower classes in former protectorates and similar areas are very few and far between.

For the case of Oman, Buckingham (2015: 414) explains that non-Arabic speaking expatriates use commercial signage in English, to "address the South Asian community in Oman, even when the products advertised cater specifically, or even exclusively, for the needs of this community." Southeast Asian migrant workers are mainly from the Philippines, and South Asian workers originate from India, Pakistan and Bangladesh. As a result, English "has emerged as one of the principal [...] lingua francas between multilingual speakers in the region" (2015: 411) and is used also "in low-skilled sectors such as small-scale street retailers and manual workers" (2015: 411). Schaub (2000) finds that in Egypt "[e]ven the poorest of street merchants or juice sellers stand to greatly increase profits, and sometimes prices, if they are able to communicate with the affluent visitors who themselves primarily use English for all transactions in Egypt." She uses the term "tourist English" to refer to uses of formulaic phrases by "street hustlers", which have also been described by Stevens (1994), who examines pragmatic failure in the use of formulaic phrases used between Egyptian street hustlers and international tourists and foreign residents in Egypt. Akhidenor (2013) describes code-switching between Chinese traders and their customers in Botswana.

Meierkord and Schneider (2021a) provide a first collection of empirical studies into behaviours at the grassroots. Contributions to their volume that concern themselves with former PPSMTs are the following: Mohr (2021) discusses trajectories of English acquisition by young Zanzibaris who work in the tourism industry. Meierkord (2021) compares grassroots users of English from Uganda and South Africa, with a focus on the impact that access to formal instruction in English has on the resulting forms of English used by individuals. Bamidele-Akhidenor (2021) investigates interactions that take place at Manama Souq in Bahrain, between the local Arab traders and their international customers, discussing how strategies of intercultural communication and negotiation are employed to ensure successful communication. Chowdhury and Erling's (2021) study is located in the Middle east and centers around the question of whether proficiency in English is a factor that positively constrains the influence of Bangladeshi's economic migration.

## 4.3 The Grassroots in Uganda

As explained above, English serves as the main MOI in Uganda and becomes the sole MOI from year 6 (the pre-final year of primary school in Uganda). As a result, Ugandans who have completed the lower secondary level after eleven years in school can be held to have obtained a stable, intermediate level of English (Namyalo et al. 2016: 23). However, many Ugandans do not reach this stage. Whilst education has been free at primary level from 1997 and at secondary level from 2007, many children drop out of the education system, despite primary education being compulsory. This is typically due to the fact that children are required to assist their parents with agricultural work, to help care for their younger siblings while their parents are at work, or because they need to work themselves to add to the family income or because their parents have passed away. As a result, only 35.5 percent of

Ugandan primary school attendants stay on to the last grade of primary education in 2016.[5]

At the same time, the amount of money that Uganda can invest in the education sector is low. In 2017, Uganda had a GDP of $1,868 per capita and spend 2.64 percent of its GDP on education. As a result, high dropout rates in Uganda combine with a comparatively under-resourced education system with large classrooms and lowly trained teachers in many rural areas (see Ssentanda 2016), and there exists a huge urban-rural divide (cf., Meierkord 2020b for details).

Nevertheless, uses of English as a lingua franca within the country can also be observed at grassroots level. As Ssempuuma (2019: 46) explains, English serves as such "especially in urban areas among Ugandans and between Ugandans and foreigners" in the homes, residential areas, and at the work place for trade and business transactions. In Uganda, interethnic marriages between individuals speaking non-mutually intelligible L1s, e.g., Luganda and Acholi, are common, and English is then chosen as a neutral language between the spouses. Similarly, particularly the capital Kampala is home to vast numbers of work migrants from all parts of Uganda, resulting in multiethnic and multilingual residential areas, which further fuels the use of English as a lingua franca. In the field of trade and business, the recent influx of returnee Indian and new Chinese traders and business people creates further transactions that take place across Englishes at the grassroots. As Ssempuuma (2019: 47) reports, he "observed that in shops owned by Indians in Kampala, the shop proprietors who are Indians use English to communicate to the shop attendants who were Baganda. The shop attendants then communicated in Luganda to the customers who could not express themselves in the English language."

Another area where English serves as a lingua franca is that of tourism, which typically affects the rural areas where Uganda's national parks are located. Schneider (2016) explains that tourism is a field where interactions between grassroots speakers of English and tourists are frequent, and Uganda is no exception. Whilst the staff at most hotels and tour operators (e.g., drivers and guides) can probably be better described as belonging to Uganda's middle class, there are many shop owners and artisans selling their produce to tourists, using English in the process (albeit often restricted to some formulaic phrases only).

## 4.4 The Grassroots in Maldives

As in Uganda, English in Maldives is used as a MOI. Different from what is the case in Uganda, however, English is acquired by children of all social backgrounds through its use as the almost sole MOI from the first grade of primary school onwards. Education in Maldives is free and compulsory throughout primary and secondary education, which means that all young Maldivians will be constantly exposed to English for the twelve years of their education. Typically, more than 90 percent of all students stay on to the last grade of primary school (see Meierkord 2020b). By contrast with Uganda, Maldives is much more affluent and is in a position to invest considerably in its education system. In 2016, the country had a GDP of $16,688 per capita and spent 4.07 percent of its GDP to support the education sector. There is however, as Meierkord (2020b) explains, an urban rural divide, which in Maldives is a divide between the capital island of Malé and the more remote atolls. Tertiary education is available in Malé and a few other islands, meaning that students from most islands will need to migrate, making further access to English available only for those who can afford this.

However, most young Maldivians continue to encounter English at work, as it has emerged as "a second working language" widely used in the government (Yadav 2014: 79), but also in most commercial businesses and, overwhelmingly, in the tourism industry. The use of English in the various sectors has, unfortunately, not been adequately researched so that precise figures for its use at grassroots level are not available. However, since "there is a dearth of qualified Maldivians to fill technical, middle and senior management positions in the tourism sector" (May 2016: 7) and since large numbers of Bangladeshi, Indian and Sri Lankan staff are employed in the construction sector as well as in fishing, trade, and transport, it is highly likely that English serves as a lingua franca across workers in these sectors. In the tourism sector, English is typically used by staff on the various resort islands (islands which have no local, Maldivian, populations but are essentially hotels), including restaurant staff, room attendants and cleaning personnel. From 2009, when the local inhabited islands were opened to tourism, English has also increasingly been used by Maldivians as well as migrant workers establishing and operating hotels, guest houses, excursion companies and dive schools on such islands. Similarly, many inhabitants of these islands now manage food stalls or small cafés where they interact with tourists of diverse L1 backgrounds, whilst artisans sell their handicrafts (see Meierkord 2018 for details).

## 5. Conclusion: Former PPSMTs, the Grassroots and Models of World English(es)

Over the decades, research investigating and comparing international varieties of English has proposed a number of models to conceptualize what Mesthrie and Bhatt (2008), following McArthur (2003), call the English language complex. Integrating former PPSMTs as well as uses of English at the grassroots is, I argue, likely to make a valuable contribution to this enterprise, towards modelling the full English language complex such as to comprehensively account for the similarities and differences between the contexts in which English is employed.

### 5.1 Recent Modelling of World Englishes and its Limitations

Whilst Sridhar and Sridhar (1986) argued for an integrated approach to English as a second language (ESL) and English as a foreign language (EFL) more than 30 years ago, the two have typically been treated separately. Recently, research (e.g., the papers in Mukherjee and Hundt 2011; Edwards and Laporte 2015; Gilquin 2015) has found that "[a]n integrated and comprehensive approach to non-native Englishes is particularly relevant to the future agenda of English linguistics because today the English language is used to a much larger extent as a non-native language (ESL/EFL) than a native language (ENL)" (Hundt and Mukherjee 2011: 2). Buschfeld and Kautzsch (2017: 113) propose to do so by extending Schneider's Dynamic Model such as to describe Englishes in both postcolonial and non-postcolonial areas in a model of Extra-and Intra-territorial Forces, in which "the group of extra-territorial forces includes any factor entering the country from the outside and intra-territorial forces are such that mainly operate on a local, that is, national or regional, level and therefore influence the cultural and linguistic development from within" and include colonization and attitudes to it, language policies and attitudes, globalization and its acceptance, foreign policies and socio-demographic background. Together with its further refinement in Buschfeld et al. (2018), the model assumes that, like postcolonial Englishes, non-postcolonial Englishes go through stages of foundation, stabilization and nativization. However, there is a need to assess to what extent nativization in different types of former PPSMTs is reshaped when uses of English are predominantly non-intranational but international IaEs, involving ever-changing speakers of various varieties of English, and typically not leading to stable linguistic patterns (see Meierkord 2012: 158–94).

## 5.2 Former PPSMTs and Models of World Englishes

While Buschfeld et al. (2018) combine postcolonial and non-postcolonial contexts in one model, they do so maintaining the ESL-EFL and the outer circle-expanding circle dichotomies. This, however, ignores that there is an in-between (see Mesthrie and Bhatt 2008: 9) and that there might exist a cline between ESL and EFL contexts, with post-protectorates being one point on it, which may be home to a further type of varioversals (Szemrecsanyi and Kortmann 2009). At yet another point seem to be those nations that have made English their official language and MOI but have no history of English usage (through colonial personnel, settlers, etc.). Models of world Englishes do not yet cater well for these contexts, in which uses and users of English differ as a result of education systems, socio-economic and demographic factors (cf., Meierkord 2018, 2020b and 2021), and where there is often a previous history of another exogenous language (e.g., Afrikaans in Namibia (cf., Buschfeld and Kautzsch 2014, Schröder and Kautzsch 2016). Here the acquisition of English frequently implies processes of third language acquisition (cf., the papers in Cenoz et al. 2001 and Aronin and Hufeisen 2009), and complex interactions of the previously acquired languages with the English acquisition process (e.g., Siemund et al. 2018).

Furthermore, whilst speakers of English in all contexts are increasingly of various socio-economic backgrounds, models of English as well as the corpus data underlying them have typically been based on what has been labelled the "educated" speaker. However, fully assessing the status of English and describing the forms in which it is used requires looking beyond the (upper) middle class "elite" of societies, at the "grassroots".

## 5.3 The "Grassroots" in Models of World Englishes

There is a growing awareness of the need to integrate the grassroots in models of world Englishes (e.g., Mair 2018). However, as a consequence of the paucity of descriptive research addressed above, "non-educated" forms of English have typically been excluded as pointed out in the Introduction. However, there is clear evidence that "elite" and "grassroots" uses of English do in fact differ, as shown by, e.g., Darvin (2017) on Filipino immigrants in Vancouver, Toefy (2017) on pronunciation differences in speakers of Colored South African English, Myrick (2014) as regards rhoticity in speakers of English on the Caribbean island of Saba, and Ofori and Albakry (2012) on attitudes towards English in Ghana. Finally, a comparison of Mesthrie (2010) and Meierkord (2012) reveals that in fact "grassroots" speakers accommodate differently to the accents of others than "elite" speakers. These differences do not only need to be acknowledged and described but also integrated into theories and models. The integration of Englishes at the "grassroots" offers a lot of potential for English Linguistics, particularly for its variationist and its World Englishes branches, to catch up and draw level with recent advances in sociolinguistics. As Saraceni (2015: 6) explains, it is particularly those developments associated with the sociolinguistics of the "grassroots" which World Englishes does not integrate at the same speed as other fields.

Against the above concerns and based on the research available on former PPSMTs and on the grassroots, I propose a research agenda to describe these Englishes and to integrate them into current theorizing. This includes, but is not limited to:

- (Comparative) studies into the present-day sociolinguistics and the histories of English in former PPSMTs of inner circle countries.
- Rigorous data collection and, based on these, (comparative) studies of the structural and pragmatic features of English spoken in these former PPSMTs, as well as attitudinal studies.
- Descriptions of those factors (political, economic, social and developmental) that, besides a history of English teaching and/or informal acquisition, determine access to and use of English at all levels of society.
- Based on the above, a cogent discussion of whether and how English in former PPSMTs ranges on a cline between typical postcolonial and expanding circle contexts.
- At a more applied level, this raises the question as to which factors contribute towards inclusion or marginalization of members of societies through English, either as a gatekeeper or as a link language.

Clearly, all of the above are best approached in collaboration with local researchers residing in the individual countries, as proposed earlier by Bolton, Graddol and Meierkord (2011).

# Appendix 1

**Table 4.1** Uses of English in Former Protectorates, Protected States, League of Nations (LoN) Mandates and United Nations (UN) Trust Territories under Inner Circle Countries' Rule

| Current State name | Protectorate etc. name | Type, e.g. protectorate | Status of English today |
|---|---|---|---|
| **Africa** | | | |
| Botswana | Bechuanaland Protectorate 1885–1966 | British protectorate | OL, MOI from grade 5 |
| eSwatini | Swaziland 1902–1968 | British protectorate | OL with Swazi, MOI from grade 5 |
| Gambia | Gambia Protectorate 1894–1965 | British protectorate | OL, MOI from grade 4 |
| Malawi | Nyasaland Protectorate 1893–1964 | British protectorate | OL, sole MOI |
| Mozambique | no history of British involvement; former Portuguese colony | Commonwealth member since 1995 | no OL, no MOI |
| Namibia | Walvis Bay 1878–1884; South West Africa 1915–1990 | British protectorate LoN Mandate 1915–1966, direct South African administration until 1978, full independence of entire territory in 1994 | OL, MOI from grade 4 |
| Rwanda | no history of inner circle rule | Commonwealth member since 2009 | OL with Kinyarwanda, Kiswahili and French, MOI since 2008 |
| Somalia | British Somaliland, 1884–1960 | British protectorate | no OL, MOI from secondary |
| Sudan | Anglo-Egyptian Sudan, 1899–1956 | British protectorate | OL |
| Tanzania | Tanganyika Territory, 1922–1946 Trust Territory of Tanganyika, 1946–1964 | British LoN Mandate for East Africa, UN trust territory | OL (with Kiswahili), MOI from primary onwards |
| | Sultanate of Zanzibar, 1890–1963 | British protectorate | |
| Uganda | Uganda Protectorate, 1894–1962 | British protectorate | OL, MOI from grade 5 |
| Zambia, declared independent | Barotseland, 1900–1964 | British protectorate | OL, MOI from grade 5 |
| Zimbabwe | Northern Rhodesia, 1924–1964 | British protectorate | OL with 15 others, MOI from grade 8 |
| **Arab world** | | | |
| Bahrain, Kuwait, Qatar, UAE States (Abu Dhabi, Ajman, Dubai, Ras Al Khaimah, Muscat and Oman) | British Residency of the Persian Gulf (various, but generally 1822–1971) | British protested states | no OL but MOI in tertiary education in Bahrain, most Universities in Kuwait, |

| Current State name | Protectorate etc. name | Type, e.g. protectorate | Status of English today |
|---|---|---|---|
| Egypt | Khedivate of Egypt 1882–1914 | British occupation with no legal basis but *de facto* protectorate | |
| | Sultanate of Egypt, 1914–1922 | British protectorate | no OL, MOI in some schools and at tertiary level in dentistry, engineering, medicine |
| | Kingdom of Egypt 1922–1956 | British protectorate | |
| Iraq | Mandatory Iraq, 1922–1932 | mandate not enacted, but Anglo-Iraqi Treaty | no OL, MOI for medicine and engineering |
| Jordan | Emirate of Transjordan, 1921–1946 | British LoN mandate | no OL, MOI in some schools and universities |
| South Yemen | Aden Protectorate, 1872–1963 | British protectorate | no OL, MOI in tertiary in technical, natural sciences and medicine |
| **Asia** | | | |
| Afghanistan | Emirate of Afghanistan, 1879–1919 | British protected state | no OL, MOI at tertiary level |
| Brunei | Brunei 1888–1984 | British protected state | no OL, main MOI in secondary and tertiary level |
| Kingdom of Bhutan | Bhutan 1910–1949 | British protected state | no OL, MOI |
| Maldives | Maldive Islands, 1796–1886 | British protected area | no OL, MOI from grade 1 |
| | Maldive Islands, 1887–1965 | British protectorate | |
| Nepal | Kingdom of Nepal, 1816–1923 | British protected state | no OL, MOI in many private schools, no MOI in most public schools |
| Tibet (Autonomous Region of the People's Republic of China) | Kingdom of Tibet, 1904–1910; 1912–1921 | British protected state | no OL, no MOI |
| **Caribbean / Central America** | | | |
| Nicaragua & Honduras | Mosquito Coast, 1655–1787 & 1844–1860 | British protectorate | OL with Spanish, Miskito and five other languages in Nicaragua; no OL in Honduras; MOI |
| **Pacific** | | | |
| Cook Islands | Cook Islands, 1888–1902 | British protectorate | OL with Cook Islands Maori, MOI in upper secondary and tertiary |
| Republic of Kiribati / Tuvalu | Gilbert and Ellice Islands, 1892–1916 | British protectorate | OL with Kiribati, main MOI; Tuvalu: OL with Tuvaluan; MOI from year 4 |

## Extending the Scope of World Englishes

| | | | |
|---|---|---|---|
| Republic of the Marshall Islands | Trust Territory of the Pacific Islands | UN trust territory (US) | OL with Marshallese, MOI from grade six |
| Federated States of Micronesia | Trust Territory of the Pacific Islands | UN trust territory (US) | OL |
| Nauru | Nauru; Trust Territory of Nauru | 1914 captured by Australian troops, British control until 1920; LoN mandate from 1923 (Australia-UK-NZ), UN trust territory after liberation from Japanese occupation in WWII (Australia-UK-NZ) from 1947 | OL with Nauruan; MOI |
| Niue | Niue, 1900–1901 | British protectorate | OL with Niuean |
| Republic of Palau | Trust Territory of the Pacific Islands | UN trust territory (US) | OL with Palauan, MOI with Palauan |
| Papua New Guinea | Territory of New Guinea Territory of Papua 1884–1888 | 1884 British protectorate; 1888 British annexation, 1902 transfer to Commonwealth of Australia, 1906 as "Territory of Papua" with Australian admninistraion; British LoN mandate 1920; 1946 UN mandate under Australia mandate; 1947 UN trust territory | OL with Tok Pisin & Hiri Motu; MOI from year 3 |
| Samoa | Western Samoa; Trust Territory of Western Samoa (NZ) | | OL with Samoan, MOI from year 5 primary |
| Solomon Islands | British Solomon Islands, 1893–1978 | British protectorate | OL |
| Tokelau | Tokelau, 1877–1916 | British protectorate | OL with Tokelauan, MOI with Tokelauan |
| Tonga | Tonga, 1900–1970 | British protected state | OL with Tongan, MOI from grade 7 |

## Notes

1 The notion of the "educated speaker" was established by Quirk (1972), Kachru (1976) and Strevens (1977).
2 For the remainder of this chapter, I use the acronym PPSMTs to refer to protectorates, protected states, mandates and trust territories together.
3 The model does not cater for interactions that involve L1 speakers of English. Such interactions have been shown to crucially differ from those among L2 and FL speakers (Knapp 2002; House 2003).
4 Exeptions do exist. For example, in the case of Egypt, Britain unilaterally declared a protectorate that lasted from 1914 to 1922.

5   Data have been taken from UNESCO Institute for Statistics 2019a and 2019b http://uis.unesco.org/en/country/mv and uis.unesco.org/en/country/ug

## References

Abouelhassan, R. S. M. and L. M. Meyer (2016), "Economy, modernity, Islam, and English in Egypt," *World Englishes*, 35 (1): 147–59.

Akhidenor, A. (2013), "Code-switching in the conversations of the Chinese trading community in Africa: the case of Botswana," *English Today*, 29 (4): 30–6.

Alomoush, O. I. S. (2019), "Is English on mobile landscape resources no longer viewed as a linguistic threat to Arabic in Jordan? Exploring functions of English on printed shopping bags in Jordan," *English Today*, First View. Available online: https://doi.org/10.1017/S0266078419000282

Aronin, L. and B. Hufeisen, eds. (2009), *The Exploration of Multilingualism. Development of Research on L3, Multilingualism and Multiple Language Acquisition*, Amsterdam: John Benjamins.

Arua, A. E. (1998), "Some syntactic features of Swazi English," *World Englishes*, 17 (2): 139–51.

Bamidele-Akhidenor, A. (2021), "Facets of intercultural communication employed in the conversations of local Arab traders in Bahrain," in C. Meierkord and E. W. Schneider (eds.), *World Englishes at the Grassroots*, 143–64, Edinburgh: Edinburgh University Press.

Bernstein, J. (1994), "English and Shona in Zimbabwe," *World Englishes*, 13 (3): 411–18.

Biewer, C. (2015), *South Pacific Englishes. A Sociolinguistic and Morphosyntactic Profile of Fiji English, Samoan English and Cook Islands English*, Amsterdam: John Benjamins.

Blommaert, J. (2008), *Grassroots Literacy. Writing, Identity and Voice in Central Africa*, London: Routledge.

Blommaert, J. (2010), *The Sociolinguistics of Globalization*, Cambridge: Cambridge University Press.

Bolton, K, D. Graddol and C. Meierkord (2011), "Towards Developmental World Englishes," *World Englishes*, 30 (4): 459–80.

Bolton, K. and C. Meierkord (2013), "English in contemporary Sweden: perceptions, policies, and narrated practices," *Journal of Sociolinguistics*, 17 (1): 93–117.

Buchstaller, I. and N. D. Wilson (2018), "Marshallese English: a first sketch," *World Englishes*, 37 (2): 356–83.

Buckingham, L. (2015), "Commercial signage and the linguistic landscape of Oman," *World Englishes*, 34 (3): 411–35.

Buschfeld, S. and A. Kautzsch (2014), "English in Namibia: A first approach," *English World-Wide*, 35 (2): 121–60.

Buschfeld, S. and A. Kautzsch (2017), "Towards an integrated approach to postcolonial and non-postcolonial Englishes," *World Englishes*, 36 (1): 104–26.

Buschfeld, S., A. Kautzsch and E. W. Schneider (2018), "From colonial dynamism to current transnationalism. A unified view of postcolonial and non-postcolonial Englishes," in C. Deshors (ed.), *Modeling World Englishes: Assessing the Interplay of Emancipation and Globalization of ESL Varieties*, 15–44. Amsterdam: John Benjamins.

Cane, G. (1994), "The English language in Brunei Darussalam," *World Englishes*, 13 (3): 351–60.

Cenoz, J., B. Hufeisen and U. Jessner, eds. (2001), *Cross-Linguistic Influence in Third Language Acquisition. Psycholinguistic Perspectives,* Bristol: Multilingual Matters.

Chowdhury, Q.H. and E.J. Erling (2021). "The value of grassroots English for Bangladeshi migrants to the Middle East," in C. Meierkord and E.W. Schneider (eds.), *World Englishes at the Grassroots,* 165–85, Edinburgh: Edinburgh University Press.

Coluzzi, P. (2016), "The linguistic landscape of Brunei," *World Englishes,* 35 (4): 497–508.

Darvin, R. (2017), "Social class and the inequality of English speakers in a globalized world," *Journal of English as a Lingua Franca,* 6 (2): 287–311.

Dashti, A. (2015), "The role and status of the English language in Kuwait: How is English used as an additional language in the Middle East?," *English Today,* 31 (3): 28–33.

Deshors, S. D., ed. (2018), *Modeling World Englishes. Assessing the Interplay of Emancipation and Globalization of ESL Varieties,* Amsterdam: John Benjamins.

de Swaan, A. (2002), *The World Language System: A Political Sociology and Political Economy of Language,* Cambridge: Polity.

de Swaan, A. (2010), "Language systems," in N. Coupland (ed.), *The Handbook of Language and Globalization,* 56–76, Malden, MA: Blackwell.

Deterding, D. and S H. Sharbawi (2012), *English in Brunei: A new Variety in a Multilingual Society,* Dordrecht: Springer.

Edwards, A. (2016), *English in the Netherlands. Functions, Forms and Attitudes,* Amsterdam: John Benjamins.

Edwards, A. and S. Laporte (2015), "Outer and Expanding Circle Englishes: The competing roles of norm orientation and proficiency levels," *English World-Wide,* 36 (2): 135–69.

Firth, A. (1996), "The discoursive accomplishment of normality: On "lingua Franca" English and Conversation Analysis," *Journal of Pragmatics,* 26 (2): 237–260.

Fussell, B. (2011), "The local flavour of English in the Gulf: In a matter of fifty years, English has attained its own distinctive features in the Gulf," *English Today,* 27 (4): 26–32.

Gilquin, G. (2015), "At the interface of contact linguistics and second language acquisition research: New Englishes and Learner Englishes compared," *English World-Wide,* 36 (1): 91–124.

Gnanadesikan, A.E. (2017), *Dhivehi. The Language of the Maldives,* Berlin: De Gruyter Mouton.

Gordon, R. (2013), "Mandates," *Max Planck Encyclopedia of Public International Law* (MPEPIL), Oxford: Oxford University Press.

Graddol, D. (1999), "The decline of the native speaker," *AILA Review,* 13: 57–68.

Hamdan, J. M. and W. A. Abu Hatab (2009), "English in the Jordanian Context," *World Englishes,* 28 (3): 394–405.

House, J. (2003), "English as a lingua franca: A threat to multilingualism?" *Journal of Sociolinguistics,* 7: 556–78.

Hundt, M. and J. Mukherjee (2011), "Discussion forum. New English and Learner Englishes—quo vadis?," in J. Mukherjee and M. Hundt (eds.), *Exploring Second-Language Varieties of English and Learner Englishes,* 209–18, Amsterdam: John Benjamins.

Isingoma, B. (2021), "The sociolinguistic profile of English at the grassroots level: A comparison of Northern and Western Uganda," in C. Meierkord and E. W. Schneider (eds.), *World Englishes at the Grassroots,* 49–69, Edinburgh: Edinburgh University Press.

Jourdan, C. (1989), "Nativization and anglicization in Solomon Islands Pijin," *World Englishes,* 8 (1): 25–35.

Kachru, B. B. (1976), "Indian English: A sociolinguistic profile of a transplanted language," *Studies in Language Learning*, 1 (2): 139–89.

Kachru, B. B. (1985). "Standards, codification and sociolinguistic realism: the English language in the outer circle," in R. Quirk and H. G. Widdowson (eds.), *English in the World: Teaching and Learning the Language and Literatures*, 11–30. Cambridge: Cambridge University Press and The British Council.

Kamwangamalu, N. M. (1996), "Sociolinguistic aspects of siSwati-English bilingualism," *World Englishes*, 15 (3): 295–305.

Kamwangamalu, N. M. and T. Chisanga, (1996), "English in Swaziland: Form and function," in V. De Klerk (ed.), *Focus on South Africa*, 285–300. Amsterdam: John Benjamins.

Kamwendo, G. (2003), "Is Malawi guilty of spoiling the Queen's language?," *English Today*, 19 (2): 30–33.

Khubchandani, L M. and P. Hosali (1999), "Grassroots English in a communication paradigm," *Language Problems and Language Planning*, 23 (3): 251–72.

Khuwaileh, A. A. and A. Al-Shoumali (2001), "Private tuition in English: The case of two universities in Jordan," *English Today*, 17 (1): 31–5.

Kirkpatrick, A. (2007), *World Englishes. Implications for International Communication and English Language Teaching*, Cambridge: Cambridge University Press.

Knapp, K. (2002), "The fading out of the non-native speaker," in K. Knapp and C. Meierkord (eds.), *Lingua Franca Communication*, 217–44. Frankfurt: Peter Lang.

Ladefoged, P., R. Glick and C. Criper (1972), *Language in Uganda*, London: Oxford University Press.

Mahboob, A. (2009), "English as an Islamic language: A case study of Pakistani English," *World Englishes*, 28 (2): 175–89.

Mair, C. (2018), "Stabilising domains of English-language use in Germany. Global English in a non-colonial languagescape," in S. Dehors (ed.), *Modeling World Englishes. Assessing the Interplay of Emancipation and Globalization of ESL Varieties*, 45–75, Amsterdam: John Benjamins.

Masters, T. (2009), *Maldives*, London: Lonely Planet.

May, J. F. (2016), *Maldives" Population Dynamics: Policy Prospects for Human Growth and Opportunity*, Malé: United Nations Population Fund (UNFPA) Maldives Country office and National Bureau of Statistics Maldives.

McArthur, T. (2003), "World English, Euro English, Nordic English?," *English Today*, 19 (1): 54–8.

McGinley, K. (1987), "The future of English in Zimbabwe," *World Englishes*, 6 (2): 159–64.

Meierkord, C. (1996), *Englisch als Medium der interkulturellen Kommunikation*, Frankfurt: Peter Lang.

Meierkord, C. (2012), *Interactions across Englishes. Linguistic Choices in Local and International Contact Situations*, Cambridge: Cambridge University Press.

Meierkord, C. (2016), "A social history of English(es) in Uganda," in C. Meierkord, B. Isingoma and S. Namyalo (eds.), *Ugandan English: Its Sociolinguistics, Structure and Uses in a Globalising Post-protectorate*, 51–71, Amsterdam: John Benjamins.

Meierkord, C. (2018), "English in paradise: The Maldives," *English Today*, 34 (1): 2–11.

Meierkord, C. (2020a), "The spread of English at the grassroots," in D. Schreier, M. Hundt and E. W. Schneider (eds.), *The Cambridge Handbook of World Englishes*, 311–38, Cambridge: Cambridge University Press.

Meierkord, C. (2020b), "Spread of English at the grassroots? Sociolinguistic evidence from two post-protectorates: Maldives and Uganda," in A. Kirkpatrick (ed.), *The Routledge Handbook of World Englishes*, London: Routledge

Meierkord, C. (2021), "Access to English and the Englishes of the disadvantaged: Examples from Uganda and South Africa," in C. Meierkord and E.W. Schneider (eds.), *World Englishes at the Grassroots*, 91–114, Edinburgh: Edinburgh University Press.

Meierkord, C. and E. W. Schneider, eds. (2021a), *World Englishes at the Grassroots*, Edinburgh: Edinburgh University Press.

Meierkord, C. and E. W. Schneider (2021b), "Introduction: English spreading at the grassroots," in C. Meierkord and E.W. Schneider (eds.), *World Englishes at the Grassroots*, 1–22. Edinburgh: Edinburgh University Press.

Melnyk, A. Y. (2013), "United Nations trusteeship system," *Max Planck Encyclopedia of Public International Law [MPEPIL]*, Oxford: Oxford University Press.

Mesthrie, R. and R. M. Bhatt (2008), *World Englishes: The Study of New Varieties*, Cambridge: Cambridge University Press.

Mesthrie, R. (2010), "Socio-phonetics and social change: Deracialisation of the GOOSE vowel in South African English," *Journal of Sociolinguistics*, 14 (1): 3–33.

Mlambo, M. (2009), "A survey of the language situation in Zimbabwe," *English Today*, 25 (2): 18–24.

Mohamed, N. (2013), "The challenge of medium of instruction: a view from Maldivian schools," *Current Issues in Language Planning*, 14: 185–203.

Mohr, S. (2021), "English language learning trajectories among Zanzibaris working in tourism," in C. Meierkord and E.W. Schneider (eds.), *World Englishes at the Grassroots*, 70–90, Edinburgh: Edinburgh University Press.

Mohr, S. and D. Ochieng (2017), "Language usage in everyday life and in education. Current attitudes towards English in Tanzania: English is still preferred as medium of instruction in Tanzania despite frequent usage of Kiswahili in everyday life," *English Today*, 33 (4): 12–18.

Mufwene, S. (2001), *The Ecology of Language Evolution*, Cambridge: Cambridge University Press.

Mukherjee, J. and M. Hundt, eds. (2011), *Exploring Second-Language Varieties of English and Learner Englishes*, Amsterdam: John Benjamins.

Mustafa, Z. (1995), "Using Arabic and English in science lectures," *English Today*, 11 (4): 37–43.

Myrick, C. (2014), "Putting Saban English in the map. A descriptive analysis of English language variation on Saba," *English World-Wide*, 35 (2): 161–92.

Nakayiza, J. (2016), "The sociolinguistic situation of English in Uganda: A case of language attitudes and beliefs," in C. Meierkord, B. Isingoma and S. Namyalo (eds.), *Ugandan English: Its Sociolinguistics, Structure and Uses in a Globalizing Post-Protectorate*, 75–94, Amsterdam: Benjamins.

Namyalo, S., B. Isingoma and C. Meierkord (2016), "Towards assessing the space of English in Uganda's linguistic ecology: Facts and issues," in C. Meierkord, B. Isingoma and S. Namyalo (eds.), *Ugandan English: Its Sociolinguistics, Structure and Uses in a Globalizing Post-Protectorate*, 19–49, Amsterdam: John Benjamins.

Ochieng, D. (2015), "The revival of the status of English in Tanzania: What future does the status of the English language have in Tanzania?," *English Today*, 31 (2): 25–31.

Ofori, D. M. and M. Albakry (2012), "I own this language that everybody speaks. Ghanaians' attitude toward the English language," *English World-Wide*, 33 (2): 165–84.

Pine, P. and W. Savage (1989), "Marshallese and English: Evidence for an immersion model of education in the Republic of the Marshall Islands," *World Englishes*, 8 (1): 83–94.

Quirk, R. (1972), *Linguistic Bonds across the Atlantic. The English Languages and Images of Matter*, London: Oxford University Press.

Randall, M. and M. A. Samimi (2010), "The status of English in Dubai," *English Today*, 26 (1): 43–50.

Rathore-Nigsch, C. and D. Schreier (2016), "Indian English in Uganda: The historical sociolinguistics of a migrant community," in C. Meierkord, B. Isingoma and S. Namyalo (eds.), *Ugandan English: Its Sociolinguistics, Structure and Uses in a Globalising Post-Protectorate*, 251–74, Amsterdam: John Benjamins.

Richmond, E. B. (1989), "African English expressions in The Gambia," *World Englishes*, 8 (2): 223–8.

Saraceni, M. (2015), *World Englishes. A Critical Analysis*, London: Bloomsbury.

Schaub, M. (2000), "English in the Arab Republic of Egypt," *World Englishes*, 19 (2): 225–38.

Schmied, J. (1996), "English in Zimbabwe, Zambia and Malawi," in V. De Klerk (ed.), *Focus on South Africa*, 301–21, Amsterdam: John Benjamins.

Schneider, E. W. (2007), *Postcolonial English. Varieties around the World*, Cambridge: Cambridge University Press.

Schneider, E. W. (2011), *English Around the World. An Introduction*, Cambridge: Cambridge University Press.

Schneider, E. W. (2016), "Grassroots Englishes in tourism interactions," *English Today*, 32 (3): 2–10.

Schröder, A. and A. Kautzsch (2016), "English in multilingual and multiethnic Namibia: Some evidence on language attitudes and on the pronunciation of vowels," in C. Ehland, I. Mindt and M. Tönnies (eds.), *Anglistentag 2015 Paderborn. Proceedings*, 277–88. Trier: WVT.

Siemund, P., S. Schröter and S. Rahbari (2018), "Learning English demonstrative pronouns on bilingual substrate: Evidence from German heritage speakers of Russian, Turkish, and Vietnamese," in A. Bonnet and P. Siemund (eds.), *Foreign Language Education in Multilingual Classrooms*, 381–405, Amsterdam: John Benjamins.

Sridhar, K.K. and S.N. Sridhar (1986), "Bridging the paradigm gap: Second language acquisition theory and indigenized varieties of English," *World Englishes*, 5 (1): 3–14.

Ssempuuma, J. (2019), *Morphological and Syntactic Feature Analysis of Ugandan English. Influence from Luganda, Runyankole-Rukiga, and Acholi-Lango*, Berlin: Peter Lang.

Ssentanda, M. (2016), "Tensions between English medium schools and mother tongue education in rural Ugandan primary schools. An ethnographic investigation," in C. Meierkord, B. Isingoma and S. Namyalo (eds.), *Ugandan English: Its Sociolinguistics, Structure and Uses in a Globalizing Post-protectorate*, 95–117, Amsterdam: John Benjamins.

Stell, G. (2014), "Uses and functions of English in Namibia's multiethnic settings," *World Englishes*, 33 (2): 223–41.

Stevens, P. B. (1994), "The pragmatics of street hustlers" English in Egypt," *World Englishes*, 13 (1): 61–73.

Strevens, P. (1977), *New Orientations in the Teaching of English*, Oxford: Oxford University Press.

Szmrecsanyi, B. and B. Kortmann (2009), "Vernacular universals and angloversals in a typological perspective," in M. Filppula, J. Klemola and H. Paulasto (eds.), *Vernacular Universals and Language Contact. Evidence from Varieties of English and Beyond*, 33–53. London: Routledge.

Toefy, T. (2017), Revisiting the KIT-split in Coloured South African English. *English World-Wide*, 38 (3): 336–63.

Trilsch, M. (2011), "Protectorates and protected states," *Max Planck Encyplopedia of Public International Law (MPEPIL)*, Oxford: Oxford University Press.
Tripathi, P.D. (1990), "English in Zambia," *English Today*, 6 (3): 34–8.
UNESCO-IBE (2012), *World Data on Education: Seventh edition 2010–11*, Geneva, Switzerland: UNESCO International Bureau of Education.
Völkel, S. (2016), "Tongan-English language contact and kinship terminology," *World Englishes*, 35 (2): 242–58.
Watson-Gegeo, K. A. (1987), "English in the Solomon Islands," *World Englishes*, 6 (1): 21–32.
Yadav, R. (2014), *Tourism in Asia: A Study of Maldives*, New Delhi: G.B. Books.

# 5

# Contact, Asia, and the Rethinking of Englishes in Multilingual Ecologies

Lisa Lim and Umberto Ansaldo

## 1. Rethinking Contact in World Englishes

What warrants this call for a rethinking of contact issues in Englishes in multilingual ecologies? The English language has, after all, been explicitly recognized as being contact-derived[1]—already from its very beginnings, that is, from the emergence of Old English from the contact of the Germanic dialects; and in the shaping of the language varieties on the British Isles, as a result of contact between Germanic, Celtic, and Romance languages, to give the present-day standardized and non-standardized English dialects (Filppula 2008; Davis 2010; Venneman 2011). Such contact has been foregrounded recently in collections such as that of Schreier and Hundt (2013), and in Onysko (2016), who argues that language contact be considered an underlying mechanism for all Englishes.

Even more so then, the statement that world Englishes, as the collection of English varieties around the world, and World Englishes, as the field of research, collectively owe their existence to language contact hardly needs mention nowadays. The evolution of Englishes in the non-settler, exploitation colonies in Asia, in particular, has been viewed as the epitome of language contact dynamics (e.g., Lim and Ansaldo 2012; Lim 2020; Ansaldo and Lim 2020)—because of the range of typologies of the indigenous languages in multilingual ecologies, which make for radically diverse Englishes, as well as because of language policies which have afforded the spread and penetration and thus evolution of the new varieties. The significance of a language contact analysis of Englishes in multilingual ecologies for the theorization of World Englishes is however sometimes understated. In this chapter, in distilling several of these contributions, we call for a revisiting of several dimensions in research.

In much of our approach to this issue, we have highlighted the importance of valuing the ecology within which different languages operate. Ecology is a broad—and potentially vague—notion. We use it to summarize all those aspects that are in danger of being forgotten when one takes an essentialist view of language as one, isolated, discrete set of linguistic features. That view is to us incompatible from a contact linguistics approach, which recognizes the importance of multiple dimensions in the evolution of any language. Most important among these are:

i) The historical context
ii) The typological context
iii) The sociolinguistic context

In what follows, we consider the role these dimensions play in World Englishes research, given the multilingual ecologies within which New Englishes emerge, by outlining an agenda for rethinking some of the historical circumstances in the evolution on Englishes, rethinking assumptions that may be held regarding the possible typologies of Englishes, and rethinking the language practices of the communities of speakers/users of Englishes. In our discussions, we draw parallels with other contact scenarios to underscore how the dynamics and outcomes in world Englishes align with general patterns of contact and evolution. In so doing, we call for greater attention not just to the significance of the multilingual ecology in investigating world Englishes, but also to the positioning of World Englishes scholarship more broadly within language contact, for a more unified theorizing in the discipline.

## 2. Rethinking History

The historical spread of the English language via the first and second diasporas in the establishment of settlement, trade and exploitation colonies is a story that is widely known and has been well recounted in many sources (see, e.g., Schneider 2007; Hickey 2020; Schreier et al. 2020). In this section, we leave aside the usual account of contact between the English-speaking and indigenous language communities during Britain's trade and colonization ventures from the seventeenth through nineteenth centuries, and instead highlight circumstances which receive far less attention, including the role of specific communities who were early adopters of English in the colonies, and ecologies pre-dating and separate from that of British colonization, involving contact between other Asian and European parties, notably the Portuguese.

### 2.1 Lesser-known Players

It has long been recognized that, in the exploitation colonies, the English language was largely introduced through formal channels of English-medium education. The significant historic event that is usually noted in this connection is Macaulay's Minute on Education, promulgated in India in 1835, in which Lord Macaulay, President of the Committee of Public Instruction, Calcutta, India, advocated the central place of English in education because "English is better worth knowing than Sanscrit [Sanskrit] or Arabic; [as] the natives are desirous to be taught English ... we must ... do our best to form a class of interpreters between us and the millions whom we govern—a class of persons, Indian in blood and colour, but English in taste, in opinion, in morals and in intellect."[2] Absolute primacy was consequently given to teaching English and teaching in English, and within 50 years, by the late 1800s, a majority of Indian primary schools were English-medium institutions (Kachru 1994: 507). This policy was also extended to British Malaya (i.e., present-day Malaysia and Singapore), where, in the latter, it has been said that it was "exclusively through the schools that English spread" (Bloom 1986: 348), as well as to Hong Kong. There the first English-medium schools were set up in the nineteenth century, accessible to an elite minority during colonial rule, though enrolment gradually increased over the decades as the population recognized the value of such a resource.

It is in such a domain that we find the first group deserving of further attention. In these territories, English-medium mission schools comprised headmasters or headmistresses and senior staff from Britain (while in the Philippines teachers were American), and the presence of regional and dialectal variation of British English as input has certainly been acknowledged, for example, recognizing Irish priests and nuns in the mission schools. What is worth noting for our purposes is the fact that many teachers were from more local bases: some of the earliest teachers of English—as well as clerks in the civil service—in Singapore, Malaysia, Brunei, and Hong Kong were South Asians, employees in the British-administered government from India or Sri Lanka (then Ceylon) (Platt and Weber 1980: 23; Gupta 1994: 44; Mesthrie and Bhatt 2008: 19). And in Singapore, until the early 1920s, the largest single racial group of teachers was in fact the Eurasians, followed by roughly equal numbers of Europeans (comprising a majority of English, Irish, and Scottish; Gupta 1994: 43) and South Asians. The contribution of these more Asian Englishes as input varieties, especially in the formal school system, warrants further attention in the study of the evolution of Englishes in the region.

Another group of peoples who deserve serious consideration are those communities in Singapore and Malaysia who very early on acquired English as their dominant language. These tended to be the non-European elite to whom the English-medium schools primarily catered. One such community were the Straits-born Chinese or Peranakans, who shifted from their vernacular Baba Malay to (Peranakan) English (Lim 2010a: 24–5, 2010b). The fact that they were early adopters of English in the region is not for mere token mention: such a position resulted in their having significant influence on the emerging New Englishes in other communities of the territory, with the dominance that they wielded through their English-language capital being reinforced by other factors, such as political and social prominence in society (for elaboration, see Lim 2010b, 2016). Evidence can be found in a study of the role of the Peranakans in the development of Singapore English (SgE) prosody (Lim 2010b, 2011, 2016). Now, the prosody of all other New Englishes and learner English varieties with tone language vernaculars have H (High) tones located on accented syllables; in contrast, SgE prosody has H tones located word- and phrase-finally. This apparent exception can be accounted for: Peranakan English (PerE) prosody displays a pattern of prominence (usually in terms of higher pitch) of the penultimate and/or final syllable of the word and/or phrase—a pattern which is found across numerous Malay/Indonesian varieties including their own vernacular Baba Malay. In the ecology paradigm, the Peranakans, as early adopters of English, and politically and socially dominant in the context of the time, would be clearly recognized as a founder population in the ecology—which would account for why PerE had such a persistent influence on the evolving SgE.

The other significant early-English-adopting community in Singapore were the Eurasians, originally from Malacca, who shifted from their heritage language Kristang, or Malacca Creole Portuguese, to (Eurasian) English (Gupta 1994: 43; Lim 2010a: 25–6; Wee 2010). In addition to their presence as teachers, the community was also prominent in the theatre scene (Wong 2019). Elsewhere, groups such as Christian Malayalis from Kerala in India and Tamils from Jaffna in Sri Lanka were English-educated and worked in the civil and educational services. These early English adopters in the region would have had significant influence on the emerging New Englishes in other communities of the territory—as demonstrated in the case of the Peranakans and Singapore English above—and further thinking and research in this direction would inform our understanding in this regard. More generally, this highlights the significance of considering lesser-known varieties of English (Schreier et al. 2010) in investigations of influence on world Englishes.

## 2.2 Lesser-known Chains

In most accounts of language contact in the evolution of world Englishes, attention is given to the outcome of contact of substrate languages with the English language introduced in the situations of settler, trade, or exploitation colonization. A significant context that has often been overlooked comprises contact occurring before the era of British colonization, typically involving a chain of contact—that is, where a feature is initially transmitted from one language into another, and only later into a language of the European colonizer, usually Portuguese in the first instance (they being the earliest), and thence into English. As recently highlighted (Lim 2020), a substantial proportion of lexicon, such as *congee, godown, shroff, catty*, and *tael*, for example, are characteristic of Asian Englishes, but their origins do not always stem directly from contact between the English language in the territories and the language(s) of the local peoples, but are in fact a few times removed. The following illustrations are drawn from Lim (2020).

A word such as *shroff*, for example, is one which is no longer used in modern English—but is still in currency in two Asian Englishes (Lim 2017a). Indian English still uses *shroff* with its original meaning. In colonial writings on India dating back to the early 1600s, it refers to a local, i.e., Asian, banker or money changer in the British East Indies. In Hong Kong, a *shroff* in 1872 was a police court official to whom monies were paid, but the word underwent semantic narrowing, and in contemporary Hong Kong English (also Sri Lankan English and, previously, Singapore English) it refers to a cashier, cashier's office or payment booth, in government offices, hospitals or, especially, carparks. The word's origins ultimately lie in Arabic فَرَّاص *ṣarrāf* 'money-changer', entering Persian as *ṣarrāf*, and Gujarati as *šaraf*, in the large-scale Perso-Arabic influence on the language during the mid-thirteenth to mid-nineteenth centuries of Persian Muslim rule—the Delhi Sultanate and the Mughal Empire—in the Indian subcontinent. It thence also entered Portuguese, during their long occupation of India from mid-sixteenth century, as *xaraffo*, referring to customs officers and money-changers, also giving *xarafaggio*, i.e., *shroffage*—the *xaraffo*'s commission as noted in a 1585 colonial report from Goa. With Indo-Portuguese as the lingua franca not only between the Portuguese and locals, but also widely adopted by subsequent European travelers and colonizers, including the British, numerous words would have been introduced into Anglo-Indian English, subsequently entering British English, including *sharaf*, via this Portuguese contact language variety.

Similarly, if one considers the word *congee* (Lim 2017b), one associates this clearly with Asia, in particular, East Asia—"congee houses" are ubiquitous across Hong Kong, for example. A staple dish found across Asia, depending on its local traditions, it is a preparation of rice (though there are versions using other grains or legumes) boiled in water (though some versions use milk or coconut milk), using grains that may be long or short, whole or broken, which is served plain and accompanied by side dishes (ranging from salted duck egg or seafood, to pickled vegetables, to braised meat) or is cooked together with ingredients (such as chicken, or preserved egg, or herbs), with as many names in Asian languages as varieties. As a dish, it is documented in ancient East and South Asian texts: the earliest reference to the dish is in the Zhou Dynasty (first century BCE). It is also mentioned in the Chinese *Record of Rites* (c. first century CE), and is also noted in India in Pliny's seventh century CE writings. As a word in English, *congee* has its origins in Tamil *kanji* (also Telugu and Kannada *gañji*, Malayalam *kaṇṇi*, Urdu *ganji*), from *kanjī* 'boilings', referring to the water in which rice has been boiled. The word was encountered by the Portuguese in their colonies, and first documented in Portuguese as *canje* in *Colóquios dos simples e drogas da India* by physician and botanist Garcia de Orta in 1563, the earliest treatise on the medicinal and economic plants of India. And it was via Portuguese that the word entered English: early English documentation is found in the 1698 *A New Account of East-India and Persia*, and the 1800 English translation (from the German translation of the original Italian) of *A Voyage to the East Indies*, based on the Carmelite missionary Paolino da San Bartolomeo's 1796 observations in India, which describes "Cagni, boiled rice water, which the Europeans call Cangi."

As these examples—just two of many—illustrate, such rethinking brings us to more nuanced consideration of the contact of communities and languages beyond and before the usual groups of English-speaking and indigenous peoples, and afford a richer, fuller appreciation of contact histories in world Englishes.

## 3. Rethinking Typology

A number of factors have been identified as relevant for the consideration of the evolution of world Englishes. Historical and political events, sociolinguistic determinants, and identity constructions are certainly recognized as important parameters (Lim and Gisborne 2009: 124), which may well define different phases or eras of an ecology—these would affect the dynamics of contact and the structural features that emerge in the evolving English differently at different points in time (see e.g., Schneider 2007 for a model for Postcolonial Englishes; Lim 2007, 2010a for Singapore English; Gonzales 2017 for Hokaglish). Factors which have been identified as more primary in the contact dynamics involve the variety/ies of the English lexifier that entered the local context; the nature of transmission of English to the local population; and the local, i.e., indigenous/ local languages of the community in which the New English emerges (Hickey 2005: 506; Lim and Gisborne 2009).[3]

Ansaldo (2009) further underlines the importance of situating any contact linguistic analysis within a 'typological matrix', that is, as comprehensive a picture as possible of the linguistic diversity in which languages come into contact and undergo change. This is in line with an ecological approach to language change, as pioneered in Croft (2000) and Mufwene (2001), in which linguistic features from different varieties enter a competition and selection process that defines the contact dynamics. In such an approach then, the outcomes of contact are not constrained to what might be considered features of 'English', but can result in any kind of restructuring, as long as the typological matrix allows for it.

In what follows, we illustrate this with two features of New Englishes: tone and particles, features often used as the poster child for contact in Asian ecologies (see, e.g., Lim and Ansaldo 2012; Lim 2020; Ansaldo and Lim 2020), precisely because they are most instructive, demonstrating as they do how features of the New Englishes can evolve to be as rich and radical as the typologies of the substrates.

## 3.1 Tone

The acquisition of the feature of tone has long been recognized in the fields of historical linguistics, contact linguistics, and creole studies.

Suprasegmental features, including tone, are documented as being susceptible to being acquired in contact situations (Curnow 2001): tone is often acquired in a non-tonal language by borrowing or imitation due to the presence of tone in the broader linguistic environment (Gussenhoven 2004: 42–3), such as in Middle Korean due to the prestigious status of Chinese in society then (Ramsay 2001). Tone is thus noted to be an areal feature, occurring in genetically unrelated languages spoken by geographically contiguous speech communities, as in Africa and Southeast Asia (Nettle 1998; Svantesson 2001).

Several creole language varieties are recognized as having tone, acquired from their tone-language substrates, as a result of contact situations involving European accent languages and African tone languages. One example is Saramaccan, an Atlantic maroon creole spoken mostly in Surinam, generally classified as an English-based creole (though its lexicon shows substantial Portuguese influence), with Gbe and Kikongo as substrates, where there is evidence for a split lexicon, in which the majority of its words are marked for pitch accent, with an important minority marked for true tone (Good 2004a/b, 2006). Papiamentu spoken in the Netherlands Antilles, with superstrates of Spanish, Portuguese and Dutch, and West African Kwa and Gbe languages as substrates, shows use of both contrastive stress and contrastive tonal features which operate independently from stress (Kouwenberg 2004; Rivera-Castillo and Pickering 2004; Remijsen and van Heuven 2005). Pichi, also known as Fernando Po Creole English, an Atlantic English-lexicon Creole spoken on the island of Bioko, Equatorial Guinea, which is an offshoot of Krio from Sierra Leone, and shares many characteristics with its West African sister language Aku from Gambia, as well as Nigerian, Cameroonian and Ghanaian Pidgin, has also been documented as having a mixed prosodic system which employs both pitch-accent and tone (Yakpo 2009). The Austronesian language Ma'ya is also documented as a hybrid system involving both contrastive stress and tone, a result of contact with tonal Papuan languages (Remijsen 2001).

It is somewhat surprising that only very recently has there been some attention and systematic investigation in the field of World Englishes in this regard.[4] Work on Nigerian English has described it as a mixed prosodic system that stands "between" an intonation/ stress language and a tone language (Gut 2005), with its pitch inventory described as reduced compared to British English, and the domain of pitch appearing to be the word, with high pitch triggered by stress, thus resembling a pitch accent language. Work on New Englishes which have emerged in ecologies where Sinitic languages are dominant has also demonstrated the emergence of (lexically based) tone. In Hong Kong, Cantonese has always been dominant through colonial rule and after the handover in 1997 to today, while in Singapore, Hokkien was prominent as the Chinese intra-ethnic lingua franca and a widely used interethnic lingua franca in colonial and early independence eras, with Mandarin gaining importance as one of the nation's four official languages, and Cantonese seeing a resurgence in the late 1980s and 1990s, due to Cantonese popular culture and significant immigration from Hong Kong (see details in Lim 2010a). In short, both ecologies have tone in their majority and dominant languages, making tone salient in the feature pool. As anticipated, the effect of this is that both HKE and SgE both exhibit (Sinitic-type) tone, at the level of the word and phrase (Lim 2009a, 2011). In HKE, stress and intonation is a process of transforming the system into one based on tones, by assigning (lexical) tone to syllables for word stress (Luke 2000; Wee 2008).[5] In SgE, the patterning of the H and L tones is further tempered by other systems in the ecology: in this case, the right-edge prominence of Malay varieties and Peranakan English, as already mentioned in Section 2, position the prominent H tones at word- and phrase-final position.

(1)  in'tend                    LH       (HKE, Wee 2008: 488)
     'origin, 'photograph       HLL
     o'riginal                  LHLL

(2)  I saw the manager this morning    LHHHHHHHL! (HKE, Luke 2008)

(3)  'manage, 'teacher          MH       (SgE, Wee 2008: 490)
     in'tend, a'round           LH
     'origin, bi'lingual        LMH
     o'riginal, se'curity       LMMH

(4)  I think happier            LHLLM    (SgE, Lim 2004: 44)

A call for revisiting English prosody was made by Lim (2009a, 2011) in the light of such findings, as well as, inter alia, considerations for the study of Asian Englishes with a keen eye on typology and ecology.

## 3.2 Particles

Another area which provides a strong impetus for a consideration of typology in research on world Englishes comprise the use of particles. Particles have been established as a discourse-prominent feature, and are consequently very easily transferred in contact-induced change (Matras 2000). They comprise a prominent feature of many languages in Asia, found in languages such as Cantonese, Hokkien, Mandarin, Malay, Tagalog, and Hindi, and are used widely in those languages to communicate pragmatic functions of various types (see Lim 2007; Lim and Borlongan 2011). Once again, it does not come as a surprise that, as a consequence of contact, where substrate typologies include particles in their grammars, particles figure as a characteristic feature in the New Englishes (Lim and Ansaldo 2012; Lim 2020.

Hindi's particles *yaar* and *na* (5, 6) are documented in Indian English, noted to be used in IndE by speakers regardless of mother tongue, i.e., not constrained to Hindi mother tongue speakers (Lange 2009). Many of Tagalog's 18 enclitic particles occur frequently in Philippine English, with findings from the Philippine component of the International Corpus of English (ICE-PH) attesting to consistent usage of particles (in decreasing order of frequency) such as *na*, which signals a relatively new or altered situation, *pa*, which denotes a relatively old or continuing situation (7), and *ba*, a question marker obligatory in formulaic yes-no questions (8) (Lim and Borlongan 2011. And Cantonese's rich set of particles appear prominently in Englishes with Cantonese in their ecology, such as HKE (9, 10).

(5) You'll you must be really having good patience *yaar* (IndE, Lange 2009: 216)

(6) Sunday will be more convenient *na* (IndE, Lange 2009: 213)

(7) We have an idea *na* of who we'll get yeah pero we're waiting *pa* for the approval. (Lim and Borlongan 2011: 68)

  'We already have an idea of who we'll get yeah but we're still waiting for the approval.'

(8) You find this fulfilling *ba* (Lim and Borlongan 2011: 62)

  'Do you find this fulfilling?'

(9) may be LG1 [Lower Ground 1st Floor] is much better *wor*. . . . noisy *ma*. . . . at G/F. . . also u seem used to study there *ma* (HKE, James 2001)

(10) K: How are you *a33?* (HKE, Multilingual Hong Kong Corpus, K. Chen p.c.)

It hardly needs to be emphasized how particles—from Asian language typologies—are clearly robust features of those New Englishes (Lim and Ansaldo 2012), with their widespread occurrence across several Englishes easily accountable by an appeal to typology. Moreover, particles have been increasingly noted in more formal contexts, suggesting that they are obtaining wider sociolinguistic currency. Given this ubiquity, in addition to their easy transfer in language contact situations, particles have been identified as comprising one of the features most likely to spread not only from the substrates to the New Englishes, but, subsequently, also horizontally across such Englishes (Lim and Ansaldo 2012). Such horizontal spread and the potential of particles to be an areal feature of Asian Englishes is certainly a direction of interest for World Englishes research.

One additional observation bears noting, illustrated in the case of SgE (a comprehensive account is found in Lim 2007), namely, that the particles are a clear demonstration of how a category in New Englishes can have origins in different substrates. Two well established SgE particles are the *lah* and *ah* particles (11, 12), with *lah* as a SgE particle included in the *Oxford English Dictionary* almost two decades ago; these particles are also common in Malaysian English. These two particles are noted as having emerged early in the development of SgE, with their origins shown to lie in Malay and/or Hokkien (Platt 1987; Gupta 1992; Lim 2007), languages prominent in Singapore's ecology during that era. In addition, there is a second, larger set of particles—*hor, leh, lor, ma,* and *meh* (13, 14)—which emerged in SgE in a later period (Lim 2007): notably, these stemmed from a different source, viz. Cantonese, shown to have had prominence in Singapore's ecology in the latter part of the twentieth century.

(11) I don't know *lah*, I very blur *lah*. (SgE, Lim 2004: 46)

'I don't know, I'm very confused.'

(12) Then you got to do those papers again *ah*? (SgE, Lim 2004: 46)

(13) My parents old fashion *a21*? Then your parents *le55*? (SgE, Lim 2007: 451)

'Are you saying that my parents are old-fashioned? Then what about your parents?'

(14) No *la21*! He's using Pirelli, you don't know *mɛ55*? (SgE, Lim 2007: 451)

'No, he has Pirelli tyres; didn't you know that?' [incredulously]

In short, attention to ecology, or rather, specific eras of an ecology, and the typological matrix of the time, clearly affords us a more nuanced investigation.

## 4. Rethinking Usage

The Asian contexts introduced in the previous section are clearly highly multilingual and typologically diverse ecologies, in which the outcomes of language contact, as demonstrated above, even if "diverging" from a traditional typology of "English," are accountable through ecology and typology, and entirely expected. In this section, we discuss two areas of multilingual practice which warrant attention in research in World Englishes.

## 4.1 Mixed Codes

The World Englishes paradigm has traditionally couched its research in terms of discrete, usually national, or regional, varieties of English—e.g., the "dialectology and sociolinguistics of English-speaking communities" (*EWW* 2020), "Englishes in their cultural, global, linguistics and social contexts" (*World Englishes* n.d.). Where the multilingual ecology is given consideration, it is usually positioned in terms of the substrate languages' influence on the nativized variety of English, and instances of co-occurrence of any additional language(s) alongside English have traditionally been considered codeswitching or mixing. The various corpora of the International Corpus of English (ICE), which are widely used in world Englishes research, are built by research teams "preparing electronic corpora of their own national or regional variety of English" (*ICE Project* 2016), each comprising a million words of spoken and written English, but which, crucially, tend to exclude data which involve other languages. Such approaches tend to erase the multilingual language practices that are, in fact, a widespread reality in many world Englishes communities. Indeed, as has been pointed out by scholars such as Canagarajah (2009), hybrid varieties, mixed codes or plurilingual practices have been natural and embraced in regions such as South Asia since pre-colonial times.

In the 1990s, such practices did start being recognized not as switching between languages but as single hybrid codes in their own right. Canagarajah (1995) provides a striking analysis of the emergence of a plurilingual English, also referred to as "Englishized Tamil," in Jaffna, northeast Sri Lanka. The code is an outcome of strong social pressure amongst Tamils against excessive use of English, but where the speaking of Tamil on its own could be considered excessively formal. Crucially, this is noted to be the unmarked everyday code, even used in what would be considered formal domains, as in the interview between a senior professor (P) and a junior lecturer (L), illustrated in (15).

(15)

1 P:  So you have done a masters in sociology? What is your area of research?

2 L:  **Naan** sociology of religion-**ilai taan** interested. **enTai** thesis topic **vantu** the rise of local deities in the Jaffna peninsula.

'**It is in** the sociology of religion **that I am** interested. **My** thesis topic **was** the rise of local deities in the Jaffna peninsula.'

3 P:  Did this involve a field work?

4 L:  **oom, oru** ethnographic study-**aai taan itay ceitanaan. kiTTattaTTa** four years-**aai** field work **ceitanaan.**

'**Yes, I did this as an** ethnographic study. **I did** field work **for roughly** four years.'

5 P:  **appa kooTa** qualitative research **taan ceiyiraniir?**

'**So you do mostly** qualitative research?'

Similarly, Li Wei (1998) argues that the mixed code of second-generation bilinguals, such as the *Cantonese*-English code used by younger generation British-born Chinese in the north of England, originally from Ap Chau, a small island near Hong Kong, illustrated in (16), does not constitute switching, but is in itself a distinctive linguistic mode.

(16)

A: Yeo    hou    do    yeo contact
   have   very   many  have contact

'We have many contacts'

G: We always have opportunities *heu xig kei ta dei fong gaowui*
   keep in contact will know that other place church

*di yen. Ngodei xixi dou*
POSS person. we time always

'We always have opportunities to get to know people from other churches. We always keep in contact.'

Thereafter, through the 2000s, similar mixed codes have received increased attention in World Englishes scholarship. The mixed code encompassing English and Tagalog, known as Taglish, is documented as being extensively used by urban Filipinos comfortable in both languages (Bautista and Gonzales 2006: 137). A tight and fluid mix involving English, Mandarin, and Hokkien is described as being commonly used by ethnically Chinese Singaporeans, illustrated in (17) (here only the English idiomatic gloss is provided: **Hokkien**, *Mandarin*, English, <u>Sinitic particles</u>; from Lim 2009b: 60).[7] Significantly, these are viewed not only as single codes in their own right (Lim 2009b; Lim and Ansaldo 2012), or as one manifestation of a New English (Lim 2009b): in the case of Taglish, illustrated in (18), such a code is reported to be the usual code amongst Filipinos, with 'pure' [sic]—i.e., what is considered unmixed—*Tagalog* or English seldom heard (McFarland 2008: 144).

(17)

Mei: Seng <u>a21</u>, time to get a job <u>ho24</u>? Pa and Irene spend all their savings on you already <u>le21</u>. Are you waiting for Pa *to buy Toto [the lottery] and get it all back* <u>me55</u>?

Pa: You say other people for what? You are just a secretary.

Irene: <u>Aiya</u>, never mind, never mind. Anyway Seng already has a job interview on Monday.

Pa: <u>Wah</u>, real or not?

Seng: I arranged the meeting through email. Now American degrees *all in demand*.

CB: <u>Wah</u>, congratulations, man.

Seng: Thanks.

Ma: **What did they just say?**

Mei: *Seng said that on Monday...*

Pa: Now you've come back, you can't play the fool anymore, okay? *What if* you end up selling insurance like this guy? **Don't make me lose face!**

(18) Then they ask me, *ano pa daw* capabilities *ko* in singing... I did not told them... *gusto ko sila mag* find out.

'Then they ask me, what other capabilities I have in singing... I did not tell them... I wanted them to find out for themselves'

Most recently, such a mixed code has been observed in domains where it was not previously found, such as newspaper reports, as illustrated in an article for Yahoo! News Philippines (Tordesillas 2013) shown in (19).

(19) Never have I felt so *kawawa* reading the statements of Defense Secretary Voltaire Gazmin justifying his plan to allow American and Japanese military access to military facilities in the Philippines to deter China's aggressive moves in the South China Sea.

[Entire article in English]

*Ano ba naman tayo?*

As noted in Lim (2020), in recent sociolinguistic scholarship, the fluidity of language boundaries, premised on the possibility that language is never normative but instead always negotiable, has been amply recognized in the translingual turn (see, e.g., Cummins 2008; García 2009; Blommaert 2010; Creese and Blackledge 2010; Baker 2011; García and Li Wei 2014; Lee and Jenks 2016). Even while translingual scholarship and the World Englishes paradigm, with its discrete varieties, may at traditional face value seem to be positioned at odds with each other (Lim 2020: 83), the time is more than overdue for World Englishes research to explore what the translanguaging approach can offer, in order to better appreciate the increasing assemblages and entanglements involved. To that end, research such as Canagarajah (2013) and the collection by Jenks and Lee (2020) certainly comprise an important step in the right direction in the field.

## 4.2 New Media

Another context of great current interest transcends regions and varieties and is found in computer-mediated communication (CMC). It is particularly significant where World Englishes research is concerned because of the flexibility and creativity of expression that the platform affords, which, crucially, allows for the articulation of multilingual repertoires, notably in situations involving an emergent English and languages using different orthographic traditions, and, consequently, novel contact dynamics, as recent scholarship has highlighted (Lim 2015; Lim and Ansaldo 2016).

In CMC, while advances have certainly been made and continue to be made in developing keyboards for various scripts, such as Chinese characters or Devanagari script, users very often prefer to use a Latin-based keyboard, and/or English, due to the constraints of the keyboard or the comparative efficacy compared to using character keystrokes. Thus, young Hongkongers, for instance, who are normally Cantonese-dominant in non-CMC domains, overwhelmingly find English easier as an input (74.3%) than Chinese (25.7%), and report a significant preference for using English, or English and Cantonese (60.6%), rather than Chinese (Lin 2005). In other words, CMC promotes significantly greater English usage than what there would normally be for a community dominant in another language—this has two major consequences in the evolution of New Englishes.

In the first place, because CMC platforms comprise a site quite distinct from the community's usual communicative practices, where there is more widespread use of English than in non-CMC contexts, there is more frequent mixing of codes—for Hongkongers, English is used to a greater extent in CMC, alongside Cantonese—and this naturally affords the conditions for language contact dynamics and the evolution of the English variety. In the online chat of young Hongkongers, illustrated in (20, 21) (from Wong 2009),[8] a number of linguistic practices, the outcome of contact, are noted. Common Cantonese phrases are used in Romanized form, such as *mafan* 'troublesome' for 麻煩 *maa4faan4* (20, turn 5), and morpheme-for-morpheme translation or relexification, such as *gum is you dun ask* (21, turn 3), and *or. . . gum you continue lo* (21, turn 5).

(20)

1R: head ask for resume??

 'the department head asked you for your resume?'

2R: how come ge

 'how come [ge2]?'

3L: yes ar

 'yes [aa3]'

3L: he said he ask all people la wor

 'he said he had asked everyone for their resume already [aa3 wo5]'

4R: what for

 'what is that for?'

5R: ma fan

 'it's so troublesome'

6L: not my head

'he is not my supervisor'

7L: programmer head

'my supervisor is the head of the programming department'

(21)

1A: did u ask Wilson to pick you up in the train station?

2B: ah...not yet...hahaaa

3A: gum is u dun ask. ...

咁 係 你 唔 問

gam2 hai6 nei5 ng4 man6

'then it's you who don't ask him to pick you up'

4A: dun say wt danger later ar...ghaa

唔 好 話 咩 危 險 一 陣 呀

ng4 hou2 waa6 me1 ngai4 him2 jat1 zan6 aa3

'don't say it is dangerous later (*laugh)'

[...]

5A: or...gum u continue lo

哦 咁 你 繼 續 囉

ngo4 gam2 nei5 gai3 zuk6 lo1

'ok...then you continue working on your assignment [lo1]'

One instance of restructuring is instructive for the evolution of a New English in CMC: the direct translation or calquing of the Cantonese expression 加油 *ga1yau4* 'add oil', into English 'add oil', by younger Cantonese-English bilingual Hongkongers. In its original Cantonese, 加油 *ga1yau4* is widely used as a general exhortation or cheer to persevere or to work hard, both in spoken Cantonese discourse and in CMC (22 and 23 respectively) (Lim 2015).

(22)

A: *Ngo chin gei yat sin tong kui lao yuen gao*

'I argued with him just a few days ago'

B: *Hah? Again? For what?*

A: *You know, just like zi chin gor d lor*

'You know, just like what happened before'

B: *Ai, kui d* temper really... ***gayau ah!***

'Sigh, his temper is really bad... be strong!'

(23)

A: Doin *meh?*

'What are you doing?'

B: *Hea gun ah, u?*

'Just taking some rest, and you?'

A: Gonna finish some readings. Need slp earlier, tmr *faan gong*

'I'm going to finish some readings and need to sleep earlier. I need to work tomorrow.'

B: Oh *hai wor, ho chur ah,* ***gayau!***

'Oh right, you're so busy. Just hang in there!'

However, an interesting pattern emerges if we compare Cantonese 加油 with its English calque *add oil*, also used in CMC and spoken discourse, illustrated respectively in (24) (Wong 2009) and (25) (Lim 2015).

(24)

A: 7.00am...

'I have to work at 7.00am'

A: very sh*t le

'it's very bad [ne]'

B: ahaha ~~~ ***add oil!***

'[laugh] work hard!'

B: Then goodnight and sweet dreams la

A: talk to you next time

(25)

A: Are you ready for tomorrow's Chinese test?

B: Not yet. Mom's forcing me to drink bedtime milk.

A: Then you should probably sleep too. ***Add oil*** for the test.

B: Yeah.

It is found (Lim 2015) that, with young Cantonese-English bilingual Hongkongers, Cantonese 加油 is used less regularly in CMC than in spoken communication, while the English calque *add oil* is reported as being used "quite often" whether texting in Cantonese, or in English or Cantonese-English, and, crucially, is used more than its original Cantonese expression. This is significant for World Englishes research: a CMC platform does enable language contact and prompt the development of HKE, in this case, in the use of particular HKE phrases, here calqued from Cantonese. An examination of microblogging sites such as Instagram, Twitter and Tumblr attest to this: a search for the hashtag #addoil turns up infinite numbers of posts.

There is a second and significant finding of such CMC research. More English-dominant bilinguals—e.g., Hongkongers who emigrated several years ago and then returned to Hong Kong, or Hongkongers of mixed parentage—exhibit a different pattern compared to the local Hongkongers: the English calque *add oil* is used significantly more often when speaking. In other words, this feature appears to have spread from CMC to non-CMC domains.

In effect, the increased use of English in the CMC domain comprises a drive in the direction of the community employing English in the bilingual mix to a greater extent, first in that domain, and then in others, which is the road to further nativization of a restructured New English in a contact context, and subsequent endonormative stabilization. CMC clearly serves as a vital platform and catalyst for the evolution of multilingual English varieties—favoring the use of English, promoting significantly more mixing with and calquing into English compared to spoken discourse, and prompting subsequent spread to other domains—and is identified as one of the forces in this knowledge economy that can drive the evolution of a new variety (Lim 2015). Continued attention to such a domain should prove rewarding in World Englishes research.

## 5. Concluding Thoughts

This chapter has highlighted several dimensions in which a rethinking leads us to more nuanced, enlightened, and forward-looking investigations in World Englishes research. In drawing parallels with other contact scenarios, such as those of creole language varieties, and with other approaches in other fields, such as translanguaging, we underscore how the dynamics and outcomes in world Englishes align with general patterns of language practices, contact, and evolution. In so doing, we call for greater attention not just to the significance of the multilingual ecology in investigating Englishes, but also to the positioning of World Englishes scholarship more broadly within language contact, and within sociolinguistics, for a more unified theorizing in the discipline.

## Notes

1  It has been widely noted that "[m]ost, if not all, languages have been influenced at one time or another by contact with others" (Winford 2003: 2), and that "language contact

is everywhere: there is no evidence that any languages have developed in total isolation from other languages' (Thomason 2001: 8).
2   "Minute by the Hon'ble T. B. Macaulay, dated the 2nd February 1835." See http://www.columbia.edu/itc/mealac/pritchett/00generallinks/macaulay/txt_minute_education_1835.html.
3   As pointed out by Schneider (2007: 25), settlement and transmission types are clear-cut and important mostly for the early phases of settlement, but tend to become increasingly blurred with time in the increasing complexity in the development of society.
4   Observations have of course been made by scholars for some decades, e.g., that Singapore English has been anecdotally described as if it "sounds like Chinese" (Bloom 1986: 430, citing Killingey 1968), and that in Hong Kong "the English intonation system is reinterpreted on the basis of the Cantonese tone system" (Luke and Richards 1982: 60).
5   Here tone accents are used as in the sources for examples (1) to (4), where L = Low tone, M = Mid tone, and H = High tone.
6   In several of the examples, tones are represented as pitch level numbers 1 to 5 where, in the Asianist tradition, the larger the number the higher the pitch; thus *33* in example (10) represents a mid level tone, and in examples (13) and (14), *21* and *55* represent respectively a low or low falling tone and a high level tone.
7   Example (17) derives from the script of the award-winning Singapore film *Singapore Dreaming* (Woo, Goh and Wu 2006) whose dialogues are vouched for by Singaporeans as being completely authentic.
8   In these examples, Cantonese tones, as represented in the Yale and Jyutping systems, are as follows: in open syllables, *1* high level or high falling, *2* medium rising, *3* medium level, *4* low falling or very low level, *5* low rising, *6* low level, and, for checked syllables, *7* high level, *8* medium level, and *9* low level.

# References

Ansaldo, U. (2009), *Contact Languages: Ecology and Evolution in Asia*, Cambridge: Cambridge University Press.
Ansaldo, U and L. Lim (2020), "Language contact in the Asian region," in E. Adamou and Y. Matras (eds.), *Routledge Handbook of Language Contact*, 434–61, London: Routledge.
Baker, C. (2011), *Foundations of Bilingual Education and Bilingualism*, 5th edition, Clevedon: Multilingual Matters.
Blommaert, J. (2010), *The Sociolinguistics of Globalization*, Cambridge: Cambridge University Press.
Bloom, D. (1986), "The English language and Singapore: A critical survey," in B. K. Kapur (ed.), *Singapore Studies*, 337–458, Singapore: Singapore University Press.
Bautista, M., S. Lourdes and A. B. Gonzalez (2006), "Southeast Asian Englishes," in B. B. Kachru, Y. Kachru and C. L. Nelson (eds.), *Handbook of World Englishes*, 130–44, Oxford: Wiley-Blackwell.
Canagarajah, A. S. (1995), "The political-economy of code choice in a revolutionary society: Tamil/English bilingualism in Jaffna," *Language in Society*, 24 (2): 187–212.
Canagarajah, A. S. (2009), "The plurilingual tradition and the English language in South Asia," in L. Lim and E.-L. Low (eds.), *Multilingual, Globalising Asia: Implications for Policy and Education, AILA Review*, 22: 5–22.

Canagarajah, A. S. (2013), *Translingual Practice: Global Englishes and Cosmopolitan Relations*, London: Routledge.

Creese, A. and A. Blackledge (2010), "Translanguaging in the bilingual classroom: a pedagogy for learning and teaching," *Modern Language Journal*, 94: 103–15.

Croft, W. (2000), *Explaining Language Change: An Evolutionary Approach*, Harlow, Essex: Longman.

Cummins, J. (2008), "Teaching for transfer: Challenging the two solitudes assumption in bilingual education," in J. Cummins and N. Hornberger (eds.), *Encyclopaedia of Language and Education*, 2nd edition, 65–76, New York: Springer.

Curnow, T. J. (2001), "What language features can be 'borrowed'?," in A. Y. Aikhenvald and R. M. W. Dixon (eds.), *Areal Diffusion and Genetic Inheritance: Problems in Comparative Linguistics*, 412–36, Oxford: Oxford University Press.

Davis, D. R. (2010), "Standardized English: The history of the earlier circles," in A. Kirkpatrick (ed.), *The Routledge Handbook of World Englishes*, 39–58, London: Routledge.

*English World-Wide*. 2020. A Journal of Varieties of English. Amsterdam: John Benjamins. https://doi.org/10.1075/eww [Accessed 6 Oct 2020]

Filppula, M. (2008), "The Celtic hypothesis hasn't gone away: New perspectives on old debates," in M. Dossena, R. Dury and M. Gotti (eds.), *English Historical Linguistics*, 153–70, Amsterdam: John Benjamins.

García, O. (2009), *Bilingual Education in the 21st Century*, Oxford: Wiley Blackwell.

García, O. and Li, W. (2014), *Translanguaging: Language, Bilingualism and Education*, Basingstoke: Palgrave Macmillan.

Gonzales, W. D. W. (2017), "Language contact in the Philippines: The history and ecology from a Chinese Filipino perspective," *Language Ecology*, 1 (2): 185–212.

Good, J. (2004a), "Tone and accent in Saramaccan: Charting a deep split in the phonology of a language," *Lingua*, 114: 575–619.

Good, J. (2004b), "Split prosody and creole simplicity: The case of Saramaccan," *Journal of Portuguese Linguistics*, 3: 11–30.

Good, J. (2006), "The phonetics of tone in Saramaccan," in A. Deumert and S. Durrleman (eds.), *Structure and Variation in Language Contact*, 9–28, Amsterdam: John Benjamins.

Gupta, A. F. (1992), "The pragmatic particles of Singapore Colloquial English," *Journal of Pragmatics*, 18: 31–57.

Gupta, A. F. (1994), *The Step-Tongue: Children's English in Singapore*, Clevedon: Multilingual Matters.

Gussenhoven, C. (2004), *The Phonology of Tone and Intonation*, Cambridge: Cambridge University Press.

Gut, U. (2005), Nigerian English prosody. *English World-Wide*, 26 (2): 153–77.

Hickey, R. (2005), "Englishes in Asia and Africa: Origins and structure," in R. Hickey (ed.), *Legacies of Colonial English: Studies in Transported Dialects*, 503–35, Cambridge: Cambridge University Press.

Hickey, R. (2020), "The colonial and postcolonial expansion of English," in D. Schreier, M. Hundt and E. W. Schneider (eds.), *The Cambridge Handbook of World Englishes*, 25–50, Cambridge: Cambridge University Press.

ICE Project (2016), *International Corpus of English*, http://ice-corpora.net/ice/index.html [Accessed 6 Oct 2020]

James, G. (2001), "Cantonese particles in Hong Kong students' emails," *English Today* 17 (3): 9–16.

Jenks, C. and J. W. Lee, eds. (2020), "Special Issue: Translanguaging and World Englishes," *World Englishes*, 39 (2).

Kachru, B. B. (1994), "English in South Asia," in R. Burchfield (ed.), *The Cambridge History of the English Language, Volume V. English in Britain and Overseas: Origins and Development*, 497–553, Cambridge: Cambridge University Press.

Kouwenberg, S. (2004), "The grammatical function of Papiamentu tone," *Journal of Portuguese Linguistics* 3: 55–69.

Lange, C. (2009), "Discourse particles in Indian English," in T. Hoffmann and L. Siebers (eds.), *World Englishes: Problems, Properties, Prospects*, 207–26, Amsterdam: John Benjamins.

Lee, J. W. and C. Jenks (2016), "Doing translingual dispositions," *College Composition and Communication*, 68 (2): 317–44.

Li, W. (1998), "The 'why' and 'how' questions in the analysis of conversational code-switching," in P. Auer (ed.), *Code-Switching in Conversation: Language, Interaction and Identity*, 156–79, London: Routledge.

Lim, J. H. and A. M. Borlongan (2011), "Tagalog particles in Philippine English: The cases of *ba, na, no,* and *pa*," *Philippine Journal of Linguistics*, 42: 59–74.

Lim, L. (2004), "Sounding Singaporean," in L. Lim (ed.), *Singapore English: A Grammatical Description*, 19–56, Amsterdam: John Benjamins.

Lim, L. (2007), "Mergers and acquisitions: On the ages and origins of Singapore English particles," *World Englishes*, 27 (4): 446–73.

Lim, L. (2009a), "Revisiting English prosody: (Some) New Englishes as tone languages?," *English World-Wide*, 30 (2): 218–39.

Lim, L. (2009b), "Beyond fear and loathing in SG: The real mother tongues and language policies in multilingual Singapore," in L. Lim and E.-L. Low (eds.), *Multilingual, Globalising Asia: Implications for Policy and Education, AILA Review*, 22: 52–71.

Lim, L. (2010a), "Migrants and 'mother tongues': Extralinguistic forces in the ecology of English in Singapore," in L. Lim, A. Pakir and L. Wee (eds.), *English in Singapore: Modernity and Management*, 19–54, Hong Kong: Hong Kong University Press.

Lim, L. (2010b), "Peranakan English in Singapore," in D. Schreier, P. Trudgill, E. W. Schneider and J. P. Williams (eds.), *The Lesser-Known Varieties of English: An Introduction*, 327–47, Cambridge: Cambridge University Press.

Lim, L. (2011), "Revisiting English prosody: (Some) New Englishes as tone languages?," in L. Lim and N. Gisborne (eds.), *The Typology of Asian Englishes*, 97–118, Amsterdam: John Benjamins.

Lim, L. (2015), "Catalysts for Change: On the Evolution of Contact Varieties in the Multilingual Knowledge Economy," unpublished manuscript, The University of Hong Kong.

Lim, L. (2016), "Multilingual mediators: The role of the Peranakans in the contact dynamics of Singapore," in L. Wei (ed.), *Multilingualism in the Chinese Diaspora World-Wide*, 216–33, New York: Routledge.

Lim, L. (2017a), "Money minded," *Language Matters. Post Magazine, South China Morning Post*, March 19, 2017. Online version: Where the word "shroff" came from, and its many meanings, March 17, 2017. http://www.scmp.com/magazines/post-magazine/short-reads/article/2079497/where-word-shroff-came-and-its-many-meanings

Lim, L. (2017b), "Boiling point," *Language Matters. Post Magazine, South China Morning Post*, November 12, 2017. Online version: Where the word congee comes from—the answer may surprise you, November 10, 2017. http://www.scmp.com/magazines/post-magazine/article/2119163/where-word-congee-comes-answer-may-surprise-you

Lim, L. (2020), "The contribution of language contact to the emergence of World Englishes," in D. Schreier, M. Hundt and E. W. Schneider (eds.), *The Cambridge Handbook of World Englishes*, 72–98. Cambridge: Cambridge University Press.

Lim, L. and U. Ansaldo (2012), "Contact in the Asian arena," in T. Nevalainen and E. C. Traugott (eds.), *The Oxford Handbook of the History of English*, 560–71, New York: Oxford University Press.

Lim, L. and U. Ansaldo (2016), *Languages in Contact*, Cambridge: Cambridge University Press.

Lim, L. and N. Gisborne (2009), "The typology of Asian Englishes: Setting the agenda," *English World-Wide*, 30 (2): 123–32.

Lim, L., A. Pakir and L. Wee (2010), "English in Singapore: Policy and prospects," in L. Lim, A. Pakir and L. Wee (eds.), *English in Singapore: Modernity and Management*, 3–18, Hong Kong: Hong Kong University Press.

Lin, A. M. Y. (2005), "New youth digital literacies and mobile connectivity: Text messaging among Hong Kong college students," *Fibreculture*, Issue 6. Available online: http://journal.fibreculture.org/issue6/index.html

Luke, K.-K. (2000), "Phonological re-interpretation: The assignment of Cantonese tones to English words," Paper presented at the *9th International Conference on Chinese Linguistics*, National University of Singapore.

Luke, K.-K. (2008), "Stress and intonation in Hong Kong English," Paper presented at the *14th Conference of the International Association for World Englishes* (IAWE), Hong Kong.

Luke, K.-K. and J. Richards (1982), "English in Hong Kong: Functions and status," *English World-Wide*, 3 (1): 47–63.

Matras, Y. (2000), "How predictable is contact-induced change in grammar?," in C. Renfrew, A. McMahon and L. Trask (eds.), *Time Depth in Historical Linguistics*, vol. 2, 563–83, Oxford: MacDonald Institute for Archaeological Research.

McFarland, C. D. (2008), "Linguistic diversity and English in the Philippines," in M. L. S. Bautista and K. Bolton (eds.), *Philippine English: Linguistic and Literary Perspectives*, 131–55. Hong Kong: Hong Kong University Press.

Mesthrie, R. and R. M. Bhatt (2008), *World Englishes: The Study of New Linguistic Varieties*, Cambridge: Cambridge University Press.

Mufwene, S. S. (2001), *The Ecology of Language Evolution*, Cambridge: Cambridge University Press.

Nettle, D. (1998), *Linguistic Diversity*, Oxford: Oxford University Press.

Onysko, A. (2016), "Language contact and World Englishes," *World Englishes* 35 (2): 191–95.

Platt, J. (1987), "Communicative functions of particles in Singapore English," in R. Steele and T. Threadgold (eds.), *Language Topics: Essays in Honour of Michael Halliday*, vol. 1., 391–401, Amsterdam: Benjamins.

Platt, J. and H. Weber (1980), *English in Singapore and Malaysia*, Kuala Lumpur: Oxford University Press.

Ramsay, R. (2001), "Tonogenesis in Korean," in S. Kaji (ed.), *Proceedings from the Symposium Cross-Linguistic Studies of Tonal Phenomena: Historical Development, Phonetics of Tone, and Descriptive Studies*, 3–17, Tokyo: Tokyo University of Foreign Studies, Institute for Language and Cultures of Asia and Africa.

Remijsen, B. (2001), *Word Prosodic Systems of Raja Ampat Languages*, Utrecht: LOT.

Remijsen, B. and V. van Heuven (2005), "Stress, tone and discourse prominence in Curacao Papiamentu," *Phonology*, 22 (2): 205–35.

Rivera-Castillo, Y. and L. Pickering (2004), "Phonetic correlates of stress and tone in a mixed system," *Journal of Pidgin and Creole Languages*, 19 (2): 261–84.

Schneider, E. W. (2007), *Postcolonial English: Varieties Around the World*, Cambridge: Cambridge University Press.

Schreier, D. and M. Hundt, eds. (2013), *English as a Contact Language*, Cambridge: Cambridge University Press.

Schreier, D., M. Hundt and E. W. Schneider, eds. (2020), *The Cambridge Handbook of World Englishes*, Cambridge: Cambridge University Press.

Schreier, D., P. Trudgill, E. W. Schneider and J. P. Williams, eds. (2010), *The Lesser-Known Varieties of English: An Introduction*, Cambridge: Cambridge University Press.

*Singapore Dreaming* (2006), [Film] Dir. Woo Yen Yen, Colin Goh, Singapore.

Svantesson, J.-O. (2001), "Tonogenesis in South East Asia: Mon-Khmer and beyond," in S. Kaji (ed.), *Proceedings from the Symposium Cross-Linguistic Studies of Tonal Phenomena: Historical Development, Phonetics of Tone, and Descriptive Studies*, 45–58. Tokyo: Tokyo University of Foreign Studies, Institute for Language and Cultures of Asia and Africa.

Thomason, S. (2001), *Language Contact: An Introduction*, Edinburgh: Edinburgh University Press.

Tordesillas, E. (2013), "Gazmin makes the Philippines look pathetic," *Yahoo! News Philippines*, July 1. Available online: http://ph.news.yahoo.com/blogs/theinbox/gazmin-makes-philippines-look-pathetic-163745294.html

Wee, L.-H. (2008), "More or less English? Two phonological patterns in the Englishes of Singapore and Hong Kong," *World Englishes*, 27(3–4): 480–501.

Wee, L. (2010), "Eurasian Singapore English," in D. Schreier, P. Trudgill, E. W. Schneider and J. P. Williams (eds.), *The Lesser-Known Varieties of English: An Introduction*, 313–26, Cambridge: Cambridge University Press.

Winford, D. (2003), *An Introduction to Contact Linguistics*, Oxford: Blackwell.

Wong, K. M. (2019), "Na kaza, greza kung stradu: The Kristang language in colonial Singapore, 1875–1926," *Language Ecology* 3 (2): 157–88.

Wong, Y. T. (2009), "The Linguistic Function of Cantonese Discourse Particles in the English Medium Online Chat of Cantonese speakers," MA dissertation, University of Wollongong.

*World Englishes*. n.d. Wiley Online Library. https://onlinelibrary.wiley.com/journal/1467971x [Accessed 6 Oct 2020]

Venneman, T. (2011), "English as a contact language: Typology and comparison," *Anglia* 129 (3–4): 217–57.

Yakpo, K. (2009), *A Grammar of Pichi*, Berlin: Isimu Media.

# 6

# Multilingualism and the Role of English in the United Arab Emirates, with views from Singapore and Hong Kong

Peter Siemund, Ahmad Al-Issa, Sharareh Rahbari, and Jakob R. E. Leimgruber

## 1. Introduction

The United Arab Emirates (UAE) has witnessed remarkable growth since its foundation in 1971. Initially fueled by the discovery of oil, the economic development of the past decades has come hand in hand with significant foreign labor and investment, resulting in a resident population comprised of no less than 85 percent of foreign citizens. These highly transient migrant workers exert a strong impact on the local linguistic ecology, with many languages present in the public sphere. English holds the position of the unchallenged lingua franca, being used as a first, second, additional, and foreign language by speakers from a multitude of linguistic backgrounds. In this context, English exists in its British and American forms, but also in several others, mainly South Asian varieties. The official language of the UAE is Arabic, but there is an ongoing language shift towards English.

Much as in Singapore and Hong Kong, the present high-tech belt of conurbations in the UAE, which stretches from Abu Dhabi in the West to Ras al-Khaimah in the East, was forged out of small settlements that primarily engaged in agriculture, fishing, and pearling. Today's UAE territory is divided between seven sheikdoms (Abu Dhabi, Ajman, Dubai, Fujairah, Ras al-Khaimah, Sharjah, and Umm al Quwain) that entered a political alliance in 1971, thus giving rise to a new country (Hawley 1971: 129). However, while the development from an agrarian to a modern high-tech society took more than one hundred years in Singapore and Hong Kong, the UAE achieved this change within just a few decades. Singapore came under British control in 1819 and Hong Kong started its colonial history in 1842. Although British interest in the Gulf Region can similarly be traced back to the early nineteenth century, Britain's prime concern in the region were local tribes that impacted their shipping routes to India (Pacione 2005: 255). Rapid urbanization in the UAE only started in the 1960s with the discovery of oil whose revenues were channelled into far-sighted infrastructure projects.

The current multilingual texture and also the history of multilingualism are quite different in the three territories compared here. Before colonization, Singapore was a sparsely populated island of primarily indigenous Malays speaking at best a few related Malayo-Polynesian varieties (Siemund and Li 2020). After it was turned into a British trading post, it quickly attracted Chinese immigrants from Southern China and colonial possessions further north (Malacca, Penang). Moreover, the British relocated sizeable numbers of Indians to Singapore, especially from Tamil speaking Southern India. As of today, Malay, Mandarin and various Chinese dialects, as well as Tamil define the linguistic landscape of Singapore.

In a similar way, Hong Kong used to be an island with low population density before colonization where different forms of Chinese co-existed. During colonial times, it was officially English-speaking in spite of the fact that the vast majority of its population spoke Cantonese (who were attracted from the neighboring Guangdong province). This lasted until 1979 when Chinese (meaning Cantonese) was made a co-official language on a par with English. After the handover to mainland China in 1997, Mandarin or Putonghua has gained prominence in conjunction with a policy that promotes trilingualism (Cantonese, Putonghua, English) and biliteracy (English, Chinese).

## 2. Dubai and the UAE

The discovery of oil in the late 1960s, requiring an expanded workforce, led to a major immigration initiative in Dubai and the entire UAE, which continues to this day. Even though oil is not the main source of revenue anymore, the need for personnel continues. The main income for Dubai today is real estate and tourism, both of which bring in vast quantities of currency and people. Statistics today show that only about 10 percent of the residents of Dubai are Emirati (Adomaitis 2014; Government of Dubai 2019; Kennetz and Carroll 2018; Piller 2018; Solloway 2019); the remainder are all immigrants from many different countries. Beyond the oil industry, workers, particularly from Asia, can easily find jobs in construction, hospitality, and retail, while managerial and teaching positions are often offered to Americans, Britons, other Westerners, and Arabs from various countries. Dubai is extremely diverse in terms of the languages, cultures, and traditions mixed together as the influx of immigrants from all over the world continues to descend on the emirate, as workers, tourists, students, and more. While Arabic is the official language of the UAE, there are more than one hundred languages spoken in the country, some of those include Bengali, Farsi, Hindi, Malayalam, Pashto, Singhalese, Tagalog, and Urdu (Habboush 2009; Baker 2017).

Due to the diverse population in Dubai, a common language was needed to help people communicate. Although Arabic is spoken by the Emiratis and other Arabs who work and reside in Dubai, English has become the lingua franca. While Arabic is the official language of the UAE, English is widely used in business, education, tourism, and government offices. In both the public and private sector, English is spoken in banks, hospitals, universities, shops, and transportation. Indeed, English is almost required in the UAE, especially in higher education. Due to the large expatriate population of the nation, many with some understanding of English, the UAE has essentially offered English a central role. Immigrants who move to the UAE have no need to speak or comprehend Arabic, and it is presumed that most expatriates working in the country will be able to use English for all types of communication (Al-Issa and Dahan 2011). This has had the effect of Arabic being consigned to a lower status among the population. The relationship between the two languages in the UAE is unequal and there are undertones of uncertainty about what the role of English actually is (see Al Hussein and Gitsaki 2018; Findlow 2006; Troudi and Jendli 2011). As Al Hussein and Gitsaki (2018: 106) point out, "It is often unclear whether the status of English in the UAE is one of an official second language or that of a foreign language whose learners could easily do without."

The UAE's language policy and planning have been at the center of helping English proliferate in the country. As the nation continually seeks to modernize and expand, English has become the lingua franca in many, if not all, domains. This has given English a place of prestige, leading Emiratis to view the language as necessary in order to advance economically (see Abendroth-Timmer and Hennig 2014; Randall and Samimi 2010). The push to ensure English as the language of instruction in higher education comes from the country's desire to prepare Emiratis for building a knowledge-based economy and be more competitive regionally and worldwide.

In order to achieve the UAE's education and economic goals, English is taught very early in the curriculum and English is now the medium of instruction (EMI) in higher education. English has an elevated status in the UAE, and this has marginalized Arabic. English is connected to modernity including education, business, and globalization, while Arabic, on the other hand, has a lower status and is considered the language of traditions, family, home, and religion (Al-Issa 2017; Al-Issa and Dahan 2011; Findlow 2006; Kazim 2000). Since English is considered more important for global success and is prestigious, many UAE families send their children to private schools to study in English (Kenaid 2011; Nazzal 2014; Pennington 2015). Emirati children hear English from the time they are very young through personal nannies, tutors, and the television. Despite the fact that public schools, available only to Emirati nationals, are supposed to teach in Arabic, they have nevertheless begun implementing a bilingual curriculum. In fact, nearly 45 percent of weekly instruction in government schools is communicated in English (Carroll and Combs 2016). This is done in order to help Emirati nationals have a chance to compete with their fellow Emiratis who attend private English medium schools.

Emirati high school graduates must take a federal English exam in order to apply to college or university. Without the proper score (180+ on the Common Educational Proficiency Assessment) (Farah and Ridge 2009), they are unable to matriculate into the higher education institutions, which are free. The graduates that fail on this threshold are instead forced to take intensive English language classes to improve their scores. However, many young Emiratis are still unable to improve to the required levels. This is due to the poor English instruction they often receive in the public high schools. For those who cannot improve, this burden causes them to drop out. The position of English at government institutions of higher education has a negative impact on young Emiratis' desire for higher education. Overall, Emirati students have very low marks on local and international standardized tests (Fox 2007). This seems counterintuitive to all the English they are supposedly learning in public schools; however, these low scores usually result from the standards and practices received at the secondary level (Moore-Jones 2015). Furthermore, without an option to study higher education in Arabic, these young Emiratis lose the potential to study at university in their own country in their native language. Three recent studies carried out in the UAE showed that Emirati youth would prefer the option of studying in Arabic or in a bilingual curriculum (Belhiah and Elhami 2015; Kennetz and Carroll 2018; Solloway 2019). These studies reveal that Emirati youth want the ability to choose what language they will study in, and some have now been demanding that option.

There are concerns among many in the UAE that English is becoming an imposition in higher education. Their worries mirror those of scholars in the field of linguistics who point out that language is not neutral and is always attached to its culture and politics (see Block 2007; Findlow 2006; Pennycook 1994; Phillipson 2001). The UAE's language policy is one of "linguistic dualism." This is most apparent in higher education, but its effect has been to lead Emirati youth to look at English as a language superior to their native Arabic. English is used in the UAE for all things modern, such as business, engineering, and sciences, while on the other hand, Arabic becomes less powerful outside of its role in the home and for religious and traditional uses.

To understand the complex sociolinguistic situation in the UAE, it is important to be aware of the role of Arabic, not only in the UAE but in all Arabic-speaking nations. Arabic holds a central role in the history of the Arab world, and many view it as the main marker of a true Arab identity (see Ahmed 2010; Al-Issa 2011; Al Mutawa 2008; Eisele 2017). As the UAE continues to support and expand the role of English within its borders, the place of Arabic continues to diminish. Another factor that has emerged from this dichotomy is a decline in Arabic literacy. While the school curricula continue to increase English classes, Arabic has not been protected or promoted. In addition to its historical role, Arabic in the United Arab Emirates, and in all Arab nations, is a diglossic language. This refers to the different varieties of Arabic used, depending on the situation. There is a "high" language, which is formal and used in writing, and there is a "low" version, which includes vernaculars (Ferguson 1959). In the UAE there have been scholars who claim that the country is actually triglossic (Carroll, Al Kahwaji and Litz 2017). Emiratis speak an Arabic dialect at home, known as *khaleeji* or Gulf Arabic. They also use Modern Standard Arabic (MSA), the "high" version of Arabic when they write, at conferences, and in Arabic classes. Finally, English has entered the mix as a third language in the Emirates.

This mix of languages, used in various situations within the UAE, has had a negative effect on young people and students. They are confronted with Modern Standard Arabic upon entering school. Prior to that they only used their *khaleeji* dialect. Therefore, children in the UAE learn a language which is rather foreign to them when they begin school. This is further confused by the addition of English early in their curriculum. Due to how difficult it is to learn MSA, it is important that it plays a central role in young Emiratis' lives. However, this does not occur on a consistent basis and there are signs that Emiratis are having difficulties with their Arabic literacy skills (Saiegh-Haddad and Spolsky 2014).

In the long term, it is incumbent upon the UAE government to determine how they wish to proceed with their language policies. The decision to make English the medium of instruction in all institutions of higher education has not necessarily been beneficial for all. Certainly, there are students who are quite capable in English, but, even for them, it can be rather difficult to study in a second language. According to several scholars, there can certainly be negative consequences when using exclusionary practices with language policies, and some even question if these exclusions are ethical or legitimate (see Hewson 1998; Markee 2002; Williams and Cooke 2002). Additionally, many Emirati students are unable to enrol in universities when their English levels are low. This will affect their ability to find jobs in the future, especially in the private sector. Furthermore, the consistent focus on English will have negative implications for Arabic literacy and on Emiratis' feelings towards their native language.

## 3. Language Attitudes and Repertoires in the UAE

Existing research on the linguistic situation in the UAE has focused on the complex multilingualism extant in the country and in the Gulf as a whole (Randall and Samimi 2010; Boyle 2011; O'Neill 2014; Thomas 2017; Cook 2017; Drodz 2017; Piller 2018). Most of these studies, however, have focused on Emirati nationals who, as noted above, are in fact a minority in their own country. The premise of our study is to supplement the promising sociolinguistic studies of Drodz (2017) and Piller (2018) with an investigation of language repertoires, attitudes, and usages among people of the Emirates.

The multilingualism of the UAE, we argue, can be illustrated by looking at residents' language repertoires as well as the attitudes they hold towards the languages in the local ecology. In order to do so, we conducted a study in March and April 2019 among students of the American University of Sharjah. This is a private university which draws its student population from a wide range of local backgrounds: both Emiratis and non-citizens attend, the latter being mostly resident aliens. The study consisted of two major components: an online questionnaire on language use and face-to-face semi-structured interviews. The online questionnaire was disseminated among the entire student body by the second author and further advertised on social media. Of the 692 students that took part in the questionnaire, 119 were interviewed face-to-face. The description of the survey, as well as the analysis of language repertoires in this section are based on the descriptions in Siemund, Al-Issa and Leimgruber (2020).

Four sections were included in the questionnaire: (i) a demographic background section, (ii) a language use section, (iii) an educational and socio-economic section, and (iv) a language attitude section. The first section collected basic information such as the year and country of birth, citizenship, and gender. It also queried participants' migration history, in that they could list all countries in which they had lived for more than twelve months (a particularly relevant item in the UAE, a globalized society with high rates of transnational migration). The section on language use records the languages that the informants acquired or came into contact with over their lifetime: this includes language use with family members and peers, languages learnt at school, as well as language use in daily activities (reading, watching television, dreaming, counting, etc.). It also asked participants to self-assess their proficiency in their languages in the four skills (passive reading and listening, and active reading and speaking). The third section attempts to ascertain socioeconomic background by querying the occupation of the participants' parents; it further documents their educational journey from kindergarten to university. Finally, attitudes towards both English and Arabic are gathered in the form of nine statements for each language, drawing on the common dimensions of status and solidarity. In what follows, after a description of the demographic background, we will concentrate on the language repertoires as well as the language attitudes of our informants.

To a large extent, the online questionnaire was inspired by those used in Siemund, Schulz and Schweinberger (2014) and Leimgruber, Siemund and Terassa (2018) in the context of Singapore. Specifically, Leimgruber, Siemund and Terassa's use of the online tool SoSci Survey (SoSci Survey GmbH, 2016) was replicated here because of the powerful customization made possible by the system: among other things, dynamic capabilities prevent participants from being presented with questions that do not apply to them (filtering). Also, language choices selected as part of their repertoires early on in the questionnaire could then be fed back into subsequent questions (e.g., those on proficiency). The average completion time was 15.6 minutes, which was similar to the estimated length given in the invitation e-mail.

## 3.1 Demographics

Our database consists of 692 unique participants, of which 440 (64%) were women and 252 (36%) men. These participants were between the ages of 19 and 37, with a mean and median of 21 (SD = 1.3). The students were primarily undergraduates, with only thirteen enrolled in Master-level degrees. All top-level divisions of the university are represented in the sample: the Achievement Academy (7 participants), the College of Architecture, Art and Design (55), the College of Arts and Sciences (195), the College of Engineering (274), and the School of Business Administration (161). Students also self-reported their Grade Point Average (GPA), with the following distribution across our four categories: 3.5–4 (23%), 3–3.49 (28%), 2.5–2.99 (32%), and below 2.5 (17%).[1]

In terms of migration background, our participants are citizens of forty-nine different countries. In this chapter, we use this measure as a factor to differentiate between Emiratis (30% of our sample) and non-Emiratis. Table 6.1 shows the distribution across citizenship and gender.

Table 6.1 Citizenship and Gender

|  | Emirati | Non-Emirati |
|---|---|---|
| Female | 141 | 299 |
| Male | 67 | 185 |

## 3.2 Language Repertoires

The participants in our sample reported knowledge of an average of 2.8 languages. Several of them, however, indicated more (see Figure 6.1), including 53 informants who claimed to know five languages or more. There are only seven monolinguals in the sample. Non-Emiratis appear consistently more multilingual than Emiratis, a difference that was confirmed to be statistically significant (t = −3.2059, df = 450.15, p-value = 0.001442).

As shown in Figure 6.2, English and Arabic were the languages reported most often. All students reported knowledge of English—an unsurprising result, as the questionnaire was administered in English at an English-medium university. In second place comes Arabic, with differences observed between Emiratis (of whom only two said they did not know Arabic) and non-Emiratis (among whom 345 out of 484 (71%) reported knowledge of Arabic). This high proportion among non-Emiratis, while significantly lower than among Emiratis, warrants closer investigation in future research. Following English and Arabic, the next most frequent languages in our sample are, in decreasing order, Hindi, Urdu, and French.

Participants also self-reported their proficiency in their highest-ranked languages, along a Likert scale with the choices "beginner," "elementary," "intermediate," "upper intermediate," "advanced," and "mastery," in line with the scale of the Common European Framework of Reference (CEFR 2020). As shown in Figure 6.3, the proficiencies in both English and Arabic are generally quite high. Overall, there is a higher proficiency in English, as well as a narrower range than in the case of Arabic. We interpret this wider range of proficiencies in Arabic as a result of its status as an additional language for many students in our sample.

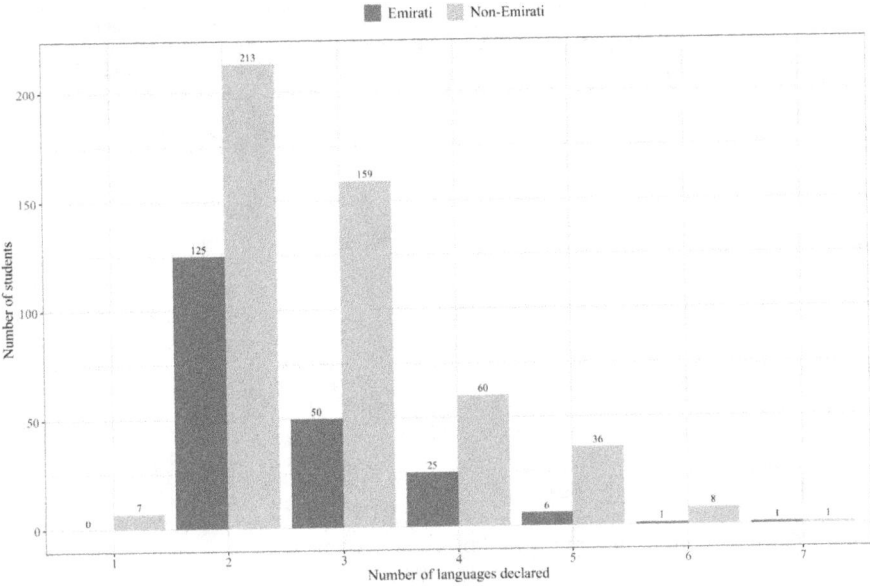

**Figure 6.1** Number of languages declared, by citizenship

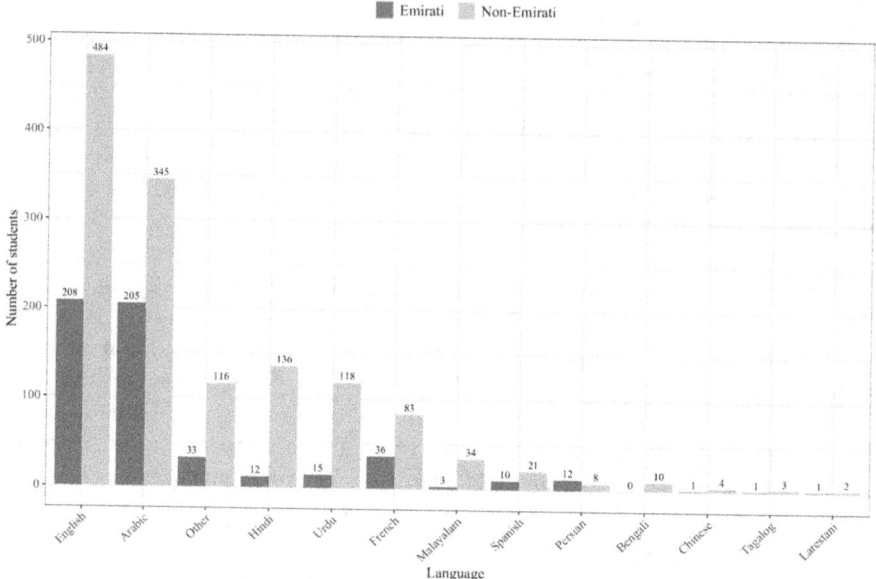

**Figure 6.2** Languages used by citizenship

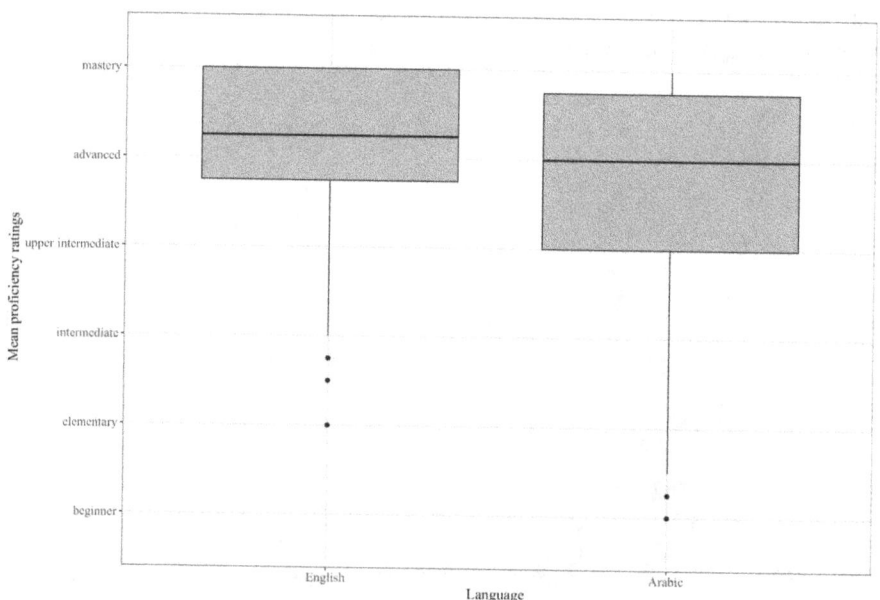

**Figure 6.3** Mean proficiency rating for English and Arabic

In our analysis of the self-reported proficiencies, a more nuanced picture emerges when discriminating between Emiratis and non-Emiratis. Further, given the high demographic weight of South Asian citizens in the UAE, we now consider them a separate category in our interpretation. As can be seen in Figure 6.4, for instance, this distinction is warranted, as there is quite a dramatic difference in Arabic proficiency: while Emiratis and non-South Asian non-Emiratis show a very similar mean proficiency of 4.8 and 4.7 respectively, South Asians rate themselves much lower with a mean proficiency of 3.5. The opposite is true with regard to English: here the South Asians rate themselves more proficient than our other citizenship groups, with more of them estimating their proficiency at "mastery" level than, especially, the Emiratis (see Section 2 above). These differences reveal something about the status of the English language within the countries our participants hail from; it certainly is the case that English enjoys wide currency as a lingua franca, a medium of education, and a language of upward social mobility in South Asia, and has done so for a considerably longer time than in the Arab World. By contrast, Arabic plays a minor role in South Asia, where it is likely restricted in use to its role as a religious language in Muslim communities.

More information can be gleaned from the individual language combinations used by the informants in our sample. The profile Arabic + English, as shown in Figure 6.5, is the most widespread by far, with 302 out of 692 (44%) reporting knowledge of these two languages. This most common profile is followed by the combination Arabic + English + French, which is reported by a mere 63 (9%). The third-most used profile is Arabic + English + Other, which was chosen by 58 (8%) of the respondents. These three most widely reported combinations amount to 61 percent of the sample. All of them contain both English and Arabic, highlighting the crucial role of these two languages in the Emirates.

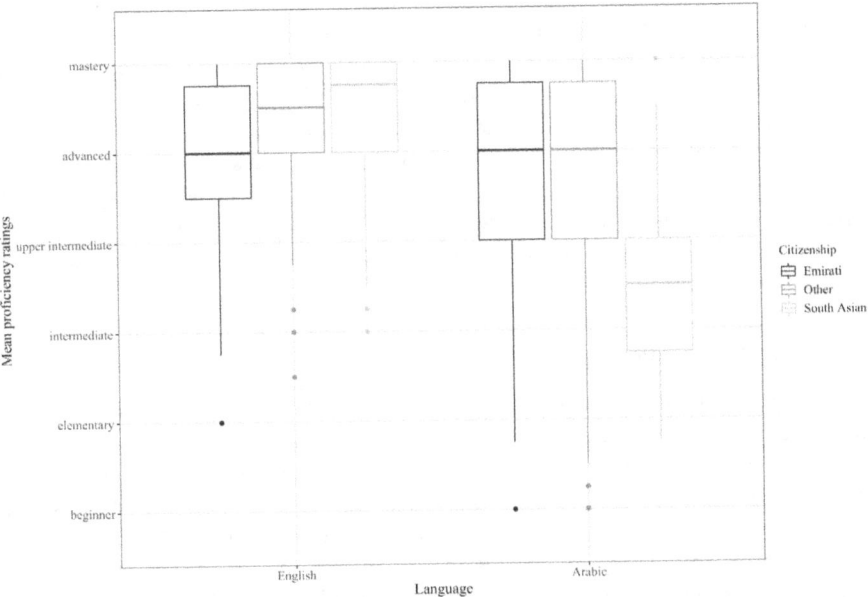

**Figure 6.4** Self-reported proficiency in English and Arabic, by citizenship

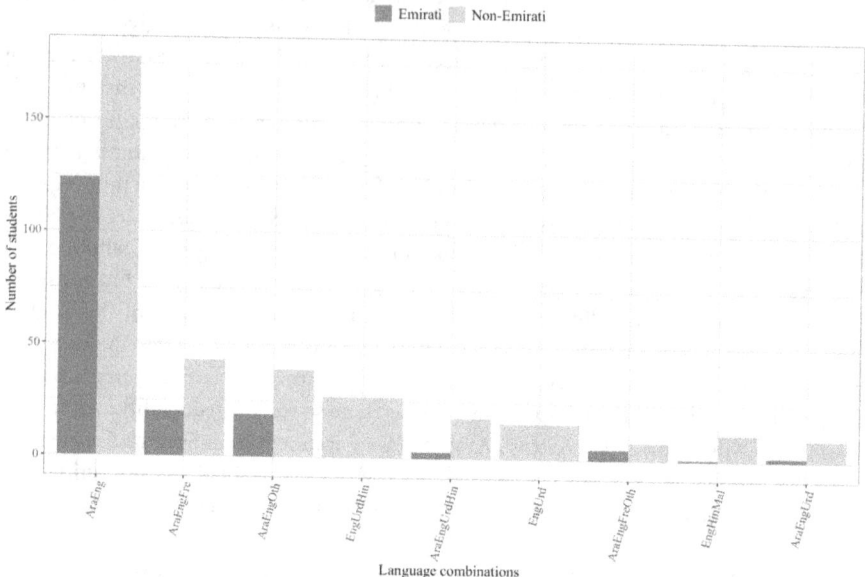

**Figure 6.5** Most frequent language combinations, by citizenship (Ara = Arabic, Eng = English, Fre = French, Urd = Urdu, Hin = Hindi, Mal = Malayalam, Oth = Other)

Citizenship is not a good predictor of repertoire. The first three profiles in Figure 6.5 remain the same among Emiratis and non-Emiratis. Some differences can, however, be observed in the less common profiles: for instance, the combination English + Hindi + Urdu is used by 27 non-Emiratis, whereas it is not used at all by Emiratis. The other profiles too are mostly found among non-Emiratis. We note that among the named languages in Figure 6.5 there are, besides Arabic and English, primarily South Asian languages (Hindi, Malayalam, Urdu), as well as French. This presence of French is probably due to its widespread use as a foreign language in the education system in many private schools of the UAE, as well as to the presence in the country of migrants from former French colonial polities in the Maghreb, Sub-Saharan Francophone Africa, and Lebanon.

### 3.3 Language Attitudes

Language attitudes were queried along the common status and solidarity dimensions, with statements about English and Arabic presented to participants. The Likert scale offered seven levels of agreement or disagreement, including a "neutral" option. For both languages, five statements from each dimension were presented. Our focus here will be on three of these statements. As can be gleaned from Figure 6.6 and Figure 6.7, the first statement, "Knowing Arabic/English will increase my opportunities to find employment" found high levels of agreement in both languages. While English scores

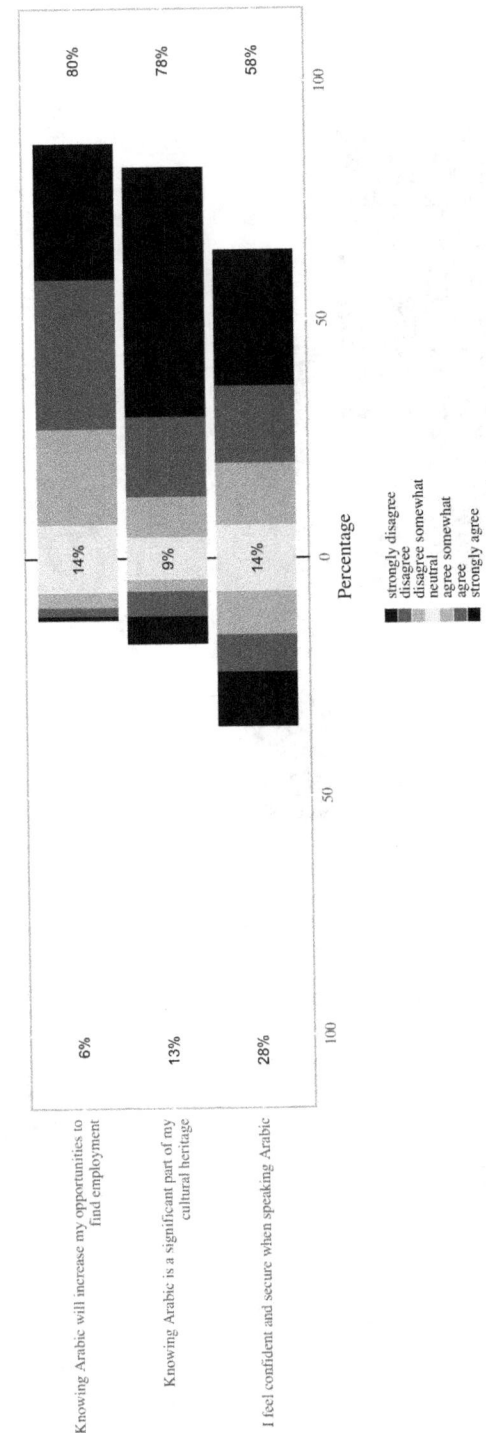

**Figure 6.6** Selected attitudes towards Arabic

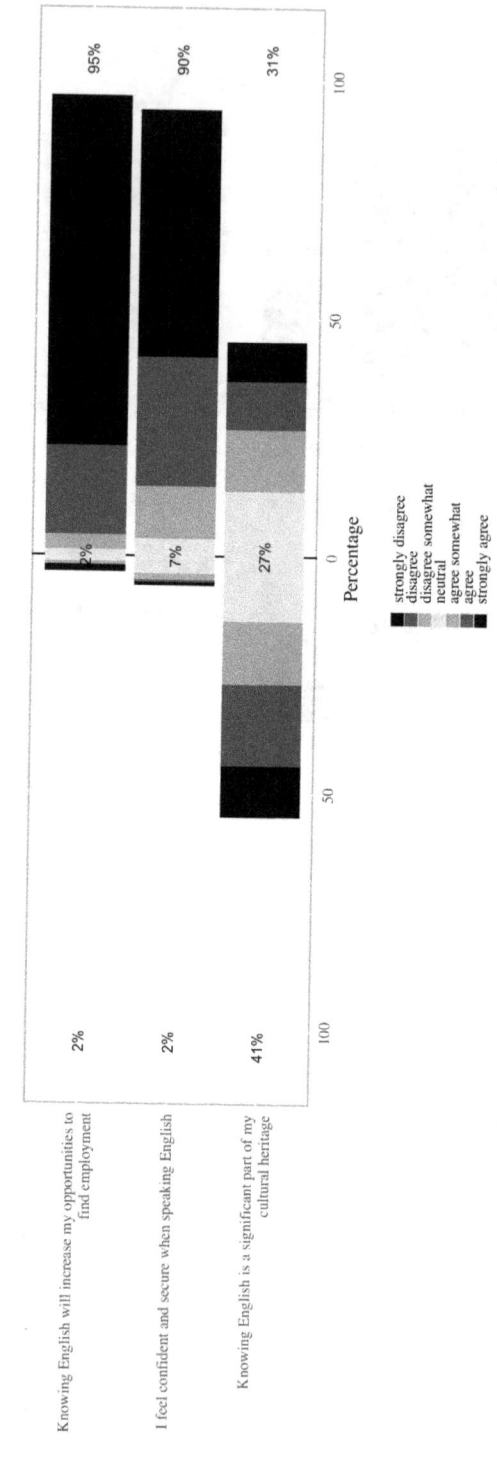

**Figure 6.7** Selected attitudes towards English

were slightly higher than Arabic, participants consider knowledge of both languages valuable in terms of status, particularly when it comes to employability. Interesting differences, however, emerge in answers to the statement "I feel confident and secure when speaking Arabic/English": 90 percent agreed that they did so for English, whereas only 58 percent did so for Arabic. This is perhaps not an unsurprising distribution in view of the self-reported proficiencies discussed above, where English consistently ranked higher than Arabic. Conversely, the statement "Knowing Arabic/English is a significant part of my cultural heritage" received 78 percent agreement in the case of Arabic, but only 31 percent (and 41 percent disagreement) in the case of English. This suggests that while English is preferred over Arabic for day-to-day communication, Arabic retains a certain prestige as a heritage language in a way that English does not. The prevalence of Arabic as a marker of cultural identity is due to the fact that while Emiratis and several migrants have Arabic as a traditional cultural language, this is only partly the case for English.

## 3.4 Gulf English

While the sociolinguistic functions of English in the Emirates (as a lingua franca, a medium of education, and, increasingly, as a second language) are perhaps better understood, the *form* of the English or the Englishes used in the country is less than clear. Previous research has proposed the terms "UAE English" (Boyle 2012) and "Gulf English" (Fussell 2011), both of which suggest a higher degree of homogeneity than can be found empirically. Among the features commonly ascribed to a putative Gulf English are lexical borrowings from Arabic such as those in Boyle (2012: 321): *jebel* 'mountain', *souk* 'market', *guthra* 'traditional male headgear', *abayah* 'black outer garment for females', and the phrase *Inshallah* 'hopefully, lit. God willing'; one might add *wasta* 'social connections'. Grammatical features listed in Boyle (2011: 150–57) include non-finite complement clauses in which the *-to* form is preferred over the *-ing* form (see (1) below), flexibility in verbal transitivity (see (2)), and uncountable as countable nouns (exemplified in (3)).

(1) Do you envisage <u>to carry out</u> this major project in phases? (Boyle 2011: 151)

(2) He <u>appealed</u> not to panic and assured that the authorities were keeping a close vigil on the progress of the depression. (Boyle 2011: 153)

(3) The duo exchanged verbal <u>abuses</u>. (Boyle 2011: 155)

More recent research on less acrolectal speech by Parra-Guinaldo and Lanteigne (2021) finds many more non-standard forms used in lingua franca situations. The morpho-syntactic features they analyzed include omissions (of auxiliary DO, auxiliary or copular BE, adverbial particles, determiners) illustrated in examples (4) to (7), non-standard tense (present simple instead of progressive, perfect, or future, V-*ing* for stative verbs, one example shown in (8)), left-dislocation, negation without DO-support (9), as well as non-standard plural marking and 3rd-person singular inflections (all examples from Parra-Guinaldo and Lanteigne 2021).

(4) What [do] you call that?

(5) This madam [is] now going, car also [is] selling.

(6) This one you want me to switch [off]?

(7) [A] Shukran card you have?

(8) For how long are you [have you been] here?

(9) Plastic no have. [We do not have plastic ones.]

The features of the putative Gulf English variety, therefore, are not surprisingly different from other Englishes found in ELF or even outer-circle settings. It can be assumed that the linguistic and geographical origin of migrants in the UAE plays a central role in the resulting variety. The extent to which these various Englishes coalesce into a single variety, perhaps through a modified form of dialect levelling, are not yet fully clear. Presently available data suggests a range of different ethnolinguistic forms of English co-existing in near isolation, with convergent accommodation towards out-group norms taking place in inter-cultural communication. The extent of this convergence remains unclear and is left for future research.

## 4. Singapore and Hong Kong

This section evaluates the situation in Dubai and the UAE from the perspectives of Singapore and Hong Kong. There are many similarities, though also important differences, in relation to the multilingual texture and the role of English therein, language policy and planning, as well as language change and shift. We will address these areas below.

### 4.1 Multilingualism and the Role of English

The economic logic behind the multiculturalism and multilingualism in the UAE can be contrasted to that in Singapore, where the nation as a whole defines itself as composed of three main ethnic groups (Malays, Chinese, and Indians). The representation of these groups is ensured by governmental decree in different domains such as housing, education, and politics. According to the 2019 Census of Population (Singapore Department of Statistics), the Chinese form the biggest group with 76.0 percent of the population, while Malays and Indians are significantly smaller contributing 15.0 percent and 7.5 percent, respectively. The remaining 1.5 percent are formed by various other groups, mainly Eurasians, Europeans, Japanese, and Arabs. This ethnic distribution has been surprisingly stable for many decades. The three main ethnic groups of Singapore are assigned official "mother tongues," namely Mandarin for the Chinese, Malay for the Malays, and Tamil for Indians. In principle, each member of these ethnic groups is expected to speak these languages, but there are considerably more complex individual language repertoires (Siemund, Schulz and Schweinberger 2014; Leimgruber, Siemund and Terassa 2018). Besides Mandarin, the Chinese speak a host of other Chinese languages ("dialects" in the official parlance), especially Cantonese, Hainanese, Hakka, Hokkien, and Teochew. The Indian population speaks various other Indian languages besides Tamil (Bengali, Gujarati, Hindi, Punjabi, and Urdu; see Cavallaro and Ng 2021).

Although Hong Kong is predominantly Chinese regarding the ethnic background of its population, there are many smaller immigrant groups, including Indians, Nepalis, Filipinos, Indonesians, and Westerners. In 2016, 94.6 percent of the Hong Kong population reported proficiency in Cantonese and 48.6 percent in Putonghua or Mandarin (Bolton, Bacon-Shone and Lee 2021: 162). The most widespread mother tongue or first language is Cantonese.

The Chinese population in both Singapore and Hong Kong is undergoing language shift, though for different reasons and in different directions (see Section 4.3). Both Singapore and Hong Kong are cities in which we find pervasive bilingualism of English and another language. However, the two cities differ in relation to the knowledge, proficiency, and use of English. Moreover, the extent to which English has been localized or nativized clearly diverges. As of today, English is widely used as one or the only home language by many Singaporean families. Recent estimates report home language use of English of around 40 percent (Leimgruber, Siemund and Terassa 2018: 283). By comparison, the status of English in Hong Kong is more aptly described as that of a foreign or second language, contingent on the population group considered. Its use as a home language is very low (below 5%; Fuchs 2021: 293) and there are even fewer speakers who learnt it as their mother tongue (0.6%; Bacon-Shone, Bolton and Luke 2015: 18). An important source of English home language use in Hong Kong are English-speaking nannies from the Philippines. Accordingly, proficiency in English, especially academic proficiency, is higher in Singapore than Hong Kong.

Regarding nativization, it has generally been easier to make a convincing case for Singapore English than Hong Kong English, even though the literature knows both terms. English in Singapore is subject to considerable register differences, ranging from Colloquial Singapore English (Singlish) to Standard Singapore English. Colloquial Singapore English is a contact language with strong influences from especially Chinese (Cantonese) and Malay. There can be no doubt that Colloquial Singapore English has far advanced on the trajectory assumed in Schneider's Dynamic Model (2007), currently being positioned at stage three (nativization) or four (endonormative stabilization), and perhaps even five (internal differentiation; see Buschfeld 2021 for data suggesting such an interpretation). During the early colonial decades, the status of English must have been that of a lingua franca, much as it is today in the UAE. A reliable indicator of the nativization of Colloquial Singapore English is that it is generally imbued with positive connotations and regarded as a symbol of national identity by many Singaporeans (Ortmann 2009: 36). Given the political developments in Hong Kong since the handover to China in 1997, it is not plausible to assume increasing degrees in the nativization of English there. It may be more plausible to use verbalizations like "English in Hong Kong" rather than "Hong Kong English," and to whatever extent English had nativized in Hong Kong, it may currently rather be de-nativizing. Having said that, English is without doubt the most important foreign language in Hong Kong and carries extensive overt prestige.

## 4.2 Language Policy and Planning

As we saw above, language policy measures in the UAE nearly exclusively pertain to the educational sector and concern—perhaps not even intentionally—what is known as "status planning" (Goundar 2017: 85). The main issue is the selection of the medium of instruction in the education system with English typically being the first choice. Determining the medium of instruction has also been a prominent topic in Singapore and Hong Kong, but, in these cities, several additional policy measures have been implemented.

A remarkable decision of far-reaching consequences was taken in Singapore in 1987 when the language of instruction was determined to be English for primary, secondary, and tertiary education. This ended a system in which education in Chinese, Malay, Tamil, and English coexisted, usually looked after by the respective ethnic groups. An important consequence of this decision was that the so-called "mother tongues" now came to be learnt as second languages in the education system, producing a devaluation of Chinese, Malay, and Tamil quite similar to that of Arabic currently observable in the UAE.

Hong Kong to this day has English-medium and Chinese-medium schools working side-by-side obliging parents to decide what they consider best for their offspring besides the problem of what they can afford. Another pertinent problem in Hong Kong lies in the moniker "Chinese," as this can mean either Cantonese or Putonghua. This, again, forces parents to take an important decision as to which strand their children should follow. The official backbone upholding English, Cantonese, and Putonghua is the biliterate/trilingual (BT) policy.

Besides selecting the language of instruction for the education system, the Singaporean government has for a long time been concerned with funneling the original migration-induced language diversity into a system of individual bilingualism involving one of the mother tongues and English. This preoccupation primarily concerns the Chinese community and entailed a profound language shift from various southern Chinese languages (or dialects) towards Mandarin (see next section). The main policy measure to achieve this is the Speak Mandarin Campaign (initiated in 1979) that needs to be conceptualized as an annual campaign placed under captivating slogans comprising a host of status planning and language learning activities.

Hong Kong currently faces a similar tension between what the Beijing government considers a dialect (Cantonese) and Putonghua, there being an increasing devaluation of Cantonese and a concomitant valorization of Putonghua. Interestingly enough, the Singaporean population has always been quite pragmatic regarding this prescribed shift towards Mandarin whereas Hong Kong has maneuvered itself into a veritable identity crisis. Hong Kong is currently entangled in a double divide where Eastern and Western values are forcefully being renegotiated, but also Northern and Southern China oppose one another within the city bounds.

Another important language policy initiative in Singapore is the Speak Good English Movement whose target is Colloquial Singapore English (Singlish), which the government views as "broken English" in need of rectification (see Wee 2011). Again, this campaign is placed under captivating slogans that especially address the younger generations, contending that only Standard English is appropriate for international communication. Curiously, the Speak Good English Movement has been much less successful than the Speak Mandarin Campaign, as Singaporeans have developed strong affection for Colloquial Singapore English and embrace it as a local solidarity code that conveys their Singaporean identity (Leimgruber, Siemund and Terassa 2018: 286). In Hong Kong, English is not really used as a local identity symbol with Cantonese essentially assuming this function. As Bolton, Bacon-Shone and Lee (2021: 179) explain, Hong Kongers typically "have a strong attachment to Cantonese, and the language also serves as a crucial marker of Hong Kong identity."

Singapore and Hong Kong also differ in the extent to which English is used or even prescribed for official documentation. The language choice for the relevant functional domains in Singapore is unanimously English, which is consistently used in institutions of the government, including ministries, schools, the armed forces, government-linked companies, and grassroots organizations. Government websites are typically English-only, and so is policy-making, public communication, and the drafting of bills. Hong Kong is different here in that such official communication is usually available in both English and Chinese. Bolton, Bacon-Shone and Lee (2021) report a certain stratification with English being preferred at the top governmental layers, while the amount of Chinese, especially Cantonese, increases for the regulation of more local affairs.

## 4.3 Language Change and Language Shift

At least since the founding of Singapore in 1965, its three main ethnic groups have experienced a situation of continuous language shift whose target is individual bilingualism in one of the mother tongues (Malay, Mandarin, Tamil) and English. The Chinese community has been going through the most severe shift, as the original Chinese immigrant languages ("dialects") have been replaced by Mandarin. The reasons are clearly political, and regarding the language shift of the Chinese community, they can be immediately recovered in the Speak Mandarin Campaign. The former Prime Minister Lee Kuan Yew, in a televised debate in 1980, left no doubt about the government's language policy:

> We must not burden our children with dialects. Drop dialects, don't let children speak dialects. In fact, dialects have no economic value in Singapore. Their cultural value is also very low. English has economic value. Mandarin has cultural value and will also have economic value 20 years later.
> Tan, November 17, 1980

As a consequence, home language use of the vernaculars (Cantonese, Hainanese, Hakka, Hokkien, and Teochew) has dropped below 20 percent from originally well over 70 percent (see Figure 6.8). During the same period, (dominant) home language use of

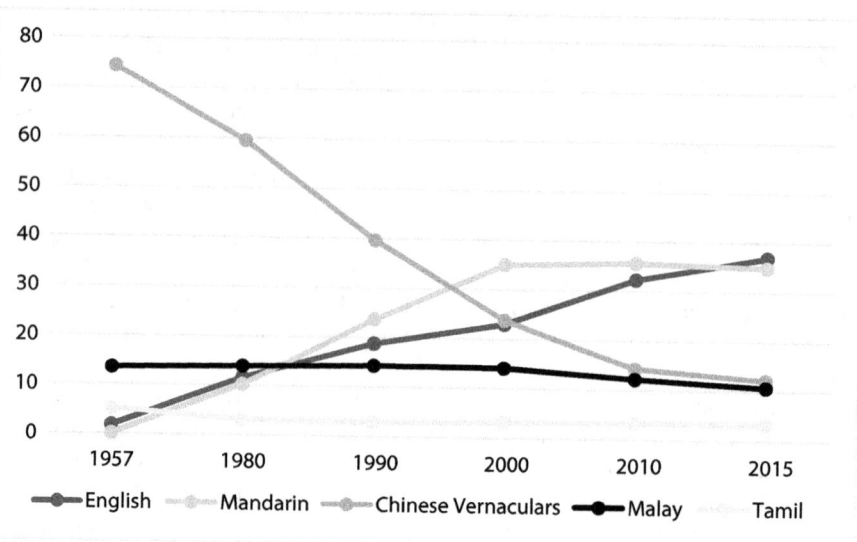

**Figure 6.8** Home language use in Singapore, in percent (data from Wong 2011; Siemund et al. 2014; Leimgruber et al. 2018; Cavallaro and Ng 2021; Singapore Department of Statistics 2020)

English and Mandarin increased to levels between 30 and 40 percent. Interestingly, home language use of Malay and Tamil have been more or less constant, but more detailed recent studies also indicate a shift towards English in these communities.

Although Hong Kong has witnessed a strong increase in the ability of its population to speak Mandarin as a second language, from under 10 percent in 1991 to more than 30 percent in 2016 (Fuchs 2020: 293), the share of the respective first or usual spoken languages has remained practically constant. Figure 6.9 illustrates a moderate decrease in the use of other Chinese dialects and some increase in the use of English and Putonghua (Mandarin). The trend as such mirrors that of Singapore, but the language spoken by the vast majority of the population remains Cantonese.

Whereas the official bilingual policy entailed stronger English learning efforts for the Indian and Malay communities in Singapore, the Chinese speakers have been going through a situation of double language shift, namely from the Chinese vernaculars to both English and Mandarin. The temporal developments shown in Figure 6.8 are also reflected in the language use of different age cohorts. Again, focusing on the Chinese community, the age-related data in Figure 6.10 demonstrate a strong use of the vernaculars in the oldest cohorts and a very strong dominance of English and Mandarin in the youngest cohorts. The use of Malay and Tamil practically do not differ across the age groups distinguished.

The above governmental figures are quite revealing but do not reflect the entire language repertoires of Singaporean speakers. Focusing on three diverse student samples collected at Nanyang Technological University, various polytechnics, and the Institute of Technical Education (ITE), Siemund, Schulz and Schweinberger (2014) as well as Leimgruber, Siemund and Terassa (2018) record substantial, socially and

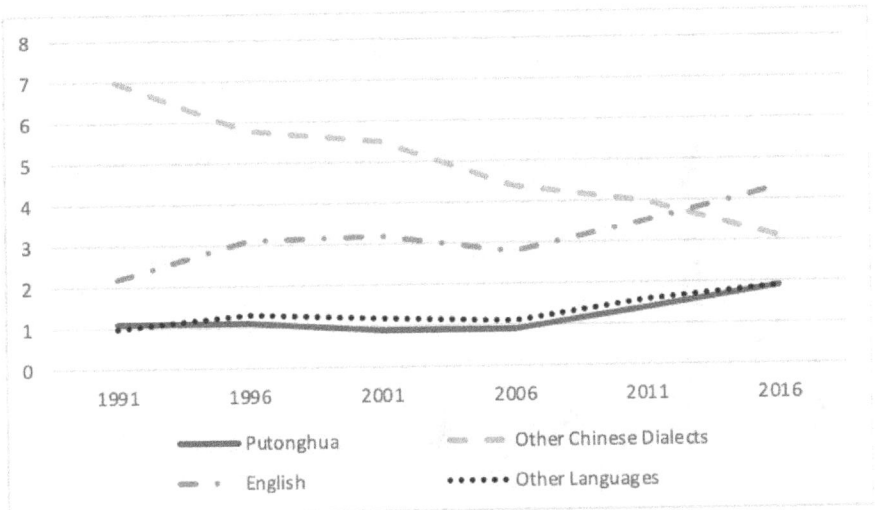

**Figure 6.9** Usual spoken language, in percent (population aged 5 or older), without Cantonese (Census and Statistics Department, 2018: Items A107, censuses and by-censuses 1991–2016; reproduced and adapted from Fuchs 2021: 293)

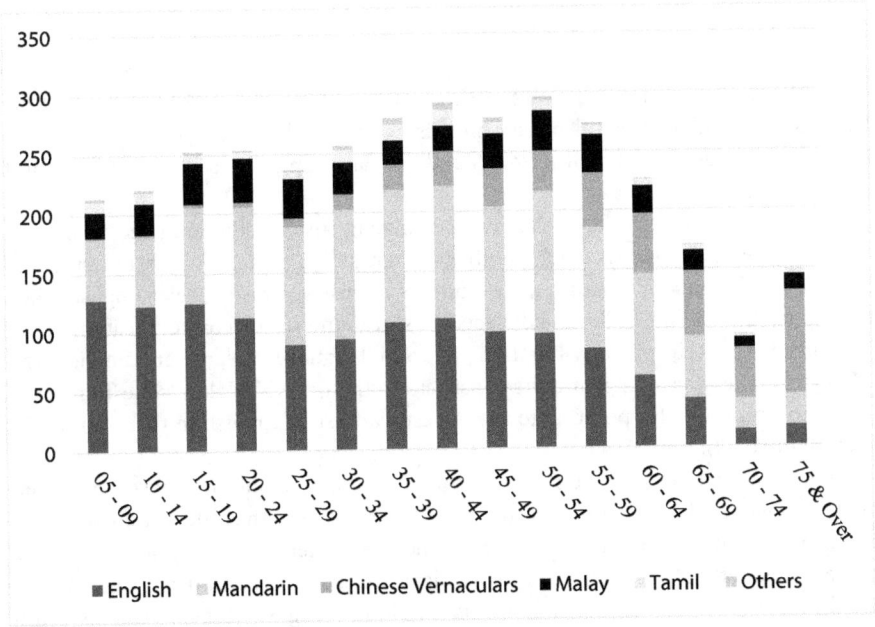

**Figure 6.10** Differences in home language use according to age, in thousand (Singapore Department of Statistics 2020, General Household Survey 2015)

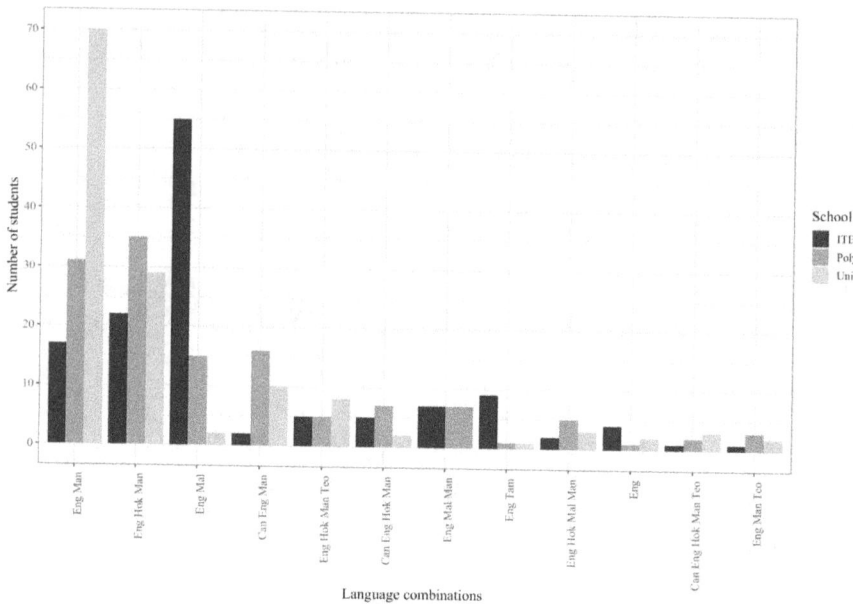

**Figure 6.11** Language combinations among university, polytechnic, and vocational training (ITE) students that occur at least five times (Leimgruber, Siemund and Terassa 2018: 293) (Can = Cantonese, Eng = English, Hok = Hokkien Chinese, Mal = Malay, Man = Mandarin Chinese, Tam = Tamil, Teo = Teochew Chinese)

ethnically dependent language diversity amongst students. Figure 6.11 shows that the Chinese vernaculars are still present in this age group, but they are mostly used as spoken languages. Bilingualism of Mandarin and English is strongest amongst university students.

The same survey also offers data on the language use in different generations and with diverse social interactants (mother, father, siblings, etc.). While the students' parents speak a mix of languages, the students themselves vastly prefer English when talking to their siblings. Chinese dialects are still found in the communication of the students with their parents, but the preferred languages clearly are English and Mandarin. The Malays appear quite consistent in their use of Malay, while Tamil does not figure prominently, pointing to the widespread use of English in this community (see Figure 6.12).

In sum, Singapore is well on its way from an originally multilingual society to one that embraces individual bilingualism of English and one of the mother tongues. Since English is the unanimous language of the education system and many other sectors of society, the mother tongues have been practically relegated to second languages mainly used in non-official and spoken contexts. In Hong Kong, Cantonese remains firmly entrenched in the population, but Mandarin becomes increasingly used as a second language besides English.

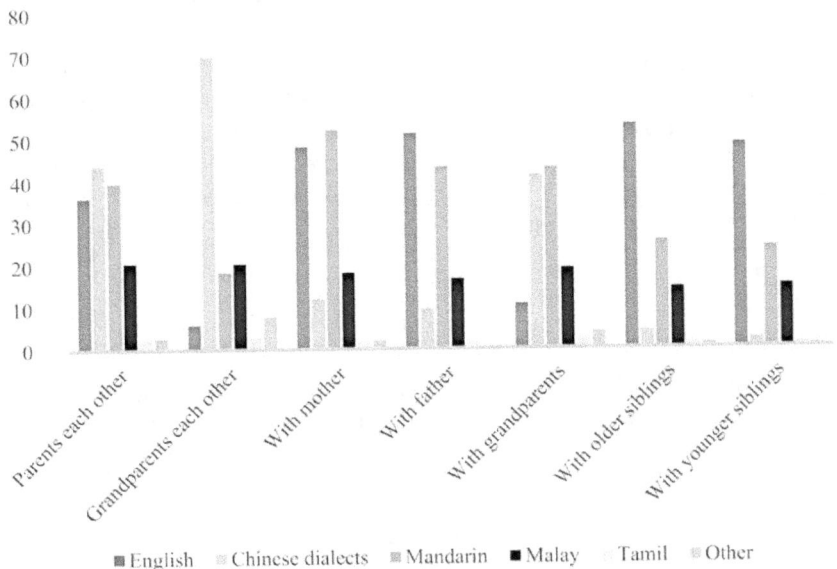

**Figure 6.12** Differences in home language use (own data, total, in percent)

## 5. Conclusion and Outlook

We conclude this chapter by considering Dubai, Singapore, and Hong Kong in the context of Kachru's (1985) well-known Circle Model as well as Schneider's (2007) Dynamic Model. Both the Englishes in Singapore and Hong Kong have often been analyzed as so-called "outer circle" varieties where English is widely used as a second language and shows signs of nativization and endonormative stabilization. Should the current increase of English as a home language in Singapore continue, the city-state is bound to join the "inner circle" countries in the long run. However, the situation will be different from Great Britain, North America, Australia, and New Zealand inasmuch as Singapore's population can be expected to maintain its bilingualism and multilingualism which, in turn, ensures a situation of sustained language contact with the other languages spoken in the area. Current tentative signs of internal differentiation (Schneider's stage five) are likely to become more noticeable in the future.

Regarding Dubai, we are currently witnessing a move from the expanding circle into the outer circle that—depending on the population group considered—may already be complete. In spite of the fact that there are some modest signs of localization, we consider it unlikely that what is here referred to as "Gulf English" will nativize and endonormatively stabilize to the extent that Singapore English has. For that to happen, the currently highly transient population of the UAE would need to settle and English would need to become part of the UAE identity. Having said that, the UAE has developed into a global dialect laboratory replicating on a global scale what could be observed some decades ago in artificial cities like Milton Keynes in the context of British dialects.

Hong Kong, as argued here, is presently perhaps best viewed as moving in the opposite direction. Even though English is considered of high instrumental value there, its importance in the local context—measured in terms of usage domains—is decreasing. Whichever stage English in Hong Kong ever reached in Schneider's model, for the great majority of the Hong Kong population it is moving towards being a foreign language under exonormative pressure.

## Notes

1   A GPA of 4.0 is the highest category in the US university system of grading; it is comparable to a letter grade A or 95–100%. A GPA of 3.5 equals 87.5% or a high B grade.

## References

Abendroth-Timmer, D. and E. M. Hennig (2014), "Plurilingualism and multiliteracies: Identity construction in language education," in D. Abendroth-Timmer and E.M. Hennig (eds.), *Plurilingualism and Multiliteracies: International Research on Identity Construction in Language Education*, 23–37, Frankfurt: Peter Lang, (ebook).

Adomaitis, K. (2014), "What is the true size of Dubai?," *Euromonitor International*, March 15. Available online: http://blog.euromonitor.com/2014/03/what-is-the-truesize-of-dubai.html (accessed December 15, 2019).

Ahmed, A. (2010), "Being taught in English 'undermines local identity'," *The National*, October 6. Available online: http://www.thenational.ae/news/uae-news/education/being-taught-in-english-undermines-local-identity (accessed September 10, 2019).

Al Hussein, M. and C. Gitsaki (2018), "Foreign language learning policy in the United Arab Emirates: Local and global agents of change," in S. K. C. Chua (ed.), *Un(intended) Language Planning in a Globalizing World: Multiple Levels of Players at Work*, 97–113, Warsaw, Poland: De Gruyter Open. Available online:https://doi.org/10.1515/9783110518269 (accessed September 10, 2019).

Al-Issa, A. (2011), "Global migrations, global English, and the transformation of identity in the UAE," in A. Temimi and A. Daoudi (eds.), *Arabic Language and the Internet*, 21–35, Durham, UK: Center for the Advanced Study of the Arab World (CASAW), University of Durham.

Al-Issa, A. (2017), "English as a medium of instruction and the endangerment of Arabic: The Case of the UAE," *Arab World English Journal*, 8 (3): 3–17.

Al-Issa, A. and L. S. Dahan (2011), "Global English and endangered Arabic in the United Arab Emirates," in A. Al-Issa and L. S. Dahan (eds.), *Global English and Arabic*, 1–22, Bern, Switzerland: Peter Lang.

Al Mutawa, M.A. (2008), "Fostering a national identity," *Gulf News*, November 23. Available online: http://gulfnews.com/news.gulf.uae/fostering-a-national-identity (accessed September 10, 2019).

Bacon-Shone, J., K. Bolton and K. K. Luke (2015), *Language Use, Proficiency and Attitudes in Hong Kong*. Hong Kong: Social Sciences Research Centre, The University of Hong Kong.

Baker, F.S. (2017), "National pride in the New School Model: English language education in Abu Dhabi, UAE," in R. Kirkpatrick (ed.), *English Language Education Policy in the Middle East and North Africa*, 279–91, Cham: Springer.

Belhiah, H. and M. Elhami (2015), "English as a medium of instruction in the Gulf: When students and teachers speak," *Language Policy*, 14: 3–23.

Block, D. (2007), *Second Language Identities*, London and New York: Continuum.

Bolton, K., J. Bacon-Shone and S. L. Lee (2021), "Societal multilingualism in Hong Kong," in P. Siemund and J. R. E. Leimgruber (eds.), *Multilingual Global Cities: Singapore, Hong Kong, Dubai*, 160–84, Abingdon: Routledge.

Boyle, R. (2011), "Patterns of change in English as a Lingua Franca in the UAE," *International Journal of Applied Linguistics*, 21 (2): 143–61.

Boyle, R. (2012), "Language contact in the United Arab Emirates," *World Englishes*, 31 (3): 312–30.

Buschfeld, S. (2021), "Multilingual language acquisition in Singapore," in P. Siemund and J. R. E. Leimgruber (eds.), *Multilingual Global Cities: Singapore, Hong Kong, Dubai*, 205–28, Abingdon: Routledge.

Carroll, K. S., B. Al Kahwaji and D. Litz (2017), "Triglossia and promoting Arabic literacy in the United Arab Emirates," *Language, Culture and Curriculum*, 30 (3): 317–32.

Carroll, K.S. and M. C. Combs (2016), "Bilingual education in a multilingual world," in G.S. Hall (ed.), *Routledge Handbook of English Language Teaching*, 191–205, New York: Routledge.

Cavallaro, F. and Ng B. C. (2021), "Multilingualism and multiculturalism in Singapore," in P. Siemund and J. R. E. Leimgruber (eds.), *Multilingual Global Cities: Singapore, Hong Kong, Dubai*, 133–59, Abingdon: Routledge.

CEFR 2020. *Common European Framework of Reference for Languages*. Council of Europe. https://www.coe.int/en/web/common-european-framework-reference-languages/home

Cook, W. R. A. (2017), "More vision than Renaissance: Arabic as a language of science in the UAE," *Language Policy*, 16 (4): 385–406.

Drodz, O. (2017), "Language Shift in Dubai: A Sociolinguistic Survey," MA Thesis, University of Hamburg.

Eisele, J. (2017), "Whither Arabic?," in A. Gebril (ed.), *Applied Linguistics in the Middle East and North Africa*, 307–42, Amsterdam: John Benjamins.

Farah, S. and N. Ridge (2009), "Challenges to curriculum development in the UAE," *Dubai School of Government Policy Brief*, 16: 1–8. Available online: https://www.researchgate.net/profile/Natasha_Ridge/publication/242611859_Challenges_to_Curriculum_Development_in_the_UAE/links/554072760cf2736761c2778d/Challenges-to-Curriculum-Development-in-the-UAE.pdf (accessed September 10, 2019).

Ferguson, C.A. (1959), "Diglossia," *Word*, 15 (2): 325–40.

Findlow, S. (2006), "Higher education and linguistic dualism in the Arab Gulf," *British Journal of Sociology of Education*, 27 (1): 19–36.

Fox, W. H. (2007), "The United Arab Emirates: Policy choices shaping the future of public higher education," *Research & Occasional Paper Series*, 13: 1–14. Available online: https://cshe.berkeley.edu/publications/united-arab-emirates-policy-choices-shaping-future-public-higher-education (accessed May 29, 2019).

Fuchs, R. (2021), "Hong Kong English: Structural features and future prospects," in P. Siemund and J. R. E. Leimgruber (eds.), *Multilingual Global Cities: Singapore, Hong Kong, Dubai*, 285–302, Abingdon: Routledge.

Fussell, B. (2011), "The local flavour of English in the Gulf," *English Today*, 27 (4): 26–32.

Habboush, M. (2009), "Classical Arabic makes a comeback," *The National*, March 22. Available online: http://www.thenational.ae/news/uae-news/education (accessed September 10, 2019).

Goundar, P. R. (2017), "The characteristics of language policy and planning research: An overview," in X. Jiang (ed.), *Sociolinguistics—Interdisciplinary Perspectives*, 81–8, Rijeka, Croatia: InTech.

Hawley, D. (1971), *The Trucial States*, New York: Twayne Publishers, Inc.

Hewson, M.G. (1998), "The ecological context of knowledge: Implications for learning science in developing countries," *Journal of Curriculum Studies*, 20 (4): 317–26.

Kachru, B. (1985), "Standards, codification and sociolinguistic realism: The English language in the outer circle," in R. Quirk and H. Widdowson (eds.), *English in the World: Teaching and Learning the Language and Literatures*, 11–30, Cambridge, UK: Cambridge University Press.

Kazim, A. (2000), *The United Arab Emirates A.D. 600 to the Present: A Sociodiscursive Transformation in the Arabian Gulf*, Dubai, UAE: Gulf Books.

Kenaid, K. (2011), *In Search of a Good Education: Why Emirati Parents Choose Private Schools in Dubai*, Dubai, UAE: Knowledge and Human Development Authority.

Kennetz, K. and K. S. Carroll (2018), "Language threat in the United Arab Emirates? Unpacking domains of language use," *International Journal of the Sociology of Language*, 254: 165–84.

Leimgruber, J. R. E., P. Siemund and L. Terassa (2018), "Singaporean students' language repertoires and attitudes revisited," *World Englishes*, 37 (2): 282–306.

Markee, N.P. (2002), "Language in development: Questions of theory, questions of practice," *TESOL Quarterly*, 36 (3): 265–74.

Moore-Jones, P. J. (2015), "Linguistic imposition: The policies and perils of English as a medium of instruction in the United Arab Emirates," *Journal of ELT and Applied Linguistics*, 3 (1): 63–74.

Nazzal, N. (2014), "Why Emiratis pick private schools," *Gulf News*, April 27. Available online: http://gulfnews.com/news/uae/education/why-emiratis-pick-private-schools-1.1324786 (accessed December 15, 2019).

O'Neill, G. T. (2014), "Just a natural move towards English: Gulf youth attitudes towards Arabic and English literacy," *Learning and Teaching in Higher Education: Gulf Perspectives*, 11 (1): 1–21.

Ortmann, S. (2009), "Singapore: The politics of inventing national identity," *Journal of Current Southeast Asian Affairs*, 28 (4): 23–46.

Pacione, M. (2005), "Dubai," *Cities*, 22 (3): 255–65.

Parra-Guinaldo, V. and B. Lanteigne (2021), "Morpho-syntactic features of English as a lingua franca in Dubai and Sharjah," in P. Siemund and J. R. E. Leimgruber (eds.), *Multilingual Global Cities: Singapore, Hong Kong, Dubai*, 303–20, Abingdon: Routledge.

Pennington, R. (2015), "Emirati parents increasingly turning to private schools," *The National*, January 5. Available online: http://www.thenational.ae/uae/education/emirati-parents-increasinglyturning-to-private-schools (accessed September 10, 2019).

Pennycook, A. (1994), *The Cultural Politics of English as an International Language*, Harlow, Essex, UK: Pearson.

Phillipson, R. (2001), "English for globalisation or for the world's people?," *International Review of Education*, 47 (3/4): 185–200.

Piller, I. (2018), "Dubai: Language in the ethnocratic, corporate and mobile city," in D. Smakman and P. Heinrich (eds.), *Urban Sociolinguistics*, 77–94, London: Routledge.

Randall, M. and M. A. Samimi (2010), "The status of English in Dubai," *English Today*, 26 (1): 43–50.

Saiegh-Haddad, E. and B. Spolsky (2014), "Acquiring literacy in a diglossic context: Problems and prospects," in E. Saiegh-Haddad and R. M. Joshi (eds.), *Handbook of Arabic Literacy*, 225–40, Dordrecht: Springer.

Schneider, E. W. (2007), *Postcolonial English. Varieties Around the World*, Cambridge: Cambridge University Press.

Siemund, P., and L. Li (2020), "Multilingualism and language policy in Singapore," in H. Klöter and M. Söderblom Saarela (eds.), *Language Diversity in the Sinophone World*, 205–28, London: Routledge.

Siemund, P., A. Al-Issa and J. R. E. Leimgruber (2020), "Multilingualism and the role of English in the United Arab Emirates," *World Englishes*. https://doi.org/10.1111/weng.12507

Siemund, P., M. E. Schulz and M. Schweinberger (2014), "Studying the linguistic ecology of Singapore: A comparison of college and university students," *World Englishes*, 33 (3): 340–62.

Singapore Department of Statistics. 2020. https://www.singstat.gov.sg.

Solloway, A.J. (2019), "Toward increased professionalism in teaching English as a second or other language through pre-service trainee teacher mentoring in the United Arab Emirates," *UKH Journal of Social Sciences*, 3 (1): 14–27.

Tan, B.H. (1980), "Drop dialects at home and help your child do better in school," *The Strait Times*, November 17: 9. Available online: http://eresources.nlb.gov.sg/newspapers/Digitised/Article/straitstimes19801117-1.2.39 (accessed September 10, 2019).

Thomas, S. (2017), "The Case of the 'Innocuous' Middle-class Migrant Employee: English Language Use and Attitudes in Dubai, United Arab Emirates," PhD Thesis, Purdue University. Available online: ProQuest Dissertations and Theses database. UMI No. 10179969 (accessed September 10, 2019).

Troudi, S. and A. Jendli (2011), "Emirati students' experiences of English as a medium of instruction," in A. Al-Issa and L.S. Dahan (eds.), *Global English and Arabic: Issues of Language, Culture, and Identity*, 23–48, Bern: Peter Lang.

Wee, L., (2011), "Metadiscursive convergence in the Singlish debate," *Language & Communication*, 31: 75–85.

Williams, E., and J. Cooke (2002), "Pathways and labyrinths: Language and education in development," *TESOL Quarterly*, 36 (3): 297–322.

Wong, W. K. (2011), "Census of population 2010 statistical release 1: Demographic characteristics, education, language and religion," *Department of Statistics*. Available online: www.singstat.gov.sg (accessed September 10, 2019).

# The History of English Language Attitudes within the Multilingual Ecology of South Africa

Susan Coetzee-Van Rooy and Bertus Van Rooy

## 1. Introduction

The English language is regarded very favorably by most South Africans living in the early twenty-first century (Dalvit and De Klerk 2005; De Kadt 1993, 2005; De Klerk 1999; Alexander 2000; Bowerman 2000; Kamwangamalu 2002), and despite its equal status as one among eleven official languages, it is by far the most widely used language outside the home domain. English is the principal language in education, government, business, and industry. Although it appeared to be a matter of debate in the 1980s and early 1990s in the build-up to the political transition that culminated in the election of a new government in 1994 (Du Plessis 1985; Prinsloo 1985; Reagan 1984, 1986; Reagan and Ntshoe 1987; Alexander 1989; Eastman 1990; Beukes 1992; Cluver 1992; Webb 1994, 1996, 1999; Heugh 1995; Titlestad 1996), it became clear in the latter half of the 1990s that the role of English would be extensive and other languages could not compete with English, not even in education, or as Rudwick and Parmegiani (2013: 92) put it, "the hegemony of English has become entrenched in the post-apartheid state."

Prior to the 1990s, statements of attitude by politicians and educationalists can be found easily, and opinion pieces or position statements also exist, but empirical research on language attitudes was not pursued, with the exception of Vorster and Proctor (1976) on the attitudes of black university students towards English and Afrikaans, and HSRC work on the language loyalties of white South Africans (Hauptfleisch 1977, 1979). The early 1990s also saw a surge in research activity into language attitudes. Three main strands of research can be identified. One set of studies, continuing the earlier work by Vorster and Proctor (1976) and Hauptfleisch (1977, 1979), focuses on "attitudes towards English," often in comparison with other languages. De Kadt (1993) records very favorable, but instrumentalist, attitudes towards English among students and domestic workers who were native speakers of isiZulu. In a matched-guise experiment, De Klerk and Bosch (1994, 1995) find the most positive attitudes are reserved for English in comparison to Afrikaans and isiXhosa. English doesn't replace the home language and other indigenous languages from the repertoire, though. For purposes of social cohesion, languages other than English are still regarded very favorably (Coetzee-Van Rooy 2012).

A second strand of research focuses specifically on attitudes towards English and other languages in "particular domains," among which the domain of education is particularly important (Barkhuizen and Gough 1996; Granville, Janks, Mphahlele, Reed, Watson, Joseph and Ramani 1998; Alexander 2000, 2003; Mclean 1999; Plüddemann 1999, 2015; Banda 2000; Heugh 2000, 2002, 2013; Desai 2001; Coetzee-Van Rooy 2018). Rudwick and Parmegiani (2013) present the typical finding that students who speak isiZulu have strong affinities for their home language and lament the limitations on the use thereof, but still favor English as language of education and public life, while their affinity for isiZulu is limited to its use in private domains.

A third strand of research concerns the study of attitudes towards different "varieties" of English, and possible shifts in attitudes. Cooper (1989) investigates attitudes towards "Conservative" (British-oriented) and "Extreme" (locally-oriented) native white SAfE and finds a consistent preference for the Conservative guise in her matched-guise experiment among Black participants in the second last year of secondary school. Lanham (1996: 27) claims, based on his experience going back to the 1960s, that "Queen's English" is strongly favored as target variety by black South Africans. Subsequent research points to a shift in attitude. Smit (1996) records changes in attitudes towards varieties of English that are consistent with changes in the social status of speakers that happened from 1994 onwards. Van Rooy, Van Rooyen and Van Wyk (2000) find that some forms of Black South African English (BSAfE) are regarded as favorably (mesolectal BSAfE) or more favorably (acrolectal BSAfE) to black listeners, although English and Afrikaans-speaking white South African listeners still favor the variety of the white native-speaker of SAfE in the experiment. Coetzee-Van Rooy and Van Rooy (2005) report that black listeners regard native-speaker WSAfE and acrolectal BSAfE equally highly, but also report favorable attitudes towards an Indian native-speaker of acrolectal Indian SAfE.

At the same time, a "critical strand" of inquiry can be detected, focusing not so much on the empirical analysis of language attitude data sampled from the general population, but on the analysis of texts and publicly communicated viewpoints that seem to support the colonial project, and included in the scope was an examination of the role of English in the colonization of South Africa (e.g., De Kock 1996; Higgs 1997). For instance, in keynote addresses to the English Academic of South Africa, Mphahlele (1984) and Ndebele (1987) call for a more critical attitude towards the English language on the eve of political liberation. More recently, empirical research on and critical discussions of language in education policy also point to the negative effect that the use of English has on students' understanding of the work and progress through the education system (for school education, see Pretorius 2000, 2002; for higher education see Favish 2005; Ncgobo 2009; Huysamen 2000; De Beer 2006; Downs 2005; Barnes, Dzansi, Wilkenson and Viljoen 2009; CHE 2010; Van Rooy and Coetzee-Van Rooy 2015), and the stifling effect that the presence of English has on the development of African languages in education and other public domains (Desai 2001; Probyn 2004, 2009; Koch and Burkett 2005; Webb 2004, 2013; Webb, Lafon and Pare 2010; Wildsmith-Cromarty 2012; Makoe and McKinney 2014; Antia and Dyers 2016).

Studies of the attitudes of black South Africans towards English since the 1990s are reasonably comprehensive, but studies of language attitudes from the preceding centuries are under-represented. What evidence there is comes from detailed case studies of particular individuals or political movements, and such evidence is contested. Some analysts find evidence for a critical opposition to the extending role of English, but other evidence points to a very favorable (if uncritical) attitude towards all things English.

This chapter aims to answer the historical question of what the attitudes of Black South Africans have been toward English since they first came into contact with the language, and whether these attitudes show signs of change over time. A better understanding of the past, and of developments into the present, can shed light on current attitudes that are still being lamented as extensively favorable towards English, to the detriment of the development of indigenous African languages in higher status domains. Language-in-education policy scholars are struggling to interpret the overt discrepancy between multilingual policies for education and the lack of implementation of these policies in the post-1994 South Africa. At least four lines of argumentation have emerged to explain the lack of implementation. Lack of political will to implement multilingual policies in education has been mentioned. The lack of clear language plans that would enable the implementation of multilingual policies in education has been raised. Some arguments focus on the unassailable prominence of English in high status functions in the society that inhibits the development of indigenous African languages. Lastly, there is the argument that the heritage of colonization and Apartheid simply makes it impossible for Black South Africans to imagine quality education in a language other than English.

It is with this last reason offered as explanation of the discrepancy between overt multilingual education policies and the lack of implementation of these policies that this chapter wants to engage. If we believe that language attitudes are embedded in the past, then it is imperative that we undertake historical studies to deepen our understanding of how the language attitudes of Black South Africans developed and how it contributes to an explanation of current language attitudes. The next section of the article presents the historical context in which the data should be situated. This is followed by a description of the corpus data and the method of analysis, before the results are presented and conclusions drawn.

## 2. Historical Context

Historical study of the attitudes of the indigenous black community of South Africa towards English has received attention in the course of historical or literary studies of important authors and/or politicians, but the focus is mostly on the work and political engagement of the individual, such as Higgs' (1997) study of DDT Jabavu, or White's (1993) study of ZK Matthews. Likewise, biographies and autobiographies offer detailed perspective on language issues, such as Mphahlele's *Down Second Avenue* (1959) and Frieda Matthew's *Recollections* (1995) that are in part autobiography and in part biography of her husband ZK Matthews. Older work on language in education policy (e.g., statements, letters, and unpublished papers by ZK Matthews, examined by White 1993) and closer to the present, the study by Hirson (1981) can also be identified. The general thrust of these studies is the view that English has been viewed very favorably as the language of education, but because of the education and the advantages in terms of employment, and the promise of future political and economic equality held, what Higgs (1997) terms the "ghost of equality."

White (1993: 197) and Higgs (1997: 48) both point out that the mission-trained African elite of the early to mid-twentieth century were assimilationist and gradualist in their political views. They accepted the dominant position of Europeans in the South African society as a given in the specific time that they lived, and aimed to assimilate and fit into that society, while expecting that the complete assimilation of the entire African population will happen over the course of several generations. In the assimilation, English had a very important role to play, as ZK Matthews explained to a fellow leader of the liberation struggle, W. G. Champion, in a letter in 1944: he accepted the unavoidable presence of Europeans in South Africa, and therefore, to participate in the broader society, access adequate education, and become part of the (white-defined) society, English had to play an important role in education.[1] Matthews (n.d.) argued for the use of the vernacular in the lower levels of education, but pointed to the limited reading matter available in the indigenous languages, and also qualified the call for the use of the vernacular languages by stating that it should not displace adequate access to the official languages. In higher education, Matthews (1959) advocated strongly for the continued use of English, both to accommodate students from several mother tongues in the same university (to avoid becoming an ethnic college), and more importantly for access to knowledge of the developed countries, in order to fast-track the educational development of people who had been left behind in the progress of world-wide formal education. Several decades later, Ndebele (1987: 14) lamented such equation of English and education, and called anew for a different language in education dispensation.

Much of the favorable view of the English language derived from the association between the language and its speakers, particularly the so-called "friends of the natives," who were settler politicians in the nineteenth century Cape parliament that appeared to promote the franchise and broader interest of educated Africans (Higgs 1997), alongside the missionaries who brought Christianity and formal school education to the indigenous population (Woeber 2012). In contrast to these "friends of the natives" stood the white Afrikaners, who were brutal in their repression of black South Africans and their fear to allow them any political rights. Frieda Matthews (1995: 35) notes that her husband ZK Matthews believed "that the Afrikaner in South Africa is ruthless in his deep-seated fear of the Black man having some power of any kind." However, there was also an awareness by prominent black leaders of the late nineteenth and twentieth centuries that the English settlers and missionaries were also racist and did not ultimately believe in the equality of the indigenous South Africans (De Kock 1996: 84; Matthews 1995: 43). Yet, the prospects were always perceived to be better under English rule than under Afrikaner rule (Higgs 1997: 6–7).

By contrast to the mission-educated Black elite, white Afrikaans speakers have held negative attitudes towards English in the corresponding period. Van Rooy (2020) traces this attitude back to the nineteenth century. Attempts by the English colonial government since the 1820s to anglicize the white Afrikaans community has not just failed, but has engendered a counter-reaction of Afrikaner nationalism (White 1993:

34) with fierce insistence on the use of Afrikaans. When the Afrikaner gained complete control of the South African government in the middle of the twentieth century, it embarked on a range of policy measures to curtail the influence of English, especially in education for black South Africans, under the policy of Bantu Education (White 1993: 36-7; Matthews 1995: 98). White (1993: 42-6) analyzes the public position articulated by the architect of Bantu Education, H. F. Verwoerd, in the 1950s, and notes that Verwoerd set out to reduce the influence of English and its speakers on education for black South Africans. Verwoerd, according to newspaper reports from the time (Voice of the City 1957; Whittock 1957), wanted to ensure that black students would not "be educated into Black Englishmen to struggle against the Afrikaner."

Researchers are confronted with the question of whether the African literate elite of the late nineteenth and early twentieth centuries were naïve in their unquestioning support of the colonial cause. De Kock (1996: 123) poses the question explicitly and answers in the negative, with reference to texts by JT Jabavu that show the understanding of the moral ambiguity and deceit of the missionaries. De Kock (1996: 63) nonetheless concedes that Jabavu and others had to wage the battle in borrowed terms. However, Hirson (1981: 222) has a less favorable reading of the evidence and views of JT Jabavu as proxy for the liberal interest. Switzer (1997) likewise refers to the mission-educated elite of the late nineteenth and early twentieth centuries, whom he calls the Black petty bourgeoisie, as believers in a Western-oriented future. They attempted through constitutional petition and independent newspapers to oppose government steps to limit the franchise or opportunities for the educated Black elite, but their "petitionary protest" (Switzer 1997: 21) was shown to be a failure by the 1930s, when the Herzog acts to remove black voters from the voter's role was passed, thereby ending the ideal of becoming assimilated into the dominant society. This marked a watershed moment, after which a more confrontational form of resistance emerged in the liberation movements, and the old guard lost their controlling influence over Black political organizations.

One way of understanding the development of Black people's response to colonization and the introduction of English into the linguistic ecology of multilingual South Africa, is to view the progression as that from tutelage, to protest, to resistance. This idea is developed in Visser and Couzens (1985) in their analysis of the collected works of H. I. E. Dhlomo. Visser and Couzens (1985: xi) argue that "'Progressivism' is the basis of much of Dhlomo's earlier writing." "Progressivism" included a positive attitude towards Western education and "it meant most of all a position of tutelage for black writers and politicians" (Visser and Couzens 1985: xi). "Tutelage" entailed the advantages of sponsorship and guidance provided by white South African liberals who took an interest in the development of a specific kind of Black elite. Visser and Couzens (1985) argue that Dhlomo's oeuvre displays an early phase of tutelage (where he displayed rather naïve positions in his writing that all progress is good). The next phase of his writing could be viewed as a gradual disillusionment where he discovered and articulated the implications of tutelage which included the development of "protest" against the "control" exercised by white liberals (Visser and Couzens 1985: xi). The final phase of his writing could be seen as a phase of "resistance" where he focused increasingly on "contemporary themes and conditions" (Visser and Couzens 1985: xiii). This development trajectory demonstrated in the writing of the pioneer of black

African drama in South Africa, from tutelage to protest to resistance, provides a productive frame for the analysis of attitudes towards English in the historical corpus of Black South African writing analyzed in this chapter.

In order to deepen our understanding of the past, we undertake a thematic analysis of the historical corpus of Black South African English, analyzing the attitudes towards English expressed by the writers of the texts in this corpus, extending back to 1867. The corpus was originally developed to enable research on language change in Black South African English, but given its size and diversity of texts, it turned out to provide a good number of relevant statements that offer insight into the development of attitudes towards English over time. Such use of a historical linguistic corpus for a thematic analysis is in keeping with recent work at the intersection between corpus linguistics and critical discourse analysis, along the lines of Baker (2006), and Baker and McEnery (2015).

## 3. Method

### 3.1 Description of the Corpus

We use the historic corpus of Black South African English (BSAE) writing that was compiled at the North-West University in South Africa in 2012–2014 (see Piotrowska 2014 for the most complete description). The corpus consists of English writing done by Black South African people ranging from 1867 until 2010. The corpus includes 663,695 words (Piotrowska 2014: 88) that consist of several types of texts (Piotrowska 2014: 85–6). The "newspaper writing" (414,718 words in total) includes: (a) writing from the *Imvo* (for the periods 1884–1888, 1914–1918 and 1944–1948); (b) writing from the *Drum* magazine (1951–1952); (c) writing from the *Sowetan* newspaper (1996, 2006); and (d) newspaper articles taken from newspapers edited by Sol Plaatje in the first two decades of the twentieth century. The "fiction" (136,426 words in total) included in the corpus consists of extracts from novels and short stories in the periods of 1920, 1930 and 1940 by writers such as Sol Plaatje, H. I. E Dhlomo and R. R. R Dhlomo (Piotrowska 2014: 85). Short stories were sourced from issues of the *Drum* magazine in the period 1951–1959; fiction from the *Staffrider* for the period 1991 to 1996; and additional samples of fiction by different authors in the period 1970 to 2000 (Piotrowska 2014: 85). The "letters" (112,551 words in total) in the corpus amount to 439 letters in total (from the period 1867 to 1965) and consist of personal, business and application letters (Piotrowska 2014: 85–6).

The corpus cannot be taken as representative of the opinion of the entire indigenous South African population. It represents, to the extent that archival data could be accessed, a diverse selection of authors over time, who were sufficiently literate to write letters or publish newspapers and fiction in English. Thus, especially before the middle of the twentieth century, the corpus largely represents the work of the mission-educated elite. However, they were the political leaders and the major players in shaping an African response to the development of the colonial and early apartheid order, until the rise of the more militant resistance of the ANC Youth League leaders and representatives of industrial workers from the middle of the twentieth century (see Higgs 1997).

## 3.2 Analysis

The first step in the analysis was to identify all texts in which the word "English" is used, which was done in WordSmith (version 8). In this manner, 51 texts were identified, which were subjected to the second step of the analysis, a thematic analysis done in ATLAS.ti (version 8.0). We analyzed the thematic content of the word "English" as used in the texts to investigate the attitudes of the writers toward English as a language and the English people in their lives. The content analysis of the attitudes expressed towards English in the texts in the historic corpus of BSAE writing provides us with a historic perspective of the attitudes of the writers whose work was included in the corpus from the nineteenth century to the present.

A very simple coding structure was followed in the content analysis of the identified texts in the corpus. The broad codes "attitudes towards the English 'language'" and "attitudes towards English 'people'" were the starting point for the analysis. In other words, upon reading of the specific sections in texts where the word "English" was contained in the corpus, we first of all tried to see if the content could be coded as, for example, "a positive attitude towards the English language" (or conversely a negative attitude). As the coding process developed, additional codes emerged related to the writers' "perceptions of English language proficiency." These codes were easy to identify because writers, for example, specifically referred to their own (or others') proficiency in "writing English" or "reading English" etc. The third set of codes relate to references in the texts by the writers that refer to societal language practices like interpreting, translation, language mixing and bilingualism. The last set of codes refers to attitudes expressed by the writers in the corpus towards the use of languages in education in South Africa or the development of literacy in English or the African languages. The codebook that was developed for each of these codes, their definitions and the frequencies of each code in the corpus are presented in Table 7.1 in the Appendix.

## 4. Findings and Discussion

Writers' attitudes towards "English people" and their customs was the more frequent association with the word "English" that emerged from the data analysis. The majority of the references expressed a positive attitude towards English people. Although these attitudes do not relate to the English language in the first instance, understanding the attitudes of the writers in the corpus towards English people, the speakers of the English language, informs our understanding of the power relations between people present in the society. As Bourdieu (1991: 503) observes, the power of an utterance in a language is not determined in linguistic terms alone, but also depends on the social power of its users. In other words, languages do not have power—people have power, and the languages used by powerful people are perceived as important because of the power of the people using these languages.

Three specific themes emerged when a finer analysis of this code was conducted. First of all, there are several examples where the writers in the corpus express their "loyalty" towards the English nation. The chief of the Amangwane, Nowadi

Luhlongwane, who resided in the Upper Tugela region, is reported to have said to the Upper Tugela Magistrate, Douglas G. Giles, on September 13, 1899:

(1) I told Umzakaziwa I was wedded to the English. [1899 Luhlongwane interpreted decl N45][2]

In the same year, James Magubelu, expressed his loyalty in a letter to Dr. Stewart at Lovedale College:

(2) I consider that it is a folly for the Native People to separate themselves from the English. What would we have been had it not been for the English. One has no words to describe the condition of the Native People, if the English had not come and lifted us up to what we are. [1899 Magubelu Letter C167.28 Pgs2C_docx]

The following report in the *Imvo* newspaper describes the passionate loyalty demonstrated by the Imidushane people who attended a meeting at their "Great Place at Tamara" on February 19, 1915 to discuss the request of the British Government for the people of the tribe to go to Prieska to assist with the building of the railway.

(3) Three cheers were given for the King, and also for our Magistrate. An amusing incident occurred at the end. The strong wave of loyalty carried one heathen man to suggest that we must all join in singing the song the English used to sing during the Boer war, when they were drivers of wagons and leaders. He meant God save the King. Of course, it was sung, the great concourse of heathens humming with big voices as if they were singing their war songs. It was a fitting occasion. Thus ended one of the most patriotic meetings held by the Natives of the Imidushane tribe. [Imvo1915]

These positive attitudes should be interpreted in the context of the late nineteenth century political history of the Cape Colony, where the constitution granting self-rule to the colony extended the franchise to all literate men who met the property and/or income qualification. This meant in practice that a minority of black men gained the vote, which they retained until the second quarter of the twentieth century, when the Herzog laws led to the withdrawal thereof (Higgs 1997). The franchise represented symbolically (because its real political power was limited) the possibility of acceptance in the mainstream of the middle class for the "New African," alongside opportunities offered by education and the promise of white-collar employment. The favorable image of the English was often in contrast to the Afrikaner, under whom black South Africans were given no rights, and their legal ability to earn property was gradually eroded in the twentieth century by the land reform acts (Higgs 1997; Matthews 1995). The introduction of Bantu education by mid-century served to further strengthen the positive attitude towards the English vis-à-vis the Afrikaner (Matthews 1995; White 1993).

In addition to these very positive attitudes of loyalty towards the English people, the writing in the corpus also expresses admiration for some of the "social habits" of

English people and admiration for English officials. In the section "Native Opinion" in the *Imvo* (1885), the virtue of punctuality is related to English people and the native people are judged negatively for not being punctual:

(4) Punctuality is said to have been taught to the English by the railways, and if so we may live in hope of being more regardful of time in South Africa; but at present the native people of this colony are notoriously unpunctual. [Imvo1885_docx]

The virtues of justice and equality are valued by some of the writers in the corpus. The case of the dismissal of Chief Mbovane Mabandla and his treatment by the Ministry of Native Affairs was discussed in the *Imvo* (1885). The case was brought to the Secretary of Native Affairs (a Mr De Wet) for investigation and the commencement of this process was reported in the *Imvo*.

(5) In interesting ourselves in the case of this Native chief we have been urged only by a desire to see that justice, which is the boast of every Englishman, and which Natives are no[t] incapable of understanding or being grateful for, measured out to one of Her majesty's liege subjects. And as we have known the present Secretary for native Affairs for years as a man keenly sensitive of committing an injustice we knew we would not appeal to him in vain. We shall watch, as every Native will do, the progress and result of the inquiry with rapt interest, only fervently desiring that justice may be done. [Imvo1885_docx]

While justice is highlighted in extract (5), the English are also hailed as champions for the equality of all citizens in a report in *Imvo* on September 20, 1888, dealing with elections in the King Williamstown region. Specific candidates are commended for the principles that they uphold:

(6) The chief characteristic of the principles they avow consists, so far as we can see, in this; that in the administration of public affairs they would know no Dutchman, Englishman or Native, neither Bond nor Free; but would still insist upon the fundamental principles of the British Constitution, broad-based in the equality of the citizens in the eyes of the Government as the only safe-guard and condition [o]f the peace, contentment, and prosperity of the Colony. [Imvo1888_docx]

In this report, the virtue of the equality of all citizens is ascribed to the English nation via their constitution. A general admiration of English civilization is in evidence in the historical sources, especially in the early phases of missionary education (De Kock 1996), before the turn towards industrial education in the late nineteenth century, which gradually shifted the aim of education towards the needs of the white-dominated economy (Switzer 1997: 24). However, several decades after the reorientation, ZK Matthews (1926) would write about Adam's College, of which he was principal at the time, that there were two strands of thought about African education—an industrial and an academic route. The possibility of a liberal education was still entertained by an influential figure such as Matthews—the first black school principal in South Africa, and later deputy principal of Fort Hare, the first university for black students. The English values inculcated in the education received by the early generations of African students seemed to have made a lasting impression and remained a model to emulate for a long time to come. White (1993: 48) refers to the nostalgia for the old mission schools and what they represented that developed anew in the middle of the twentieth century as the apartheid government was in the process of implementing the system of Bantu education.

Lastly, there are numerous examples in the historic corpus of BSAE where the writers express their admiration for specific English Government "officials." For example, on January 11, 1916, *Imvo* reported on the annual honours bestowed on members of the British Empire, and said the following about the Knighthood of Sir Umhlali Reynolds:

(7) The other South African Knighthood is that of Sr. F. Umhlali Reynolds who, last election, had the singular distinction of being the only S.A. Party member retained unopposed for the Natal constituency, of UMzimkhulu; and moreover is of the useful kind of Englishmen in that most English Province, who are leading their race to political co-operation with those of other races. As Natives we rejoice to have a Knight with a Native name. Sir Umhlali is very satisfactory. [Imvo1916_docx]

While the attitudes towards the English nation and the English people are positive overall, some negative attitudes are also present in the data. In *Imvo* of October 15, 1918 the German treatment of native people is discussed. The views of an "esteemed European correspondent" on the matter are reported as follows:

(8) An esteemed European correspondent who has been reading an account of the treatment of Natives in German East by the Bishop of Zanzibar, not during the war, but in the normal life of the Colony, calls our attention to it. <u>Some of the English actions in dealing with Natives have been questionable</u>, but at least we have as a nation meant to be fair and the majority of us wish to give them a share in our knowledge and civilization and Religion. It will be well to give our people some idea of the German methods to compare them with the English. It will at any rate comfort them a little when they are rubbed the wrong way by rough people, or have a real hardship to beat—to think how infinitely harder their lot will be if ever the German gets hold of South Africa. [Imvo1918, emphasis added]

Although this expression of negative attitudes towards the English nation or English people are not expressed by a Black South African writer, the editors of the *Imvo* allowed this view to be included in the newspaper which speaks to an attempt to present a balanced view of English virtues. Criticism of English actions can be found across various historical studies and biographies. Frieda Matthews (1995: 43) remarks on the advantage that the South African English took of their racial privilege during the twentieth century, knowing that the "laws" and the Afrikaner will be blamed.

The social power and the attractiveness of the characteristics of the English nation and English people are overtly present as a theme in the historic BSAE corpus, and this provides the basis for the positive attitudes towards the "English language" also expressed in the writing investigated in this chapter. The attitude to the people gradually lost some of its strong positive overtones from the 1930s onwards, but in contrast to the Afrikaner, the English always seemed more favorably disposed towards Africans.

The second major theme that emerged from the analysis is the attitudes towards the English language, especially, very positive attitudes towards "knowledge of the English language" and one's ability (language proficiency) to use English effectively. The positive attitudes towards the high status of English in the society are expressed in fiction and in newspaper reports. An illustration of the attitude that English is related to upward social mobility is presented in a short story by Dyke H. Sentso that was published in the *Drum* in June 1951 where a young character discusses the progress that he observed when a young man from the village returned for a visit from Johannesburg:

(9)  -Father ... !
-Yes, son ... ?
-Did you see Molole's son?
-Yes, my boy.
-He is well dressed father, is he not?
-Yes, my son.
-He speaks English and jingles money in his pockets.
-Yes, my son.
-He is a pride to be a man's son, he not?
-Yes, my son. [Drum 195106 fiction]

The juxtaposition of the visitor's fancy clothes with the money in his pockets and the fact that he speaks English expresses the positive views that English is associated with upward social and economic mobility in this short story.

In a brief report entitled "No more quacks?" in *Drum*, a traditional medicine man by the name of L.S. Khontsiwe is predicting the co-existence of Western and African medicine in the near future:

(10) SOONER or later medicine men (African version) and lily-white jacketed, Western-trained medical doctors may find themselves competing to save souls in the same wards in our national hospitals. That's exactly what'll happen if the Rand's primitively-garbed, hairy, barefooted, L S Khontsiwe, African Doctors Associations' mastermind who speaks English with an Oxford accent under his tribal blanket, is the shrewd judge of time and events that he seems to be. [Drum 195211 reports]

The magazine's comment about Khontsiwe's "Oxford English" is associated with his wisdom about the nature of how medicine will be practiced in the future in South

Africa, and contrasted with his primitive way of dressing, his unkempt hair and the fact that he goes barefoot.

The very positive attitudes towards knowledge of English are expressed in two ways in the corpus. On the one hand, some of the writers report on "advanced proficiency" in English skills such as reading, writing or speaking. On the other hand, the "lack of English skills" in reading, writing or speaking is expressed as a problem by some writers. From both these types of expressions, we can infer that the presence of skills in English is viewed positively. This evidence from the corpus is consistent with the historical importance attached to English proficiency. The English language was key to educational opportunities, which in turn provided access to better employment. Comaroff (1999: 10–11) notes that an acknowledged linguist and polyglot such as Sol Plaatje became active in the South Africans Improvement Society in Kimberly in 1895, to improve his speaking and writing skills in English, which contributed to his employment as court interpreter in Mafeking in 1898. For example, in the following excerpts, writers in the corpus lament their seeming "lack of English abilities" and beg the forgiveness of their readers for this shameful condition:

(11) P.S. Please don't be discouraged because I have not written with my own hand, I am not quite up to the mark in English letter writing. [Letter written by W. Soyi to Dr. Steward at Lovedale College on 3 September 1984] [1874 Koyi Letter C252.4 Pg2C_docx]

(12) I am sorry to say I have no best news to tell you, here, but I feel very kind to speak with you with a letter. The only thing that is pity is, that I am very poor in English and in spelling English words, I hope that you shall take great trouble in reading this letter, I cannot express my heart about you farther, I can simply say all the privilege I have got here, I have them on account of you. Dearest Sir, pray for us and that we should pray for you also ... I hope that you will excuse me, Sir for my bad English in writing I remain with kind regards to you all. [Letter written by Ias Mashologu at Lovedale College to Dr. Stewart who is travelling to Scotland with his family on 20 May 1893] [1893 Mashologu Letter C252.25 Pg2C_docx]

(13) Dear Sir please be merciful on me about what I am going to ask. I ask any Daily Soul's bread from you, which is the blood of Christ and Body. I ask my religious London Congregational.
And please give it to me or let me in you don't know the day I'll be summoned at. Let me in let me in let me in. I am only sorry because I am short in English.[3] [1898 Cindi Letter C252.33 Pg1C_docx]

The extent of the proficiency constraint for some writers is quite evident in the following extract, in which the writer, who is already employed as teacher, laments the limitations of his own education, and articulates his desire to have been able to study for longer:

(14) Since I had left the Lovedale I am getting on well, but only one thing which I am not pleased for it, that I am had left school without get education, now I am wish to be back Lovedale again it is because I am very shame to have half education from high school such as Lovedale how I am still teaching a children of Spande Kroon Missionary Station Umzinga Natal.
I had been commence my school at the first day of August last and Dr Dalzell gave me that work and I am teacher there only Zulu and English, but I have many children in my school 54 children although I am the teacher there I not pleased my heart like very much to have more education I have nothing to say now god may be with you and bless you and all your family, may God bless also all the Lovedale people and increase the Lovedale education more than before. Remember me when you pray, I am remember you. I send my good compliments to you and all Lovedale's people. [1890 Zulu letter C252.24]

Particularly noticeable is the lack of verb inflection and very rudimentary mastery of tense, aspect and modality in the passage ("am had left," "without get education," "had been commence"). Articles are also used in inconsistent ways, both in cases where the article would not conventionally be used ("the Lovedale") or where it would conventionally be used ("to have half ___ education from ___ high school such as Lovedale"). Repetition and lack of punctuation indicate a writing style that is very close to oral interaction, and serves as further testimony to the limitations that this teacher had in expressing himself.

The opposite sentiment is also present in the corpus, where writers reflect on the good writing abilities of writers in English, for example, in a letter to the editor of *Imvo*:

(15) A Gospel Minister of long standing and considerable experience in South Africa thus writes us on the 15th December "I write a line to say that my copies of Native Opinion have duly reached me, and also to say that the articles and get up are good. I can only speak of the English part, and I am bound to say that I think it highly creditable. What is written is in good English, and the spirit and tone are of that moderate firm tone to which no one can fairly object, and if the same course is continued all well-wishes of the natives will approve and commend the publication."[4] [Imvo1884_docx]

The third prominent theme that emerged from the coding process is related to attitudes towards "specific language practices" in the society of the writers. There are instances in the corpus where writers refer to the bilingualism in the society and language practices like interpreting and translation that are used often. These attitudes indicate an awareness by the writers in the corpus (and the members on the society) of the linguistic diversity and complexity of the South African context. There is evidence in the corpus of the widespread use of bilingual addresses at events in the society. For example, at an event in the Libode district in 1918, the Governor was addressed by the Regent of Western Pondoland, Mangala Ndamase. The following excerpt from *Imvo* in 1989 indicates what language arrangements were made at the event to ensure that all attendees were able to understand the address:

(16) His Excellency then sat down with his Party (Lady Buxton, Miss XXX[5] His Aid-de Campe and the Chief Magistrate's Chief Clerk—Colonel Muller). The latter introduced His Excellency to the Natives and Europeans present. His Excellency then asked Chief Magala to come under the verandah near His Excellency which he did. Colonel Muller narrated this history of the Buxton family, their philanthropic spirit towards the Natives and backward nations, after which His Excellency made a lengthy speech which was, however attentively listened to. Before His Excellency's speech, addresses were read out in Kafir and English by Messrs I.G. Mtingane and R.G. Ntloko respectively (as space will not allow of the Kafir address being published as it is the same as the one in English). [Imvo1918]

From this excerpt it is clear that bilingualism prevailed at this public address and reports in the *Imvo* (1918) also depended on a bilingual audience who would be able to read the English version of the address.

The omnipresence of the multilingualism of people in the society and the practice of interpretation at events and translation of documents are also present in the corpus. On October 26, 1953, Elliott Koza writes a letter to the Town Clerk in Kimberley to request consideration for the job of interpreter:

(17) I hereby beg for admission into your department, as an interpreter clerk or Beer Hall Manager.
I am married and 24 years of age, the following languages, I can speak read and write, Setswana, Sotho, Afrikaans and English.
The only language, I am weak is Xhosa; but not that I can't hear and speak it.
[1953 Koza Letter N57.5 Pg1C_docx]

Half a century earlier, Sol Plaatje was appointed court interpreter in Mafeking, on the back of his fluency in English, Dutch, isiXhosa, German and Sesotho, alongside his native Setswana (Comaroff 1999: 11). The same form of deep individual multilingualism is reported in the obituary of Isaiah Budiwana Mbelle, Plaatje's contemporary and his brother-in-law, who passed away on July 16, 1947:

(18) A Short Review of Bud Mbelle's Life Story
In the humble town of Burghersdorp, Cape Province, in the year 1870 was born on June 24 Isaiah Budiwana Mbelle who became South Africa's greatest African pioneer clerk interpreter. On his early days he attended the Wesleyan Methodist Primary School, and showed great promise. From 1886 to 1888 he was a student at Healdtown where he distinguished himself as a scholar and passed the Teacher's Examination with Honors.
For five years he taught in Herschel and in Colesberg. In both places he won the hearts of his pupils and the community at large. In those days a teacher had to play many parts in the life of the community especially in church affairs. Thus that love of work and church became part and parcel of his life. To quote Inspector Satchel's words Mr Mbelle was not "a Walking cabbage," but sought to

improve himself every day. In 1892 he was the first African to pass the Cape Civil Service Examination. He passed in English, Dutch (Afrikaans) Xhosa, Sesotho, Sechuana and Zulu. [Imvo1947]

The language repertoire of Elliott Koza looks similar to the multilingual repertoires of urban citizens in the Gauteng Province in the present, where Sotho and Nguni languages as well as Afrikaans and English form part of the repertoires of citizens of Johannesburg (Coetzee-Van Rooy 2012, 2016).

In the societies that the writers of the corpus lived in and wrote about, multilingualism seems to have extended to white people who lived and worked in South Africa at that time as well. In a speech by Reverend John Knox Bokwe on July 21, 1916 to commemorate the 75th anniversary of the opening of the Lovedale College, he proposed the following language arrangements:

(19) IN ENGLISH
Chairman of the Gathering!
Since I have been chosen to speak at this Anniversary in the name of the NATIVE PEOPLE, I feel that I must speak what I have to say in my Native Xosa instead of using a strange language. Therefore I request the Rev. B.J. Ross to translate for me. [1916 Bokwe Letter BC293 B22.3 Pg11C_docx]

The reference to English as a "strange language" indicates some distance between the language and Bokwe, but the letter also shows his confidence that a white minister was competent to interpret from isiXhosa to English.

In 1910, Manyaki Renge in Queenstown wrote a letter to his Chief Magistrate, Mr. Walter Stanford. The first part of the letter is written in part in English and the larger second part in isiXhosa, a clear case of code-switching, which is premised on the ability of the magistrate to read both languages:

(20) Know that I shall mix English and Kafir,[6] because you are XakaXaka. [1910 Renge Letter BC293 B174 Pg2C_docx]

The excerpts discussed in this section provide evidence of the widespread bi- and multilingualism in the societies that the writers of the historic BSAE corpus write about.

The fourth theme that emerged from the coding process is not quantitatively prominent, but in terms of gravitas, it cannot be ignored in this discussion. As is clear from the frequencies of codes reported in the Appendix, there are a small set of references to the issue of "languages in education" in the society of the writers included in the corpus. There are two prominent passages in the corpus that discuss the issue of language in education policies, both written by D. D. T. Jabavu, the first African who became professor at the University of Forth Hare (and hence in all of South Africa) in the *Imvo* of November 1916 and May 1918. In both of these texts, Jabavu maintained that native children should be taught literacy in their home languages, and that English and/or Dutch should be added to their repertoires only after literacy in the home language was achieved. The argument for literacy in the home language was built by first of all referring to the success of early missionary education, as viewed by Jabavu:

> (21) The salient feature of their system [early missionary education] was the education of the Natives in their mother tongue, until pupils had mastered the reading of the Scriptures, which were then, as now, the only advanced text book in the language. The pupil dared not be allowed to begin the Alphabet in English or Dutch, where those were the alternative languages, before they had shown proficiency in their own lingo. [Imvo1916_docx]

Jabavu specifically lamented the influence of Dr. Thomas Muir (Superintendent-General of Education in the Cape Colony, later the Cape Province, from 1892 until 1915) on the language in education arrangements made in missionary education:

> (22) It is a thousand pities Missionary bodies allowed themselves to be dictated to by Dr Muir in this [decisions about the language of teaching and learning in missionary schools] and in the matter of taking unconverted Teachers for Mission Schools. For the result has simply been deplorable. Dr Muir commenced with pragmatic contempt of the pupils' mother tongue when he insisted on Native children being examined only in Standard made for European pupils. The result has been that a type of educated Native has been produced which has been taught from infancy to look down upon its own language and is either unable to read it intelligently or will not read it at all. On the other hand these Natives have received but the smattering of the English language, and nothing more. How, in the circumstances, was a Native lad or lass to be expected to be grounded in the Scriptures when he or she was not particularly versed in any of the languages in which they are written? [Imvo1916_docx]

Jabavu's description of the lack of proficiency of pupils in neither the home language, nor English, is eerily similar to definitions of the now criticised concept of "semilingualism," defined as having a "low level [of proficiency] in both languages" known (Valadez, MacSwan and Martínez 2000: 238).

In a second passage in the data, Jabavu defended the value of African languages in comparison to English and Dutch, as part of his critique of Loram's (1917) book, *Education of the South African native*. He focused his attention on the section titled, "The Ultimate Supremacy of the European Language" in Loram (1917) and he specifically challenged Loram's (1917) ideas about the fate of the Bantu languages. Jabavu took issue with Loram's (1917) claim that African languages in South Africa would not be maintained and that people would eventually shift to English or Dutch. He offered an example of the maintenance of African languages in the Eastern Cape, despite co-existence with white people for a long time.

> (23) In districts thickly populated by Natives like Bechuanaland, Swaziland, Transkei and Pondoland it is certain that English and Dutch will never oust the Bantu

language as a means of intercourse any more than they have done in Kaffraria where the white man's occupation extends over two centuries. [Imvo 1918]

Next, Jabavu questioned Loram's (1917) claim that white people would not acquire and learn African languages. He called into question the empirical basis of Loram's (1917) claims, and provided insights into the language attitudes towards bi- and multilingualism of the society of his time.

(24) That all Europeans are unwilling to learn them [African languages] is yet to be proved. In Basutoland there is hardly a Frenchman who is unable to speak se-Suto as well as any mo-Suto. Dutchmen who live in Native areas in the Cape Province generally know Xosa well. It is Englishmen who are notorious for their unwillingness to learn even other European languages. [Imvo 1918]

The unwillingness of white English-speaking South Africans to acquire or learn additional languages (neither African languages nor European languages) described by Jabavu above is also reported in language attitude studies in the 1970s in South Africa. Hauptfleisch (1979: 42–3), for example, found that English-speaking South Africans were not interested in being proficient in a second language in general, even though they were positive about the idea of bilingualism.

Thirdly, Jabavu reminded readers of the Loram (1917) text that although there were some topics which could not yet be described and discussed in African languages, there were also many topics which could be described and discussed more effectively in African languages than in English or Dutch.

(25) Granting that they "are not capable of expressing the ideas which the new civilization has brought to the country" it is a fact acknowledged by Bantu scholars that the European languages on the other hand cannot express many ideas peculiar to the African mind. Just as Chopin cannot take the place of Mozart so English and Dutch can never be substitutes for the XXX and eloquence to be found in Xosa. [Imvo 1918]

Jabavu concluded that for as long as the African languages carried the identity of its people, these languages would be maintained.

(26) To abolish the present bilingual system amongst the Europeans would be child's play to any attempt to destroy the Native languages. The survival of Welsh in Wales or of Polish in Poland is proof enough that the Bantu languages will persist as long as the Bantu maintain their racial identity. [Imvo 1918]

The importance of African home languages as carriers of cultural identity in South Africa today (see for example Coetzee-Van Rooy 2012) vindicates the arguments made by Professor Jabavu one hundred years ago.

The evidence presented in the analysis makes it clear that the writers of the historic BSAE corpus valued the use of African languages in education and predicted that

African languages will be maintained in the presence of English and Dutch (later Afrikaans). These attitudes position English as an important language in the repertoires of multilingual African home languages speakers in South Africa across almost 150 years.

One should mention briefly that the views articulated by Professor Jabavu in the extracts above are juxtaposed to the very different view of his colleague and second African professor at Fort Hare, Z. K. Matthews. Although the corpus does not include examples of the writing of Professor Matthews, it is important to consider his view about the language in education policy here briefly in the interest of a balanced picture.

On the one hand, Matthews was extremely clear that he valued and respected African languages and culture. In response to the use of African languages as media of instruction proposed by the Nationalist government in the 1940s in South Africa, Matthews wrote the following in a letter to the Natal Congress leader (W. G. Champion):

(27) Of course it will be argued that any opposition to this emphasis upon Bantu Language is based upon a disrespect for our languages. Nothing is further from the truth. (Hirson 1981: 226)

Furthermore:

(28) The serious defect of early native education was the use of a foreign language as a medium of instruction. It was believed—as it is in many respectable quarters today—that the Native child had to learn English as early as possible [if] its future education was to be successful. The Natives aided and abetted this attitude by insisting that they sent their children to school, not to learn the vernacular, which they claimed could best be learnt at home and from themselves rather than from the representatives of a foreign culture, but to learn to read and write English and to assimilate some of the white man's ways of doing things (Hirson 1981: 224)

These statements clearly indicate that Matthews valued African home languages and viewed them as the most appropriate media of instruction in the early years of education. On the other hand, Matthews clearly favored the use of English after the completion of the early years of school education:

(29) It is therefore of the utmost importance that the vernacular should receive its proper place in Native Schools. And yet nothing ought to be done to give the Native the impression that he is to [be] denied the opportunity of learning the official languages. Nothing is calculated to destroy interest in the Native languages among them than an attempt to minimise the importance of learning English and Afrikaans and to disparage their efforts in this direction ... The present system in which the vernacular is the medium of instruction in lower classes and a subject of study in the higher classes seems to me highly commendable. (Matthews, n.d.)[7]

In conclusion, one is reminded that Matthews' views about language clearly indicate the political objectives of African people of his day: successful access to political and economic empowerment rightfully dwarfed all other issues, including the language question.

## 5. Conclusion

We combined a corpus study with a close textual reading of historical documents identified as relevant through a pre-screening of the data using a corpus retrieval tool. The selection of fifty-one texts offered a number of insights, some of which could have been expected on the basis of historical research, but some are new. The combination of corpus data with close attention to detail from a qualitative perspective appears to be profitable to yield a kind of balanced picture that might allude conventional scholarly methods for selecting texts to understand viewpoints historically.

The most important insights are the favorable attitudes towards a language which are closely related to favorable attitudes, or even loyalty, towards the people who speak that language. This loyalty has complex political and socio-economic causes, but the evidence from the data shows that issues of political freedom and economic opportunity were far more pressing in the history of Black South Africans' contact with English than the language issue as such. Thus, while attitudes are conveyed towards language, the political and economic dimensions drive the attitudes towards language. Even as far as education is concerned, the desire for the best possible education usually weighs more than the language in which that education is offered, and only enhances the need and intent to improve proficiency in the language of education.

Attitudes towards English people, and through that towards the English language, were influenced by the presence of Afrikaans people and the Afrikaans language (including its earlier, colonial Dutch, forms). Because of the comparatively more favorable interaction with English people, and because of deliberate steps taken by an Afrikaans government to limit access to English, the attitudes towards Afrikaans were comparatively unfavorable, and increasingly so over time, but conversely, attitudes towards the English language became increasingly more favorable.

Attitudes towards the indigenous African languages were not unfavorable. The value of using these languages especially in the early phases of education was expressed overtly by two authors (see extracts 21, 22, 28 and 29), although this was not a prominent concern articulated in the corpus. However, due to external factors of an educational, economic, and political nature, these languages were just not deemed useful after the early phases of education or ultimately as potential vehicles for economic mobility and obtaining political rights. They remain a part of the linguistic ecology of South Africa, counter to the expectation of Loram (1917), for reasons aptly explained by Professor D.D.T. Jabavu in 1918. These languages still perform important attitudinal and identity functions today.

# Appendix

**Table 7.1** Codebook for the Analysis of Attitudes towards English People and the English Language in the Historic Black South African English Corpus

| Broader theme | Code | Definition | Freq. |
|---|---|---|---|
| Attitudes towards **English people** [total occurrences=50] | Positive attitudes towards English people | Any reference by the writer that indicates positive attitudes towards English people. | 39 |
| | Negative attitudes towards English people | Any reference by the writer that indicates negative attitudes towards English people. | 11 |
| Attitudes towards the **English language** [total occurrences=38] | Positive attitudes towards the high status of English | Any *positive* reference to the high status of English, or expressions that being able to speak English is a symbol of upward mobility or modernity. | 9 |
| | Negative attitudes towards English language proficiency concerning writing | Any reference by the writer towards her/his own inability or negative writing proficiency in English; or the ineffective writing proficiency in English of fellow South Africans. | 7 |
| | Positive attitudes towards English language proficiency concerning talking | Any references by the writer that he/she can talk English well. | 4 |
| | Positive attitudes towards English language proficiency concerning writing | Any reference by the writer towards her/his own good ability or positive writing proficiency in English; or the effective writing proficiency in English of fellow South Africans. | 4 |
| | Positive attitudes towards English language proficiency concerning reading | Any reference by the writer towards her/his own effective reading proficiency in English; or the effective reading proficiency in English of fellow South Africans. | 3 |
| | Positive attitudes towards knowledge of English | Any reference by the writer about the knowledge of his own English or the knowledge of the English of fellow South Africans. In this specific case, knowledge of English is seen as a positive element that might influence the employability of people or might demonstrate their allegiances towards English people / the English government. | 3 |
| | Negative attitudes towards English language proficiency concerning reading | Any reference by the writer that he/she or fellow South Africans cannot read English. | 2 |

# English Language Attitudes in South Africa 141

| | | | |
|---|---|---|---|
| | Positive attitudes towards English language proficiency concerning expressing views | Any reference by the writer that he/she or fellow South Africans can express their views well/effectively in English. | 1 |
| | Negative attitudes towards English language proficiency concerning talk | Any reference by the writer of a "deficiency" to express oneself in English. | 1 |
| | Negative attitudes towards the status of English | Any negative reference by the writer about the high status of English and how using English in inappropriate contexts is not socially acceptable. | 1 |
| | Attitude towards standard English | Any reference to "standard English." | 1 |
| | Attitude towards English as an international language | Any reference by the writer of the use of English in an international context. | 1 |
| | Attitude towards South African English | Any reference by the writer of typical characteristics of SA English. | 1 |
| Attitudes towards **language practices** [total occurrences=17] | Attitudes towards bilingualism with English | Any reference by the writer of attitudes towards bilingualism in the pair with English, for example, Dutch English bilingualism. | 4 |
| | Attitudes towards interpretation ability | Any reference by the writer about her/his positive ability to do interpreting between languages that include English. | 3 |
| | Attitudes towards translation from or to English | Any reference by the writer that expresses an attitude towards the translation of English texts into other languages. | 3 |
| | Attitudes towards Afrikaans and English requirements | Any reference by the writer that knowledge of Afrikaans and English are requirements for a position. | 2 |
| | Attitudes towards multilingual language proficiency | Any reference by the writer of her/his or a fellow South African's multilingual abilities. | 2 |
| | Attitude towards the necessity of interpretation | Any reference by the writer that it is necessary to interpret into a specific language. | 1 |
| | Attitude towards the presence of interpretation in the community | Any reference by the writer that interpretation was done in the community or at a specific event. | 1 |
| | Attitude towards language mixing | Any reference by the writer that language mixing will occur with the implication that this is natural and positive. | 1 |
| Attitudes towards **languages in education** [total occurrences=6] | Attitudes towards the usefulness of languages in education in South Africa | Any reference by the writer of the usefulness of different languages in education in SA. | 3 |

| Broader theme | Code | Definition | Freq. |
| --- | --- | --- | --- |
| | Attitude that English for education is not good enough | Any reference by the writer that his/her level of education, including her/his education in English, is not enough or should be advanced. | 1 |
| | Attitudes towards English literacy classes | Any reference by the writer to English literacy classes. | 1 |
| | Attitudes towards African languages literacy classes | Any reference by the writer to literacy classes in African languages. | 1 |

## Notes

1. Extracts from Matthews's unpublished 1944 letter are quoted at length in both Hirson (1981: 226) and White (1993: 201), from where the summary above has been formulated.
2. Each quotation from the historic corpus of Black South African English writing is referenced to assist researchers to find the same document if they analyze the corpus. The reference includes the date of publication and, where applicable, additional referencing information from the original archives from where the document was sourced.
3. Letter written by Andrew Cindi to a Magistrate in Mafikeng on March 22, 1898 to beg forgiveness for smoking dagga which he did not know was a sin.
4. Comment reported in the Native Opinion section of the *Imvo* in December 1884.
5. XXX in the transcript represent illegible text in the source document that could not be transcribed.
6. No adjustments are made to the original source texts to accommodate the contemporary judgement of taboo values of words used by historical authors.
7. Undated manuscript, which can be dated to approximately 1940 based on the information and historical references in the text.

## References

Alexander, N. (1989), *Language Policy and National Unity in South Africa/Azania*, Cape Town: Buchu Books.

Alexander, N. (2000), "English unassailable but unattainable," *PRAESA Occasional papers*, 3.

Alexander, N. (2003), "Language education policy, national and sub-national identities in South Africa," *Strasbourg: Council of Europe*, 17–18.

Antia, B. E. and C. Dyers (2016), "Epistemological access through lecture materials in multiple modes and language varieties: The role of ideologies and multilingual literacy practices in student evaluations of such materials at a South African University," *Language Policy*, 15 (4): 525–45.

Baker, P. (2006), *Using Corpora in Discourse Analysis*, London: Continuum.

Baker, P. and T. McEnery, eds. (2015), *Corpora and Discourse Studies: Integrating Discourse and Corpora*, London: Palgrave Macmillan.

Banda, F. (2000), "The dilemma of the mother tongue: Prospects for bilingual education in South Africa," *Language Culture and Curriculum*, 13 (1): 51–66.

Barkhuizen, G. P. and D. Gough (1996), "Language curriculum development in South Africa: What place for English?," *Tesol Quarterly*, 30 (3): 453–71.

Barnes H., D. Dzansi, A. Wilkenson and M. Viljoen (2009), "Researching the first-year accounting problem: Factors influencing success or failure at a South African higher education institution," *Journal for New Generation Sciences* 7 (2): 36–58.

Beukes, A. M. (1992), "Moedertaalonderrig in'n demokratiese Suid-Afrika," *Per Linguam*, 8 (1): 42–51.

Bourdieu, P. (1991), *Language and Symbolic Power*, Harvard University Press.

Bowerman, S. A. (2000), "Linguistic Imperialism in South Africa: The 'Unassailable' Position of English," PhD diss., University of Cape Town.

Cluver, A. D. D. V. (1992), "Language planning models for a post-apartheid South Africa," *Language Problems and Language Planning*, 16 (2): 105–36.

Coetzee-Van Rooy, S. (2012), "Flourishing multilingualism: Evidence from the language repertoires in the Vaal Triangle region," *International Journal of the Sociology of Language*, 218: 87–119.

Coetzee-Van Rooy, S. (2016), "Multilingualism and social cohesion: Insights from South African students (1998, 2010, 2015)," *International Journal of the Sociology of Language*, 242: 239–65.

Coetzee-Van Rooy, S. (2018), "Dominant language constellations in multilingual repertoires: Implications for language-in education policy and practices in South Africa," *Language Matters*, 49: 19–46.

Coetzee-Van Rooy, S. and B. Van Rooy (2005), "South African English: labels, comprehensibility and status," *World Englishes*, 24 (1): 1–19.

Comaroff, J. (1999), "Introduction," in J. Comaroff and B. Willan (eds.), *The Mafeking Diary of Sol T. Plaatje*, 8–16, Cape Town: David Philip.

Cooper, P.A. (1989), "An evaluation of attitudes towards conservative and extreme dialects of South African English," *English Usage in Southern Africa*, 20: 39–53.

Council on Higher Education (CHE) (2010), "Higher Education Monitor: Access and throughput in South African Higher Education: Three case studies," *HE Monitor*, Number 9, Pretoria: CHE.

Dalvit, L. and V. De Klerk (2005), "Attitudes of Xhosa-speaking students at the University of Fort Hare towards the use of Xhosa as a language of learning and teaching (LOLT)," *Southern African Linguistics and Applied Language Studies*, 23 (1): 1–18.

De Beer, K. J. (2006), "Open access, retention and throughput at the Central University of Technology," *South African Journal for Higher Education*, 20 (1): 33–47.

De Kadt, E. (1993), "Attitudes towards English in South Africa," *World Englishes*, 12 (3): 311–24.

De Kadt, E. (2005), "English, language shift and identities: A comparison between 'Zulu-dominant' and 'multicultural' students on a South African university campus," *Southern African Linguistics and Applied Language Studies*, 23 (1): 19–37.

De Klerk, V. (1999), "Black South African English: Where to from here?" *World Englishes*, 18 (3): 311–24.

De Klerk, V. and B. Bosch (1994), "Language attitudes in the Eastern Cape: A tri-lingual survey," *South African Journal of Linguistics*, 12: 50–9.

De Klerk, V. and B. Bosch (1995), "Linguistic stereotypes: Nice accent—nice person?," *International Journal for the Sociology of Language*, 116: 17–37.

De Kock, L. (1996), *Civilising Barbarians: Missionary Narrative and African Textual Response in Nineteenth-Century South Africa*, Johannesburg: Wits University Press.

Desai, Z. (2001), "Multilingualism in South Africa with particular reference to the role of African languages in education," *International Review of Education*, 47 (3–4): 323–39.

Downs C. T. (2005), "Is a year-long access course into university helping previously disadvantaged black students in biology?," *South African Journal for Higher Education*, 19 (4): 666–83.

Du Plessis, L. T. (1985), "The state of the art of language planning in South Africa," *South African Journal of Linguistics*, 3 (sup2): 1–23.

Eastman, C. M. (1990), "What is the role of language planning in post-apartheid South Africa?," *TESOL Quarterly*, 24 (1): 9–21.

Favish J. (2005), "Equity in changing patterns of enrolment, in learner retention and success at the Cape Technikon," *South African Journal of Higher Education*, 19 (2): 274–91.

Granville, S., H. Janks, M. Mphahlele, Y. Reed, P. Watson, M. Joseph and E. Ramani (1998), "English with or without g(u)ilt: A position paper on language in education policy for South Africa," *Language and Education*, 12: 254–72.

Hauptfleisch, T. (1977), *Language Loyalty in South Africa. Volume 1: Bilingual Policy in South Africa: Opinions of White Adults in Urban Areas*, Report no. TLK/L-6, Pretoria: Human Sciences Research Council.

Hauptfleisch, T. (1979), *Language Loyalty in South Africa. Volume 3: Motivations to Language Use: Opinions and Attitudes of White Adults in Urban Areas*, Report no. TLK/L-10, Pretoria: Human Sciences Research Council.

Heugh, K. (1995), "Disabling and enabling: Implications of language policy trends in South Africa," *Language and Social History: Studies in South African Sociolinguistics*, 329–50.

Heugh, K. (2000), *The Case Against Bilingual and Multilingual Education in South Africa*, Vol. 3, Cape Town: PRAESA.

Heugh, K. (2002), "The case against bilingual and multilingual education in South Africa: Laying bare the myths: Many languages in education: Issues of implementation," *Perspectives in Education*, 20 (1): 171–96.

Heugh, K. (2013), "Multilingual education policy in South Africa constrained by theoretical and historical disconnections," *Applied Linguistics*, 33: 215–37.

Higgs, C. (1997), *The Ghost of Equality: The Public Lives of D.D.T. Jabavu of South Africa, 1885–1959*, Athens: Ohio University Press.

Hirson, B. (1981), "Language in control and resistance in South Africa," *African Affairs*, 80 (319): 219–37.

Huysamen, G. K. (2000), "The differential validity of matriculation and university performance as predictors of post-first-year performance," *South African Journal of Higher Education*, 14 (1): 146–51.

Kamwangamalu, N. M. (2002), "The social history of English in South Africa," *World Englishes*, 21 (1): 1–8.

Koch, E. and B. Burkett (2005), "Making the role of African languages in higher education a reality," *South African Journal of Higher Education*, 19 (6): 1089–107.

Lanham, L. W. (1996), "A history of English in South Africa," in V. De Klerk (ed.), *Focus on South Africa*, 19–34, Amsterdam: John Benjamins.

Loram, C. T. (1917), *The Education of the South African Native*, Longmans, Green, and Company. Available at: https://archive.org/details/educationofsouth00lorauoft/page/n6/mode/2up

Makoe, P. and C. McKinney (2014), "Linguistic ideologies in multilingual South African suburban schools," *Journal of Multilingual and Multicultural Development*, 35 (7): 658–73.

Matthews, F. (1995), *Remembrances*, Bellville: Mayibuye Books.

Matthews, Z. K. (1926), "The crisis in university education in South Africa. Handwritten notes of presentation," ZK Matthews papers (ACC101), document number C1/2, University of South Africa, Documentation Centre for African Studies. Available at: http://uir.unisa.ac.za/bitstream/handle/10500/6091/ZKM_C1_2.pdf

Matthews, Z. K. (1959), "The crisis in university education in South Africa," Unpublished typescript, ZK Matthews papers (ACC101), document number C4/16, University of South Africa, Documentation Centre for African Studies. Available at: http://uir.unisa.ac.za/bitstream/handle/10500/5774/ZKM_C4_16.pdf

Matthews, Z. K. n.d. [1940s?], "The aims of native education," Unpublished typescript, ZK Matthews papers (ACC101), document number C4/6, University of South Africa, Documentation Centre for African Studies. Available at: http://uir.unisa.ac.za/bitstream/handle/10500/5774/ZKM_C4_6.pdf

Mclean, D. (1999), "Neocolonizing the mind? Emergent trends in language policy for South African education," *International Journal of the Sociology of Language*, 136: 7–29.

Mphahlele, E. (1959), *Down Second Avenue*, London: Faber and Faber.

Mphahlele, E. (1984), "Prometheus in chains: The fate of English in South Africa," *English Academy Reviews*, 2 (1): 89–104.

Ncgobo S. (2009), "Lecturers' and students' reflections on a bilingual programme," in B. Leibowitz, A. Van der Merwe and S. Van Schalkwyk (eds.), *Focus on First-Year Success: Perspectives Emerging from South Africa and Beyond*, 209–55, Stellenbosch: SUN Media.

Ndebele, N. S. (1987), "The English language and social change in South Africa," *English Academy Review*, 4: 1–15.

Piotrowska, C. M. (2014), "A Diachronic Analysis of the Progressive Aspect in Black South African English," MA diss., North-West University, South Africa.

Plüddemann, P. (1999), "Multilingualism and education in South Africa: One year on," *International Journal of Educational Research*, 31 (4): 327–40.

Plüddemann, P. (2015), "Unlocking the grid: Language-in-education policy realisation in post-apartheid South Africa," *Language and Education*, 29 (3): 186–99.

Pretorius, E. J. (2000), "What they can't read will hurt them: Reading and academic achievement," *Innovation*, 21: 33–41.

Pretorius, E. J. (2002), "Reading ability and academic performance in South Africa: Are we fiddling while Rome is burning?," *Language Matters*, 33: 169–96.

Prinsloo, K. P. (1985), "A proposed agenda for language planning in South Africa," *South African Journal of Linguistics*, 3 (sup2): 24–31.

Probyn, M. (2004), "Making sense of science through two languages: A South African case study," *School Science Review*, 86 (314): 49–59.

Probyn, M. (2009), "Smuggling the vernacular into the classroom: Conflicts and tensions in classroom codeswitching in township/rural schools in South Africa," *International Journal of Bilingual Education and Bilingualism*, 12 (2): 123–36.

Reagan, T. (1984), "Language policy, politics, and ideology: The case of South Africa," *Issues in Education*, 2 (2), 155–64.

Reagan, T. (1986), "The role of language policy in South African education," *Language Problems and Language Planning*, 10 (1): 1–13.

Reagan, T., and I. Ntshoe (1987), "Language Policy and Black Education in South Africa," *Journal of Research and Development in Education*, 20 (2): 1–8.

Rudwick, S., and A. Parmegiani (2013), "Divided loyalties: Zulu vis-à-vis English at the University of KwaZulu-Natal," *Language Matters*, 44: 89–107.

Smit, U. (1996), "South African English in the 1900s: A field study on status, roles and attitudes," *English World-Wide*, 17 (1): 77–109.

Switzer, L. (1997), "Introduction: South Africa's alternative press in perspective," in L. Switzer (ed.), *South Africa's Alternative Press: Voices of Protest and Resistance, 1880–1960*, 1–53, Cambridge: Cambridge University Press.

Titlestad, P. (1996), "English, the Constitution and South Africa's language future," in V. De Klerk (ed.), *Focus on South Africa*, 163–73, Amsterdam: John Benjamins.

Valadez, C. M., J. MacSwan and C. Martínez (2000), "Toward a new view of low-achieving bilinguals: A study of linguistic competence in designated 'semilinguals'," *Bilingual Review/La Revista Bilingüe*, 25 (3): 238–48.

Van Rooy, B. (2020), "Present-day Afrikaans in contact with English," in R. Hickey (ed.), *English in Multilingual South Africa: The Linguistics of Contact and Change*, 241–64, Cambridge: Cambridge University Press.

Van Rooy, B. and S. Coetzee-Van Rooy (2015), "The language issue and academic performance at a South African University," *Southern African Linguistics and Applied Language Studies*, 33 (1): 31–46.

Van Rooy, B., S. Van Rooyen and H. Van Wyk (2000), "An assessment of high school pupils' attitudes towards the pronunciation of Black South African English," *South African Journal of Linguistics*, 18(sup38): 187–213.

Visser, N. and T. Couzens, eds. (1985), *H.I.E. Dhlomo: Collected Works*. Johannesburg: Ravan Press.

Voice of the City (1957), Newspaper clipping, ZK Matthews papers (ACC101), document number C5/2, University of South Africa, Documentation Centre for African Studies. Available at: http://uir.unisa.ac.za/bitstream/handle/10500/8513/ZKM_C5_2.pdf

Vorster, J. and L. Proctor (1976), "Black attitudes to 'white' languages in South Africa: A pilot study," *The Journal of Psychology*, 92 (1): 103–8.

Webb, V. (1994), "Language policy and planning in South Africa," *Annual Review of Applied Linguistics*, 14: 254–73.

Webb, V. (1996), "English and language planning in South Africa: The flip-side," in V. De Klerk (ed.), *Focus on South Africa*, 175–90, Amsterdam: John Benjamins.

Webb, V. (1999), "Multilingualism in democratic South Africa: The over-estimation of language policy," *International Journal of Educational Development*, 19 (4–5): 351–66.

Webb, V. (2004), "African languages as media of instruction in South Africa: Stating the case," *Language problems & Language Planning*, 28 (2): 147–73.

Webb, V. (2013), "African languages in post-1994 education in South Africa: Our own Titanic?," *Southern African Linguistics and Applied Language Studies*, 31 (2): 173–84.

Webb, V., M. Lafon and P. Pare (2010), "Bantu languages in education in South Africa: An overview. Ongekho akekho!–The absentee owner," *Language Learning Journal*, 38 (3): 273–92.

White, T. R. H. (1993), "Z.K. Matthews and the Politics of Education in South Africa," MA diss., University of York.

Whittock, T. G. (1957), "Black Englishmen, Letter to the editor," *Daily Dispatch*, March 21. Newspaper clipping, ZM Matthews papers (ACC101), document number C5/3, University of South Africa, Documentation Centre for African Studies. Available at: http://uir.unisa.ac.za/bitstream/handle/10500/8513/ZKM_C5_3.pdf

Wildsmith-Cromarty, R. (2012), "Reflections on a research initiative aimed at enhancing the role of African languages in education in South Africa," *Journal for Language Teaching= Ijenali Yekufundzisa Lulwimi= Tydskrif vir Taalonderrig*, 46 (2): 157–70.

Woeber, C. (2012), "The mission presses and the rise of black journalism," in D. Attwell and D. Attridge (eds.), *The Cambridge History of South African Literature*, 204–25, Cambridge: Cambridge University Press.

# 8

# Transnational Dialect Contact and Language Variation and Change in World Englishes

Rebecca Lurie Starr

## 1. Introduction

Despite the accelerating pace of transnational mobility and connectivity in the current era of globalization, the nature and consequences of transnational dialect contact have received relatively little attention within the study of language variation and change. The present chapter focuses on this phenomenon as it relates to world Englishes; due to their ideological and geopolitical positionalities, these varieties experience substantial effects of contact that differ crucially from those experienced among "native" varieties of English.

Theoretical models of world Englishes may be divided into frameworks that account for variation within world Englishes-speaking communities and those that classify varieties of English around the world and their patterns of change. In the latter category is Kachru's (1985) Three Circles of English model, which divides English-speaking nations into an Inner Circle (e.g., the United States), in which English is natively spoken as a first language, an Outer Circle (e.g., India), consisting of postcolonial nations in which English is extensively used in institutions, and the Expanding Circle (e.g., China), in which English is commonly learned as a foreign language. This model has been critiqued in prior work for its static nature, its focus on nation-states, and its inadequacy in classifying nations such as South Africa, in which different segments of the population differ substantially in their histories with and use of English (Bruthiaux 2003; Park and Wee 2009). Despite these issues, Park and Wee (2009) make the case that the model retains considerable utility from an ideological perspective, as Outer Circle Englishes continue to be perceived as less legitimate, non-native, and of lower status than Inner Circle varieties, even in cases such as Singapore, in which English is now primarily acquired as a first language.

In contrast to the static Three Circles Model, Schneider's (2007) Dynamic Model of postcolonial Englishes proposes several phases of development in which varieties become increasingly stable, nativized, and locally-oriented. Crucial to the present discussion is the phase of endonormative stabilization, in which the community shifts its orientation from upholding external norms to accepting local norms (Schneider

2007: 48–52); a number of world Englishes, including Singaporean, Jamaican, Bajan, Indian, and Philippine English are proposed by Schneider to either be moving through this phase or to be on the cusp of entering it. This "cusp" status is suggestive of the difficult and piecemeal process of abandoning standard language ideologies that valorize Inner Circle Englishes, as also highlighted by Park and Wee (2009). As a result, many communities of world Englishes speakers are currently in a state of ideological flux, with rising endonormativity influencing some segments of the population and certain domains, but not yet reaching others.

Aside from rising endonormativity, a second major change proposed by some scholars to be underway in English worldwide is Americanization (Gonçalves et al. 2018), meaning the adoption of American lexical, grammatical, phonological, and orthographic conventions for English. The potential implications of parallel trends towards endonormative stabilization and Americanization for world Englishes, many of which historically orient towards British English norms, are consequential and multifaceted. The proposed ongoing global adoption of American English features also raises questions regarding the mechanisms and extent of such a change, in light of prior theorizations in sociolinguistics on the limitations of language change via media exposure (e.g., Trudgill 2014). As in the case of rising endonormativity, there is substantial scope within shifts toward American norms for individual differences in attitudes and use among speakers in the community.

The two proposed sociolinguistic changes outlined above, rising endonormativity and Americanization, introduce further complexity into already complex systems of language use within world Englishes-speaking communities. These systems have historically been modelled using a range of approaches. Given the common observation across world Englishes-speaking regions of the coexistence of standard and colloquial varieties, early theorizations of variation in these communities argued for either a diglossic model involving a High and Low variety (Gupta 1991), or a less discrete post-creole/lectal continuum (DeCamp 1971; Platt 1975). Theorization and debate in this area have been particularly intense among scholars of Singapore English, in which the High or acrolectal variety in these traditional frameworks is commonly referred to as Standard Singapore English and the Low variety as Colloquial Singapore English (or "Singlish"). Alternative approaches to variation in Singapore have included the Expanding Triangles Model (Pakir 1991), which sought to distinguish between the factors of formality level and English proficiency, and the Cultural Orientation Model (Alsagoff 2010), which proposed that the High variety, redubbed "International Singapore English," indexes a global orientation, authority, formality, and other related attributes, while "Local Singapore English" indexes a local orientation, closeness, informality, and so on (39).

Although Alsagoff's model allows for hybridity of language use among individual speakers, more recent work argues that the global-local dichotomy is insufficient to capture the fluid nature of language use in Singapore (Leimgruber 2012; Starr 2019a, 2019b, forthcoming). Scholars with this view, including myself, have called for a rejection of code-based models for world Englishes and a shift to the indexical, feature-focused approaches used in variationist sociolinguistics. Greater integration of sociolinguistic approaches into world Englishes has also been advocated for by researchers who argue for the key role of social variation in communities such as South Africa (Mesthrie 2020: 10).

The present chapter explores how developments in world Englishes due to transnational dialect contact bolster the case for a variationist sociolinguistic approach. Following an introduction of the central principles and assumptions of variationist traditions and how they might be applied to world Englishes, the chapter surveys three major sources of transnational dialect contact: institutional exonormativity, transnational mobility, and media consumption, and considers evidence regarding their implications for language variation and change.

## 2. Investigating World Englishes Through the Lens of Language Variation and Change

As pioneered by Labov (1966, 1972, et seq.), the study of language variation and change centers around the empirical investigation of probabilistic patterns in inter- and intra-speaker language use. Eckert (2012) identifies three waves of variationist scholarship, referring to three research traditions that are roughly chronological in origin, but which all continue to inform variationist work. The first wave, initiated by Labov's (1966) study of the Lower East Side of New York City, examines geographically defined settings via surveys and sociolinguistic interviews; this tradition seeks to identify quantitative patterns in the social distribution and changing trajectories of linguistic variants, focusing on broad demographic categories such as social class and gender. The second wave incorporates ethnographic methodologies to explore more locally-defined social categories and the ways in which vernacular features reflect membership in these local social groups, as in Rickford's (1986) work on Estate Class and Non-Estate Class residents of Cane Walk, Guyana. Finally, the third wave reframes linguistic variation not as a reflection of social place, but rather as in a co-constitutive relationship with identity; research in this wave shifts its attention from communities to styles, and examines how individuals draw upon linguistic and other social-semiotic resources, juxtaposing them in various configurations to index social meanings and construct personae. Crucial in this framework is the notion of the indexical field (Eckert 2008), referring to an evolving set of distinct but ideologically linked stances, social types, and characteristics that may be invoked via a particular linguistic feature. For example, Podesva's (2008) third wave work on the speech of an American gay medical student highlights how features including falsetto and released -t/d can be deployed in combination with other features to construct various styles, including "caring doctor" and "gay diva."

In addition to language production, scholars informed by these variationist traditions have also examined language perception and attitudes, addressing questions surrounding the role of sociolinguistic information in cognition in addition to providing a more robust view of the social functions of language. Campbell-Kibler (2008), for example, underscored the utility of the indexical field by demonstrating listeners' agency in attributing diverse or even conflicting attributes to a speaker based on their use of the same linguistic feature. Labov et al. (2011) investigated listeners' sensitivity to the frequency of sociolinguistic variants, identifying a logarithmic pattern in which only one or two tokens of a variant have a substantial impact on listener evaluation. Work of this type supports the view that listeners are highly sensitive to fine-grained patterns of language use, and that quantitative examination of the deployment and collocation of individual features, when integrated with ethnographic and other qualitative methodologies, can fruitfully advance our understanding of sociolinguistic phenomena in all communities, including those in which world Englishes are spoken.

Due in part to the American origins of the variationist tradition, the majority of research in this field has focused on communities in the United States and Canada, and to a lesser extent the United Kingdom (although many significant studies have been carried out involving other languages in various parts of the world) (see Stanford 2016). Only a limited number of studies (e.g., Rickford 1986; Blake 1996) have examined Englishes or English-based contact languages outside of the Inner Circle using a variationist approach (see Farquharson and Migge 2017 for a review). The dearth of variationist research on world Englishes and contact languages is arguably due to a lack of integration between the academic traditions of contact linguistics, world Englishes, and sociolinguistic variation, rather than the unsuitability of variationist approaches to these settings and language varieties. In fact, a variationist sociolinguistic approach, and particularly an indexical approach typical of the third wave, can account for phenomena among speakers of world Englishes that are not well-captured by other frameworks.

As pointed out by Leimgruber (2012), one of the major advantages of a variationist approach to world Englishes is a shift of focus from codes (i.e., varieties or lects) to individual linguistic variants. For example, taking the case of Singapore English, this approach means shifting away from analyzing speakers' use of so-called Standard Singapore English versus Colloquial Singapore English and instead analyzing their use of particular features, such as the merger of the COT/CAUGHT/COURT vowels (see Starr forthcoming), in various settings and in combination with other features to index particular social meanings. This change allows researchers to investigate styles of language use that incorporate a range of features with distinct indexical fields—styles that, in other approaches, may be characterized as "hybrid" or "leaky" (Gupta 1994; Leimgruber 2012).

The adoption of the indexical field framework also avoids the limitations of one-dimensional continua and scalar models that range from acrolect to basilect or standard to non-standard, as well as models in which attributes such as informality can only be evoked by local variants, as in Alsagoff's (2010) Cultural Orientation Model. Instead, in the third wave approach, single variants may be indexically linked to a wide range of possible stances, attributes, and social types; moreover, clusters of features may become enregistered as a socially-recognized style linked to a persona or a more widely-circulating characterological figure (Agha 2007: 177). In this view, sociolinguistic variation among speakers of world Englishes is no longer interpreted as purely a matter of "standard" versus "non-standard," or "local" versus "global," thereby acknowledging that these speakers do more with language than signal affiliation with or distance from dominant norms.

Another related notion that may be usefully adopted from scholarship in variationist sociolinguistics to a world Englishes context is that of the repertoire (Benor 2010; also see Blommaert 2010). Used primarily in Inner Circle variationist research in reference to "ethnolinguistic repertoires" associated with speakers of varieties such as Chicano English, the repertoire approach reimagines enregistered sociolects as a pool of linguistic features from which speakers selectively draw, rather than a uniform code that speakers codeswitch in and out of. Again, this approach emphasizes the meaning-making potential of individual linguistic features, rather than holistic codes. In Starr and Balasubramaniam (2019), we adopt the ethnolinguistic repertoire framework to account for variation in the realization of English /r/ among Tamil Indian Singaporeans. We argue that this variation is not best conceived of as shifting from Indian Singapore English to Standard Singapore English, but rather reflects a speaker's selection of social-semiotic resources from their repertoire, in this case tapped or trilled /r/ versus approximant /ɹ/, to index a range of possible social meanings, including the construction of Tamil Indian identity. Outside the realm of ethnolects, this same repertoire approach can be adapted to features traditionally associated with lects along a continuum in any world Englishes context (e.g., Standard Singapore English versus Colloquial Singapore English).

The increasing flexibility afforded by variationist approaches is particularly valuable in recent work on world Englishes due to key developments in many of these communities that have upended traditional systems of sociolinguistic meaning. As discussed in the introduction, the trend towards endonormative stabilization across many postcolonial Englishes means that features formerly unambiguously classed as non-standard are now in a state of flux, with some community members evaluating them as acceptable in formal contexts and others disagreeing with that assessment. Another set of major ongoing changes in these communities are societal shifts, including changing media consumption patterns and rising transnational mobility, that all serve to increase non-local, and particularly transnational dialect contact. The Americanization of world Englishes, as discussed in the introduction, is just one of the potential impacts of this phenomenon. The introduction of non-local forms linked with various social types and stances has the potential to radically broaden the repertoires of speakers in these communities, transform the indexical fields associated with particular variants, expand speakers' range of sociolinguistic knowledge, and lead to the enregisterment of new styles and personae. Bearing in mind the significance of rising transnational dialect contact for world Englishes, the following section considers various sources of such contact and discusses their respective sociolinguistic impacts.

## 3. World Englishes and Sources of Transnational Dialect Contact

There are a variety of channels through which speakers may come into contact with external linguistic norms and speakers of non-local dialects. In a homogeneous community populated primarily by native speakers, such exposure is generally limited, and would come from consumption of non-local media, travel outside the community, and interpersonal ties with speakers who had migrated from elsewhere. Members of a community in which a marginalized dialect is spoken might also be exposed in school to a standard variety perceived as "non-local." Given national language policies and migration patterns, the majority of non-local exposure within homogeneous native-speaker communities would likely consist of dialects spoken within the same country, rather than international varieties.

In communities where world Englishes are spoken, including both the Outer and Expanding circles, the extent and nature of transnational English contact is considerably different from the circumstances described above. Moreover, the ideological positioning of non-local Englishes in this context is distinct from how non-local varieties are perceived in communities that are ideologically construed as "native-speaking." In the following sections regarding sources of transnational dialect contact, each discussion will consider the extent to which community members receive exposure from these sources, and the impact that this exposure might have on language use, sociolinguistic knowledge, and attitudes in the community. Work in the variationist tradition will be introduced along with other research that demonstrates the utility of moving beyond traditional models for world Englishes. Although studies of other settings will be referenced, this discussion highlights recent and ongoing work on Singapore, which has been at the forefront of variationist approaches to world Englishes.

## 3.1 Institutional Exonormativity

In the context of world Englishes, institutional exonormativity refers to the use of non-local, Inner Circle curricular materials and linguistic norms in Outer and Expanding circle schools, extra-curricular classes, language campaigns, and other institutional domains. The adoption of textbooks developed in Britain for English classes in a community outside of the UK, for example, would be a case of such exonormativity. While Kachru's Inner Circle includes a number of countries ideologically constructed as "natively" English-speaking, in the case of English education and promotion, orientation towards a non-local norm almost always refers to the promotion of standard US or UK English (although there are some notable exceptions, such as the influence of New Zealand English curricula and teachers in the South Pacific [Crocombe 1992: 96]).

Despite longstanding calls in the study of Teaching English as a Foreign Language and other related fields for a shift towards "English as an International Language" and other approaches to English language teaching that do not valorize native speaker norms (see Jenkins 1998; Holliday 2006), the promotion of US and UK English remains *de rigeur* in English programs in the Expanding Circle. While some countries have longstanding orientations exclusively towards the US or UK due to their colonial histories, geographical proximity, or other sociohistorical factors, many Expanding Circle nations, such as China, make use of curricular materials from both regions (He 2017: 130). Thus, learners in certain segments of the Expanding Circle receive considerable exposure to both US and UK varieties in educational settings. Whether such exposure increases their explicit sociolinguistic knowledge of these dialects, however, is another matter; materials from different regional sources are often incorporated into curricula with no clear provenance provided to students, limiting the degree to which students might link features to regions. At the same time, certain types of EFL programs, particularly those designed to prepare students for study abroad and standardized English exams, such as those offered by the British Council, are explicitly associated with specific regional norms. Moreover, although standardized English exams such as the TOEFL and IELTS purport to be international in orientation and to accept any "native" variety of English, students are routinely advised to focus their preparation on the variety associated with the makers of the exam (e.g., US English for the TOEFL test), and to avoid mixing spelling standards or regional accent features (Recine 2016). Therefore, we expect a minority of students learning English in an Expanding Circle setting, and specifically those aiming to study abroad, to gain some explicit sociolinguistic knowledge regarding the features associated with US and UK English.

Turning to the Outer Circle, despite long-established local conventions for English in these communities and ongoing progression towards endonormative stabilization, standard language ideologies and pragmatic concerns both contribute to the widespread upholding of Inner Circle norms for English in institutional settings. In other words, these Inner Circle varieties are perceived as both more legitimate and more "useful" than the local variety, thereby rationalizing their continued institutional promotion. Due to the legacy of British colonialism and imperialism, with the exception of the Philippines and a few other cases, the variety targeted as an ideological norm in Outer Circle nations is specifically a conservative form of standard British English (i.e., "Received Pronunciation"); while the recent dominance of American media has resulted in minor concessions in education policy, such as tolerance for American spelling on exams in some countries (e.g., Singapore), British English remains the notional standard in most respects. In Hong Kong, for example, Chan (2018: 35) finds that 68 percent of students agree that Hong Kong examinations target British English, while only 7 percent and 6 percent identify American and Hong Kong English, respectively. One participant reports, "since my early schooling days, I have been told again and again that we should learn British English" (Chan 2018: 35). Similarly, Kenya promotes British norms in schools and discourages the use of Kenyan English in formal settings (Ni Chonghaile 2012).

This institutional exonormative orientation is maintained even in societies with well-established local English norms. In Singapore, where English is the most commonly-spoken home language (Singapore Department of Statistics 2015) and locally-developed English textbooks are used (Singapore Ministry of Education 2020), the education system continues to position standard British English as Singapore's target variety (Rubdy 2010); governmental policies and campaigns in Singapore, most notably the Speak Good English Movement, similarly promote standard British English (often presented in aregional terms as "universally understood" English) and frame Singapore English as illegitimate and problematic for national development (Park and Wee 2009; Gupta 2010).

In terms of transnational dialect contact, the impact of exonormative institutional practices in the Outer and Expanding Circles is threefold: (1) increasing the community's exposure to Inner Circle varieties, (2) increasing their sociolinguistic knowledge of the distinctions between these varieties and the local variety, and

(3) ideologically constructing the acquisition of Inner Circle varieties as desirable. Regarding increased exposure, the majority of contact with Inner Circle varieties due to institutional exonormativity comes via educational media consumption, meaning videos, textbooks, and other learning materials. In a minority of settings, exonormativity also leads to increased interpersonal interaction with Inner Circle English teachers; this is the case in Japan, for example, where thousands of native English speakers are hired to teach in local schools via the Japan Exchange and Teaching program (JET Programme 2019).

Although the two modalities of transnational dialect contact due to institutional exonormativity are media consumption and interpersonal contact resulting from transnational mobility, each of which will be examined further in their respective sections below, it is nonetheless worth considering these institutional cases separately from the more general effects of media exposure and interpersonal contact. Such contact within institutions is crucially distinct in that it is often accompanied by explicit metalinguistic discussion of local versus non-local features (see Starr 2017); moreover, language exposure within institutional contexts carries with it both the benefits and drawbacks of institutional authority. Watching an educational video in class, for example, may have a greater influence on a student than a video they watch for leisure at home because they know they may be assessed on it later; on the other hand, the video may have less influence in the classroom setting, due to decreased engagement and less intrinsic motivation on the part of the student.

As to whether students actually absorb anything from media presented in an institutional context, a large body of evidence suggests that students do engage with and show learning benefits from multimedia in English language curricula (Mayer 2005; Ismaili 2013; Kabooha and Elyas 2018; i.a.). Whether this sort of multimedia exposure, or exposure to teachers from various international dialect backgrounds, translates into shifts in speakers' sociolinguistic awareness, attitudes, or variation patterns has not been extensively assessed in scholarly work. In my own research on expatriate and local children in Singapore, I find that children show significant effects of school setting in both perception and production, with expatriate children attending local government schools acquiring significantly different patterns from those in international schools, underscoring the role of educational institutions in shaping children's sociolinguistic knowledge and patterns of use (Starr et al. 2017; Starr 2019a). At the same time, the majority of expatriate children attending local schools were not observed to acquire local Singapore English norms in their phonological production, even if they had been born in Singapore; I argue that this phenomenon reflects persistent institutional exonormativity that discourages children from Inner Circle backgrounds from acquiring Outer Circle features (Starr 2019a). The same study also finds significant effects of endonormative versus exonormative orientation among Singaporean children; children who rate speakers of Singapore English as likely to be English teachers and children who report that they do not feel they have an accent in their own speech are both more likely to use phonological features typical of Singapore English. This finding suggests that the ideological messages children receive from institutions about the legitimacy and normativity of Outer Circle Englishes have significant impacts on their language use.

## 3.2 Mobility

As transnational mobility has accelerated in the twenty-first century, scholarly interest in mobility and its consequences has also expanded, as is reflected in the proliferation of novel frameworks and terms, including "superdiversity" (Vertovec 2007) and "metrolingualism" (Otsuji and Pennycook 2010), intended to capture diverse contact settings. However, transnational flows of people and languages under globalization are not a new phenomenon; indeed, such mobility underlies the very existence of world Englishes. As noted by Johnstone and Pollack (2016: 255), mobility is a broad term that encompasses a wide variety of travel and migration phenomena. These different types of mobility, ranging from individual overseas holidays, to study abroad experiences, to short-term expatriate stays, to permanent migration, to colonization, vary significantly in their sociolinguistic consequences due to differences in power, geography, demographics, extent and length of contact, ideologies, and other factors. The consequences of mobility can be assessed on an individual level or a broader societal level, investigating diverse topics such as the acquisition of second dialect features by a particular migrant, the broadening of sociolinguistic knowledge resulting from increasing contact with non-local speakers, or the development of a contact dialect in a community over generations.

A large body of prior work in variationist sociolinguistics examines geographic mobility in the Inner Circle and its impact on the use of local features by native-born residents and newcomers. Of particular relevance to world Englishes research are studies involving the acquisition of stigmatized regional features, including work on immigration into the American South, such as Wolfram et al.'s (2004) study of Latinx acquisition of /ay/ monophthongization and Dodsworth and Kohn's (2012) study of newcomer and local children in North Carolina, as well as various studies of Polish migrants' acquisition of regional dialect features in the UK (Schleef et al. 2011; Drummond 2013). Crucially, outcomes of contact in these Inner Circle settings are found to be constrained not only by age of acquisition, degree and length of exposure, and complexity of the linguistic feature, but also by the relative legitimacy and status of each variety. Dodsworth and Kohn (2012), for example, find that it is local children in North Carolina who shift towards the more prestigious features used by their newcomer peers, and not the other way around. These findings in Inner Circle settings suggest that transnational migration in world Englishes-speaking communities will be similarly shaped by ideological factors, and illustrate the necessity of examining the consequences of mobility not only for migrants, but also the native-born population.

The present discussion of transnational mobility and its consequences for world Englishes is divided into two sections, the first focusing on short-term mobility, including overseas travel and study abroad, and the second on longer-term or permanent migration.

### 3.2.1 Short-term Mobility

In research on Inner Circle settings and in popular discourse within those communities, it is generally assumed that changes in a speaker's habitual language use due to geographic mobility would only result from long-term migration involving sustained interpersonal contact with a new community, rather than from a short-term sojourn elsewhere. In world Englishes-speaking communities, however, the notion that a speaker who spends a limited time overseas in an Inner Circle nation may retain (or affect) that non-local accent upon their return is a commonly circulated discourse. These ideologies appear to be longstanding in communities where overseas study in the Inner Circle is a long-established practice; in several countries formerly colonized by Britain, including Guyana and Nigeria, the stereotype of a returnee who exhibits exaggerated US or UK English speech and mannerisms was enregistered by the mid-twentieth century as a characterological figure known as a "been-to" (Obiechina 1973: 54; p.c., John Rickford, February 18, 2014).

More recent iterations of this discourse include the 2013 Malaysian video "Your Accent Come From Where?"[1] by YouTube comedy group TheMingThing, which portrays several Malaysian characters who have acquired US and UK accents from improbably brief exposure, including one young man who has returned with an accent after four days abroad ("I brought back with me so many brilliant memories!" "Yeah, that's not the only thing you brought back."). The video also highlights that Malaysians do not pick up local accents when visiting India or other non-Inner Circle countries. The same observation is made by Ntarangwi (2009), who reports a common joke among Kenyans about those who study abroad: "the ones who go to the United States and United Kingdom come back with thick American and British accents, while those who go to India never do" (54). This emphasis on the selectivity of non-local dialect acquisition reflects the ideology that speakers who engage in this behavior are doing so as an affectation resulting from a desire to affiliate themselves with a more prestigious dialect. Discourse on the impact of overseas study or travel can also serve as a means of rejecting elite local speech patterns by casting them as non-local; Mesthrie (2020: 6) describes the case of South African politician Lindiwe Mazibuko, whose educated speech patterns were attributed in the media to the gap year she spent in London and characterized as "un-African."

Despite the pervasiveness of "been-to" discourse, only limited scholarly work assesses the extent to which Outer Circle returnees maintain non-local features after sojourns overseas. Starr (2019b), a survey-based study of Singaporeans' own pronunciation of BATH- and TRAP-class words and their knowledge of how those words are pronounced in the US and UK, does not find any evidence that Singaporeans who have spent time in the US are more likely to use an American English-like /æ/ vowel for BATH-class words. Starr (forthcoming) similarly finds no effect of US travel experience on Singaporean use of postvocalic /r/, another salient feature of American English. On the other hand, Chua's (2016) analysis of data drawn from the Voices of Children in Singapore project observes that adolescents born in Singapore who have spent at least five months overseas do retain certain phonetic features of their second dialect after their return. While it is unsurprising to find children acquiring some features of a second dialect, it is noteworthy that they have retained those second dialect features after returning to Singapore, given their young age when they rejoined the Singapore English-speaking community. The limited evidence for an impact of overseas experience in speakers' language use data may be partially accounted for by the additional adoption of Inner Circle English features by those speakers who consume US and UK media but have no overseas travel experience; this possibility is considered in Section 3.3.

Short-term travel does not only potentially affect production, but also sociolinguistic knowledge; interpersonal experience with speakers of a particular region should increase an individual's knowledge of that region's dialect features. Indeed, Starr (2019b) finds that Singaporeans with experience traveling to the UK show significantly greater accuracy in reporting which words in the BATH and TRAP classes are pronounced with the /ɑ:/ vowel in London. US travel experience is also observed to correlate with Singaporeans' knowledge of the BATH-TRAP merger in American English.

While the discussion above has focused on the impact of short-term overseas stays among native-born members of Outer Circle communities, a related subject worthy of mention here is the situation of Expanding Circle learners of English who spend time studying overseas in an Outer Circle English-speaking setting. One major context in which this occurs is the Philippines, which has increasingly positioned itself as a global center for English language education (Choe 2016). Due to the Philippines' ideologically precarious situation in the Outer Circle, individual learners may hold differing views regarding the acquisition of Philippine English features, depending upon their learning goals and social ties with local Filipinos. Imperial (2016), an investigation of Korean learners of English in Baguio City, found that learners who interacted more with Filipino peers and reported greater engagement with their English classes produced English voiceless stops with shorter voice onset times, meaning in a manner more consistent with local Philippine English (110). The study also observed that Korean learners who were better able to identify the regional origin of a speaker of Philippine English in a listening task also used significantly longer voice onset times, thereby distancing themselves from local norms (140); this finding underscores that familiarity with the local variety is not sufficient to trigger a shift towards that variety in a learner's speech, but may conversely assist in a learner's efforts to avoid the acquisition of stigmatized features. Imperial's (2016) work on this Outer Circle setting is consistent with studies of other languages in the field of Second Language Acquisition indicating that most L2 learners strongly orient towards what they perceive to be standard varieties, avoiding acquisition of regional and non-standard features even if they are prevalent in the speech of teachers and native-speaker peers (Starr 2017). This learner tendency, along with the institutional exonormativity described in the section above, means that the typical student studying abroad in an Outer Circle setting is unlikely to acquire many features of the local variety unless they develop substantial community ties.

### 3.2.2 Migration

Rising transnational migration across the socioeconomic spectrum in recent decades has transformed existing world Englishes-speaking communities and forged new communities of diverse English speakers. Many of the nations serving as major sources of out-migration are traditionally placed in the Outer Circle, including the Philippines,

India, and Bangladesh; others, such as Mexico and China, are members of the Expanding Circle (United Nations, Department of Economic and Social Affairs, Population Division 2017). The significance of smaller-scale migration from Inner Circle nations, such as Australia, into world Englishes-speaking communities should also not be overlooked, particularly given the socioeconomic power of these "expatriate" migrants and the status granted to Inner Circle varieties in institutional contexts.

The impact that transnational migration is expected to have on a local community's sociolinguistic practices, knowledge, and attitudes is constrained by the relative number of migrants, their social status, the legitimacy granted to their language variety, and their level of integration. For example, although expatriates have had a longstanding presence in Singapore, in recent years the social spheres of the expatriate and local communities have increasingly intersected as migration to the country has risen. As a result of these changes, 45 percent of young Singaporeans now report having a close friend of another nationality (National Youth Survey 2016). Starr et al. (2017) argues that this increased contact has led to expanded sociolinguistic knowledge among Singaporeans; we demonstrate that Singaporean children are now very skilled at explicitly associating speakers of various Englishes with their regional origin, and at identifying the likely occupations of such speakers.

Crucially, however, we should not expect local exposure to international varieties of English to necessarily result in local shifts towards those varieties. In Starr and Balasubramaniam (2019), we consider the impact of the recent rise in foreign workers and immigrants from South Asia on Singapore's longstanding Tamil Indian community. We argue that the rise in newcomers from South Asia is one of several factors that account for the precipitous drop we observe in the use of tapped and trilled /r/ in English among Tamil Indian Singaporeans. While tapped/trilled /r/ is an established variant in Singapore English, it has now become linked with non-local South Asian identity, leading younger speakers to prefer approximant /ɹ/ to index their identity as locals and distance themselves from recent arrivals.

One sector of the transnational labor market that has attracted scholarly attention in sociolinguistics is foreign domestic workers (i.e., maids). Foreign domestic workers from the Philippines constitute a major source of exposure to English for children in some societies in Asia and the Middle East; in Hong Kong, standard language ideologies and the devaluing of Outer Circle Englishes have led to concern among laypeople that exposure to Filipino maids could be a "bad influence" on children's English acquisition. Leung (2012) assesses whether any impact of exposure to Filipino English can be identified, comparing Hong Kong kindergarteners and secondary school students who have had a Filipino maid versus those who have not. He finds that children with maids from the Philippines show no deficit in listening tasks involving stimuli using American, British, or Hong Kong English; moreover, they show an advantage with stimuli spoken in Philippine English. In Singapore, Starr et al. (2017: 15) finds no correlation between having a Filipino maid and children's ability to identify Philippine English or other English varieties; rather, all local children regardless of home exposure are found to be skilled at identifying Philippine English, perhaps reflecting the major presence of Filipino workers in the service sector and other areas of the labor market. Other ongoing work on the same Voices of Children in Singapore data suggests no influence of having a Filipino maid on children's patterns of language use. When taken together with the Tamil Indian Singaporean findings above, it seems clear that the influx of speakers of other Outer Circle Englishes into communities such as Singapore and Hong Kong is not triggering a vast levelling of Outer Circle features into a panregional dialect; to the contrary, these migration phenomena are raising sociolinguistic awareness of local vs. non-local varieties and encouraging young speakers to highlight their local identity using various social-semiotic resources.

Another significant implication of transnational migration in relation to world Englishes is the potential for the creation of new contact varieties. In many regions with significant levels of migration, English is the lingua franca used for communication among foreign workers and between foreign workers and locals, even when another language is dominant in the local community. In the Gulf states of the Middle East, for example, English rather than Arabic serves as the lingua franca of transnational migrants, who constitute the majority of the labor force there (Alharbi 2018; also see Siemund, Al-Issa, Rahbari and Leimgruber, this volume). Research on the impact of migration on the formation of new English as a Lingua Franca (ELF) varieties includes Boyle (2011), a study of the English used in the United Arab Emirates. Using data from the UAE's largest English-language newspaper, Boyle demonstrates that the English of the region contains innovative features (e.g., novel transitive patterns, as in "to alert a fire accident"[153]) and that the community is converging on these novel conventions, indicating that a new variety is emerging. Siemund, Al-Issa and Leimgruber (2020) draw a similar conclusion based on a survey of university students in the UAE, arguing that speakers show signs of convergence on a developing "Gulf English." The widespread use of English as a lingua franca in these emerging transnational migrant communities underscores the need for updated models of world Englishes that better account for new mobility patterns.

### 3.2.3 Media

Traditional sociolinguistic frameworks center interpersonal interaction as the core mechanism of language variation and change (Labov 2007). These approaches argue that sustained interpersonal contact is required to provide speakers with sufficient exposure and motivation for the acquisition of complex sociolinguistic patterns. As such, the potential role of media as a source of language change has been treated with skepticism, particularly in light of social dialectology studies demonstrating that regional variation has continued to thrive despite widespread mass media consumption (Trudgill 2014).

A growing body of research, however, has reconsidered the role of media in community language change and speakers' patterns of language use (Stuart-Smith et al. 2013; Sayers 2014; Androutsopoulos 2014; Nycz 2019; i.a.). Critiquing the characterization of media consumption as lacking in social interactivity, the work of Stuart-Smith and colleagues (2013) points to scholarship in communication studies that approaches media consumption as a form of parasocial interaction in which individuals may become highly emotionally engaged with the characters and stories they consume. Stuart-Smith et al.'s (2013) study of the diffusion of *th*-fronting and *l*-vocalization from the London area to Glasgow, Scotland identifies a significant effect of engagement in the popular London-based television program *EastEnders*; however, this work also takes the view that the role played by media consumption is primarily that of accelerating changes already introduced via interpersonal ties. Building upon the observation that certain types of linguistic features, such as lexis, would appear to be more straightforward to acquire from media exposure than others, such as phonological constraints, scholars in this area have increasingly queried exactly what aspects of language can be picked up via media contact, and to what extent this expanded sociolinguistic knowledge shapes speakers' attitudes, perception abilities, and/or production patterns (Stuart-Smith et al. 2013; Androutsopoulos 2014; Starr 2019b).

Due to a number of factors, the impact of media consumption on speakers in world Englishes-speaking communities may differ from the patterns observed in Inner Circle nations. First, speakers of world Englishes typically consume a higher proportion of non-local English-language media than local English-language media (if such local media exists at all). While Singapore has its own domestic media industry, for example, viewership is low relative to consumption of American and British film and television programs (Jagdish 2017). Additionally, due to continued institutional exonormativity and the reification of Inner Circle norms as desirable, "standard" English, world Englishes-speaking consumers may be more likely to attend to and/or adopt features they observe in Inner Circle media. A final key factor is the global dominance of American cultural and economic products, including hip-hop, Hollywood films, professional sports, and multinational corporations. Indeed, the desire to affiliate with American culture and the widespread consumption of American media have been identified in lay discourse and scholarly work as the primary explanations for the worldwide Americanization of English (Rindal 2010; Leow 2011; Gonçalves et al. 2018). Potential shifts toward American English norms are particularly salient in popular discourse due to the continued institutional dominance of British English in much of the Anglophone world, leading to conflicts over spelling conventions and vocabulary that are of interest not only to linguists but also stakeholders in education, media, and language policy.

In sum, greater relative exposure to Inner Circle varieties than local varieties in media, the ideological positioning of local varieties, and the desirability of American English may all encourage world Englishes speakers to engage with and show sociolinguistic influence from international media consumption; however, this prediction has yet to be extensively tested.

### 3.2.4 Traditional Media

Despite the hesitation in sociolinguistics to attribute language change to media exposure, it is not uncommon in the field of contact linguistics to find claims regarding change resulting from "distant contact" via media exposure (Winford 2003: 31). In Singapore, for example, an observed rise in postvocalic /r/ has been speculated to result from American media influence (Poedjosoedarmo 2000; Tan 2012). Recent work supports the view that the subset of world Englishes speakers who do consciously target American English frequently cite media as a motivating factor; this observation is made by Rindal (2010) about Norwegian learners of English, and by Hansen Edwards (2016: 209) about Hong Kong, in which 90 percent of students who reported targeting American English mentioned media in their questionnaire responses (e.g., "The media has helped shape my accent. I watch a lot of American TV shows and movies in my free time" [209]).

At the same time, other scholars have cautioned against attributing innovative features in English varieties to diffusion from American English when these features may have developed via independent drift (Meyerhoff and Niedzielski 2003; Trudgill 2014). In fact, evidence for American media influence on speakers of world Englishes is quite limited, as very few studies have directly assessed whether individuals who consume more American media are more accurate in their knowledge of American English features, have more positive attitudes towards them, or use more of them in their own speech. Regarding the rise in postvocalic /r/ in Singapore, in Starr (forthcoming), an analysis of the low back vowels in Singapore English and how these interact with rhoticity, I argue that several factors cast doubt on whether increasing postvocalic rhoticity truly represents a shift towards American English norms due to media influence. First, there is no correlation observed in these data between participants who consume more US media and the use of postvocalic /r/. Secondly, postvocalic /r/ does not appear to be increasing in all stylistic contexts, but only in careful, read speech, suggesting that it may be rising in popularity because it is a "spelling pronunciation" that indexes correctness. Moreover, some degree of postvocalic /r/ use is present among all age groups in the data, and therefore it does not appear to be a novel variant introduced by recent American media dominance. Most notably, the vowel used by young Singaporeans in COURT-class words, even in careful speech, is a low [ɒ] associated with Colloquial Singapore English, rather than the mid vowel used in American English. As a result, young Singaporeans' production of words in this class, such as *sport* and *norm*, bear very little resemblance to their form in American English, even when postvocalic rhoticity is present. If Singaporeans were modelling American English based on aural exposure from media speech, we would expect use of postvocalic rhoticity to consistently co-occur with an American English-like preceding vowel, as these two segments are heavily co-articulated. Thus, while it is clear that young Singaporeans are shifting away from British features in careful speech, what they are moving toward is not a wholesale adoption of American English features, but rather something distinctly Singaporean.

Additional phonological features of Singapore English investigated in other work also show no signs of a broad shift towards American norms. Returning to the realization of the BATH and TRAP vowel classes examined in Starr (2019b), this survey of 1,167 native-born Singaporeans reveals the maintenance of a conservative distinction between these vowels consistent with standard British norms and inconsistent with American English, despite the fact that 92 percent of the survey respondents reported consuming US media at least occasionally. However, although overall levels of /æ/ responses for BATH words were low, frequent consumption of US media did in fact significantly correlate with greater self-reported use of /æ/ for BATH-class words (Starr 2019b: 66). This finding appears to constitute the first piece of empirical evidence of a media consumption effect for language use by speakers of world Englishes. On the other hand, even frequent consumers of US media in the data were not producing a complete phonological merger of BATH and TRAP as is typical of American English, underscoring the limited nature of this effect.

As previously discussed in the section on mobility, Starr (2019b) also assessed respondents' knowledge of how the BATH and TRAP vowels are produced in standard US and UK English. While accuracy for UK English was significantly predicted by more frequent consumption of UK media (69), performance on the US task was less expected. First, despite the high levels of US media consumption reported among respondents, only 137 of 1,167 participants were able to accurately report the merger of BATH and TRAP to /æ/ in US English (71). Equally unexpectedly, although accuracy in the US task did correlate with US media consumption, this effect was rendered statistically insignificant by the much larger effect of UK media consumption. In other words, respondents who consumed more UK media had much more accurate sociolinguistic knowledge of US English features, although exposure to UK media is unlikely to improve sociolinguistic knowledge of American English. In light of the particular UK media programs that were popular at the time of the survey (e.g., *Sherlock*), I proposed that respondents who frequently consumed UK media were more likely to be high-engagement viewers with a stronger Western orientation, and therefore outperformed other respondents in their explicit knowledge of Inner Circle English features (76). This incongruous finding reflects the difficulties inherent in attempting to identify specific impacts of media exposure that are independent of speaker identity and attitudes. Because media consumption is generally a leisure activity, individuals will naturally consume more media from a region that they find interesting and hold positive attitudes towards; in the absence of experimental methods in which individuals are assigned media to view, this correlation of consumption and interest presents considerable challenges to the researcher.

One indirect means through which media may potentially facilitate language change is by shifting a community's attitudes towards a dialect (e.g., by presenting it as a prestige variety) (Stuart-Smith 2007). This role of media is particularly relevant in the context of world Englishes-speaking communities in which British English is the historical standard, where rising endonormativity and Americanization mean that different community members may indexically link dramatically different sets of features with standardness and formality.

In ongoing work, I have been investigating the role of Singaporeans' media consumption habits in shaping sociolinguistic perceptions of variation in the COT-CAUGHT-COURT vowel set. This set of variables is particularly useful in distinguishing US, UK, and Singapore English norms, because their configuration differs in each variety, with COT distinct from CAUGHT-COURT in the UK, COURT distinct from COT-CAUGHT (which are merged or distinct, depending on region) in the US, and all three sets merged to [ɒ] in traditional descriptions of Singapore English (Deterding 2007). This ongoing study employs a digital matched-guise newscaster paradigm adapted from Labov et al. (2011), in which participants are told that they will hear clips of three Singaporeans preparing audition tapes to be newsreaders on local radio. Participants are asked to help the auditioners improve by giving each audio clip a rating on a six-point scale from "totally professional" to "totally unprofessional," and then providing open-ended feedback. To create the stimuli, three female Chinese Singaporean graduate students read brief pseudo-news passages, including filler passages and target passages constructed to contain two tokens each of the COURT vowel (e.g., *report*, *sport*). A US, UK, or Singapore-like variant (meaning [ɔɹ], [ɔː], or [ɒ]) was digitally spliced in to one or both of these tokens, creating six versions of each target passage that contained COURT vowels that were either consistently produced in one way (UK, US, or Singapore), or contained one token produced one way and one produced another (e.g., US-Singapore).

The preliminary findings involving fifty-one participants born in Singapore ages 21–29 indicate significant effects of media consumption patterns on professionalism ratings. Linear mixed-effect regression modelling finds that participants who report high levels of US media consumption give significantly higher professionalism ratings to the 100 percent US and hybrid US-UK guises; also, participants with low levels of Singapore media consumption give significantly higher ratings to all guises not involving Singapore variants (US, UK, and US-UK). These findings confirm that it is not only non-local media consumption, but also level of local media consumption that shapes individuals' attitudes towards varieties. Finally, looking at the ratings overall, professionalism ratings for guises containing Singapore variants do not significantly differ from guises that do not contain those variants, supporting the notion that younger Singaporeans are more likely to view features traditionally associated with Colloquial Singapore English as appropriate to formal contexts, in line with rising endonormativity.

### *3.2.5 Social Media and other Online Language Use*

Scholars have recently begun to examine the impact of transnational dialect contact in online language use, particularly on social media sites such as Facebook, Twitter, and Instagram. Individuals may be more likely to adopt novel variants or terms in the online domain than they are to adopt non-local patterns that they encounter in person, for several reasons. First, many of the features encountered online involve lexis, which is relatively easy to acquire via limited contact. Also, as illustrated by the phenomenon of digital blackface (Hess and O'Neill 2017), the disembodied nature of online language use allows users to express themselves in ways that would be perceived as inauthentic to their embodied social identities (Turkle 1995). The innovative and casual nature of online language use also encourages the adoption of novel terms and constructions. Finally, the globalized nature of many online communities, such as Twitter, leads to increased transnational contact and a global experience of shared online systems and affordances (e.g., "retweeting," "likes"), giving rise to a repertoire of shared terms.

Some of the most compelling evidence regarding the transnational Americanization of English comes from Gonçalves et al. (2018), which presents largescale analyses of Twitter data and the Google Books corpus. Within their corpus of over thirty million geolocated English-language tweets, American English vocabulary dominated in every nation examined, across all three Circles, with the exceptions of India, Ireland, and the UK; British spelling, on the other hand, retained influence across more nations, reflecting the continued role of British norms in formal education. At the same time, other research on American regional variation on Twitter concludes that, far from being a uniform, globalized community, in fact Twitter shows substantial variation by region consistent with conventional dialect boundaries identified by dialectologists (Huang et al. 2016). While impressive in their scope, the lexically-focused methodologies of these studies limit the extent to which they can definitively capture region-based sociolinguistic variation.

Smaller-scale research investigating language use on social media sites has examined how world Englishes speakers draw upon local sociolinguistic resources and juxtapose them with non-local features to construct various online personae. In the context of Singapore, Ooi and Tan (2014) and Chong (2020), analyzing Facebook and Instagram respectively, both observed the use of American slang terms, some originating in online culture (e.g., *LOL*) and others from African American Vernacular English (e.g., *woke*) (or, in many cases, originating from the intersection of both communities). As pointed out by Chong (2020: 19), the African American origins of many of these terms are lost on most Singaporean internet users, who simply view them as globalized "internet" slang. In her comparison of the Instagram accounts of female undergraduate students versus a younger group of adolescent girls, Chong found that the younger group used few features associated with Colloquial Singapore English, instead preferring to engage in globalized linguistic and paralinguistic practices (e.g., respelling, use of creative fonts) to index their youthful identities. Specifically, Chong argues that these adolescents use sociolinguistic resources to construct several different personae associated with the broader characterological figure of the Xiao Mei Mei ("younger sister"), an immature, trendy teenaged girl. Young Singaporeans' recruitment of American-origin features to construct casual, cool styles in interactions among themselves illustrates the limitations of traditional models that associate Inner Circle norms with correctness, formality, and an outward orientation.

A final language change phenomenon that has been observed to result from online contact is the nativization of non-local features. Using a large corpus of WhatsApp messages supplemented with online social media data, Chee (2019) investigates the innovative term *toh* in Singapore English; originally meaning "to fall" in Hokkien, she argues that the current use of this term has evolved from a loan translation of the American internet slang term *dead*, which carries a range of related meanings, including, "that's so funny." Chee's analysis is a reminder that language change under globalization does not necessarily mean homogenization. Rather, young speakers of world Englishes are drawing upon features they encounter via contact and transforming them, creating new social-semiotic resources with which to express their identities.

## 4. Concluding Remarks

The preceding discussions have provided a broad, but incomplete overview of three major channels of transnational dialect contact in world Englishes-speaking communities: institutional exonormativity, transnational mobility, and media consumption. Throughout these sections, the interactions of rising endonormativity, Americanization, and accelerating transnational flows of people and information have been shown to hold major implications for the language use, ideologies, and sociolinguistic knowledge of world Englishes speakers. Moreover, rather than a rapid global levelling of Englishes, what we are instead witnessing is a more nuanced and multifaceted set of variation and change phenomena, in which rising contact with non-local varieties can trigger the innovation of new features, an increasing emphasis on the performance of local identity, as well as the adoption of non-local features and the expansion of speakers' sociolinguistic repertoires.

The transformative impacts of these developments in world Englishes-speaking communities affirm the need for approaches that move beyond codes and lectal continua. While it is debatable whether the sociolinguistic situation in any community has ever been simple enough to be effectively captured by a unidimensional continuum from non-standard to standard lects, such models are manifestly unable to account for the sociolinguistic patterns observed in world Englishes today. There is no longer a single way of doing "standard language" in these communities, nor is there a single way of being colloquial; moreover, different community members have diverging views regarding what social meanings are linked with which linguistic forms. Feature-focused variationist approaches have the potential to capture the social-semiotic moves of speakers as they strategically juxtapose features that index a constellation of possible social meanings. Such approaches also recognize that speakers use linguistic features in combination with other social signifiers to construct locally-salient personae, such as the Xiao Mei Mei in Chong's (2020) Instagram study, rather than only to affiliate themselves with local or global language norms. The adoption of variationist frameworks has the additional advantage of better integrating the fields of World Englishes and mainstream quantitative sociolinguistics. This improved dialogue carries potential benefits both for World Englishes and sociolinguistics, which has long over-relied on evidence from North American settings to propose universal principles of language variation and change.

The developments discussed in this chapter also uncover certain limitations in the ability of existing models of world Englishes to incorporate recent globalization trends, and in particular to factor in the role of rising transnational mobility, which has forged new English-speaking communities and transformed existing ones. As we argue in Starr and Balasubramaniam (2019), the progress of Singapore English towards the differentiation phase, as predicted by the Dynamic Model, has been thrown off-track in certain respects by the rising salience of the dichotomy between locals and non-locals. In the Caribbean, progression from British English-oriented norms towards endonormativity has similarly been upended by the impact of contact with the US (see Ferguson 2016). In fact, every postcolonial English-speaking community is currently being transformed, to some extent, by rising transnational contact; models of the development of world Englishes must account for this reality.

The rapid changes underway in the attitudes, knowledge, and language use patterns of world Englishes speakers also speaks to the need for updated corpora and other sources of data that can inform fresh sociolinguistic analyses of evolving patterns in established and newly-formed communities. Work in progress on recently-compiled corpora of world Englishes, such as the Corpus of Singapore English Messages (CoSEM), a corpus of WhatsApp messages between young Singaporeans (Gonzales et al. n.d.; see discussion of Chee 2019 above), promises to yield new insights into how younger speakers are communicating.

Finally, as is evident in this chapter, many questions regarding the impact of transnational dialect contact on language variation and change have yet to be rigorously investigated across multiple communities, while others have not yet been addressed at all, either within world Englishes or with respect to other languages and varieties. If variationist sociolinguistics as a field can effectively work to overcome its North American, inward-looking focus, these efforts may give rise to a long overdue wave of scholarship on globalization and transnational contact.

## Notes

1   https://www.youtube.com/watch?v=mPCXixIY2kw

## References

Agha, A. (2007), *Language and Social Relations*, Cambridge: Cambridge University Press.
Alharbi, N. (2018), "English as a lingua franca in the Gulf Cooperation Council states," in J. Jenkins, W. Baker and M Dewey (eds.), *The Routledge Handbook of English as a Lingua Franca*, 126–37, New York: Routledge.
Alsagoff, L. (2010), "English in Singapore: Culture, capital and identity in linguistic variation," *World Englishes*, 29 (3): 336–48.
Androutsopoulos, J. (2014), "Mediatization and sociolinguistic change. Key concepts, research traditions, open issues," in J. Androutsopoulos (ed.), *Mediatization and Sociolinguistic Change*, 3–48, Berlin: De Gruyter.
Benor, S. B. (2010), "Ethnolinguistic repertoire: Shifting the analytic focus in language and ethnicity," *Journal of Sociolinguistics*, 14 (2): 159–83.
Blake, R. (1996), "Barbadian Creole English: Insights into class and race identity," *Journal of Commonwealth and Postcolonial Studies*, 4 (1): 37–54.
Blommaert, Jan. (2010), *The Sociolinguistics of Globalization*, Cambridge: Cambridge University Press.
Boyle, R. (2011), "Patterns of change in English as a lingua franca in the UAE," *International Journal of Applied Linguistics*, 21 (2): 143–61.
Bruthiaux, P. (2003), "Squaring the circles: Issues in modeling English worldwide," *International Journal of Applied Linguistics*, 13 (2): 159–78.
Campbell-Kibler, K. (2008), "I'll be the judge of that: Diversity in social perceptions of (ING)," *Language in Society*, 37 (5): 637–59.
Chan, K. L. R. (2018), "Washback in English pronunciation in Hong Kong: Hong English or British English?," *Proceedings of CLaSIC 2018: Motivation, Identity and Autonomy in Foreign Language Education*, 27–40, Singapore: National University of Singapore Centre for Language Studies.
Chee, H. N. (2019), "Toh: Language Contact, Identity Construction and the Proliferation of CMC amongst Singaporean Youth," BA Honours Thesis, National University of Singapore.
Choe, H. (2016), "Identity formation of Filipino ESL teachers teaching Korean students in the Philippines: How negative and positive identities shape ELT in the Outer Circle," *English Today*, 32 (1): 5–11.

Chong, C. X. J. (2020), "Glossy Girls, Calm Girls and Grown-up Girls: Comparing the Stylistic Practices of Young Singaporeans on Instagram," BA Honours Thesis, National University of Singapore.

Chua, A. M. Y. (2016), "Sociophonetic variation among local and returning Singaporean children," BA Honours Thesis, National University of Singapore.

Crocombe, R. (1992), *Pacific Neighbours: New Zealand's Relations with Other Pacific Islands*, Christchurch, New Zealand: Centre for Pacific Studies, University of Canterbury.

DeCamp, D. (1971), "Toward a generative analysis of a post-creole speech continuum," in D. Hymes (ed.), *Pidginization and Creolization of Languages*, 349–70, Cambridge: Cambridge University Press.

Deterding, D. (2007), "The vowels of the different ethnic groups in Singapore," in D. Prescott, A. Kirkpatrick, I. Martin and A. Hashim (eds.), *English in Southeast Asia: Varieties, Literacies and Literatures*, 2–29, Newcastle, UK: Cambridge Scholars Press.

Dodsworth, R. and M. Kohn (2012), "Urban rejection of the vernacular: The SVS undone," *Language Variation and Change*, 24 (2): 221–45.

Drummond, R. (2013), "The Manchester Polish STRUT: Dialect acquisition in a second language," *Journal of English Linguistics*, 41 (1): 65–93.

Eckert, P. (2008), "Variation and the indexical field," *Journal of Sociolinguistics*, 12 (4): 453–76.

Eckert, P. (2012), "Three waves of variation study: The emergence of meaning in the study of sociolinguistic variation," *Annual Review of Anthropology*, 41: 87–100.

Farquharson, J. and B. Migge (2017), "Introduction," in J. Farquharson and B Migge (eds.), *Pidgins and Creoles Volume 3: Sociolinguistics and/of Pidgins and Creoles*, 1–11, New York: Routledge.

Ferguson, G. M. (2016), "Remote acculturation and the birth of an Americanized Caribbean youth identity on the islands," In J. L. Roopnarine and D. Chadee (eds.), *Caribbean Psychology: Indigenous Contributions to a Global Discipline*, 97–117, Washington, DC: American Psychological Association.

Gonçalves, B., L. Loureiro-Porto, J. J. Ramasco and D. Sánchez (2018), "Mapping the Americanization of English in space and time," *PlosONE*, 13 (5): e0197741. https://doi.org/10.1371/journal.pone.0197741

Gonzales, W. D. W., M. Hiramoto, J. Leimgruber and J. J. Lim. (n.d.), "Corpus of Singapore English Messages (CoSEM): Description and Explorations," unpublished manuscript.

Gupta, A. F. (1991), "Acquisition of diglossia in Singapore," in A. Kwan-Terry (ed.), *Child Language Development in Singapore and Malaysia*, 119–60. Singapore: National University of Singapore Press.

Gupta, A. F. (1994), "A model for the analysis of Singapore English," in S. Gopinathan, A. Pakir, H. W. Kam and V. Saravanan (eds.), *Language Society and Education in Singapore: Issues and Trends*, 2nd edition, 119–32, Singapore: Times Academic Press.

Gupta, A. F. (2010), "Standard Singapore English revisited," in L. Wee, A. Pakir and L. Lim (eds.), *English in Singapore: Modernity and Management*, 57–90, Singapore: National University of Singapore Press.

Hansen Edwards, J. G. (2016), "Accent preferences and the use of American English features in Hong Kong: A preliminary study," *Asian Englishes*, 18 (3): 197–215.

He, D. (2017), "Perceptions of Chinese English and pedagogic implications for teaching English in China," in Xu, Z. X., D. H. Deyuan and D. Deterding (eds.), *Researching Chinese English: The State of the Art*, 127–40, New York: Springer.

Hess, A. and S. O'Neill (2017), "The White internet's love affair with digital blackface," *The New York Times*, December 22, retrieved from: https://www.nytimes.com/video/arts/100000005615988/the-white-internets-love-affair-with-digital-blackface.html

Holliday, A. (2006), "Native-speakerism," *ELT Journal*, 60 (4): 385–87.

Huang, Y., D. Guo, A. Kasakoff and J. Grieve (2016), "Understanding U.S. regional linguistic variation with Twitter data analysis," *Computers, Environment and Urban Systems*, 59: 244–55.

Imperial, R. (2016), "Speech Production and Sociolinguistic Perception in a 'Non-Native' Second Language Context: A Sociophonetic Study of Korean Learners of English in the Philippines," MA Thesis, National University of Singapore.

Ismaili, M. (2013), "The effectiveness of using movies in the EFL classroom—A study conducted at the South East European University," *Academic Journal of Interdisciplinary Studies*, 2 (4): 121–32.

Jagdish, B. (2017), "Commentary: What's wrong with 'Made in Singapore'?," *Channel News Asia*, September 30, retrieved from: https://www.channelnewsasia.com/news/singapore/commentary-what-s-wrong-with-made-in-singapore-9240738.

Jenkins, J. (1998), "Which pronunciation norms and models for English as an International Language?," *ELT Journal*, 52 (2): 119–26.

JET Programme (2019), "Participating countries," retrieved from: http://jetprogramme.org/en/countries/.

Johnstone, B. and C. Pollack (2016), "Mobilities, materialities, and the changing meanings of Pittsburgh speech," *Journal of English Linguistics*, 44 (3): 254–75.

Kabooha, R. and T. Elyas (2018), "The effects of YouTube in multimedia instruction for vocabulary learning: Perceptions of EFL students and teachers," *English Language Teaching*, 11 (2): 72–81.

Kachru, B. B. (1985), "Standards, codification, and sociolinguistic realism: The English language in the Outer Circle," in R. Quirk and H. G. Widdowson (eds.), *English in the World: Teaching and Learning the Language and Literatures*, 11–30, Cambridge: Cambridge University Press.

Labov, W. (1966), *The Social Stratification of English in New York City*, Washington, DC: The Center for Applied Linguistics.

Labov, W. (1972), *Sociolinguistic Patterns*, Philadelphia, PA: University of Pennsylvania Press.

Labov, W. (2007), "Transmission and diffusion," *Language* 83 (2): 344–87.

Labov, W., S. Ash, M. Ravindrath, T. Weldon, M. Baranowski and N. Nagy (2011), "Properties of the sociolinguistic monitor," *Journal of Sociolinguistics*, 15 (4): 431–63.

Leimgruber, J. (2012), "Singapore English: An indexical approach," *World Englishes*, 31 (1): 1–14.

Leow, S. W. (2011), "American English 'likely to prevail'," *The Straits Times*, September 7.

Leung, A. H.-C. (2012), "Bad influence?—An investigation into the purported negative influence of foreign domestic helpers on children's second language English acquisition," *Journal of Multilingual and Multicultural Development*, 33 (2): 133–48.

Mayer, R. E. (2005), "Cognitive theory of multimedia learning," in R. E. Mayer (ed.), *The Cambridge Handbook of Multimedia Learning*, 31–48, New York: Cambridge University Press.

Mesthrie, R. (2020), "Colony, post-colony and world Englishes in the South African context," *World Englishes*, 1–12. DOI: 10.1111/weng.12469

Meyerhoff, M. and N. Niedzielski (2003), "The globalization of vernacular variation," *Journal of Sociolinguistics*, 7 (4): 534–55.

National Youth Survey (2016), *A Snapshot of our Singaporean Youth*, retrieved from: https://www.nyc.gov.sg/-/media/mccy/projects/nyc/files/innitiatives/resource/2017-stats-handbook/nys2016.ashx.

Ni Chonghaile, C. (2012), "Kenya plays with language gaps," *The Guardian*, October 16, 2012, retrieved from https://www.theguardian.com/education/2012/oct/16/kenya-debates-language-identity.

Ntarangwi, M. (2009), *East African Hip-hop: Youth Culture and Globalization*, Champaign, IL: University of Illinois Press.

Nycz, J. (2019), "Media and second dialect acquisition," *Annual Review of Applied Linguistics*, 39: 152–60.

Obiechina, E. (1973), *An African Popular Literature: A Study of Onitsha Market Pamphlets*, Cambridge, UK: Cambridge University Press.

Ooi, V. B. Y. and P. K. W. Tan (2014), "Facebook, linguistic identity and hybridity in Singapore," in R. Rubdy and L. Alsagoff (eds.), *The Global-Local Interface and Hybridity*, 225–44, Bristol: Multilingual Matters.

Otsuji, E. and A. Pennycook (2010), "Metrolingualism: Fixity, fluidity and language in flux," *International Journal of Multilingualism*, 7 (3): 240–54.

Pakir, A. (1991), "The range and depth of English-knowing bilinguals in Singapore," *World Englishes*, 10 (2): 167–79.

Park, J. S.-Y. and L. Wee (2009), "The three circles redux: A market-theoretic perspective on World Englishes," *Applied Linguistics*, 30 (3): 389–406.

Platt, J. T. (1975), "The Singapore English speech continuum and its basilect "Singlish" as a 'creoloid'," *Anthropological Linguistics*, 17: 363–74.

Podesva, R. J. (2008), "Three sources of stylistic meaning," *Texas Linguistic Forum*, 51: 1–10.

Poedjosoedarmo, G. (2000), "The media as a model and source of innovation in the development of Singapore Standard English," in A. Brown, D. Deterding and L. E. Ling (eds.), *The English Language in Singapore: Research on Pronunciation*, 112–20, Singapore: Singapore Association for Applied Linguistics.

Recine, D. (2016), "Can you use non-American English on the TOEFL?," *Magoosh TOEFL Blog*, retrieved from: https://magoosh.com/toefl/2016/can-you-use-non-american-english-on-the-toefl/.

Rickford, J. R. (1986), "The need for new approaches to social class in sociolinguistics," *Language and Communication*, 6: 215–21.

Rindal, U. (2010), "Constructing identity with L2: Pronunciation and attitudes among Norwegian learners of English," *Journal of Sociolinguistics*, 14 (2): 240–61.

Rubdy, R. (2010), "Problematizing the implementation of innovation in English language education in Singapore," in L. Wee, A. Pakir and L. Lim (eds.), *English in Singapore: Modernity and Management*, 207–33, Singapore: National University of Singapore Press.

Sayers, D. (2014), "The mediated innovation model: A framework for researching media influence in language change," *Journal of Sociolinguistics*, 18 (2): 185–212.

Schleef, E., M. Meyerhoff and L. Clark (2011), "Teenagers' acquisition of variation: A comparison of locally-born and migrant teens" realisation of English (ing) in Edinburgh and London," *English World-Wide*, 32 (2): 206–36.

Schneider, E. W. (2007), *Postcolonial English: Varieties Around the World*, Cambridge: Cambridge University Press.

Siemund, P., A. Al-Issa and J. R. E. Leimgruber (2020), "Multilingualism and the role of English in the United Arab Emirates," *World Englishes*, 1–14. https://doi.org/10.1111/weng.12507

Singapore Department of Statistics (2015), *General Household Survey 2015*, retrieved from: http://www.singstat.gov.sg/publications/publications-and-papers/GHS/ghs2015.

Singapore Ministry of Education (2020), "Approved textbook list," retrieved from: https://www.moe.gov.sg/education/syllabuses/approved-textbook-list.

Stanford, J. N. (2016), "A call for more diverse sources of data: Variationist approaches in non-English contexts," *Journal of Sociolinguistics*, 20 (4): 525–41.

Starr, R. L. (2017), *Sociolinguistic Variation and Acquisition in Two-Way Language Immersion: Negotiating the Standard*, Bristol, UK: Multilingual Matters.

Starr, R. L. (2019a), "Attitudes and exposure as predictors of -t/d deletion among local and expatriate children in Singapore," *Language Variation and Change*, 31 (3): 251–74.

Starr, R. L. (2019b), "Cross-dialectal awareness and use of the BATH-TRAP distinction in Singapore: Investigating the effects of overseas travel and media consumption," *Journal of English Linguistics*, 47 (1): 55–88.

Starr, R. L. (forthcoming), "Changing language, changing character types," in L. Hall-Lew, E. Moore and R. J. Podesva (eds.), *Social Meaning and Variation: Theorizing the Third Wave*, Cambridge, UK: Cambridge University Press.

Starr, R. L. and B. Balasubramaniam (2019), "Variation and change in English /r/ among Tamil Indian Singaporeans," *World Englishes*, 38 (4): 630–43.

Starr, R. L., A. J. Theng, N. J. Y. Tong, K. M. Wong, N. A. Binte Ibrahim, A. M. Y. Chua, C. H. M. Yong, F. W. Loke, H. Dominic, K. J. Fernandez and M. T. J. Peh (2017), "Third culture kids in the Outer Circle: The development of sociolinguistic knowledge among local and expatriate children in Singapore," *Language in Society*, 46 (4): 507–46.

Stuart-Smith, J. (2007), "The influence of the media," in C. Llamas, L. Mullany and P. Stockwell (eds.), *The Routledge Companion to Sociolinguistics*, 140–48, New York: Routledge.

Stuart-Smith, J., G. Pryce, C. Timmins and B. Gunter (2013), "Television can also be a factor in language change: Evidence from an urban dialect," *Language*, 89 (3): 501–36.

Tan, Y.-Y. (2012), "To r or not to r: Social correlates of /ɹ/ in Singapore English," *International Journal of the Sociology of Language*, 218: 1–24.

Trudgill, P. (2014), "Diffusion, drift, and the irrelevance of media influence," *Journal of Sociolinguistics*, 18 (2): 214–22.

Turkle, S. (1995), *Life on the Screen: Identity in the Age of the Internet*, New York: Simon & Schuster.

United Nations, Department of Economic and Social Affairs, Population Division (2017), *International Migration Report 2017: Highlights*, retrieved from: https://www.un.org/en/development/desa/population/migration/publications/migrationreport/docs/MigrationReport2017_Highlights.pdf.

Vertovec, S. (2007), "Superdiversity and its implications," *Ethnic and Racial Studies*, 30 (6): 1024–54.

Winford, D. (2003), *An Introduction to Contact Linguistics*, Oxford: Wiley-Blackwell.

Wolfram, W., P. M. Carter and R. Moriello (2004), "New Dialect Formation in the American South: Emerging Hispanic English," *Journal of Sociolinguistics*, 8 (3): 339–58.

# "I Don't Get It": Researching the Cultural Lexicon of Global Englishes

David Crystal

## 1. Introduction

Anyone talking to an English speaker from the UK is likely to encounter, sooner or later, such sentences as:

(1) Philippa [leaving a department store]: It was like Clapham Junction in there!
(2) David [weeding his garden, and grumbling]: This is like painting the Forth Bridge.
(3) Mary [talking about her holiday]: Our hotel made Fawlty Towers look like the Ritz.
(4) Jim [showing someone his watch]: I'm afraid it's more Portobello Road than Bond Street.

To be understood, listeners need to have the relevant cultural background. They need to know: in (1) that Philippa has found her shopping expedition chaotic (Clapham Junction in London being the busiest station in the UK for changing trains); in (2) that David is moaning about the way weeds removed at the end of one growing season always seem to reappear in the next (the bridge across the River Forth in Scotland being so large and structurally complex that by the time painters finish giving it a protective coat of paint, it is time for them to start all over again); in (3) that Mary's accommodation was absolutely awful (*Fawlty Towers* being a television comedy series in which a paranoid seaside hotel manager deals with a never-ending series of disasters, a world away from one of London's classiest hotels); in (4) that Jim is playing down the value of his watch (bought from a street-market rather than from one of the most expensive streets in London). Listeners who lack this cultural knowledge may smile politely and nod, but inside they have to admit failure: "I don't get it."

This is not just a problem for foreign learners of English. English may be your first language, but if you come from a part of the world where these expressions are unfamiliar or unknown, you will be just as lost. And British visitors to other English-speaking countries will face similar difficulties. I can recall many situations where I have been at a loss because I have no idea what to make of the cultural reference the speaker has unconsciously used. I have reported some of these experiences in past papers (Crystal 2011, 2014, 2017). Native speakers often make allowances for possible misunderstanding by speaking more slowly or simplifying syntax, but cultural allusions are so deeply embedded in their linguistic sensibility that they are usually unaware they have made them. Being a linguist, of course, I ask speakers to explain, and invariably they are surprised at my apparent ignorance. To take just one example: in New Zealand, I repeatedly had to ask for explanations of the cultural allusions used in the "Yeah Right" advertising campaign for Tui beer (Tui 2005), in which a sentence was followed by a dismissive "yeah right" (i.e., "I don't believe it"). I understood the first of the following examples, because I shared the cultural background, but not the second:

> The cheque is in the post. Yeah Right.
> Let Paul fly you there. Yeah Right!

My interlocutor could not believe I did not know who Paul was. (I then learned he was the breakfast host on *Newstalk ZB*, the country's main breakfast show, who owned a plane which he crashed—and survived. He then got another plane, which he crashed—and survived.) Similar incomprehension surfaced in the USA when allusions were made to baseball personalities I did not know, and in Switzerland, the Czech Republic, and The Netherlands.

I choose these last three locations to make the point that local cultural references are not restricted to countries where English is the first language of the population, but can surface anywhere that people carry on fluent conversations in the language—which of course means virtually anywhere, these days. The global spread of English has significantly increased the likelihood of encountering instances of cultural incomprehension—either when visiting a country physically or engaging with it through the internet. The "new Englishes" of the world display the phenomenon most dramatically, for when a country adopts English as a means of communication it rapidly adapts it to meet its needs. Words for local fauna and flora, food and drink, myths and legends, politics, broadcasting, sports, religion, and every facet of daily life soon generate a local vocabulary that is opaque to most people outside the country. So when I find myself listening to an informal conversation among a group of locals—such as a group of teachers at an English Language Teaching (ELT) conference, or a group of managers at a reception following a business meeting—I am very likely going to hear references to local shops, suburbs, bus-routes, institutions, television programs, personalities, and so on that escape me. The participants may allude to an advertising jingle, the lyric of a popular song, a proverb, a childhood story or nursery rhyme, and many other shared topics of local culture, none of which I recognize. After a while, even I begin to nod politely, for one cannot always be intervening to say, "Excuse me, but what does that mean?"

A more awkward situation arises when I *think* I have understood, and interpose a comment, only to find, from the puzzled responses of my interlocutor, that I have got things totally wrong. The instance I reported in Crystal (2017) provides a brief illustration:

## "I Don't Get It"

A couple of years ago I was lecturing in Leiden. The country was in the grip of exceptionally cold weather. The canals were frozen and people were skating on them. The previous time the canals had frozen over like this, it seems, was 1997. So it wasn't surprising that after the lecture the dinner-time talk—four Dutch colleagues, my wife and me, with a conversation entirely in English—at one point turned to the ice skating. Which bits of the ice were safe? Which weren't? Under the bridges was dangerous, for it was warmer there. Our knowledge of ice-skating was increasing by the minute. It was a lively and jocular chat, and the exceptional weather formed a major part of it. Then one of them said something that I didn't quite catch, and the four Dutch people suddenly became very downcast and there was a short silence. It was as if someone had mentioned a death in the family.

I had no idea how to react. Somebody commented about it being such a shame, about the—I now know how to spell it—*Elfstedentocht*. One of the four noticed my confused face. "The 11-cities tour was cancelled," he explained, adding "because of the ice." Ah, so that was it, I thought. Some sort of cultural tourist event taking in 11 cities had been called off because the roads were too dangerous. I could understand that, as the roads were so slippery that I'd had to buy some special boots a few days earlier to keep myself upright. But why were my colleagues so upset about it? "Were you going on it?" I asked. They all laughed. I had evidently made a joke, but I'd no idea why. "Not at our age!" said one of them. I couldn't understand that answer, and didn't like to ask if it was a tour just for youngsters. Then I got even more confused, for someone said that it was the south of the country that was the problem because the ice was too thin. But why was thin ice a problem? That would mean the travelling would be getting back to normal. I was rapidly losing track of this conversation, as the four Dutch debated the rights and wrongs of the cancellation. It might still be held . . . ? No, it was impossible. It would all depend on the weather . . . And eventually the talk moved on to something else.

What I'd missed, of course, was the simplest of facts—and cultural linguistic differences often reduce to very simple points—which I discovered when I later looked up *Elfstedentocht* on the Internet. It firstly referred to a *race*, not a tour (*tocht* in Dutch has quite a wide range of uses) and moreover an *ice* race, along the canals between the eleven cities. It is an intensive experience, only for the fittest and youngest—hence the irony of my remark. But the semantics of the word was only a part of it. The cultural significance of the word I had still to learn. I discovered it in the website of the *Global Post*.[1]

> It's hard to overestimate the grip that the Elfstedentocht has on the Dutch psyche. For sports fans in the Netherlands the epic 200-kilometer (125 mile) skating race is like the World Series, Super Bowl and Stanley Cup combined. Its mythical status is enhanced by the fact that it can only be held in exceptional winters when the canals are covered by 15 cm (6 inches) of ice along the length of the course.... If the Elfstendentocht, or "11 cities tour," goes ahead, organizers expect up to 2 million spectators—one in eight of the Dutch population—could line the route. The race has only been held 15 times since the first in 1909, and winners become instant national heroes. The legendary

1963 contest was held in a raging blizzard. Just 136 finished out of 10,000 starters.

A stronger cultural affirmation is difficult to imagine. The fact that it was an ice race was so obvious, to the Dutch people at the table, that they took it completely for granted, disregarding the fact that for me, coming from Wales, the significance of the thickness of ice on canals would totally escape me.

## 2. The Need for Cultural Lexicons Across World Englishes

As instances of this kind accumulate, the question arises as to how to deal with them, both in research and in teaching. I do not know of any survey describing this kind of lexicon, or the cultural settings that give rise to it, or reporting the frequency with which it is used in everyday conversation, for a particular country, and it is not immediately obvious how one would set about making such a survey. Nor does there exist what might be called a "cultural syllabus" in ELT, in which the lexical features that identify a particular country are organized and graded in some way. All ELT coursebooks include a certain amount of cultural encounter, of course—a visit to a restaurant, perhaps, or a trip to the Houses of Parliament—but these are sporadic, with the domains (in the sense of 'areas of subject-matter') chosen as a means of making a grammatical point interesting, or as an opportunity to introduce a swathe of new vocabulary. There may be a visit to the shops in Bond Street, but the commercial world of that part of London is not related to other shopping experiences of a contrasting kind, such as would be encountered in the street-markets of Portobello Road or the stalls of Covent Garden. To help develop such intuitions, the learner would need a cultural dictionary or thesaurus of shopping—ideally, both.

Shopping is but one of a large number of domains where people readily make cultural allusions. How many such domains are there, and how might they be organized for a research project? We need a comprehensive descriptive framework within which all the cultural allusions encountered in a country can be located and classified: a cultural taxonomy. And this research task should also have a comparative dimension, to allow the cultural backgrounds of speaker and listener to be brought into some sort of correspondence. We might think of it as a translation task. What is the equivalent of *Clapham Junction* (in the sense of 'chaos') in other global English varieties? *Is* there an equivalent? Which domains in a country give rise to cultural allusions not shared by other countries? For example, I would expect a country that regularly suffers from earthquakes to have a host of cultural memories of places and events that would be immediately meaningful to the people there; whereas I would not expect the domain of earthquakes to have any great cultural resonance in Britain. Culture is usually defined positively: the features that make a community recognizable. It can also be viewed negatively: the features that a community does not have.

There has been a definite trend, since the 1980s, to increase the amount of cultural information in English language studies. There has always been a strong cultural element in historical lexicography, of course, as the entries in the unabridged *Oxford English Dictionary* routinely illustrate; and American dictionaries have from their earliest days included basic encyclopedic information in the form of entries on people, places, institutions, historical events, and so on. Dictionaries of individual language varieties also have a respected history, with Hobson-Jobson (for Indian English) first appearing in the nineteenth century (Yule and Burnell, 1886); and a selection of later examples would include dictionaries of Jamaican English (Cassidy and Le Page, 1967), South African English (Branford and Branford, 1978/1991), and Trinidad and Tobago English (Winer, 2009). The scale of these works needs to be appreciated, for they typically contain 10,000 entries or more. There have also been a few discursive publications focusing on cultural identities, such as *British English for American Readers* (Grote, 1992), *Say Again? The other side of South African English* (Branford and Venter, 2016), and the two English-orientated books in the *Coping With . . .* series—*Coping with America* (Trudgill, 1982) and *Coping with England* (Hannah, 1987). Many articles in the periodical *English Today* contain partial accounts. But these publications inevitably draw attention to the vast range of varieties for which *no* descriptive treatment yet exists. The first systematic attempt to make international variation the basis of a general dictionary for English-language learners was the *Longman Dictionary of English Language and Culture* (Summers, 1992/1998/2004), but the focus of this book was on British and American English, with other varieties receiving only sporadic mention. The recent efforts of the *Oxford English Dictionary* to represent different Englishes is another initiative in that area (see Salazar, this volume).

Regional dictionaries have a literal aim: to describe cultural phenomena as they actually exist. So, for example, the Longman dictionary does describe what Clapham Junction is, but it does not illustrate how people can use this expression in everyday speech. The entry reads (I quote from the third edition): "a very busy railway station in southwest London where a lot of people catch a train to work or change trains." This is accurate enough, in its simplicity (the entries all use the Longman defining vocabulary), but it gives no indication that people apply the notion to other situations, as in my example above. Just occasionally we see in its entries the kind of information that we need in order to capture the extended usage, as in this entry (omitting phonetic details):

**Tweedledum and Tweedledee** two characters in the book *Through the Looking-Glass* by Lewis Carroll. They are fat little men, who are both dressed in school uniform and look exactly like each other. Their names are often used to describe two people or groups who are almost exactly the same as each other, especially when they both seem to be bad: *Some voters felt there was little real difference between the two party leaders—a case of choosing between Tweedledum and Tweedledee.*

This is the kind of treatment readers have to see (along with other examples of usage) if the dictionary is to help them handle cultural adaptations.

## 3. Types of Lexicon

Only about a quarter of the entries in the Longman dictionary deal with cultural phenomena, and only a proportion of these present issues of the kind illustrated above. The coverage in fact contains four types of lexical entry. The first three are well-recognized, both in lexicology and ELT (I present the fourth type in a later section).

### 3.1 Culture-neutral Vocabulary, Regionally Unrestricted

This is the remit of a general dictionary of World English. The lexical items and proper names seem to be understood in the same way by all countries where English is spoken—*sun, tree, land, eyes, hand, enemy, government, speak, want, give, love, make, cold, tired; UNESCO, Denmark, New York, Second World War, Albert Einstein, North Pole, Google, Scrabble* ... "Seem" is important, as, in the absence of descriptive studies, it is always possible that an item has acquired an additional nuance in a country that differentiates it from usage elsewhere.

### 3.2 Culture-neutral Vocabulary, Regionally Restricted

This has been the traditional focus of English variationist lexicology: a meaning shared by more than one country is expressed by different lexical items or proper names— [car] *bonnet* (BrE), *hood* (AmE); *pavement* (BrE), *sidewalk* (AmE), *footpath* (AusE); *traffic light* (BrE, AmE), *stop light* (AmE), *robot* (SAfE); *candy floss* (BrE), *cotton candy* (AmE), *fairy floss* (AusE); [cars] *AA* (BrE), *AAA* (AmE); [film classification] *U* (BrE), *G* (AmE); [financial centre] *the City* (BrE), *Wall Street* (AmE). Related are cases where an item expresses different shared meanings, as with *gas* (BrE—natural gas, AmE—petrol); *flyover* (BrE—of roads, AmE—of planes); *subway* (BrE—of roads, AmE—of underground trains). The point to appreciate here is that the various items are not culturally distinctive, for the countries named, as the referents are shared—both Britain and the USA have passageways under roads and trains beneath the ground, for example. It would make no sense to answer the question "Name a feature that uniquely identifies British culture" by saying "traffic light" or "pavement."

### 3.3 Culture-specific Vocabulary, Used Literally

This is the indefinitely large set of lexical items or (especially) proper names associated with a country, traditionally covered by an encyclopedia rather than a dictionary (though lexicographical traditions differ, as mentioned above: proper names have been an important feature of American dictionaries, whereas British dictionaries on the whole have avoided them). Using British and American English examples, this category can be illustrated by terms to do with government (*House of Lords; Capitol Hill*), national symbols (*Union Jack; Uncle Sam*), broadcasting companies (*BBC; NPR*), television programs (*Fawlty Towers; Mister Rogers' Neighborhood*), geographical locations (*the Fens, Bond Street, the Forth Bridge; the Prairies, Broadway, the Grand*

*Canyon*), and historical personalities (*Winston Churchill; George Washington*). Here the "Name a unique feature" question can be answered positively.

## 4. A Cultural Taxonomy

How many cases of this kind are there, in a variety of English? And how can they be systematically studied? The first task is to construct a comprehensive descriptive framework for global variation. Such a task might seem impossibly large, for the "universe of discourse," as it is sometimes called, is infinite. We can talk or write about anything. But the challenge of organizing this vast discourse into discrete and manageable domains has long been a subject of study by the science of classification, *taxonomy*, with its many specific applications, such as the Linnaean taxonomy for biology and the Dewey taxonomy for libraries. The taxonomy I know best is the one I developed for a project called the Global Data Model (GDM), devised in the 1990s as a means of classifying content on the Internet, and which was eventually adopted and adapted by various companies as a system for dealing specifically with online advertising (Crystal, 2010). It was also used as the organizing principle for the Cambridge University Press family of general encyclopedias in the 1990s and the corresponding Penguin family in the early 2000s, so it has been well tested.

The GDM has ten top-level domains, subdivided into some 1,500 hierarchically organized subdomains:

UNIVERSE (space and space exploration)
EARTH SCIENCE (structure and surface of the Earth)
ENVIRONMENT (land care and management)
NATURAL HISTORY (plants and animals)
HUMAN BODY (physical and psychological make-up of the human being, including medical care)
MIND (knowledge, beliefs, science, technology, arts, and communication)
SOCIETY (social organization, including politics, economics, military science, and law)
RECREATION (leisure activities, including hobbies, sports, and games)
HUMAN GEOGRAPHY (world geography, travel, and geography of countries)
HUMAN HISTORY (world history, archaeology, and history of countries)

As an illustration of the approach, Table 9.1 shows the taxonomy used for the domain of EARTH SCIENCE, with some subdomains conflated, along with some indications of content and a British cultural illustration. (The complete taxonomy is provided in the Appendix.) For domains where there is no British example, I have given an instance from some other part of the world.

These subdomains show the level of discrimination that worked satisfactorily for the internet and encyclopedia projects. Whether this level works well for capturing the usages that appear in global cultural variation is an open question. An important methodological issue will be to decide how granular such a model should be. Each of

**Table 9.1** The Domain of EARTH SCIENCE Exemplified

| Domain | Example |
| --- | --- |
| Climate [atmosphere, weather ...] | the Met Office |
| Rocks and minerals [formations, mines ...] | Giant's Causeway |
| Earth dynamics | |
|     Earthquakes | Port-au-Prince (Haiti, 2010) |
|     Tsunamis | Sendai (Japan, 2011) |
|     Volcanic eruptions | Mount St Helens (USA, 1980) |
| Landscape | |
|     Mountains [hills, plateaux, passes ...] | the Downs |
|     Caves [caverns, potholes ...] | Wookey Hole |
|     Valleys [canyons, gorges ...] | Cheddar Gorge |
|     Vegetation [forests, grassland, soils ...] | the New Forest |
|     Deserts [dunes, oases ...] | Atacama (Chile) |
|     Ice [glaciers, icebergs ...] | Aletsch (Switzerland) |
|     Islands [atolls, reefs ...] | Anglesey |
|     Coastline | Chesil Beach |
| Freshwater bodies | |
|     Groundwater [springs, geysers ...] | Bath Hot Springs |
|     Inland [lakes, swamps ...] | the Lake District |
|     Rivers [estuaries, streams ...] | River Severn |
|     Waterfalls | Gaping Gill |
|     Control [dams, reservoirs, canals ...] | the Thames Barrier |
|     Bridges | the Humber Bridge |
| Saltwater bodies | |
|     Seas [oceans, currents, tides ...] | the Channel |
|     Coastline [gulfs, bays, fjords ...] | the Wash |
|     Control [harbours, breakwaters ...] | Dover Harbour |

these domains could be broken down further, if required for a particular country—for example, different kinds of vegetation. Conversely, it may be that most of a domain, such as HUMAN BODY, will not need to be represented, as the vocabulary (*hand, foot, head* ...) will be shared across countries without any cultural implication (apart, perhaps, from their metaphorical use in fixed expressions, such as proverbs). It is impossible to say how a cultural adaptation of the GDM taxonomy will develop, without descriptive application. Similarly, although each line is illustratable by an indefinitely large set of items, only some of these will be sufficiently frequent and country-wide in awareness to justify inclusion. Corpus-based studies should help here.

There will be some unexpected outcomes. One way of quantifying the extent of cultural presence is to take an extract from a country's English language output and identify the number of expressions in it that an outsider would fail to understand. When I did this, using an extract from an online forum in Zurich in which people were complaining (in English) about traffic problems in the area (Crystal, 2014), 19 of the 129 content words (about 15 percent) were culturally opaque. I was not expecting the figure to be so high. The impression I get, from such occasional pieces of analysis, is that, the more local and specific the domain of inquiry, the greater the number of culturally opaque expressions.

Another unexpected outcome relates to choice of domain. For example, in the GDM model the domain of NATURAL HISTORY is divided into 156 subdomains. It might be thought that this domain would be of less importance in a cultural dictionary, and that such a level of granularity would be unwarranted; but that is to underestimate the minute way in which cultures actually manifest themselves. There are 43 categories of symbol for the USA listed in one website <https://statesymbolsusa.org/us/symbols/state>, and that domain is one of the most fruitful. There are some overlaps and duplications, but around 700 entities are recognized, which would populate a goodly number of the natural history subdomains.

These lists are encyclopedic in character. Whether one understands a sentence in which the items occur depends on real-world knowledge, which can be provided only by someone who knows the country well, from the inside—and even then, not all the items will be known to everyone. If I have had a good education, and travelled a bit, I will of course know some of the equivalents in other countries, but I will have no intuition about their local usage. For example, in Britain I know that the Meteorological Office is usually referred to as *the Met Office*; but I do not know whether there are similar everyday ways of referring to the equivalent organization in the USA (the National Weather Service), Australia (the Bureau of Meteorology), or elsewhere—or whether these names turn up in everyday English at all. It would take natives or long-

Table 9.2 US-specific Cultural Symbols in the Domain of NATURAL HISTORY

| Category | Number of unique members | Examples |
| --- | --- | --- |
| Amphibians | 24 | *Arizona tree frog, Idaho giant salamander, New Mexico spadefoot toad* ... |
| Birds | 62 | *California quail, Baltimore oriole, Carolina wren* ... |
| Dinosaurs/Fossils | 60 | *Alaska woolly mammoth, Kentucky brachiopod, Mississippi petrified wood* ... |
| Cats and Dogs | 22 | *Alaskan malamute, Maine coon cat, Boston terrier* ... |
| Aquatic life | 102 | *Kentucky spotted bass, New England neptune, Oregon triton* ... |
| Flowers | 74 | *Louisiana iris, Carolina lily, Oklahoma rose* ... |
| Food and agriculture | 147 | *Texas red grapefruit, Rhode Island greening apple, Louisiana gumbo* ... |
| Horses | 17 | *Florida cracker horse, Missouri mule, Tennessee walking horse* ... |
| Insects | 68 | *California dogface butterfly, Oregon swallowtail, Carolina wolf spider* ... |
| Mammals (excluding cats, dogs, horses) | 66 | *Alaskan malamute, California grizzly bear, Virginia opossum* ... |
| Plants | 40 | *Texas purple sage, Wyoming big sagebrush, Oklahoma Indiangrass* ... |
| Reptiles | 33 | *Arizona ridge-nosed rattlesnake, New Mexico whiptail lizard, Alabama red-bellied turtle* ... |
| Trees | 59 | *California redwood, Colorado blue spruce, Ohio buckeye* ... |

Source: <https://statesymbolsusa.org/us/symbols/state> (last accessed April 14, 2020)

term residents of these countries only a few minutes to add a column to the EARTH SCIENCE domain, and fill out the subdomains with appropriate examples from their part of the world. The long-term research aim would be to create a comparative table in which this were done for all countries. If such a table existed it would solve the problem I had with, for instance, *Elfstedentocht*. I would look up this word and be directed to the subdomain SPORT, within RECREATION, and then to RINK SPORTS. I could cross-refer to The Netherlands. I would see examples there of the kind of usage I had experienced in my conversation.

This is the kind of project that could benefit from the crowd-sourcing potential of the Internet, along the lines of the Urban Dictionary, where items can be added as new associations develop and old ones die out. The third edition of the Longman dictionary (2004) includes the *Atkins Diet, Ben Affleck, the iPod,* and *Jamie Oliver,* for example, and has an extra 50 pages. Several of the entries in the first edition of the Longman Dictionary (1992) are already receding from public consciousness, such as some of the characters from television programs of the 1960s. There was an entry on *Ena Sharples*, for example, who was certainly an iconic figure in those days, but I wonder how many people today would be able to make sense of a sentence in which the name was used to characterize "an old, working class woman with strong opinions and strict ideas about other people's moral behavior, which she expressed very openly," given that her last appearance in the show was in 1980. But she's still there in the third edition.

It is difficult to predict how long a cultural memory will last. Presumably, once the generation that experienced a phenomenon has passed away, the memory will die, unless there is a really good reason to motivate intergenerational transmission. Judging by this example from the CLIMATE subdomain of Earth Science, heard in 2018, forty years is an eyeblink:

*Climate*
A "There's a big storm on its way." B "Are you sure? Who announced it? Michael Fish?"

The reference is to the unfortunate weatherman who in October 1987 announced on television that reports of a hurricane approaching Britain were false, only to be proved wrong a few hours later when the worst storm in nearly three centuries hit the southern part of England, causing huge destruction.

And a cultural reference may last long after the phenomenon itself has disappeared, as this next example illustrates:

*Bridges*
[in London] "I'll meet you on the South Bank—by the wobbly bridge."

The reference is to the Millennium Bridge across the Thames, opened in 2000, because when it was first built, the number of people crossing it caused it to sway alarmingly (the problem was fixed by 2002, but the usage has stuck).

It would be important not to delete entries that become obsolete. Cross-cultural linguistic studies are usually synchronic in character, but we need a historical cultural lexicography too. A glance at any issue of a Victorian magazine will immediately display items whose meaning is culturally opaque, such as this article, taken from *Punch* (May 24, 1862). The items that need glossing are underlined.

### Held to Anything but Esteem

A correspondent writes to the <u>*Times*</u>, complaining of the scanty supply of <u>steam</u> at the <u>Exhibition</u>. We should have thought that they could have got any supply of it with the <u>Brompton Boilers</u> so close at hand. We must say that the <u>Commissioners</u> have been most dreadfully backward all through their management of the <u>Exhibition</u> in keeping the <u>steam</u> up to the high point of the <u>Exhibition of 1851</u>.

Of the 27 content words, and ignoring duplications, eight (30 percent) need a gloss—twice as many as in the Zurich example. The older a text, it seems, the greater the degree of cultural opacity. A historical cultural dictionary, or thesaurus, to complement the general vocabulary already covered by the *OED*, would facilitate the interpretation of such passages.

However, useful as such a work would be, it would not solve the problems illustrated by Clapham Junction, Bond Street, and the Forth Bridge. The Forth Bridge would be there, in the subdomain of BRIDGES, but simply as a gazetteer entry, with information about its location, size, shape, and so on. In a fuller entry, there might indeed be some cultural references, such as to films in which it has appeared—the climax to Alfred Hitchcock's *The 39 Steps* (1935) is a famous instance. But none of this would help learners understand why someone would refer to this bridge when weeding a garden. That requires a further element in an entry, in which figurative allusions are explained, and this requires a consideration of metaphor. So in addition to the third lexical category identified above—*Culture-specific vocabulary, used literally*—we now need a fourth: *Culture-specific vocabulary, used metaphorically*

## 5. Cultural Metaphors

The classical account of metaphor (Richards, 1936) identifies the two elements that enter into this figure of speech: the *tenor* is "the underlying idea or principal subject" of the metaphorical expression; the *vehicle* is the entity which has properties that the creator of the metaphor attaches to this idea. For example, if Hilary says *Our garden is a jungle*, *garden* is the tenor, what she wants to talk about, and *jungle* is the vehicle, the metaphorical way she wants to talk about it. For a metaphor to be successful, it is crucial that both elements are known and have some evident relationship to each other. We have to know what a jungle is like to make sense of Hilary's sentence. If she had said *Our garden is a quadratic equation*, the metaphor would fail for most people (except perhaps for mathematicians and poets), because either they do not know what a quadratic equation is, or they find it difficult to see how its properties relate to the properties of a garden.

The examples at the beginning of this chapter all illustrate metaphors where the speaker assumes a level of cultural knowledge. In *It was like Clapham Junction in there*, the tenor is 'a chaotic situation', and the vehicle is 'Clapham Junction'. In the other cases, there are two vehicles (italicised):

> This is like *painting* the *Forth Bridge* [tenor: 'weeding']
> Our hotel made *Fawlty Towers* look like *the Ritz* [tenor 'hotel accommodation']
> I'm afraid my watch is more *Portobello Road* than *Bond Street* [tenor: 'cost of watch']

These are all examples from British English. An example from American English is *That was from out in left field*, said by a lecturer in response to a question that evidently took him by surprise. The tenor is 'unexpected question', and the vehicle is 'baseball', the specific allusion being to a situation where the ball is returned from the left side of the outfield, as seen from the home base, thus taking the runner by surprise. An example from South African English is *Let's go graze*, said by one hungry student to another. The tenor is 'needing to eat' and the vehicle is 'animals feeding on grass'. Examples like this illustrate the importance of understanding culturally-rooted metaphors across the Englishes-speaking world. Recent research on world Englishes has started to investigate cultural metaphors (see, e.g., contributions in Callies and Onysko 2017, and in Callies and Degani 2021). Findings from these and other future studies could help to inform the taxonomic approach to cultural metaphors.

Another important source of cultural adaptation is the catch phrase, as the original usage is readily applied to a wide variety of situations. If someone uses a catch phrase to create an effect in a conversation, or indirectly alludes to one, its success totally depends on the listener's ability to recognize its origin. Film and television provide the largest category of illustrations:

> *Star Wars*: May the force be with you. [said to someone about to clean his car]
> *Star Trek*: I'm boldly going! [said by a man about to take a first trip on a zip wire]
> *Batman* movies: Good thinking, Batman [said by a mother in response to a suggestion made by her son]
> *Monty Python*: And now for something completely different [said by a host introducing speeches at a wedding reception]
> *Blue Peter*: This is something I made earlier [hostess bringing in a plate of meringues]

In the most famous cases, the allusion may by now be so well known that we have to consider it a part of Standard English: the item would appear in a general dictionary as an idiom without a regional stylistic label. (*Catch 22* would be an example from the LITERATURE domain.) I wonder if there is any variety of English these days where *May the force be with you* would be opaque? Or *Batman*? But I imagine items deriving from *Monty Python* or *Blue Peter* would be completely missed in many places, and remain features of a specifically British cultural identity.

It is not at all obvious just how many items identified in the cultural taxonomy would give rise to this kind of metaphorical adaptation. In principle, any of them might be the vehicle of such an expression. In practice, certain domains prove to be much more exploited than others. In an analysis of all the cultural entries in the second edition of the Longman dictionary, there were 214 where I could easily find an adaptation, and 75 percent of these came from just six domains: Television (39), Literature (34), Recreation (22), Cinema (20), Society (20), Beliefs (16), Communication (12). But a personal survey of this kind is not enough, as any one person's intuition will bring to mind adaptations that reflect individual experience, and these may not be shared by others. Those who know Shakespeare or the King James Bible well will be likely to use adaptations in their conversations which reflect their knowledge of the texts and which would be missed by anyone unfamiliar with them. Only a large-scale and long-term international study could provide a robust account of the range of situations where adaptations take place, providing data on frequency of use and an evaluation of effectiveness (such as the "likes" used in social media). Constructing an online site so that the data can be easily seen, and items from different countries easily compared, will also provide a Web designer with interesting challenges.

## 6. Conclusion

These challenges have to be faced, for the problem of intercultural linguistic opacity is increasing as countries continue to adapt English to meet their needs. These needs are usually seen in relation to a country's desire to be part of the global English-speaking community. But alongside this natural drive to foster mutual intelligibility, there is the equally important drive to express national identity; and as this second force grows, it begins to interfere with the first. This is never a big problem for a "new English" in its early days of emergence; but once that initial period is over, and a country begins to "own" English in a mature manner, then the scale of the problem begins to grow. It can be seen especially in a country's literature written in English, where novelists, for example, confidently write about their home experience using local expressions, literally and metaphorically. And these days English writing is increasingly encountered in Web pages and social media, as in my Zurich example.

An intercultural perspective, finally, prompts us towards an alternative interpretation of such labels as "Brazilian English." Traditionally, these labels referred to the errors introduced into the English of learners due to interference from their mother-tongue. In the approach outlined here, "Brazilian English" is now a positive term, not a negative one: it means the expressions used by capable English speakers in Brazil which identify its unique culture and which would be a potential source of misunderstanding to outsiders. Englishes that have long established their identity no longer have a problem in being described in this way. If I talk about "American English," "British English," "Australian English," and the like, there is no hint of apology in these labels. The varieties are seen as equals in a global English-speaking world. The ultimate aim of an international cultural reference work would be to help all varieties of the language achieve this status.

## Appendix

This is a modified version of the Global Data Model taxonomy, with some of the superordinate headings in the hierarchy omitted for reasons of space. It shows 1,180 domains. Also omitted from the online version are subdomains for the geography and history of individual countries. These have been grouped into broad geographical areas, because in a cultural table these countries would provide the horizontal axis, as follows:

| Domain | British English | USA English | Indian English | Brazilian etc. English |
|---|---|---|---|---|
| ... | | | | |
| Water control | | | | |
| Rivers | | | | |
| Waterfalls etc. | | | | |

**Universe**
Cosmos
  Observation of the cosmos
  Stars & constellations
  General cosmological notions
  Non-planetary bodies
  Solar system
  Astrology
Space exploration
  Space missions
  Space vehicles
Extraterrestrial life
Time
  Measurement of time
  Time-keeping

**Earth Science**
Atmosphere
Climate
Earth general
  Earth study
  Earth history
Earth formation
  Earth dynamics
    Earth surface processes
  Earth cycles
  Earthquakes
  Earth tectonics
  Tsunamis
  Volcanoes
Earth resources
  Minerals
  Rocks
  Energy sources
Earth surface features
  Water bodies

    Freshwater bodies
      Groundwater features
      Inland water features
      Water control
      Rivers
      Waterfalls
    Saltwater bodies
      Currents
      Coastline water features
      Sea control
      Oceans and seas
  Land relief features
    Sea floor
    Caves
    Deserts
    Ice features
    Mountains
    Coastline land features
    Plateaux
    Islands
    Earth vegetation
    Valleys

**Environment**
Farming
  Farming policy
  Farming practice
  Agriculture
  Animal husbandry
Gardening
  Horticulture
    Garden design
    Garden tools
    Garden plants
    Gardening exhibitions
Environmental habitats

Rural environment
Urban environment
Environmental care
Environmental damage
Environmental protection
Environmental study

**Natural history**
  Study of natural history
  Eukaryotes [plants, fungi, animals, protoctista]
    Plants
      Bryophyta [liverworts, mosses]
      Plant diseases
      Gymnosperms [trees, shrubs]
        Cycadophyta [cycads]
        Gnetophyta [cone-bearing desert plants]
        Coniferophyta [conifers, ginkgos]
      Lycopodiophyta [clubmosses]
      Angiosperms [flowering plants]
        Dicotyledons
          Caryophyllidae [sorrel, dock]
          Dilleniidae [heathers]
          Hamamelidae [witch hazel, chestnut, oak]
          Magnoliidae [vines]
          Rosidae [hawthorn, laburnum]
          Asteridae [petunia, marigold, foxglove, chamomile]
        Monocotyledons
          Commelinidae [grasses, cereals]
          Liliidae [daffodils, bluebells, tulips]
          Arecidae [dates, palms, coconuts]
          Alismatidae [water plants]
          Zingiberidae [ginger, arrowroot, herbs]
      Pteridophyta, Filicinophyta [ferns]
      Equisetophyta, Sphenophyta [horsetails]
      Psilophyta [whiskferns]
    Fungi
      Basidiomycota [mushrooms, stinkhorns]
      Ascomycota [yeasts, truffles]
      Zygomycota, deuteromycota [moulds, pathogenic yeasts]
    Animals
      Chordates
        Cephalachordata [amphioxus, lancelet]
        Tunicata [tunicates, sea squirts]
        Vertebrates
          Birds
            Procellariiformes [petrels, albatrosses]
            Podicipediformes [grebes]
            Falconiformes [falcons, kites, eagles]
            Galliformes [chickens, peafowl, grouse]
            Sphenisciformes [penguins]
            Pelecaniformes [pelicans, gannets, cormorants]
            Coliiformes [mousebirds]
            Ciconiiformes [herons, flamingoes, spoonbills]
            Apterygiformes [kiwis]
            Coraciiformes [kingfishers, hornbills]
            Rheiformes [rheas]
            Casuariiformes [emus, cassowaries]
            Apodiformes [thorntails, swifts]
            Caprimulgiformes [nightjars, goatsuckers]
            Gruiformes [coots, cranes, buttonquails]
            Charadriiformes [curlews, guillemots, puffins]
            Cuculiformes [cuckoos, roadrunners]
            Trogoniformes [trogons]
            Columbiformes [pigeons]
            Psittaciformes [cockatoos, parrots, lovebirds]
            Anseriformes [swans, geese, ducks]
            Strigiformes [owls]
            Struthioniformes [ostriches]
            Tinamiformes [tinamous]
            Gaviiformes [loons]
            Passeriformes [garden birds]
            Piciformes [toucans, woodpeckers, puffbirds]
          Fish
            Chondrichthyes [sharks, rays, skates]
            Agnatha [lampreys, hagfish]
            Sarcopterygii [dipnoi, lungfish]
            Osteichthyes [bony fishes]
              Elopiformes [tarpons, ladyfish]
              Perciformes [angelfish, mullet, mackerel, tuna]
Clupeiformes [sardines, herrings, anchovies]
Atheriniformes [moonfish, rainbowfish, garfish]
Gasterosteiformes [sticklebacks, pipefish, snipefish]
Pleuronectiformes [flounder, halibut, plaice]
Salmoniformes [salmon, trout]
Paracanthopterygii [perch, cod]

Osteoglossiformes [featherback, butterfly fish]
Ostariophysi [minnows, carp, barbel]
Scorpaeniformes [rockfish, lumpfish, razorfish]
Tetraodontiforms pufferfish, sunfish, boxfish]
Actinopterygii, Acipenseriformes, Polypteriformes [sturgeon, reedfish]
Anguilliformes [eels]
Mammals
  Proboscidea [elephants]
  Chiroptera [bats]
  Edentata [anteaters, armadilloes]
  Perissodactyla [horses, zebras]
  Marsupialia [kangeroos, koalas]
  Lagomorpha [rabbits, hares]
  Carnivora [dogs, cats]
    Caniformia [dogs, seals, walruses, badgers, bears]
    Feliformia [cats, lions, tigers, hyaenas]
  Monotremata [platypuses]
  Primates [monkeys, humans]
  Rodentia [rats, mice]
  Insectivora [hedgehogs, shrews]
  Ectacea [whales, dolphins]
  Tubulidentata [aardvarks]
  Sirenia [manatees]
  Artiodactyla [pigs, sheep, antelopes]
Amphibia
  Urodela, Trachystomata, Caudata [hellbinders, newts]
  Gymnophonia [wormlike amphibians]
  Anura [frogs, toads]
Reptiles
  Crocodilia [crocodiles, alligators]
  Chelonia [turtles, tortoises]
  Rhynchocephalia [lizards]
  Squamata [wormlizards]
    Sauria [geckos, chameleons]
    Serpents [snakes, vipers]
Metazoa [invertebrates]
  Brachiopoda [lamp shells]
  Ctenophora [jellies, sea gooseberries]
    Tardigrada [liverworts, bearworms]
    Platyhelminthes [flatworms, flukes]
    Gnasthostomulida [intertidal marine worms]
    Nematomorpha [hairworms, gordions]
    Pentastoma [respiratory parasites in vertebrates]
    Kinorhyncha [mud dragons]
    Loricifera [microscopic marine sediment-dwelling]
    Nematoda [eelworms, hookworms, roundworms]
    Acanthocephala [spiny-headed worms]
    Priapulida [priapulus]
    Mollusca [clams, oysters, octopus, squid]
    Arthropoda [crustaceans, insects]
      Crustacea [lobsters, crabs, barnacles]
      Myriapoda [centipedes, millipedes]
      Pterygota [flies, bees]
      Arachnida [spiders]
      Gastrotricha [hairybacks]
    Entoprocta [tiny aquatic, anus inside]
    Echinodermata [urchins, starfish]
    Chaetognatha [arrowworms]
    Phoronida [horseshoe worms]
    Cnidaria [coral, jellyfish]
    Ectoprocta [moss animals]
    Onychophora [velvet worms]
    Nemertina [marine worms, ribbonworms]
    Annelida [earthworms, fanworms]
    Pogonophra [beardworms]
    Hemichordata [acorn worms]
    Rotifera [rotifers, wheel animalcules]
    Echiura [spoon worms]
    Sipuncula [peanut worms]
    Mesozoa [wormlike marine parasites]
Protoctista [*see below*]
  Myxomycota [slime moulds]
  Protophytes [*no everyday name*]
  Protozoa [*no everyday name*]
Prokaryotes [*see below*]
Bacteria
  Cyanophycota [*no everyday name*]
  Prochlorophycota [*no everyday name*]
Viruses

**Human beings**
Human body
  Human appearance
  Human movement
  Human development
  Human fitness
  Human anatomy
  Human physiology
  Human sensation

- Clothing
  - Clothes fashion
  - Clothes making
  - Clothing the body
    - Headwear
    - Clothes for the limbs
      - Clothes for the lower limbs
        - Footwear
        - Legwear
      - Clothes for the upper limbs
    - Clothes for the torso
      - Clothes for the torso as a whole
      - Clothes for the lower torso
      - Clothes for the upper torso and neck
- Body decoration
- Dangers and accidents to the body
- Medicine
  - General medical concepts
  - Medical diagnosis
    - Pathological analysis
    - General medical techniques
  - Diseases
    - Circulatory diseases
      - Blood disease
      - Immune disease
      - Lymphatic disease
      - Pulmonary disease
      - Heart disease
    - Skin disease
    - Ear disease
    - Mouth disease & dentistry
    - Gastro-intestinal diseases
      - Gastro-intestinal disease
      - Endocrine disease
      - Kidney & urinary disease
    - Reproduction
      - Pregnancy & birth
      - Childhood disease
      - Male & female reproduction
    - Eye disease
    - Connective tissue disease
    - Brain & neural disease
  - Hospital care
    - Hospitals
    - Nursing
  - Medical organizations
  - Alternative medicine
    - Acupuncture
    - Alexander technique
    - Aromatherapy
    - Art therapy
    - Auricular therapy
    - Ayurvedic medicine
    - Bach flower remedies
    - Chelation therapy
    - Chiropractic
    - Colonic irrigation
    - Color therapy
    - Cranial osteopathy
    - Crystal therapy
    - Cupping
    - Cymatics
    - Dance therapy
    - Ear candling
    - Feldenkrais method
    - Feng shui
    - Flotation therapy
    - Gestalt therapy
    - Herbalism
    - Homeopathy
    - Hydrotherapy
    - Iridology
    - Kinesiology
    - Light therapy
    - Magnetic therapy
    - Naprapathy
    - Naturopathy
    - Negative ion therapy
    - Osteopathy
    - Polarity therapy
    - Qigong
    - Rebirthing
    - Reflexology
    - Reiki
    - Rolfing
    - Sex therapy
    - Shiatsu
    - Sitz bath therapy
    - Spagyric therapy
    - Tai chi chuan
    - Thalassotherapy
    - Traditional Chinese medicine
    - Trager psychophysical integration
    - Transcutaneous Electrical Nerve Stimulation
    - Water birth
  - Psychiatry
  - Medical treatment
    - Blood services
    - General medical procedures
    - Paramedical services
    - Surgical intervention
- Nutrition
  - Cookery
    - Cookery methods
    - Cookery equipment
  - Food and drink
    - Drinks
      - Non-alcoholic drinks
      - Alcoholic drinks
    - Confectionery
      - Bakery
      - Sweets and candies
    - Dairy products

　　　　　Food flavorings
　　　　　Food provision
　　　　　　Meat
　　　　　　Seafood
　　　　　　Fruit and nuts
　　　　　　Vegetables
　　Nutritional science
　　　　　Nutritional disorders
　　　　　Diet
　　　　　Food constituency
　　Eating and drinking
　　　　Catering
　　　　　Eating locations
　　　　　Catering management
　　　　Meals
　　　　Eating implements
　　Paranormal activity
　　Drugs
　　　　Medical drugs
　　　　Recreational drugs
　　Psychology
　　　　Human behavior
　　　　Human cognition
　　　　Human emotions
　　　　Human personality
　　　　Human perception
　　　　　Human perception of sound
　　　　　Human perception of taste
　　　　　Human perception of smell
　　　　　Human perception of touch
　　　　　Human perception of vision
　　　　Study of psychology
　　Human safety

**Human activities**
　　Arts and crafts
　　　　Arts in general
　　　　Decorative arts and crafts
　　　　　Basketry
　　　　　Ceramics
　　　　　Floral arts
　　　　　Glassware
　　　　　Stained glass
　　　　　Jewelry
　　　　　Lacquerwork
　　　　　Metalwork
　　　　　Enamelwork
　　　　　Mosaic
　　　　　Carpets
　　　　　Needlework
　　　　　Tapestry
　　Literature
　　　　Literature in general
　　　　Literary study
　　　　　Literary criticism
　　　　　Literary style
　　　　Creative writing
　　　　　Drama
　　　　　Prose literature
　　　　　　Fiction
　　　　　　　Novels
　　　　　　　　Crime novels
　　　　　　　　Adventure & thriller novels
　　　　　　　　Historical novels
　　　　　　　　Romantic novels
　　　　　　　　Science fiction & fantasy novels
　　　　　　　　Supernatural & horror novels
　　　　　　　　War and spy novels
　　　　　　　　Westerns
　　　　　　　Short fiction works
　　　　　　Non-fiction literature
　　　　　　　Biographies
　　　　　　　Diaries
　　　　　　　Humorous & satirical literature
　　　　　　　Short nonfiction works
　　　　　　　Travel literature
　　　　　Poetry
　　　Music
　　　　Musicology
　　　　Recording of music
　　　　Visual representation of music
　　　　Musical composition
　　　　　Classical music composition
　　　　　　Instrumental music composition
　　　　　　Opera composition
　　　　　Popular music composition
　　　　Technical production of music
　　　　Presentation of music
　　　　　Classical music presentation
　　　　　Instrumental music presentation
　　　　　Vocal music presentation
　　　　　Modern music presentation
　　　　　Folk music
　　　　　Jazz
　　　　　Media music
　　　　　Musicals
　　　　　Popular music presentation
　　　　Religious music
　　　Performing arts
　　　　Cinema in general
　　　　　Cinema performance
　　　　　Cinema evaluation
　　　　　Cinema production
　　　　Dance in general
　　　　Dance performance
　　　　　Ballet
　　　　　Dancing
　　　　　Ethnic dance
　　　　　Study of dance
　　　　　Production of dance
　　　　Radio in general
　　　　Radio performance
　　　　　Radio evaluation
　　　　　Radio production

    Theatre in general
      Theatrical performance
        Circus
        Theatre acting
        Theatrical entertainment
        Puppetry
        Magic as entertainment
        Mime
      Theatre evaluation
      Theatre production
    Television in general
      Television performance
      Television evaluation
      Television production
Visual arts
    Graphic arts
      Graphic artworks
      Graphic art techniques
    Engraving
      Engraving artworks
      Engraving art techniques
    Photography as art
    Painting as art
      Painting artworks
      Painting art techniques
    Sculpture
      Sculpture artworks
      Sculpture techniques
Beliefs
    Mythology
      Folklore
      Legends
      Myths
    Ancient and native beliefs
      African beliefs
      American beliefs
        Middle American beliefs
        North American beliefs
        South American beliefs
      Middle Eastern beliefs
        Egyptian beliefs
        Phoenician beliefs
        Assyro-Babylonian beliefs
        Persian beliefs
      Pacific beliefs
      Prehistoric beliefs
      European beliefs
        Celtic beliefs
        Finno-Ugric beliefs
        Ancient Greek beliefs
        Ancient Roman beliefs
        Slavonic beliefs
        Teutonic beliefs
    Religion
    General religious notions
    Buddhism
      Buddhist beliefs
      Buddhist practices
      Buddhist sources
    Christianity
      Christian individuals
      Christian locations
      Christian practices
      Christian sources
      Christian beliefs
      Christian groups
        Catholics
        Protestants
          Baptists
          Millenarianism
          Mormons
          Jehovah's Witnesses
          Quakers
          Methodists
        Christian Orthodox
    Hinduism
      Hindu beliefs
      Hindu practices
      Hindu sources
    Islam
      Islamic beliefs
      Islamic practices
      Islamic sources
    Judaism
      Judaic beliefs
      Judaic practices
      Judaic sources
    Confucianism
    Jainism
    Unitarianism
    Zoroastrianism & Parseeism
    Shintoism
    Sikhism
    Taoism
    Lamaism
    Minority belief systems
      Wicca
      Divination
      Gnosticism
      New Age
      Spiritualism
      Shamanism
      Scientology
      Satanism
      Theosophy
      Voodoo
      Witchcraft
Mediums of communication
    Study of communication
    Advertising
      Broadcasting medium
      Methods of communication
        Special systems of communication
        Secret systems of communication

Alternative systems of
  communication
Means of communication
  Postal communication
  Electronic communication
  Graphic communication
Nonverbal communication
  Auditory communication
  Visual communication
Language
  Language in general
  Language in use
    Language structure
    Spoken language
    Written language
    Sign language
    Grammar
    Vocabulary
  Language evaluation
  Language disability
Publishing
  General publishing notions
  Editorial content
    Books
    Newspapers & magazines
      Content of newspapers &
      magazines
      Editions of newspapers &
      magazines
    Bookmaking
      Printing
      Papermaking
    Typography
      Page layout
      Typefaces
  Publishing sales & marketing
    Bookselling
    Selling newspapers & magazines
Knowledge
  Education
    Teaching and learning
    Educational institutions
      Further education
      Schools
        Younger schooling
        Older schooling
      Vocational training
    Educational resources
      Knowledge management
        Oral transmission of
        knowledge
        Retrieval of knowledge
          Bibliography
          Indexing
        Storage of knowledge
          Libraries
          Computer storage

Philosophy
  Classical philosophy (BC and early AD)
  Medieval philosophy
  Modern philosophy (from 16th century)
Reference science
Science & sciences
  General science
  Biology
    Biochemistry
      Biochemical elements
      Genetic chemistry
      Hormones
      Biological energy
    Biological cells
      Biological cell division
      Biological cell structures
    Genetics & heredity
    Embryology
    Biological organisms
    Ecology
    Palaeobiology
    Biological taxonomy
    Evolution
    Biological study
  Mathematics
    Mathematical graphs & charts
    Geometry & trigonometry
    Algebra
    Arithmetic
    Statistics
  Physical sciences
    Chemistry
      Chemical elements
      Analytical chemistry
      Inorganic chemistry
      Organic chemistry
      Chemical apparatus
    Physics
      Mechanics
        Classical mechanics
        Quantum mechanics
          Fundamental particles
          Atoms & nuclei
          Nuclear energy
      Relativity
      Waves (physics)
      Electromagnetism
      Acoustics
      Optics
      Properties of matter
        Fluid mechanics
        Solid state physics
        Thermodynamics
        Electricity
      Study of physics
Technology
  Building

Interior design of buildings
Soft furnishings
Upholstery
Floor coverings
Hangings and window dressing
  Household linens
Cleaning & care of buildings
  Textile cleaning in buildings
  Surface and object cleaning
    Dry cleaning in buildings
    Wet cleaning in buildings
Decoration of buildings
Furniture
  Furniture-making
  Design of furniture
  Types of furniture
  Furniture tools & materials
Buildings in general
  Planning of buildings
  Sale of buildings
  Architecture
  Dwellings
    Types of dwelling
    Structural elements of a dwelling
  Building professions
    Construction of buildings
      Construction of building interiors
      Construction of building exteriors
    General notions in building
    Security of buildings
    Safety of buildings
    Utilities in buildings
      Electricity in buildings
        Lighting in buildings
        Electricity supply in buildings
      Gas supply in buildings
      Heating in buildings
      Ventilation in buildings
      External plumbing in buildings
      Internal plumbing in buildings

Computing
  Computer science
  Computer hardware
    Computer central processing
    Computer peripherals
  Computer software
    Computer programming
    Computer systems
Electrical engineering
  Electrical equipment in general
  Audio and video equipment
Material science
Optical technology
  General optical notions
  Photographic technology
Energy & power supply
Mechanical technology
  Machines & engines
  Engineering
  Tools & devices
Textiles
Transportation
  Air transportation
    Air travel
      Air piloting
      Air services
      Air safety
    Air vehicles
      Air vehicles in general
      Air vehicle design & manufacture
        Air vehicle construction
        Air vehicle design
      Air vehicle products
      Commercial air vehicles
        Air vehicles for business
        Air vehicles for general public
      Types of air vehicle
        Balloons as air vehicles
        Air cushion vehicles
        Gliders
        Helicopters
        Aeroplanes
        Vintage air vehicles
      Aeroplane maintenance
      Aeroplane parts
    Airports and airways
      Airport construction
      Airway organization
      Air traffic control
  Goods transportation
    Containers for transporting goods

  Transporting goods
  Packaging goods for transportation
 Rail transportation
  Rail system
   Railways
    Railway tracks
    Railway organization
   Rail traffic control
  Rail travel
   Rail services
   Rail safety
   Rail journeys
  Rail vehicles
   Rail vehicles in general
   Construction of rail vehicles
   Design of rail vehicles
   Rail products
    Commercial rail vehicles
     Rail vehicles for business
     Rail vehicles for general public
    Types of rail vehicle
    Vintage rail vehicles
   Rail vehicle maintenance
   Rail vehicle parts
 Road transportation
  Driving on roads
   Requirements for driving on roads
   Road safety issues
   Road vehicle requirements
  Road management
   Roads
    Road construction
    Organization of roads
   Traffic control
    Methods of traffic control
    Highway code
  Road vehicles
   Road vehicle performance
   Road vehicle construction
   Road vehicle design
   Road vehicle products
    Commercial road vehicles
     Business & industrial road vehicles
     Public road vehicles
    Domestic road vehicles
     Bicycles
     Motorbikes
     Motorless road vehicles
     Automobiles
     Underfoot rollers
    Vintage road vehicles
   Road vehicles maintenance
   Road vehicle parts
    Road vehicle body & accessories
    Road vehicle cooling systems
    Road vehicle fuel & exhausts
    Road vehicle ignition
    Road vehicle braking systems
    Road vehicle electrical systems
    Road vehicle engines
    Road vehicle engine block
    Road vehicle engine cylinder head
    Road vehicle engine carburetor
    Road vehicle suspension and steering
    Road vehicle transmission systems
   Road vehicle marketing
 Water transportation
  Travel by water
   Water travel services
   Water travel piloting
   Water travel safety
  Water vehicles
   Water vehicles in general
   Water vehicle construction
   Water vehicle design
  Water vehicle products
   Commercial water vehicles
   Water vehicles for business & industrial
   Water vehicle for general public
   Water vehicle types
    Non-motorized, non-sailing water vehicles
    Motorized water vehicles
    Water vehicles with sails
   Vintage & ancient water vehicles
  Water vehicle maintenance
  Water vehicle parts
 Waterways
  Traffic control of waterways
  Construction of water routes
  Organization of water routes

## Society
Economics
 General economic notions
  Commerce
   Commercial profit-making
   Commercial non-profit-making
  Economic theory
  Employment
   Employment conditions
   Employment earnings
   Employment conflicts
 Finance
  Personal financial management
   Account management

- Saving and borrowing
- Foreign exchange
- Financial markets
- Government financial management
  - Accountancy
  - Taxation
- General finance notions
- Insurance
- Money
- Law
  - Lawcourt systems
    - Lawcourt procedure
    - Lawcourt organization
  - General legal notions
  - Dealing with crime
    - Criminal enquiry
      - Detection and arrest
      - Police
      - Evidence of crime
    - Crime prevention
    - Crime punishment
  - Legal domains
    - Commercial law
    - Criminal law
      - Drugs law
      - Crimes relating to people
        - Homicide
        - Sex crimes
        - Injury & threat crime
        - Crimes against children
      - Crimes relating to objects
        - Criminal damage
        - Theft
    - Family law
    - International law
    - Property law
    - Inheritance law
    - Tort
- Military affairs
  - Peace movements
  - Armed forces
    - Army
    - Navy
    - Airforce
  - Military science
  - Military technology
    - General military notions
    - Defensive weaponry
    - Offensive weaponry
  - War
- Politics
  - General political notions
  - Political beliefs
  - Political activities
    - National political activities
    - International political activities
    - Political elections
  - Political groups
    - Local political groups
    - National political groups
    - International political groups
- Sexual matters
  - Meeting and dating
  - Sexual behavior
- Society and culture
  - Anthropology
  - Social structure
    - Genealogy
    - Heraldry
    - Position in society
    - Primary social groups
    - Social rights of passage
    - Secondary social groups
    - Social institutions
    - Study of society
- Terrorism

**Recreation**
- General leisure notions
  - Leisure activities
    - Social leisure activities
      - Bellringing
      - Funfairs
      - Fireworks
      - Parties
    - Outward bound activities
      - Animal sports
      - Ballooning
      - Bungee jumping
      - Guiding and scouting
      - Mountaineering
      - Underwater diving
      - Parachuting
      - Quad biking
      - Rambling
      - Skateboarding
      - Caving & potholing
      - Whitewater rafting
      - Wakeboarding
      - Windsurfing
- Gambling
  - Gambling in games
  - Gambling in sports
    - Gambling in animal sports
    - Gambling in football
- Games
  - Board & surface games
    - Backgammon
    - Chess
    - Dominoes
    - Draughts / Checkers
    - Go (game)
    - Monopoly (game)
    - Shuffleboard

　　　　　Shogi
　　　Chance & reward games
　　　　　Bingo
　　　　　Craps
　　　　　Pachinko
　　　　　Roulette
　　　Computer & video games
　　　Card & tile games
　　　　　Baccarat
　　　　　Blackjack
　　　　　Bezique
　　　　　Canasta
　　　　　Contract bridge
　　　　　Cribbage
　　　　　Mah jong
　　　　　Poker
　　　　　Pinochle
　　　　　Rummy
　　　　　Card tricks
　　　　　Tarot cards
　　　　　Whist
　　　Projectile games
　　　　Bagatelle
　　　　Frisbee
　　　　Paintball
　　　　Quoits
　　　　Rounders
　　　　Skittles
　　　Puzzle & word games
　　　　Crosswords
　　　　Rubik's cube
　　　　Scrabble
Pastimes
　　Collecting as a pastime
　　　　Numismatics
　　　　Antiquarian books
　　　　Philately
　　Creative hobbies
　　　　Knitting
　　　　Modelling
　　　　Quilting
　　　　Origami
　　Playful activities
　　　　Kites
　　　　Models & miniatures
　　　　Toys
Sport
　　Animal sports
　　　　Equestrianism
　　　　　Cross country equestrianism
　　　　　Dressage
　　　　　Show jumping
　　　　Polo
　　　　Angling
　　　　Animal racing
　　　　　Greyhound racing
　　　　　Horse racing
　　　　　Rodeo
　　Aerial sports
　　　　Hang gliding
　　Athletic sports
　　　　Athletics
　　　　Biathlon
　　　　Orienteering
　　　　Walking as a sport
　　Ball sports
　　　Bat & ball sports
　　　　Baseball
　　　　Cricket
　　　　Softball
　　　Foot & ball sports
　　　　American football
　　　　Australian rules football
　　　　Canadian football
　　　　Soccer
　　　　Gaelic football
　　　　Rugby league/union
　　　Hand & ball sports
　　　　Basketball
　　　　Court handball
　　　　Handball
　　　　Korfball
　　　　Netball
　　　　Volleyball
　　　　Water polo
　　　Racket & ball sports
　　　　Badminton
　　　　Pelota
　　　　Real tennis
　　　　Squash
　　　　Table tennis
　　　　Tennis, lawn/court
　　　Stick & ball sports
　　　　Bandy
　　　　Croquet
　　　　Golf
　　　　Field hockey
　　　　Hurling
　　　　Ice hockey
　　　　Lacrosse
　　　Throwing/pushing/sliding ball sports
　　　　Bowls
　　　　Curling
　　　　Ten-pin bowling
　　Combat
　　　　Boxing
　　　　Fencing
　　　　Martial arts
　　　　　Kendo
　　　　　Karate
　　　　　Judo
　　　　　Sumo
　　　　Wrestling
　　Gymnastics

Gymnastics
Trampolining
Rink sports
  Roller skating
  Skating
    Figure skating/ice dance
    Distance/speed/short-track skating
Snooker, Billiards, Pool
Snow sports
  Skiing
  Toboggan, Bobsleigh, Luge
Strength sports
  Powerlifting
  Tug of war
  Weightlifting
Target sports
  Darts
  Archery
  Shooting as a sport
  Vehicle sports
    Cycling as a sport
    Motor vehicle sports
      Motorcycle racing
      Car racing
Water sports
  Open water sports
    Canoeing
    Powerboat racing
    Rowing as a sport
    Surfing as a sport
    Sailing as a sport
    Water skiing
  Swimming and diving

**Geographical locations**
Geographical studies
  Geography
  Mapping
  Travel
    Travel accommodation
    Travel destinations
    Travel guides
    Travel means and plans
      Journeys
      Travel planning
Sub-Saharan Africa-related
Asia-related
Australasia/Pacific-related
Europe-related
Middle America/Caribbean-related
North America-related
North Africa-related
Arctic/Antarctic-related
South America-related

**History**
Historical studies
Archaeology
Sub-Saharan Africa-related
Asia-related
Australasia/Pacific-related
Europe-related
Middle America/Caribbean-related
North America-related
North Africa-related
Arctic/Antarctic-related
South America-related

## Notes

1   https://www.pri.org/stories/2012–02–10/europe-s-deep-freeze-has-netherlands-buzzing-hopes-epic-elfstedentocht-ice-race, Feb 10, 2012, last accessed April 13, 2020.

## References

Ames, P. (2012), "Europe's deep freeze has Netherlands buzzing with hopes for epic Elfstedentocht ice race," *Global Post*, February 10. Available online: https://www.pri.org/stories/2012–02–10/europe-s-deep-freeze-has-netherlands-buzzing-hopes-epic-elfstedentocht-ice-race (last accessed April 13, 2020).

Branford, J. and W. Branford (1978/1991), *A Dictionary of South African English*, 4th edn, Cape Town: Oxford University Press.

Branford, J. and M. Venter (2016), *Say Again? The other side of South African English*, Cape Town: Pharos Dictionaries.

Callies, M. and A. Onysko, eds. (2017), "Metaphor Variation in Englishes Around the World," special issue of *Cognitive Linguistic Studies* 4 (1), Amsterdam: John Benjamins.

Callies, M. and M. Degani, eds. (2021), *Metaphor in Language and Culture across World Englishes*, London: Bloomsbury.

Cassidy, F.G. and R.B. Le Page (1967), *Dictionary of Jamaican English*, Cambridge: Cambridge University Press.

Crystal, D. (2010), "Semantic targeting: past, present, and future," *Aslib Proceedings*, 62 (4/5): 355–65.

Crystal, D. (2011), "The future of Englishes: going local," in R. Facchinetti, D. Crystal and B. Seidlhofer (eds.), *From International to Local English—and Back Again*, 17–25, Bern: Lang.

Crystal, D. (2014), "Making sense of sense," in E. Glaser, A. Kolmer, M. Meyer and E. Stark (eds.), *Sprache(n) verstehen*, 21–32, Zurich: vdf Hochschulverlag.

Crystal, D. (2017), "My priority for the next 50 years; an online cultural dictionary," *Teaching Language and Culture*, 1: 14–27.

Grote, D. (1992), *British English for American Readers*, Westport, CT: Greenwood Press.

Hannah, J. (1987), *Coping with England*, Oxford: Blackwell.

"Held to Anything but Esteem," *Punch, Or the London Charivari*, May 24, 1862.

*Oxford English Dictionary*. https://www.oed.com/

Richards, I.A. (1936), *The Philosophy of Rhetoric*. Oxford: Oxford University Press.

*State Symbols USA*. https://statesymbolsusa.org/us/symbols/state (last accessed April 14, 2020).

Summers, D, ed, (1992/1998/2004), *Longman Dictionary of English Language and Culture*, Harlow: Addison Wesley Longman.

*The 39 Steps* (1935), [Film] Dir. Alfred Hitchcock, UK: Gaumont British Picture Corporation.

Trudgill, P. (1982), *Coping with America*, Oxford: Blackwell.

Tui (2005), *Yeah right*, Auckland: Hachette Livre NZ.

*Urban Dictionary*. https://www.urbandictionary.com/

Winer, L. (2009), *Dictionary of the English/Creole of Trinidad and Tobago*, Quebec: McGill-Queens University Press.

Yule, H. and A.C. Burnell (1886), *Hobson-Jobson: a Glossary of Anglo-Indian Colloquial Words and Phrases*, London: John Murray.

# 10

# Colonial Cultural Conceptualizations and World Englishes

Frank Polzenhagen, Anna Finzel, and Hans-Georg Wolf

## 1. Introduction

Our chapter will explore texts written during the colonial period from a cognitive-cultural and cognitive-sociolinguistic perspective. Not only are the respective texts a window into the underlying mindset of the colonizers, but they also provide insights into the historical intellectual superstructure in which certain world Englishes developed. The contexts that will be addressed are India and sub-Saharan Africa. The text types chosen for analysis include key programmatic texts outlining the principles and objectives of colonial policies, for instance Lugard's *Dual Mandate*, League of Nations documents, reports commissioned by colonial authorities and legal texts.

In the first part of the chapter (Section 2), we will outline cultural conceptualizations and ideologies underlying British colonial policy at large with a particular focus on the conceptual construction of the "colonial subject," the local cultures and local languages. In this respect, India and sub-Saharan Africa represent quite different cases: while Indian "high culture" and Indian spirituality were generally held in high esteem by the British colonizers—at least in the academic circles—and orientalist (in the sense of Saïd) cultural conceptualizations were thriving, African spirituality and societal organization were regarded as downright "primitive." Since in both contexts many cultural practices were felt to be "disturbing" by the colonizers, the next part of this chapter (Section 3) will focus on some specific aspects of the local cultures and the way they were construed. The cultural notions we will address come from the domains of societal organization and religion/spirituality, more precisely the realms of (homo-)sexuality and witchcraft. In these realms, colonial conceptualizations drove legal regulations and efforts at cultural engineering by the colonizers, efforts which had lasting effects on some of the respective local patterns and practices.

The impact of colonial cultural conceptualizations, however, is not only one-sided but bidirectional. One straightforward linguistic manifestation of the other direction is borrowing from local languages to the so-called "common core" of English. The prime domains of borrowing and the absence of borrowing in others as well as the specific semantics of the loanwords readily reflect the colonial cultural conceptualizations under investigation. This point is addressed in Section 4. Section 5 provides some tentative conclusions.

With this scope, this chapter wishes to contribute a cognitive-sociolinguistic perspective on colonial contact situations and their repercussions in the settings and varieties of English involved.

## 2. The Metaphoric Construction of the Colonial Subject

It is a commonplace that there was no such thing as a unified philosophy or vision in Britain's attitude towards "her colonies." What we find instead is a diffuse set of various currents, some of them mutually incompatible, others reinforcing each other, and significant shifts with respect to the dominance and impact of individual currents over time. Likewise, there was no such thing as a unified stance towards all colonies; instead, the attitudes differed sharply depending on the individual context, for example India and Africa. However, a central common denominator of these attitudes and currents is the conceptual construction of the constellation between colonizer and colonized in terms of a more or less rigid US VERSUS THEM schema. This schema was spelled out in numerous dichotomies and oppositions, for instance in terms of rigid biological otherness (race, skin color), societal organization (civilized versus primitive) or moral qualities (Christian versus pagan), to name just a few. There is a wealth of studies on this colonial discourse of *othering* and on how it contributed to the construction of identity as COLONIZER and COLONIZED. The early classics in the field include Fanon (1952, 1961) and Saïd (1979). The latter, in particular, has shown that the way the OTHER is conceptualized is far more revealing about the conceptualizer than it is about the *other*. This literature has also stressed that the US VERSUS THEM schema was conceived, across the various domains, along a vertical axis, the colonizer (US) being UP (i.e., superior) and the colonized (THEM) being DOWN (i.e., inferior). However, we will argue that there was also a horizontal axis, namely with the colonizer conceptualized as AHEAD and the colonial subject as BEHIND.

In the following discussion, we will look into some of the ways this common conceptual base, that is US VERSUS THEM, combined with the image schemas UP VERSUS DOWN and AHEAD and BEHIND, was spelled out in terms of specific metaphoric conceptualizations that run through colonial discourse. In fact, the various currents and colonial attitudes can be straightforwardly characterized as different elaborations and interpretations of such conceptual metaphors.

One of our foci will be on metaphors that frame the relation between colonizer and colonized as constellations between PARENT (FATHER) and CHILD, ADULT and CHILD, or TEACHER and PUPIL. These abound in colonial discourse; below are some random illustrations from three centuries. The instantiations of the metaphors are highlighted in italics. Some of these quotes will also appear for further analysis in later sections.

> Knowing as we do the falsehood and impiety of idolatrous polytheistic superstitions, knowing the cruelties, the immoralities, the degrading extravagancies and impositions of the Hindoo system, we shall silently and calmly leave them in all the

fulness of their operation, without telling *our subjects, who ought to be our children*, that they are wrong, that they are deluded, and hence plunged into many miseries?

Grant 1796: 88

Wherever I look upon anyone connected with Africa, no matter how black his face, *I regards* [sic] *him or her as my own son or daughter.*
Robert Moffat, 1840, missionary in southern Africa, quoted in Cleall 2012: 6

He [the African] is an apt *pupil*.

Lugard 1922: 70

In brief, the virtues and the defects of this race-type are those of attractive *children*, whose confidence when once it has been won is given ungrudgingly as to an older and wiser superior, without question and without envy.

Lugard 1922: 70

The same sentiments also transpired in Article 22 of the covenant of the League of Nations, which was written around the same time as Lugard's text. It "expressed concern—as 'a sacred trust of civilization'—for the 'well-being and development' of 'peoples not yet able *to stand by themselves* under the strenuous conditions of the modern world'" (Wolf 2008: 556, italics added).

This quote at the same time points to conceptualizations of linearity sustained by a SOURCE-PATH-GOAL image schema and coupled with the EVENT STRUCTURE metaphor (see, e.g., Peña Cervel 2005), with STATES ARE LOCATIONS as one particular metaphor. Such conceptualizations are also evident in the colonial documents and will be discussed below.

The metaphors we will highlight are special in several respects. First of all, they frame the US VERSUS THEM constellation as a temporal condition; over time and given a proper "investment" on the side of the metaphoric PARENT, ADULT, TEACHER, the distance to the OTHER will reduce and eventually disappear: the CHILD will develop into an ADULT and into a PARENT; the PUPIL will reach eye level with the TEACHER, though the PARENT-CHILD relationship, as a logical entailment of the metaphor, will never cease to exist, of course.[1] Furthermore, the direction is fixed: it is a one-way route of "development," fostered by educational measures on the side of the colonizers and other agents such as missions. Moreover, these metaphors all entail the notions of a "responsibility," the PARENT or ADULT towards the CHILD, the TEACHER towards the PUPIL. Generally speaking, this metaphor system is intimately tied to and partly taken from Christian discourse, the FAMILY conceptualization in particular, evoking the notion of "family of man." US VERSUS THEM also underlies a set of cultural categories which does not allow for a reduction of distance, namely that of racial categories.

With their inherent features, or meaning foci (in the sense of Kövecses [2002] 2010), these conceptual structures are important access points to analyze the ambivalence and schizophrenia of colonial visions. They are also excellent cases in point to show the different attitudes of the colonizers towards specific colonial regions, for instance India and sub-Saharan Africa.

## 2.1 Flipped Roles Restored: The Case of India

As Trautmann (1997) aptly put it, British attitudes towards India oscillated between Indomania and Indophobia. Historically speaking, Indomania is first and foremost a product and ingredient of the early so-called New Orientalist school. The rise of New Orientalists in the second half of the eighteenth century is closely tied to the advent of Sanskrit studies at that time. Through Sanskrit, the European scholars got access to and explored the ancient Vedic literature as well as the ancient Indian texts on astronomy/ astrology, geometry, geography, and philosophy. The Orientalists' fascination with these texts was enormous. They put the ancient "Indian wisdom" and knowledge on a par with (if not above, at times) the ultimate reference points of the time, more precisely ancient Greek and Arabic scholarship, thus constructing a triad at the origin of Western culture and science. Here is how the Orientalist mathematician John Playfair concludes his comparative analysis of ancient Indian, Arab, Greek and modern Western astronomy:[2]

> That observations made in India when all Europe was barbarous or uninhabited, and investigations into the most subtle effects of gravitation made in Europe, near five thousand years afterwards, should thus come in mutual support of one another, is perhaps the most striking example of the progress and vicissitudes of science, which the history of mankind has yet exhibited.
>
> Playfair [1822] 2011: 128

In the same vein, the Orientalists' general account of Hinduism was highly favorable. As Trautmann (1997: 65) summarizes: "The main features, which are more or less the same in all the renderings, are two: that Hinduism is basically monotheistic [and hence constructed as being congenial to the Christian system; our addition], and that the benevolence of its religion and laws made India a prosperous and peaceful country before foreign conquest."

What was stressed was again the ancient origin of Hinduism and the associated societal organization, far outdating the Christian belief system and Western European "civilization." Many everyday practices and the colorful imagery of mundane Hinduism were certainly felt to be "disturbing" also by the Orientalists, but they were dismissed as later appropriations of the original spirit to the vulgar masses.

The Orientalist portrait of a perfect Indian high culture was completed, last but not least, with their admirable account of Sanskrit. Sanskrit studies were instrumental to the rise of comparative historical linguistics, with the Orientalist William Jones as its early most prominent exponent. His major achievement was a thorough account of the relatedness of Sanskrit (and Old Persian) with modern European languages of the various branches now classified as belonging to the Indo-European family.[3] Jones' view of Sanskrit could hardly be more enthusiastic: "The Sanscrit [sic] language, whatever be its antiquity, is of a wonderful structure; more perfect than the Greek, more copious than the Latin, and more exquisitely refined than either" (Jones 1786: n.p.).

What is important for our present concern is that the Orientalist construction of Indian high culture inevitably flipped the roles in the metaphor system sketched at the beginning of the section: if Indian civilization is far older than the British one, if Indian science predates the European one, if Sanskrit is the ancestral language (or close to it) of the European ones, including English, it is India that is superior and in the metaphoric role of the PARENT/ADULT while Britain is the CHILD. If ancient "Indian wisdom" is something Britain can learn from, it is India who is the TEACHER and Britain who is the metaphoric PUPIL. Hence, the Orientalist position ultimately challenges the very basics of the conceptual construction of the colonial self and the colonial subject.

Not surprisingly, the response to Orientalist positions was fierce in Britain, and within a few decades they were "killed off," as Trautmann (1997: 99) puts it. The anti-Orientalists launched a wholesale attack on virtually every aspect of Indian culture. The ideal(istic) Orientalist portrait of Indian high culture was countered with accounts of atrocities witnessed in ordinary Indian society, including practices such as child marriage, female child murder, widow burning (*sati*), or corporal punishments.[4] The following extracts from Charles Grant's ([1796] 1853)[5] *Observations on the State of Society among the Asiatic Subjects of Great Britain* provide a representative illustration of this discourse:

> The first that shall be mentioned is the shocking barbarity of their punishments. The cutting off legs, hands, noses, and ears, putting out of eyes, and other penal inflictions of a similar kind, all performed in the coarsest manner, abundantly justify our argument.
> 
> Grant [1792] 1853: 23

> But in Hindostan, mothers of families are taken from the midst of their children, who have just lost their father also, and by a most diabolical complication of force and fraud, are driven into the flames.
> 
> Grant [1796] 1853: 59

Added to such lists of actual atrocities are accounts of "immoral" practices in Indian society, including and highlighting those linked to sexuality. Again, Grant's report provides ample illustration thereof, covering the full "disturbing" range from polygamy, promiscuity, prostitution to homosexuality:[6]

> Polygamy, which is tolerated among the Hindoos, tends still more to destroy all rational domestic society.... As to the men, they are under little restraint from moral considerations. The laws of caste impose restrictions and fines for offences of the nature in question, so far as that distinction is concerned, but leave great scope for new connections, and for promiscuous intercourse, which is matter of little scruple or observation. Receptacles for women of infamous character are every where licensed, and the women themselves have a place in society. The female dancers, who are of this order, make the principal figure in the entertainments of ceremony given by the great. Indecency is the basis of their exhibitions; yet children and young persons of both sexes are permitted to be present at these shows, which have admittance even into the principal zenanas ['harem']. Licentious connections are therefore most common, though subsisting apparently without that intoxication of passion which hurries on the mind against conviction, and

carried on without much concealment, nay almost with the insensibility of brutes. On such points, the Hindoos seem to advert to no rule except what the law enjoins; there is no sentiment diffused at large through society, which attaches shame to criminality. Wide and fatal are the effects of this corruption of manners; a corruption not stopping here, but extending even to the unnatural practices of the ancient Heathens, though in these the Mahomedans are still more abandoned.

Grant [1796] 1853: 23–4[7]

The next target of Grant's attack is ordinary Hinduism, depicted by him as a conglomerate of "ridiculous," "scandalous," "filthy," "wicked" practices and imagery:

The character of the whole multitude of hindoo deities, male and female, is another source of immorality. The legends and histories of their actions are innumerable, and in the highest degree extravagant, absurd, ridiculous, and incredible. But the feature by which they are, above all, distinguished, is the abandoned wickedness of their divinities, Brahma, Vishnow, Mahadeo, (who are held to be respectively the creator, the preserver, and the destroyer of the world, ) and of all the rest, in their several subordinate capacities. The most enormous and strange impurities, the most villanous frauds and impostures, the most detestable cruelties and injustice, the most filthy and abominable conceits, every corrupt excess and indulgence, are presented to us in their histories, varied in a thousand forms. These scandalous legends are more or less known among all the millions of Hindostan; they form an immense series of adventures, which fill the imagination of a weak and credulous people; very many of them are perpetuated by images, temples, and ceremonies, and those of such a nature as it were pollution to describe.

Grant [1796] 1853: 50

Grant is unambiguous about the overall objectives of his report: it is to counter what "has suited the views of some philosophers" (Grant [1796] 1853: 20) and to make clear that their idealistic portrait of India has little to do with the Indian realities, and it is to assign to the Indian natives "their true place in the moral scale" (Grant [1796] 1853: 25). The colonial metaphoric system is firmly in place again: no flipped roles; the European is UP; the colonial subject is DOWN; the British are the ADULTS; the Indians are the metaphoric CHILDREN. Grant makes that very explicit in the following passage:

Whilst an [sic] European, deriving a *superiority* from his race, or from the station he is appointed to fill, regards only in a distant speculative way the effeminate exterior, adulatory address, and submissive demeanor of the Hindoos, he naturally enough conceives them to be a people in whom the mild and gentle qualities predominate. He is apt to consider them with a mixture of complacency and contempt; and even the bad dispositions towards each other, which he soon discovers to exist in them, *he may view with feelings analogous to those which the petty malignity of children, or of beings of a diminutive species, might excite.*

Grant [1796] 1853: 24, italics added

Grant is a fairly early proponent of a strict Anglicist position towards India, coupled with a strict Christianization stance. His *Observations* even predate Jones' major publications. The final blow in the so-called Orientalist–Anglicist debate in favor of the Anglicists came four decades later, in the 1830s. It is linked to a key text in British colonial history, Macaulay's *Minute on Indian Education* (1835). Since Grant's *Observations*, the general view of India had shifted from the romanticist picture of the New Orientalists to a pronounced Indophobia, at least with regard to the realities of the Indian colony. Macaulay could rely on this shift in public perception and could direct his decisive blow towards the very core of the Orientalist stance that was still maintained in academic circles, i.e., the great esteem held for Indian high culture. And this is what he did:

> I am quite ready to take the oriental learning at the valuation of the orientalists themselves. I have never found one among them who could deny that a single shelf of a good European library was worth the whole native literature of India and Arabia. The intrinsic superiority of the Western literature is indeed fully admitted by those members of the committee who support the oriental plan of education.
> 
> It will hardly be disputed, I suppose, that the department of literature in which the Eastern writers stand highest is poetry. And I certainly never met with any orientalist who ventured to maintain that the Arabic and Sanscrit [sic] poetry could be compared to that of the great European nations. But when we pass from works of imagination to works in which facts are recorded and general principles investigated, the superiority of the Europeans becomes absolutely immeasurable. It is, I believe, no exaggeration to say that all the historical information which has been collected from all the books written in the Sanscrit [sic] language is less valuable than what may be found in the most paltry abridgments used at preparatory schools in England. In every branch of physical or moral philosophy, the relative position of the two nations is nearly the same.
> 
> The question now before us is simply whether, when it is in our power to teach this language, we shall teach languages in which, by universal confession, there are no books on any subject which deserve to be compared to our own, whether, when we can teach European science, we shall teach systems which, by universal confession, wherever they differ from those of Europe differ for the worse, and whether, when we can patronize sound philosophy and true history, we shall countenance, at the public expense, medical doctrines which would disgrace an English farrier, astronomy which would move laughter in girls at an English boarding school, history abounding with kings thirty feet high and reigns thirty thousand years long, and geography made of seas of treacle and seas of butter.
> 
> Macaulay 1835: n.p.

His own colonial vision, which he derives from this line of argument, is well-known:

> I feel with them that it is impossible for us, with our limited means, to attempt to educate the body of the people. We must at present do our best to form a class who may be interpreters between us and the millions whom we govern,—a class of

persons Indian in blood and colour, but English in tastes, in opinions, in morals and in intellect. To that class we may leave it to refine the vernacular dialects of the country, to enrich those dialects with terms of science borrowed from the Western nomenclature, and to render them by degrees fit vehicles for conveying knowledge to the great mass of the population.

Macaulay 1835: n.p.

With this vision, Macaulay set the scene for the doctrine of indirect rule that subsequently guided British colonial policy up to the break-down of the Empire.

The debate sketched above was quite unique to the Indian case. In particular, there was no parallel hesitation about the role and position of the colonizer in the context of sub-Saharan Africa. Lugard (1922: 46), for instance, is very explicit on this point: "India's ancient civilisation and social organisation, based on and an integral part of its religions, and the culture and high intelligence of its educated classes, all combine to differentiate the problems of its vast population from those of other tropical regions of the Empire."

In the eyes of the colonizers, Africa south of the Sahara had no pre-colonial intellectual or societal achievements worth of scholarly attention. This perception prevailed well up to the middle of the twentieth century, as famously expressed in the stance of the British historian Hugh Trevor-Roper (1963: 871) that pre-colonial sub-Saharan Africa "had no history prior to European exploration and colonization, that there is only the history of Europeans in Africa. The rest is darkness." What was reported at length was the activities and "achievements" of the colonizers.

The attitudes towards traditional African belief systems were the same as for India. They were scarcely regarded as worthy of being treated as "religion" (but see below). Again, Lugard's account is representative of this mindset.

> Through the ages the African has evolved no organised religious creed, and though some tribes appear to believe in a deity, the religious sense seldom rises above pantheistic animism, and seems more often to take the form of a vague dread of the supernatural. It is curious that whereas in East Africa Sir C. Eliot observes that prayers are always addressed to a benevolent deity, in the West the prevalent idea seems to be the propitiation of a malevolent spirit. Belief in the power of the witch and wizard, and of the Juju-priest and witch-doctor, in charms and fetish, and in the ability of individuals to assume at will the form of wild beasts, are also common among many tribes.

Lugard 1922: 69

This perception started to change only in the 1930s, following the work of anthropologists such as Bronisław Malinowski.[8] Malinowski was not opposed to Lugard's vision of "indirect rule";[9] however, he disagreed with Lugard's outright dismissive view of African magic beliefs and practices. Rather than placing them merely in the realm of superstition that had to be eradicated, as it is done in Lugard's *Dual Mandate*, Malinowski found the magic belief systems to be crucial factors in societal organization and instrumental for social coherence, in particular the resolution of conflicts and maintenance of balance (see Foks 2018 for a discussion). He was hence opposed to Lugard's position that, as Foks (2018: 38) puts it, "law-making, as state-making, was reserved for white Europeans, with a hard line between customary and colonial courts."[10] Instead, Malinowski proposed that "the law itself was to be indirectly generated as a fusion of African and European customs" (Foks 2018: 39).

## 2.2 Distance Restored

As noted above, the metaphor system under analysis is special in that it presents the distance between the colonizer and the colonial subject as a temporary condition. The state of equality is postponed, its achievement a matter of natural development. Eventually, the metaphorical CHILD will evolve into a mature adult; the PUPIL will rise to the level of the TEACHER, provided that there is appropriate guidance. This metaphor system was rooted in the Christian notion of the "family of man."

Colonial discourse abounds in the programmatic commitment to the "rising of the natives" and hence to the reduction of the distance between colonizer and colonial subject (see below). At the same time, the colonizers had always been at unease with or even opposed to the very idea that they would find themselves on equal terms with their colonial subjects. Thus, although propagating the reduction of the distance to the natives, they were eager to preserve and firmly establish this distance.[11] The two stances are obviously incompatible. In the colonial discourse, we see two patterns of how this condition was dealt with.

The first pattern stays entirely within the logic of the metaphor system and insists on the distance between colonizer and colonial subject as well as on the long time-span needed to reduce and eventually close the gap. This way, the uncomfortable state of equality is postponed to the far future. Right from the start and across the centuries, colonial discourse is full of reports about the slow progress of the endeavors to "raise" the natives. Lugard (1922: 178–9), for instance, is very explicit on this point: "the era of complete independence is not as yet visible on the horizon of time.... The danger of going too fast with native races is even more likely to lead to disappointment, if not to disaster, than the danger of not going fast enough."

The notion of "the natives" lagging behind on an imagined path to Western civilization as the ultimate goal is also expressed in League of Nations documents:

> [T]he *gradual civilisation of the native populations* as well as the economic development of the countries will be furthered in the best possible manner. The Commission therefore asks the Council to call the attention of all the Mandatory Powers to this system of education as being in its opinion particularly suitable to the conditions of life of *backward* peoples.
> League of Nations 1924: 183, italics added

With social progress and material progress based on collective and individual property, and the development of products for exportation, I believe that we shall have attained the *second stage I have in view, the stage of material and social* well-being.... As soon as the people of Togoland should have *reached a civilised state of life*, they would be able to stand by themselves.

League of Nations 1925: 23, italics added

In these quotes, the STATES ARE LOCATIONS metaphor is evident. The respective League of Nations documents recorded statements by the French representative on the Commission and colonial governor of Togo, Paul Auguste François Bonnecarrère. At least according to the French ideal of assimilation of the native, the US VERSUS THEM schema ceases to exist once the colonial subjects reaches the Western state of civilization; IDENTITY OF CULTURE IS IDENTITY OF LOCATION:

From the remarkable statement made by M. Bonnecarrère, it appeared that the present policy tended to the *development of the native in the direction of European civilisation*.... M. Bonnecarrère said he did not believe in the imperfectability of the native, in spite of the sceptics who thought that it was impossible to *convert him into a civilised man*. Nevertheless, the native was greatly handicapped by the nature of his country and surroundings. In his fight against nature, which was a hard task-master and sometimes no luxuriant—a neglected road might disappear within two months under bush—the native was not so sensitive as the European, and this was lucky for him, because his present offerings, caused by the rigours of the climate and by his destitution, were only too real. However, it resulted from this, that *his development was being retarded*, and he had to struggle continually against his surroundings, simply for his livelihood and the procreation of his race. *A long time must still elapse before he could be completely assimilated to the European.*

League of Nations 1925: 25, italics added

This quote brings into play dimensions of otherness beyond those provided by the metaphor system. One dimension that was frequently evoked in the early colonial discourse is the negative impact of the local climate on the nature of the colonial people, a view still held in the previous quote.[12] This belief is also referred to by Grant (although he thought it to be overrated): "The debilitating nature of the climate of our Eastern territories, and its unfavorable influence upon the human constitution, have been already mentioned, and by others represented in strong colours" (Grant [1796] 1853: 75), and "it is reasonable to believe, that were those evils corrected which do not arise from the climate, they would in time held a much higher place among the human species than they are now capable of maintaining" (Grant [1796] 1853: 31).

Climatic conditions are a dimension external to the colonial subjects. Their obvious physical features of otherness (most prominently skin color) were always highlighted as prime markers of them being different from the colonizers. Recall the earlier quote from the missionary Robert Moffat: "Wherever I look upon anyone connected with Africa, *no matter how black his face, I regards* [sic] *him or her as my own son or daughter*" (Robert Moffat, 1840, missionary in southern Africa, quoted in Cleall 2012: 6, italics added). Here, he evokes the notion of the "family of man," but puts a reference to skin color in a no-matter construction that implies that it might indeed be taken to matter.

It is, however, important to notice that for colonial agents of this mold, the no-matter stance is meant to be truly *inclusive*, not *exclusive*: however different somebody (or a group of people) is from their implicit norm, everybody is a member of the family of man.[13] There is no undertone of superior and inferior races in this stance. Grant's account of the Indians, harsh as it is, is guided by the same spirit:

> If the character of the Hindoos proceeded only from a physical origin, there might be some foundation for thinking it unalterable; but nothing is more plain, than that it is formed chiefly by moral causes, adequate to the effect produced: if those causes therefore can be removed, their effect will cease, and new principles and motives will produce new conduct and a different character. It is unwarrantable to infer, that because the Hindoos, or to narrow the term, the Bengalese, are at present low in their sentiments, conduct, and aims, they must always remain so.... The history of many nations who have advanced from rudeness to refinement, contradicts this hypothesis; according to which, the Britons ought still to be going naked, to be feeding on acorns, and sacrificing human victims.... Let it however be again observed, that the argument maintained here supposes only a *gradual* change. If we bring into immediate contrast, the *present state* of the Hindoos, and the *full, general, accomplishment* of such a change, tacitly sinking in our comparison, a long series of years, and of slow progressive transitions, we shall indeed form to ourselves a picture of egregious contrarieties, but it will not be a just representation. Nothing is contended for, which cannot be supported from the nature of man, and the experience of past ages.
> 
> Grant [1796] 1853: 63

From the vantage point of monogenetic theories of the human kind (including their Christian version of the "family of man"), the "distance" between the colonizer and the colonial subjects was hence primarily the product of culture and social institutions, i.e., forces *external* to man; the "gap" can be closed through gradual change. This view differs sharply from the stances taken by polygenetic theories that entered the scene in the nineteenth century. These theories were truly racist in design, assuming and propagating the fundamental otherness of the races, not only in terms of outward features (skin color or physical characteristics) but also in terms of inherent intellectual and social capacities. It was the most drastic attempt at "restoring the distance" between the European colonizers and the colonial subjects. This mindset became an integral part of colonial discourse. Again, Lugard provides explicit illustrations thereof:

> It is essential to realise that tropical Africa is inhabited by races which differ as widely from each other as do the nations of Europe, and that some of the principal racial types present even greater divergence than those of Europe and parts of Asia.... All have been modified to a greater or less degree by admixture with negro blood, which has produced racial types differing from each other, and widely different from the negro type. They vary in their mental and physical characteristics according to the amount of negro blood in their veins, which has shown itself extremely potent in assimilating alien strains to its own type.
> 
> Lugard 1922: 67

The racist version of US VERSUS THEM also applied the linear idea of development, but with a separate trajectory for the colonial subject (cf., Dimier 2004: 286). Sir Donald C. Cameron, the second governor of the British mandate of Tanganyika (today Tanzania), is quoted as saying:

> Everyone, whatever his opinion may be in regard to direct or indirect rule, will agree, I think, that it is our duty to do everything in our power to *develop the native on lines which will not Westernise him* and turn him into a bad imitation of a European—our whole education policy is directed to that end. We want to make him a good African.
>
> League of Nations 1926: 137, italics added

This point, of course, begs the question of what "a good African" is supposed to be (cf., Wolf 2008: 567).[14]

A perennial problem for the colonial administrations was the so-called "half-castes," who undermined the racial categories of US VERSUS THEM. The League of Nations documents bear numerous examples of how difficult it was for the colonial administrators to deal with this group (see Wolf 2008: 568). A quote by the Belgian representative on the Permanent Mandate Commission is representative of the prevailing view and clearly expresses the underlying conceptual schemas of UP VERSUS DOWN, SOURCE-PATH-GOAL and the STATES ARE LOCATIONS metaphor:

> In the colonies, where there were two possibilities—European status and the status of a native subject to customary law—two half-castes sprung from the same mixture of blood *might follow entirely different paths in life* owning to circumstances over which they had no control, *one sinking to the position of a native, the other advancing to that of a European*—at any rate as far as his status was concerned.
>
> League of Nations 1935: 21, italics added

## 2.3 (Re)Defining the Mission

The conceptualizations that transpire from the colonial texts are not fully consistent and at times contradictory. One would think that US VERSUS THEM in terms of racial categories—as in Lugard's (1933) reference to "miscegenation" (quoted in Brutt-Griffler 2002: 58)—would not be compatible with PARENT-CHILDREN conceptualizations. Still both sets existed side by side in the colonial mind (at least in Lord Lugard's). The notion of "responsibility" goes back to the metaphoric relation of PARENT/ADULT/TEACHER vis-à-vis CHILD/PUPIL and was the anchor point for the colonial key notion of the "civilizing mission."[15] In the present section, we will access this notion from some considerations on the metaphoric concept of the CHILD and the program of "educating the native."

Lugard frames his picture of the "African native" explicitly along the lines of the CHILD metaphor:

> He lacks power of organisation, and is conspicuously deficient in the management and control alike of men or of business. He loves the display of power, but fails to

realise its responsibility. His most universal natural ability lies in eloquence and oratory. He is by no means lacking in industry, and will work hard with a less incentive than most races.

He has the courage of the fighting animal—an instinct rather than a moral virtue. He is very prone to imitate anything new in dress or custom, whether it be the turban and flowing gown of the Moslem, or the straw hat and trousers of the European, however unsuited to his environment and conditions of life. He is an apt pupil, and a faithful and devoted friend. In brief, *the virtues and the defects of this race-type are those of attractive children*, whose confidence when once it has been won is given ungrudgingly as to an older and wiser superior, without question and without envy.
Lugard 1922: 69–70; italics added

Much of *The Dual Mandate* is a program of "educating the natives," that is, the metaphorical child. The basic principles advocated by Lugard in this respect are reminiscent of the Rousseauian notions of the child and of education, cp.:

The danger of going too fast with native races is even more likely to lead to disappointment, if not to disaster, than the danger of not going fast enough.
Lugard 1922: 178–9

Nature wants children to be children before they are men. If we try to pervert this order we shall produce a forced fruit that will have neither ripeness nor flavor and that will soon spoil.
Rousseau [1762] 1979: 90

Lugard's characterization of the role of the COLONIZER/TEACHER and his position relative to the NATIVE/PUPIL reads as follows:

But if the standard which the white man must set before him when dealing with uncivilised races must be a high one for the sake of his own moral and spiritual balance, it is not less imperative for the sake of the influence which he exercises upon those over whom he is set in authority. The white man's prestige must stand high when a few score are responsible for the control and guidance of millions. His courage must be undoubted, his word and pledge absolutely inviolate, his sincerity transparent. There is no room for "mean whites" in tropical Africa. Nor is there room for those who, however high their motives, are content to place themselves on the same level as the uncivilised races. They lower the prestige by which alone the white races can hope to govern and to guide.
Lugard 1922: 59

It is reflective of the general *zeitgeist* in educational matters and again, in parts, reminiscent of the Rousseauian views:

Treat your pupil according to his age. Put him in his place from the first, and keep him there so well that he does not try to leave it.... He must know only that he is weak and you are strong, that his condition and yours put him at your mercy. Let him know this, let him learn it, let him feel it.

Rousseau [1762] 1979: 90

In this section we considered, from a cognitive-linguistic perspective, colonial attitudes and the construction of the colonial subjects by the colonizers. The following section will highlight how colonial conceptions of morality and religion collided with local practices, how the colonizers tried to deal with such practices they perceived as disturbing, and how the measures taken by the colonizer might have impacted on the cultural conceptualizations expressed in Indian, respectively African English, today.

## 3. "Disturbing" Practices and Cultural Engineering

Various cultural practices the colonizers encountered in their colonies conflicted with their moral ideology and ideas of "civilization," for example, the caste system in India and polygamy in Africa. In the following, we will focus on homosexuality and witchcraft as two fairly well-documented areas in which colonial conceptions and legal implementations left their traces on cultural conceptualizations evidenced in the Englishes in question today.

### 3.1 Homosexuality

While race was one aspect of colonial discourse that aided in justifying imperial supremacy, issues concerning sexuality (and, concomitantly, also gender) were another aspect. Industrialization and urbanization in Britain changed the concepts of FAMILY and SEXUALITY by emphasizing the role of reproduction for a stable society, in particular towards the end of the nineteenth century when the threat of the downfall of the British Empire was pervasive (see Weeks 1990). Scientific advancements in medicine and psychology and an increasing concern about public health additionally stimulated the debate. After the passing of the so-called Contagious Diseases Acts in 1864, 1866 and 1869 (cf., Bryder 1998), Acton (1870: 246), for instance, claims in a medical report on the regulation of prostitution:

> If the race of the people is of no concern to the State, then has the State no interest in arresting its vitiation. But if this concern and this interest be admitted, then arises the necessity for depriving prostitution not only of its moral, but of its physical venom also.
>
> She [the prostitute] is a woman with half the woman gone, and that half containing all that elevates her nature, leaving her a mere instrument of impurity; degraded and fallen she extracts from the sin of others the means of living, corrupt and dependent on corruption, and therefore interested directly in the increase of immorality—a social pest, carrying contamination and foulness to every quarter to which she has access.

Acton 1870: 166

Acton's statements quite explicitly plot that with medical progress and a rise in hygienic awareness, a close connection between morals and public health was drawn, in which MORAL CONTAGION was conceptualized as PHYSICAL CONTAGION. In an enterprise that Bashford (2004) calls "imperial hygiene," sanitary measures taken in the nineteenth and twentieth century represented and fostered the dichotomy between PURE versus IMPURE/POLLUTED. This dichotomy was carried across the colonies and intersected with the understanding of race, sexuality, and gender. Hence, sexuality came to the fore as an issue of administrative concern, at home as well as in the colonies, with race as an ever co-present topic. As Stoler (1995: 179) put it, "in the name of British, French, and Dutch moralizing missions, colonial authority supposedly rested on the rigor with which its agents distinguished between desire and reason, native instinct and white self-discipline, native lust and white civility, native sensuality and white morality, subversive unproductive sexuality and productive patriotic sex."

Extra-marital and non-reproductive sexuality—or sex for pleasure—thus constituted a corrupting factor because, after all, sexuality and marriage were seen as a "way Europeans sought to maintain social distance and bolster their sense of innate superiority" (Bryder 1998: 808). Where extra-marital sexuality appeared to be unavoidable, particularly among the all-male armed forces abroad, prostitution was perceived as the lesser evil compared to same-sex sexual activities.[16] Stoler (1995: 180) reports on the belief that if the common soldier were "thwarted from exercising his "natural" sexual urges, he would resort to "unnatural vices," "specifically to masturbation or sexual relations with other men" and remarks that "the dangers of a homosexual European rank and file were implicitly weighed against the medical hazards of rampant heterosexual prostitution: both were condemned as morally pernicious and a threat to racial survival." Levine's (1994: 596) account is in line inasmuch as "the constant haunting fear of homosexuality ... would undermine the manly adventure of imperial conquest" because "there was no room for even a hint of the effeminacy assumed to exist among subject men."

Two major logical strands fed into the colonizers' understanding of homosexuality in the nineteenth century: Firstly, the concept of MASCULINITY was structured according to a "hierarchy of manliness" (at least in the Indian context, see Hinchy 2014: 275), with British men as the ideal and the colonized men below them, sorted in descending order by religion, ethnicity, or class (for the latter, cf., Stoler 1995: 179f). Thus, hierarchizing men along an UP VERSUS DOWN image schema was crucial to maintaining masculinity as a social status with which superiority and colonial rule and expansion were justified (see Brady 2009).[17] As Brady argues, this had further implications for the treatment of homosexual practices among British men inasmuch as these practices undermined masculinity and were therefore denied. In the then-scandalous trial of Boulton and Park—two London cross-dressers—the initial indictment (which was later dropped) read that they "feloniously wickedly and against the order of nature with each other did commit and perpetrate that detestable and abominable crime of buggery not to be named among Christians" (initial indictment of 1870 in the Central Criminal Court, quoted in Cohen 1996: 79). Aldrich (2003) observes that homosexual relationships between colonizers and colonized also posed a threat to the colonial agenda, since they potentially enabled equal relationships and subsequently produced anti-imperialist mindsets.

As is reflected in the Boulton-and-Park indictment, the conceptualization HOMOSEXUALITY IS AN UNNATURAL CONDITION was the second strand of logic upon which the understanding of homosexuality was built. While the term *homosexuality* itself was coined only in the second half of the nineteenth century, *buggery* and *sodomy* (which included a number of non-reproductive and thus impure sexual practices) had already been criminalized through precursory British law, for example in the mediaeval treatises *Fleta* and *Britton* and Henry VIII's Buggery Act of 1533 (see Gupta 2008; Weeks 1990: 11ff.). The conceptual link to SIN is obvious: "Buggery is a detestable, and abominable sin, amongst Christians not to be named, committed by carnall [*sic*] knowledge against the ordinance of the Creator, and order of nature" (Coke 1648: 58).

The understanding of HOMOSEXUALITY as UNNATURAL along religious lines blended well into the discourse on sexuality along medical lines that was prominent particularly in the nineteenth century (see Bleys 1995: 2), when colonialism was approaching its heyday. If British superiority stood and fell with the degree of masculinity, and if sexuality between men was corruptive to masculinity, then it is not surprising that homosexual practices had to be properly codified in law. Since "buggery" and "sodomy" were no unequivocal offences, a fact which complicated legal action,[18] revising anti-sodomy laws was urgent and the colonies were an ideal testing ground for legislation at home (Gupta 2008). It was once more Macaulay who contributed to the Indian Penal Code that was installed in 1860. Clause 361 of the initial proposal for a law against homosexuality in 1837 read:

> Whoever intending to gratify unnatural lust, touches for that purpose any person or any animal or is by his own consent touched by any person for the purpose of gratifying unnatural lust, shall be punished with imprisonment of either description for a term which may extend to 14 years, and must not be less than two years.
> Report of the Indian Law Commission on the Penal Code 1837; quoted in Gupta 2006: 4822

It eventually found its expression in Section 377 of the 1860 final version, which maintained the notion of "unnaturalness":

> Unnatural offences—Whoever voluntarily has carnal intercourse against the order of nature with any man, woman or animal shall be punished with imprisonment for life, or with imprisonment of either description for a term which may extend to 10 years, and shall be liable to fine.
> Explanation—Penetration is sufficient to constitute the carnal intercourse necessary to the offence described in this section.
> Indian Penal Code 1860; quoted in Gupta 2006: 4816[19]

Section 377 was overruled only in 2018—seventy-one years after India's independence—to decriminalize homosexual behavior among consenting adults.

Turning towards Nigeria, Section 214 of the Criminal Code, which was modeled after the Queensland Penal Code, was first introduced to the Northern parts in 1904 and is still in place in the Southern territories (see Mwalimu 2007); it reads all too familiar:

> *Any person* who has carnal knowledge of any person against the order of nature or has carnal knowledge of an animal, or permits a male person to have carnal knowledge of him or her against the order of nature is guilty of a felony and liable upon conviction to 14 years imprisonment.
> Nigerian Criminal Code 1904; quoted in Ayeni 2017: 216, original emphasis

The same can be said about Section 284 of the Penal Code, which was modeled after the Indian Penal Code and still operates in the Northern territories (complemented by Shari'a law): "Whoever has carnal intercourse against the order of nature with any man or woman is liable upon conviction to fine and imprisonment for a term which may extend to fourteen years" (Nigerian Penal Code 1960; quoted in Ayeni 2017: 217).

It becomes clear that the conceptualization HOMOSEXUALITY IS AN UNNATURAL CONDITION, as still enshrined in contemporary legislation, was a colonial imposition based on a British fear, and as such it spread across the colonies (cf., Gupta 2008). As Gupta (2008: n.p.) furthermore argues, the implementation of anti-sodomy laws in the colonies "was a way of segregating the Christian, European self from alien entities that menaced it with infection."

Differing approaches existed in explaining the allegedly abnormal sexuality of the colonized, and arising discourses on INNATE VERSUS ACQUIRED, OCCASIONAL VERSUS REAL and PATHOLOGICAL VERSUS NORMAL challenged the notion of UNNATURALNESS (see Bleys 1993; Murray and Roscoe 2001). Burton, for instance, argued in his *Terminal essay* of 1885 that the climate was mainly responsible for homosexual practices, similar to Grant's observation outlined in Section 2.2. This argumentation was largely influenced by the conceptualization HOMOSEXUALITY IS AN ACQUIRED CONDITION, while at the same time suggesting that HOMOSEXUALITY IS A NATURAL CONDITION. Burton assumed an accumulation of such practices in the so-called Sotadic Zone, whereas "the races to the North and South of the limits here defined [obviously including the British] practise it only sporadically amid the opprobrium of their fellows who, as a rule, are physically incapable of performing the operation" (Burton 1885; quoted in White 1999: 145).

Notably to this chapter, he saw Hindus as opponents of "the Vice." Considering what was mentioned before, namely that particularly in the Indian colony the "hierarchy of manliness" was eagerly applied, this seems surprising. After all, ascribing unmanly homosexuality to the inferior races would aid in establishing a superior British masculinity. And in fact, according to Sinha (1995), homosexuality was part of this discourse, but astonishingly associated with the races that ranked higher on the hierarchy. Perhaps Burton's account, which is rather apologetic of homosexuality, should be considered as a late tribute to the Orientalist school. Burton furthermore deemed homosexuality a foreign import into West Africa—an idea he might have gotten from Gibbon's claim a century earlier that "the negroes, in their own country, were exempt from this moral pestilence" (Gibbon [1781] 1854: 324). The basis for this assumption was presumably the understanding of sub-Saharan African cultures as primitive and therefore "close to nature, ruled by instinct, and culturally unsophisticated," with their "sexual energies and outlets devoted exclusively to their 'natural' purpose: biological reproduction," implying that they would be "the most heterosexual" (Murray and Roscoe 2001: xi).

Obviously, the image of the colonial subjects as constructed by the British often diverged from the actual circumstances; but whatever view on the colonized cultures, claiming that homosexuality is unnatural and likewise fearing "infection" points to a rather schizophrenic perspective. In any case, the "disturbing practices" found abroad must have constituted a danger to British superiority, respectability and normality, rendering legal controls and cultural engineering even more necessary. Their existence likewise justified the colonial mission to bring civilization to the uncivilized.

At this point it is worthwhile to briefly sketch out some pre-colonial conceptualizations of HOMOSEXUALITY in India and West Africa. They are attested in traditional texts and orature and in the existence of homosexual practices as described in the research literature.[20]

In the Indian context, textual evidence in the form of scriptures from the Vedic period dates back until about 1500 BCE, followed by the emergence of Hinduism, Buddhism and Islam which provide a plethora of texts. Although Hunt (2011) warns that the existence of homosexual practices in these texts should not be romanticized and that homophobia is part of Indian history, it is undeniable that same-sex love and homoerotic activities have been explicitly described throughout the centuries. Vanita and Kidwai (2001: xxiv) observe that such relationships were rarely subject to prosecution and not labelled as "abnormal," "unnatural" or "unhealthy." Instead, Hunt (2011) refers to the insemination ceremony *Garbhadan Sanskaar*, one of the Hindu rites of passage that gives advice on how not to conceive a homosexual child, or the ancient text Rig Veda, which says that *Vikruti evam prakriti* ('what is unnatural is also natural'). These instances of HOMOSEXUALITY IS A NATURAL CONDITION are often used by Indian LGBTIQ activists to argue for their case and against conservative Hindus. The Kamasutra categorizes HOMOSEXUALITY as THIRD NATURE, and other medical texts describe it in terms of desire rather than behavior—long before this was considered in Western science (see Vanita and Kidwai 2001: xxi).

Vanita and Kidwai (2001) also assume conceptual links relating to FRIENDSHIP between conjugal and same-sex couplings, for instance with regard to the concept of the symbolic SEVEN STEPS: in traditional wedding ceremonies, the couple takes seven steps together and the last step signifies friendship. Vanita and Kidwai (2001: 7) show how the expression *saptapadam hi mitram* ('seven steps/words taken together constitute friendship') is repeatedly used in ancient texts about non-conjugal friendship, which suggests an egalitarian status of these bonds. Although the lack of procreation at first appears to be an impediment to same-sex friendships, the purity of such friendships is itself a source of (re)birth. In the epic *Mahabharata*, for example, Krishna (a Hindu god) evokes the creative power of his unspoilt friendship with Arjuna upon the stillbirth of his friend's only grandchild: "Never hath a misunderstanding arisen between me and my friend Vijaya [Arjuna]. Let this dead child revive by that truth!" (Mahabharata, Asvamedha Parva; quoted in Vanita and Kidwai 2001: 8).

In fact, sexual intercourse as a necessity for procreation is conceptualized as a degeneration of humankind, underlining that "male friendship is the purest bond":

> In those days offspring were begotten by fiat of the will. In the age that followed, Treta, children were begotten by touch alone. The people of that age, even, O monarch, were above the necessity of sexual congress. It was in the next age, Dwapara, that the practice of sexual congress originated, O king, to prevail among men. In the Kali age, O monarch, men have come to marry and live in pairs.
> Mahabharata, Santi Parva; quoted in Vanita and Kidwai 2001: 9

In other Indian myths, same-sex encounters may actually produce offspring, as is the case in some variants of the genesis of the gods Ganesha ('born by two women') or his brother Kartikeya ('born by two men'). The *Krittivasa Ramayana* tells the story of King Dilipa, two of whose widows were *sampriti* ('in extreme love') and had a child named "Bhagiratha" ('born of two vulvas' [*bhaga*]; Vanita and Kidwai 2001: xix)

However, other, partly less benevolent, conceptualizations that emphasize the important role of reproduction also existed. Kakar and Kakar (2006: 103) describe the ancient Indian category of Sanskrit KLIBA. This category included all sorts of men: sterile, impotent, castrated, with mutilated or deficient genitalia, receivers of anal sex, performers of oral sex, fathers without sons, transvestites or hermaphrodites. Hence, men who could not or refused to perform satisfactorily in the reproductive process. Das Wilhelm (2008: 37) remarks that in dictionaries published in the West, *kliba* was translated as "impotent, emasculated, a eunuch, unmanly, timorous, weak, idle, a coward," thus including the notion of STRENGTH as a component of MASCULINITY. As a final example, the Narada-smriti states that the so-called *mukhebhaga* ('he who performs oral sex on men') is "incurable" and "unmarriageable under all circumstances"—in contrast to the *paksha*, which refers in some regards to the Western concept of the BISEXUAL (Das Wilhelm 2008: 49).

In Africa, cultural knowledge is fixed to a lesser degree in written form, so it is somewhat more difficult to textually carve out pre-colonial conceptualizations of HOMOSEXUALITY. Early colonial accounts furthermore seem void of description, presumably, as Bleys (1995) argues, due to the focus on black masculinity necessitated by slave trade. Since African traditions are highly oral, folk beliefs, orature, and customary law can serve as a rich source of data for accessing cultural conceptualizations. The lack of descriptions in colonial texts can be complemented by research literature on contemporary and historical homosexual communities and patterns of same-sex relationships in Africa.

Appiah and Gates (2010) report on several examples from the West African context specifically: at the Asante courts in today's Ghana during the eighteenth and nineteenth century, cross-dressing male slaves pleased their masters. Among the Igbo in the twentieth century, women could become female husbands and take wives in order to secure their independence. Homosexuals are seen as mediators between the spiritual and the human world by the Dagari in Burkina Faso:

> Any person who is this link between this world and the other world experiences a state of vibrational consciousness which is far higher, and far different, from the

one that a normal person would experience. This is what makes a gay person gay. This kind of function is not one that society votes for certain people to fulfill. It is one that people are said to decide on prior to being born.

Somé 1993: 7; quoted in Murray and Roscoe 2001: 92

This quote proves that the conceptualization of HOMOSEXUALITY as AN INNATE AND NATURAL CONDITION is not alien to the African context. It also relates, in a wider sense, to African cosmology per se, which is discussed from a cognitive-sociolinguistic perspective in much more detail in Wolf and Polzenhagen (2009).

Furthermore, members of the *yan daudu*, a gay community among the Muslim Hausa in Nigeria, take the role of mediators between men and women where prostitution is concerned. While sometimes living in rather marginalized communities, this role secures them an economically stable position within the larger society. Although the prospect of financial security seemed to be the main reason for a self-identification as *yan daudu* in a study by Besmer in 1983 (referenced in Murray and Roscoe 2001), 7 percent of the informants still named "nature" as the reason for identification, yet another attestation of the conceptualization of HOMOSEXUALITY as A NATURAL CONDITION in the West African context.

There are yet more instances of same-sex relationships that the British colonizers encountered. Ayeni (2017) mentions records of woman-to-woman marriage among the Igbo and the people of Mbaise that go back until at least the eighteenth century. Such unions may include the payment of a bride price and their main purpose is the assurance of the family line, with the female husbands usually receiving high status and male privileges. Documents of court decisions based on customary law demonstrate their cultural rootedness.

The Yoruba, a predominantly Christian community, often claim that homosexuality is not part of their culture. While this might apply to the contemporary "Western" concept of HOMOSEXUALITY, there are various examples of traditional same-sex relationships. Aina (1991), for instance, found that HOMOSEXUAL INTERCOURSE was conceived of as a SOURCE OF POWER for otherwise heterosexually oriented men. Furthermore, Ajibade (2013) analyzed the existence of same-sex relationships in Yoruba orature. An Ifa priest he interviewed related the genesis of Orunmila, the *orisha* of wisdom, who was begotten through the intercourse of two females. Though perceived as an unsanctioned union (therefore, Orunmila is boneless), it is again the mere existence of same-sex relationships in orature which proves their cultural embedding. The same can be said about rituals in which priests (male or female) known as *iyawo orisa* ('brides of the deities') dress like women while becoming possessed by male gods. An example of an unfavorable judgment of homosexuality in Yoruba tradition is given in the following piece of orature:

> If a man is having sexual intercourse with another man
> It results into lumps, boils and yaws
> It results into various diseases
> If a woman is having sexual intercourse with another woman
> It results into murk and fowl [*sic*] odour,
> It results into mud and dirt.

Ajibade 2013: 975; translated there from Yoruba

Here, MALE HOMOSEXUALITY is conceptualized as DISEASE and FEMALE HOMOSEXUALITY as POLLUTION. Ajibade in fact notes that these practices, perceived as evils that affect the whole society, align with further findings in the Yoruba context that conceptualize HOMOSEXUALITY as UNNATURAL, PATHOLOGICAL and A RESULT OF OCCULT ACTIVITY. He continues to point out that sexual intercourse which results in procreation is favorable, for which he gives several examples. For lesbianism specifically, the conceptualization of A FEMALE GENITAL NOT USED FOR PROCREATION IS A DEAD GENITAL emerges, as expressed in the following passage:

> Any woman who engages in sexual intercourse with fellow woman
> Don't you know she is (only) gazing at a dead genital?
> Had it been that is [sic] the way we administer the community
> The community would be unbearable for the people?
>
> Ajibade 2013: 978

The genital of a heterosexual female metonymically stands for life and the continuation of society. In turn, a logical entailment of this line of reasoning is that (FEMALE) HOMOSEXUALITY means DEATH OF SOCIETY.

All the given examples offer, of course, not even a fragmentary view into the pre-colonial understanding of HOMOSEXUALITY in India and West Africa. However, they illustrate that same-sex practices formed part of the local cultures at the time colonial conceptualizations were implemented, implying that the understanding as UNNATURAL can be attributed to the colonial influence. Evidently, both cultures were not completely free from homophobia before, but the new conceptual framework changed cultural cognition with lasting effects.

These discourses are nowadays still prevalent and indeed have cross-cultural resemblance with regard to the "un-Indianness" or "un-Africanness." In both contexts, opponents consider homosexuality an import from the West that corrupts local values and traditions. This view bizarrely turns colonial laws into defenders of these values and traditions (see, for instance, Gupta 2008; Vanita and Kidwai 2001 on India; Ayeni 2017 on Nigeria).

In India, Section 377 has only recently ceased to be applied to homosexual practices between two consenting adults. Several scholars have noted that the stance on homosexuality is somewhat ambiguous in public discourse as well as in people's mindsets (e.g., Boyce 2006; Kirpal 2016). While some tolerate it, others condemn it as a "disease" (Vanita and Kidwai 2001: xxiv), as "unnatural ... acts not designed for human beings" (Hunt 2011: 322) or as "immoral" and "abysmal, absurd" (Hunt 2011: 324).

The public opinion in Nigeria, the setting where missionaries "poured their fire-and-brimstone sermons against Sodom and Gomorrha over their first converts" (Zabus 2013: 80 on the colonization of Africa), appears to be less ambivalent. The overall negative tenor is often coined in Christian and Islamic terms, that is with Western religious beliefs entering the debate, for instance when then President Olusegun Obasanjo declared homosexuality "un-Biblical, unnatural and un-African" in 2004 ("Obasanjo backs bishops" 2004). Archbishop Peter Akinola is infamously known for statements such as the following:

> Same sex marriage, apart from being ungodly, is unscriptural, unnatural, unprofitable, unhealthy, un-cultural, un-African and un-Nigerian. It is a perversion, a deviation and an aberration that is capable of engendering moral and social holocaust in this country. It is also capable of existincting [sic] mankind and as such should never be allowed to take root in Nigeria. Outlawing it is to ensure the continued existence of this nation.
>
> Brown 2009: n.p.

A number of the conceptualizations described earlier are contained in the quote: from SIN to UNNATURAL, homosexuality is seen to embody a variety of vices proclaimed in the Bible. This includes the inhibition of procreation, which might tap into previously existing cultural conceptualizations. Colonial legislation as introduced by the British is still effective in Nigeria and was even reinforced in 2013 through the Same Sex Marriage (Prohibition) Act.

The ambivalence of attitudes in India and the dismissiveness in Nigeria are mirrored in the results presented in Finzel (forthcoming). In this study, data collected through sociolinguistic interviews with Indian English and Nigerian English speakers was analyzed with regard to conceptualizations of HOMOSEXUALITY. Of all the conceptualizations in the Indian English data, around 43 percent were found to echo a negative stance and 48 percent a positive one. In the Nigerian English data in contrast, the share was 12 percent for a favorable position and 68 percent for an adverse one. It seems thus that cultural engineering in terms of HOMOSEXUALITY was successfully accomplished in both colonies, but in Nigeria with presumed sustainability—possibly because religion functioned as an implementation tool.

## 3.2 Witchcraft

Another disturbing practice in the colonies, specifically the African colonies and mandate territories (on the historical background, see Wolf 2008) was fetishism or, relatedly, witchcraft. Discussions in the League of Nations Permanent Mandate Commission bear ample evidence of how "disturbing" such practices were perceived to be despite the fact that fetishism was, perhaps hesitantly, awarded the status of a religion (see above):

> M. PALACIOS [the Spanish representative] asked for information regarding the fetishism practiced by the natives and the dangers of such a religion; he also wished to have information regarding the practices observed which were contrary to public order and good morals.
>
> M. BONNECARRÈRE stated that fetishism was a danger, as it was based on obscurantism and on the action of certain men who exploited their contemporaries.... He respected native customs and realised it was impossible to suppress fetishism; but he was endeavouring to diminish its importance, particularly by exercising supervision over the fetish groups, which were submitted to the ordinary law.
>
> League of Nations 1925: 34

Another source of dispute was the practice followed by the Animists of holding certain religious (Ju-Ju) ceremonies in the village street, which they closed for the purpose.

League of Nations 1925: 152

Lord LUGARD ... remarked that there were twenty cases of witchcraft, with nineteen sentences of imprisonment. The African, as they all knew, attributed any unusual case of sickness or death to the agency of witchcraft, and he looked upon the person who could detect the witch who had worked the spell as a benefactor and killed the man pointed out as a witch, in order to save, as he thought, the lives of others. Though it was, of course, necessary to stamp out those so-called "murders," the imprisonment or execution of the person who detected the witch was, from the native point of view, unjust, and even an encouragement to the practice of witchcraft. The subject was one of extreme difficulty ...

Mr. Hunt [acting district officer in the British Cameroons] personally had had a good deal of experience of witchcraft cases and witch-doctors in the Cameroon Province, and he fully appreciated how deeply that superstition was ingrained in the native mind. But so serious was the consequence of any leniency in that matter that he was persuaded that native susceptibilities should be overridden and severe punishment meted out to all concerned, including the witch-doctor.

League of Nations 1934: 19–20

Nevertheless, a comment made by Lugard regarding the eradication of witchcraft suggests that universal reason was also attributed to the colonial subjects: "Are any steps taken to endeavour to convince the people present at the trial of the error of their belief—for example, by pointing to the lucrative nature of the witch-doctor's profession, or by showing the true cause of death by post-mortem examination?" (League of Nations 1934: 53).

The case of witchcraft as the last example in this article once more shows how colonial engineering impacted upon local structures and perceptions: witchcraft or being a witch nowadays is a punishable offense in Nigeria (Laws of the Federation of Nigeria 1990) and other African countries. In other words, the idea of WITCHCRAFT AS A PUNISHABLE OFFENSE, as expressed in the League of Nations documents, was carried over to the legal system after independence. This "Westernization" through law may result in cognitive-cultural effects, as is for instance suggested in Finzel and Wolf (2019) and Wolf (2021). There, the semantics of *witch* and *witchcraft* in African Englishes were found to be predominantly female gendered and negatively connoted, while this was or is not the case in a traditional African context.

## 4. (Post)colonial Impact on the English Language

In the previous sections, we shed light on colonial mindsets and structures from a cultural-cognitive perspective and discussed possible consequences on how these factors might have influenced conceptualizations found in Indian and African Englishes.

However, as we stated in the introduction, the influence has not been a one-way street. Linguistic material from the formerly subjugated parts of the British empire has found its way into the common core of English, reflecting the title of Ashcroft et al.'s (1989) collective volume *The Empire writes back* (also see Wolf and Polzenhagen 2009: 26f.).

An analysis of the *Oxford English Dictionary* (2020) revealed around 850 entries from sub-Saharan Africa, ranging from *abakwetha* (of or relating to the traditional initiation period or ritual symbolizing passage into manhood among Xhosas) to *Zuluize* (to make into a Zulu). In terms of lexical domains relevant to the topics discussed above, thirty-seven items stem from "religion, tradition, ritual," with *Babalawo* (originally in West Africa: a traditional healer in the Ifa system of divination); *juju* (an object of any kind superstitiously venerated by West African native peoples, and used as a charm, amulet, or means of protection; a fetish); *malombo* (a Venda rite of exorcism and healing conducted by a diviner, accompanied by drumming, singing, and dancing, which causes a high state of nervous excitement) as representative examples. Thirty-one items are categorized as "witchcraft, superstition, mythology." Amongst these thirty-seven items, one finds, for example, *abatagati* (esp. among the Nguni peoples: witches or wizards as a class; practitioners of evil magic); *baloi* (in southern Africa (in Sotho and Tswana society): practitioners of magic or witchcraft); *mafufunya* (the evil spirits which are believed to possess a person suffering from this disorder); *mganga* (in East Africa: a doctor whose traditional functions include exorcism, prophecy, and the removal of spells); *moloi* (in southern Africa (in Sotho and Tswana society): a practitioner of magic; a wizard, a witch) and *muti* (medicine as traditionally practiced among the black peoples of Africa, usually in the form of charms or other objects to which healing or magical powers are ascribed, incorporating herbs and parts of animals and (occasionally) of human bodies).

For Indian items in the *Oxford English Dictionary* (2020), our search turned up around 780 items, ranging from *aal* (the noni or Indian mulberry) to *zho* (a hybrid bovine animal, bred from a yak bull and a common cow, used for domestic purposes in Northern India). One item pertains to "philosophy," twenty-nine items to "religion, tradition, ritual," and three to "witchcraft, superstition, mythology." Beyond these categories, two items found for Indian English relate to issues discussed above, namely *dancing girl* (a girl who dances in public; a female professional dancer; esp. in India, a nautch-girl), which insinuates prostitution, and *half-caste* (a person of mixed descent; esp. (in India) one born or descended from a European father and Indian mother).

The words mentioned in this section show at least a lexical influence of the (former) colonies on the English language. This influence can lead to further investigating the way these items were contextualized by the colonizers, i.e., to see whether conceptual influences occurred concurrently. Obvious examples of conceptual influence and cultural appropriation come from the realm of spirituality highlighted earlier in the chapter. The Western meanings of items such as *karma* or *juju*, for instance, are necessarily reduced versions of the original highly complex notions, seen through the lens of the Western observer and charged with a long history of orientalist conceptions. Rather than looking into such complex notions, we will briefly discuss a more mundane example from the Indian context, i.e., *bungalow*. The *OED* defines *bungalow* as follows:

"Originally: a one-storied house (or temporary building, e.g., a summer-house), lightly built, usually with a thatched roof. In modern use: any one-storied house."

The term derives from Hindi or Marathi *bangla*, meaning 'of Bengal'. A thorough analysis of the cultural history related to this item is given by King (1982), and the short account given here is based on his investigation. The early recorded mentions of the term come from the mid-seventeenth century, and they refer to quickly-built shelters in the style of Bengali huts. These *banglas*, as they were called, were set up temporarily for specific purposes (e.g., for wedding celebrations or meetings) rather than for permanent dwelling. We also find the term *banggol/banggolo* applied to common indigenous huts for permanent housing, e.g., in the following account from 1810:

> The style of private ediface that is proper and peculiar to Bengal, consists of a hut with a pent roof constructed of two sloping sides which meet in a ridge forming the segment of a circle so that it has a resemblance to a boat when overturned ... This kind of hut, it is said, from being peculiar to Bengal, is called by the native Banggol ... Among the natives, the poor man has one hut for himself and cattle, the richer men increase the number without altering the plan of the building.
>
> quoted in King 1982: 44

Modeled on this and other types of indigenous houses, the colonizers developed the fairly distinct type of cottage-type dwelling characteristic of Anglo-Indian colonial life style, preserving the term *bungalow*. The following account comes from J. Lockwood Kipling, the father of Rudyard Kipling:

> Our early residents in India, engaged in military, administrative or trading duties, lived a nomadic life for the greater part of the year in tents, and since there was nothing in the indigenous buildings of Bengal suited to their requirements, their first dwelling houses, designed by themselves and built of materials at site, are naturally planned on the model of the Indian service tents to which they were accustomed, i.e., a large and lofty room surrounded by double walls of canvas enclosing space between them, with partitions at two or more corners for bath or store rooms. It is probable, indeed, that in the beginning the tent itself was occasionally covered with the sun-proof thatch or 'bangla'. The name and the thatch were all we took'.
>
> quoted in King 1982: 56

This form of dwelling was reserved for the European colonizers. In its explicit opposition to the "native town," it is a prominent materialization of colonial culture; as King rightly notes:

> The spatial separation of the district officer or army subaltern from the native town expressed a social and political divide. It was also explained on cultural grounds, European beliefs leading them to perceive the 'native city' as a source of illness and disease.
>
> King 1982: 63

The bungalow-centered compound was also a materialization of other ingredients of the respective zeitgeist, in particular the desire to be close to nature.

In the nineteenth and twentieth century, the bungalow spread from India to virtually all parts of the world, as a type of dwelling in other tropical colonies (e.g., in Africa), as a country house in rural areas (e.g., as a competitor to the traditional English cottage in Britain), often as a place primarily for vacations, and, finally, as a dominant dwelling-style in the emerging suburbs (e.g., in the US and Australia). The bungalow has become a global phenomenon. In each of its manifestations it has not only been physically adapted to the respective contexts and functions, but it has also become a central element and prime marker of a particular life-style, e.g., suburban US middle-class culture (for detailed analyses, see King 1982). In other words., the notion of a 'bungalow' has been culturally appropriated and imbued with, in this case, Western middle-class values.

A parallel, though less prominent, example of such a cultural appropriation is the item *teapoy*. It is derived from Hindi *tipāi*, meaning 'three-legged' and originally referring to an Indian-style small three-legged table. *Tea-* in *teapoy* thus is a folk-etymologic interpretation of the Indian element meaning 'three', and at the same time the product of the cultural appropriation of this furniture to English tea culture, i.e., a table used to serve tea. Contemporary teapoys more often than not have four legs and they come in a wide range of styles other than Indian.

We hope to have shown with this brief discussion that loan words are a fruitful anchor and starting point for the investigation of conceptual influences, not only with the non-native varieties at the receiving end (the traditional perspective in Kachruvian research of contextualization) but also with the Western varieties as a target.

## 5. Conclusion

To the best of our knowledge, this chapter constitutes the first attempt in the field of World Englishes to consider the cultural-conceptual framework during the colonial period, or to use a different term, the zeitgeist in which second language varieties of English emerged. Our cases in point were the Indian and African contexts. First, we discussed the general philosophical and biological outlook of intellectuals and administrators towards the indigenous colonial populations. Secondly, we looked at social practices by the colonial subjects that collided with the prevalent moral beliefs (at least in theory) of the colonizers. These practices were perceived as "disturbances" that needed to be fenced in and regulated, if not eradicated. Hence, colonial policy not only created administrative and legal structures, but superimposed ideological mindsets whose traces can be witnessed in cultural conceptualizations expressed in the respective varieties of English. We tried to sketch some of these traces effected by colonialism.

For the very reason that this process of socio-cultural influence started during the colonial period—and not post-independence—alongside the, albeit restrictive (see Wolf 2008), implantation of English in the territories under British rule, we deem the term *Postcolonial English(es)*, that is gaining currency (see, e.g., Schneider 2007), highly misleading. Our examples came from the domains of marriage, (homo)sexuality, and witchcraft; others, such as polygamy, could have been included as well but were not considered for reasons of space. We argued, however, that influence was not a one-way street. In the last part of this chapter, we briefly pointed to lexical influences from the colonies on the English language per se. Interestingly enough, many of the lexical items stem from the lexical fields that represent the domains related to the socio-moral "disturbances" perceived by the colonizers. To what extent a conceptual flow from the colonies to Britain took place remains yet to be explored.

## Notes

1 The ongoing parent-child relationship can well be observed in the relation of France to its former colonies, especially in Africa, where the francophone countries until recently did not enjoy monetary sovereignty (cf., e.g., Samba Sylla et al. 2019; Maclean 2019). The British, on the other hand, *neglected their children* and eventually *abandoned* them after independence; quite literally so, if the educational system is considered (see Wolf 1999, 2001, 2008).
2 For a detailed account, see Trautmann (1997: 84–93).
3 Other than some linguists of the time who thought Sanskrit to be the *Ursprache*, that is the common ancestral language they were eagerly searching for, Jones regarded Sanskrit as one of the offsprings of this original language.
4 It is plain that these are atrocities, and it is a merit of many agents in the otherwise also atrocious colonial enterprise to have named them as what they are, i.e., atrocities covered up by cultural rules designed to preserve local power structures, and to have worked against them with a truly altruistic mindset. Colonial administration, however, was very hesitant to prohibit such practices. Even when legal regulations were issued to this effect (e.g., the Child Marriage Restraint Act 1929/30 in India), they came late, were half-hearted and were reluctantly reinforced.
5 Grant was an Evangelical, with a long carrier as a missionary in India and strong ties to the East India Company. He was an ardent proponent of the abolition of slavery. For a more detailed discussion of his positions, see Trautmann (1997: 117).
6 Here, we are obviously in the realm of double standards. In Western societies, prostitution, for instance, has always been more or less tolerated, if not institutionalized (brothels). In most time frames, successive polygamy (e.g., re-marriage) was not regarded as problematic, and promiscuity (after all, a version of simultaneous polygamy) was more or less accepted, at least when performed by men. With the issue of homosexuality, we are in the realm of overt oppression in Western societies. Note, however, that Grant is writing from the perspective of an Evangelical, i.e., against the background of a specific system of beliefs and morals.
7 We assume that the reference to "the unnatural practices of the ancient Heathens" refers to homosexuality (cf., Clark 2009).
8 An indicator of this change and of the increasing anthropological interest in Africa is the renaming of the *School of Oriental Studies* to *School of Oriental and African Studies* (SOAS) in 1938.
9 In fact, he was promoted by Lugard, who thought anthropological work necessary for the development of colonial policy and saw much of Malinowski's work as supportive of his own colonial vision. Lugard was a co-founder of the International Institute of

10  Compare: "The right to legislate is reserved. That this should remain in the hands of the Central Government—itself limited by the control of the Colonial Office, as I have described cannot be questioned" (Lugard 1922: 206).
11  This point is highlighted in the work of Homi Bhabha (e.g., 1994).
12  Climate-related "explanations" of differences between nations were thriving at the time. They were also an integral part of the discourse on the *génie de la langue*, meant to account for the specific "character" of languages. Such explanations persisted well into the twentieth century; a prominent example is Otto Herdel's account of the German consonant shifts, commonly referred to as *Hauch- und Schnauftheorie*, in which he famously relates this sound change to the new environmental conditions in the more mountainous regions the German people moved to.
13  There was a parallel rhetoric of "Indian sisters" in the context of colonial India; see Cleall (2012: 29ff.) for a discussion.
14  Racial segregation was also evident in the segregation of schools in East Africa into "three separate main racial educational systems," with different schools for Europeans, Indians and natives (Tanganyika. Administering Authority 1958: 32).
15  To be clear, we are talking of ideology here; the colonial practice on the ground can hardly be described as "responsible," at least on the side of the British (for a thorough discussion and exemplification, see Wolf 1999, Wolf 2001: 64–99, Wolf 2008).
16  However, as Weeks (1990) notes, prostitution and homosexuality were conceptually linked, especially in the second half of the nineteenth century.
17  Bleys (1993: 168) refers to a "hierarchy of civilisations," a term which is equally applicable but addresses to a lesser degree the patriarchal nature of colonization.
18  For instance, there had to be proof of penetration and emission of semen for a conviction prior to 1826, when Robert Peel loosened this requirement (Weeks 1990: 12).
19  This quote seems to slightly deviate in few very minor points (irrelevant to the present argumentation) from the actual original text (cf., https://web.archive.org/web/20070114135350/http://chddistrictcourts.gov.in/THE%20INDIAN%20PENAL%20CODE.pdf).
20  Undoubtedly, such concepts of HOMOSEXUALITY cannot be equaled with modern (let alone colonial) Western concepts. Investigations in world Englishes are therefore problematic and beneficial at the same time: problematic since English lexemes usually diverge from variety to variety in terms of the associated concepts due to contact with local concepts and may thus have different meanings; beneficial since the study of world Englishes facilitates the analysis of the cognitive concepts associated with these lexemes.

# References

Acton, W. (1870), *Prostitution Considered in its Moral, Social, and Sanitary Aspects, in London and other Large Cities and Garrison Towns. With Proposals for the Control and Prevention of its Attendant Evils*, 2nd edition, London: John Churchill and Sons.

Aina, T. A. (1991), "Patterns of bisexuality in Sub-Saharan Africa," in R. Tielman, M. Carballo and A. Hendriks (eds.), *Bisexuality & HIV/AIDS: A Global Perspective*, 81–90, Buffalo: Prometheus Books.

Ajibade, G. O. (2013), "Same-sex relationships in Yorùbá culture and orature," *Journal of Homosexuality*, 60 (7): 965–83.

Aldrich, R. (2003), *Colonialism and Homosexuality*, London and New York: Routledge.

Appiah, A. and Gates, H. L. (2010), *Encyclopedia of Africa*, New York: Oxford University Press.

Ashcroft, B., G. Griffiths and H. Tiffin, eds. (1989), *The Empire Writes Back: Theory and Practice in Post-Colonial Literature*, London: Routledge.

Ayeni, V. O. (2017), "Human rights and the criminalization of same-sex relationships in Nigeria: A critique of the Same-Sex Marriage (Prohibition) Act," in S. Namwase and A. Jjuuko (eds.), *Protecting the Human Rights of Sexual Minorities in Contemporary Africa*, 203–37, Pretoria: Pretoria University Law Press.

Bashford, A. (2004), *Imperial Hygiene: A Critical History of Colonialism, Nationalism and Public Health*, New York: Palgrave Macmillan.

Bhabha, H. K. (1994), *The Location of Culture*, London and New York: Routledge.

Bleys, R. (1993), "Homosexual exile: The textuality of the imaginary paradise, 1800–1980," *Journal of Homosexuality*, 25 (1–2): 165–82.

Bleys, R. (1995), *The Geography of Perversion. Male-to-male Sexual Behaviour outside the West and the Ethnographic Imagination, 1750–1918*, New York: New York University Press.

Boyce, P. (2006), "Moral ambivalence and irregular practices: Contextualizing male-to-male sexualities in Calcutta/India," *Feminist Review*, 83: 79–98.

Brady, S. (2009), *Masculinity and Male Homosexuality in Britain, 1861–1913*, London: Palgrave Macmillan.

Brown, A. (2009), "The latest hate speech from the Church of Nigeria," *The Guardian*, March 13, 2009. Available online: https://www.theguardian.com/commentisfree/andrewbrown/2009/mar/13/religion-anglicanism-akinola-nigeria (accessed March 6, 2020).

Brutt-Griffler, J. (2002), *World English: A Study of its Development*, Clevedon: Multilingual Matters.

Bryder, L. (1998), "Sex, race, and colonialism: An historiographical Review," *The International History Review*, 20 (4): 806–22.

Clark, D. (2009), *Between Medieval Men: Male Friendship and Desire in Early Medieval English Literature*, Oxford: Oxford University Press.

Cleall, E. (2012), *Missionary Discourses of Difference. Negotiating Otherness in the British Empire, 1840–1900*, New York: Palgrave Macmillan.

Cohen, W. A. (1996), *Sex Scandal: The Private Parts of Victorian Fiction*, Durham and London: Duke University Press.

Coke, E. (1648), *The Third Part of the Institutes of the Laws of England: Concerning High Treason, and other Pleas of the Crown, and Criminall Causes*, 2nd edition, London: Miles Flesher per William Lee and Daniel Pakeman. Available online: https://gutenberg.beic.it/webclient/DeliveryManager?pid=6495661

Das Wilhelm, A. (2008), *Tritiya-Prakriti: People of the Third Sex. Understanding Homosexuality, Transgender Identity, and Intersex Conditions Through Hinduism*, Philadelphia: Xlibris.

Dimier, V. (2004), "On good colonial government: Lessons from the League of Nations," *Global Society*, 18 (3): 279–99.

Fanon, F. (1952), *Peau Noire, Masques Blancs*, Paris: Seuil.

Fanon, F. (1961), *Les Damnés de la Terre*, Paris: Maspero.

Finzel, A. (forthcoming), "Innate or acquired? HOMOSEXUALITY and cultural models of GENDER in Indian and Nigerian English," in H.-G. Wolf, D. Latic and A. Finzel (eds.), *Cultural-Linguistic Explorations into Spirituality, Emotionality, and Society*, Amsterdam and Philadelphia: John Benjamins.

Finzel, A. and H.-G. Wolf (2019), "Conceptual metaphors as contact phenomena? The influence of local Concepts on source and target domain," in E. Zenner, A. Backus and E. Winter-Froemel (eds.), *Cognitive Contact Linguistics. Placing Usage, Meaning and Mind at the Core of Contact-Induced Variation and Change*, 187–211, Berlin and New York: De Gruyter.

Foks, W. (2018), "Bronislaw Malinowski, 'indirect rule,' and the colonial politics of Functionalist Anthropology, ca. 1925–1940," *Comparative Studies in Society and History*, 60 (1): 35–57.

Gibbon, E. ([1781] 1854), *The History of the Decline and Fall of the Roman Empire. Volume V*, Boston: Little, Brown, and Company.

Grant, C. ([1796] 1835), *Observations on the State of Society among the Asiatic Subjects of Great Britain, Particularly with Respect to Morals ; and on the Means of Improving it.—Written Chiefly in the Year 1792*, Printed as Appendix I to: Report from the Select Committee on the Affairs of the East India Company, with Minutes of Evidence, in Six Parts, an Appendix and Index to Each.

Gupta, A. (2006), "Section 377 and the dignity of Indian homosexuals," *Economic and Political Weekly*, 41 (46): 4815–23.

Gupta, A. (2008), "This alien legacy: The origins of 'sodomy' laws in British colonialism," *Human Rights Watch*, December 17, 2008. Available online: https://www.hrw.org/report/2008/12/17/alien-legacy/origins-sodomy-laws-british-colonialism (accessed February 4, 2020).

Hinchy, J. (2014), "Obscenity, moral contagion and masculinity: Hijras in public space in colonial North India," *Asian Studies Review*, 38 (2): 274–94.

Hunt, S. J. (2011), "Conservative Hindu reactions to non-heterosexual rights in India," *International Journal of Sociology and Anthropology*, 3 (9): 318–27.

Jones, W. (1786), "The third anniversary discourse" (delivered February 2, 1786, by the President, at the Asiatick Society of Bengal, on the Hindus), *Electronic Library of Historiography*. Available online: http://www.eliohs.unifi.it/testi/700/jones/Jones_Discourse_3.html (accessed April 13, 2020).

Kakar, S. and K. Kakar (2006), *Die Inder: Porträt einer Gesellschaft*, München: C. H. Beck.

King, A. D. (1982), *The Bungalow, 1600—1980. A Study of the Cultural, Social, Political and Economic Factors in the Production of a Global House-type*. PhD thesis. School of Social Sciences Brunel University, Uxbridge. Available online: https://bura.brunel.ac.uk/handle/2438/5217 (accessed August 10, 2020)

Kirpal, S. (2016), "Gay rights—are societal values really divergent from constitutional morality?," *International Academy of Family Lawyers*. Available online: https://www.iafl.com/media/1260/2016.pdf (accessed March 6, 2020).

Kövecses, Z. ([2002] 2010), *Metaphor: A Practical Introduction*, 2nd edition, Oxford: Oxford University Press.

*Laws of the Federation of Nigeria* (1990). Available online: http://www.nigeria-law.org/Criminal%20Code%20Act-Tables.htm (accessed March 12, 2020).

League of Nations (1924), "Permanent Mandate Commission. Report on the Work of the Fourth Session of the Commission Submitted to the Council of the League of Nations. Annex 12," *League of Nations Archive*, Geneva.

League of Nations (1925), "Minutes of the Sixth Session Held at Geneva from June 26th to July 10th, 1925," *League of Nations Archive*, Geneva.

League of Nations (1926), "Minutes of the Ninth Session Held at Geneva from June 8th to 25th, 1926, Including the Report of the Commission to the Council," *League of Nations Archive*, Geneva.

League of Nations (1928), "Permanent Mandate Commission. Minutes of the Fourteenth Session. Held at Geneva from October 26th to November 13th, 1928, Including the Report of the Commission to the Council and Comments by Various Accredited Representatives of the Mandatory Powers," *League of Nations Archive*, Geneva.

League of Nations (1934), "Permanent Mandate Commission. Minutes of the Twenty-Sixth Session Held at Geneva from October 29th to November 12th, 1934, Including the Report of the Commission to the Council," *League of Nations Archive*, Geneva.

League of Nations (1935), "Minutes of the Twenty-Seventh Session Held at Geneva from June 3rd to 18th, 1935, Including the Report of the Commission to the Council," *League of Nations Archive*, Geneva.

Levine, P. (1994), "Venereal disease, prostitution, and the politics of empire: The case of British India," *Journal of the History of Sexuality*, 4 (4): 579–602.

Lugard, F. J. D. (1922), *The Dual Mandate in British Tropical Africa*, Edinburgh and London: William Blackwood and Sons.

Macaulay, T. B. (1835), "Minute by the Hon'ble T. B. Macaulay, dated the 2nd February 1835." Available online: http://www.columbia.edu/itc/mealac/pritchett/00generallinks/macaulay/txt_minute_education_1835.html (accessed April 13, 2020).

Maclean, R. (2019), "West African countries take a step away from colonial-era currency," *The New York Times*, December 21. Available online: https://www.nytimes.com/2019/12/21/world/africa/west-africa-currency-france-franc.html (accessed March 17, 2020).

Murray, S. O. and W. Roscoe, eds. (2001), *Boy-Wives and Female Husbands. Studies of African Homosexualities*, New York: Palgrave Macmillan.

Mwalimu, C. (2007), *The Nigerian Legal System. Volume 1: Public Law*, New York: Lang.

"Obasanjo backs bishops over gays" (2004), *BBC News*. Available online: http://news.bbc.co.uk/2/hi/africa/3955145.stm (last accessed March 6, 2020).

*Oxford English Dictionary*, online (2020), Oxford: Oxford University Press.

Peña Cervel, M. S. (2005), "The image-schematic basis of the EVENT STRUCTURE metaphor," *Annual Review of Cognitive Linguistics*, 2 (1): 127–58.

Playfair, J. ([1822] 2011), *The Works of John Playfair*, Volume 3, edited by James G. Playfair, Cambridge: Cambridge University Press. [Digitally printed version.]

Rousseau, J.-J. ([1762] 1979), *Emile: or On Education*, transl. Allan Bloom, New York: Basic Books.

Saïd, E. W. (1979), *Orientalism*, New York: Vintage Books.

Samba Sylla, N., S. Ferguson, W. Saas and M. Seijo (2019), "Money on the left: Confronting monetary imperialism in Francophone Africa: Ndongo Samba Sylla interviewed by S. Ferguson, M. Seijo and W. Saas, *Monthly Review online*. Available online: https://mronline.org/2019/05/26/money-on-the-left-confronting-monetary-imperialism-in-francophone-africa/ (accessed March 17, 2020).

Schneider, E. (2007), *Postcolonial English: Varieties around the World*, Cambridge: Cambridge University Press.

Sinha, M. (1995), *Colonial Masculinity. The "Manly Englishman" and the "Effeminate Bengali" in the Late Nineteenth Century*, Manchester and New York: Manchester University Press.

Stoler, A. L. (1995), *Race and the Education of Desire. Foucault's History of Sexuality and the Colonial Order of Things*, Durham and London: Duke University Press.

Tanganyika. Administering Authority (1958), *Report of the United Nations Visiting Mission to Tanganyika, 1957, Observations of the Administering Authority*. The Government Printer, Dar es Salaam.

Trautmann, T. R. (1997), *Aryans and British India*, New Delhi: Vistaar.

Trevor-Roper, H. (1963), "The rise of Christian Europe," *The Listener* (November 28, 1963).

Vanita, R. and S. Kidwai, eds. (2001), *Same-Sex Love in India: Readings from Literature and History*, New York: Palgrave Macmillan.

Weeks, J. (1990), *Coming Out: Homosexual Politics in Britain from the Nineteenth Century to the Present*, revised edition, London and New York: Quartet Books.

White, C., ed. (1999), *Nineteenth-century Writings on Homosexuality: A Sourcebook*, London and New York: Routledge.

Wolf, H.-G. (1999), "The impact of British colonial policy on the forms and functions of English in Cameroon," in U. Carls and P. Lucko (eds.), *Form, Function and Variation in English: Studies in Honour of Klaus Hansen*, 219–33, Frankfurt/M.: P. Lang.

Wolf, H.-G. (2001), *English in Cameroon*, Berlin and New York: De Gruyter.

Wolf, H.-G. (2008), "British and French language and educational policies in the mandate and trusteeship territories," *Language Sciences*, 30: 553–74.

Wolf, H.-G. (2021), "East and West African Englishes: Differences and commonalities," in A. Kirkpatrick (ed.), *The Routledge Handbook of World Englishes*, 2nd edition, 216–32, London and New York: Routledge.

Wolf, H.-G. and F. Polzenhagen (2009), *World Englishes: A Cognitive Sociolinguistic Approach*. Berlin and New York: De Gruyter.

Zabus, C. (2013), *Out in Africa: Same-Sex Desire in Sub-Saharan Literatures & Cultures*, Woodbridge: James Currey.

# 11

# Individual Lives in Collectivist Faces: On Social Norms in a Radio Show

Eric A. Anchimbe

## 1. Introduction

Postcolonial African communities have been shown to have collectivist cultural frames (cf., Lienhardt 1985; Nwoye 1992; de Kadt 1998; Egner 2006; Anchimbe 2018). Social interaction norms of these societies oblige speakers to communicate in ways that portray them as deserving and acceptable members of their societies. While research has illustrated the functioning of these collectivist societies, Lienhardt (1985: 145) warns, truly so, that we should not place "too much one-sided stress on the collectivist orientation of African ideas of the person" to a point where it "deflect[s] interest from this [individual] African concern, also, on occasion, with individuals as individuals" (Lienhardt 1985: 143). A number of studies have shown that interlocutors in or from these societies often prefer to project collectivist or group faces even where the individual face would suffice, for instance, in requesting, criticizing and thanking (e.g., Nwoye 1992), in offering (e.g., Anchimbe 2018), in insulting others (e.g., Mulo Farenkia 2011), in instructing (Grainger et al. 2010), and in constructing identities (Ige 2010) among others.

This chapter illustrates how individual life experiences and faces are often submerged or subsumed into collectivist group faces during interactions in postcolonial African communities. This happens in interactions that take place in private as well as in public space. Focus in this chapter is on the radio show, "Happy Birthday," broadcast in Bamenda, Cameroon, a postcolonial collectivist context where a postcolonial English variety, Cameroon English (cf., Simo Bobda 1994; Anchimbe 2006; Kouega 2007; etc.), is used. I also demonstrate that, although English is a nativized language in this society, it is still capable of communicating the collectivist intentions speakers encode during interactions. Given that the pragmatics of Postcolonial Englishes has been slow in emerging, this chapter seeks to draw more attention to it, and to signal the need for emic multilingual approaches for studying Postcolonial Englishes.

Although the radio broadcasts take place in the public sphere, when the need to project collectivist group values and defend group social norms arises, interlocutors quickly adopt positions and construct discourses that enable them to do so. For instance, they would easily and quickly attribute and accept blame and criticism, give and receive advice on personal or private issues, and adopt and perform kinship asymmetrical roles for respect, social cohesion, etc. The adoption of kinship asymmetrical roles, social affective roles and tasks, and advice-giving roles is generally based on the interlocutor's age, social status, social hierarchy and sometimes gender. Allegiance to the group, its culture and norms is so strong that members are ready to perform private dialogue, give and take family-like advice, and enact respect behavior in the public space in ways reminiscent of the intimacy of the home. They do so in order to maintain their group face and in accordance with the social norms of their societies.

Pragmatic research on Postcolonial Englishes is not only limited but also marked by reliance on Western approaches, especially Brown and Levinson's (1987) politeness framework, Blum-Kulka et al.'s (1989a, b) cross-cultural approach, Goffman's (1967) face concept, and Austin's (1962) and Searle's (1979) speech act theories. In this group belong Lwanga-Lumu (1999) on requests in Uganda, Mustapha (2011) on compliment responses in Nigerian English, Ouafeu (2006) on pragmatic particles in Cameroon English, Anderson (2006, 2009) on requests in Ghanaian English, etc.

Yamuna Kachru (1991a, b) was among the first to consciously raise the lack of research attention on the pragmatics of New Englishes, as they were called then. Nelson (1991) on speech acts in New Englishes creative writings and Tinkham (1991) on the social variation in the use of speech acts in India, both included in Kachru's (1991a) edited volume, have as overall aim to illustrate the variation in pragmatic phenomena in New Englishes contexts. Kachru (1991a) proposes an integrated framework for research on speech acts in indigenized varieties of English. Her cry that "the speech act theory is not sufficient for research on cross-cultural interactions" (Kachru 1991b: 299) in postcolonial contexts was echoed in the 1990s by Nwoye (1992) and de Kadt (1998). In the 2000s, a few more studies pointed out the insufficiency of Western theories to postcolonial English discourses, among them, Kasanga (2003, 2006), Anchimbe (2008), and Mulo Farenkia (2010). Others have recently proposed more concise frameworks for analyzing non-Western discourses, e.g., emancipatory pragmatics (Hanks et al. 2009) and postcolonial pragmatics (cf., Janney 2009; Anchimbe and Janney 2011a/b, 2017; Anchimbe 2016, 2018). Postcolonial pragmatics approaches postcolonial discourses from the standpoint of their locatedness, historically, socially and geographically, in the lives of multilingual speakers and their collectivist postcolonial societies. I have used it in this chapter since it is built on the complex societal structure of postcolonial societies.

In line with that, the rest of the chapter is structured as follows: Section 2 presents the data used in the analysis and Section 3 explains the applicability of postcolonial pragmatics to collectivist cultures like the Cameroonian while Section 4 examines how individual lives and faces are understood in terms of the society's group face and social norms. The conclusion accentuates the importance of understanding the basic multilingual, multicultural and multiethnic structure of collectivist postcolonial societies in research endeavors about them.

## 2. The Data: *Happy Birthday* Program

The data used in this study are culled from two editions of the program "Happy Birthday"[1] broadcast on the Bamenda station of the Cameroon Radio and Television

(CRTV) network in November-December 2007. Two interviews were selected from the two editions because they contain many of the issues analyzed in this chapter. In almost all of the interviews, there is at least one instance of collectivist group priorities overriding the individual's face or privacy.

In this Saturday morning prime time broadcast, the host visits the maternity sections of hospitals in the city and wishes happy motherhood and happy birthday to mothers and babies respectively. In the exchanges with the mothers, which last on average two minutes, the host asks the mothers their names, age, marital status, education, the number of children they have or wish to have, their husbands and the delivery experience. She then offers them the chance to inform friends and/or family about the delivery of the child. The program lasts thirty minutes and is generally pre-taped although a few broadcasts are live.

The host switches between three languages during the broadcast, i.e., English, Cameroon Pidgin English and French. The major reasons for the switches are the linguistic needs of the interviewee (i.e., switching to the language she understands) and the additional social role the host wants to play (e.g., switching to Pidgin often happens to create a family atmosphere conducive for reprimanding a young mother for giving birth out of wedlock and while still in school). Such reprimands are done on radio just as they would normally be done in a home setting (see Anchimbe and Janney 2011a). Sometimes the host also asks mothers to pass on messages to loved ones or sing birth celebratory songs in their native languages. It is, therefore, a multilingual program in which choice of language is highly significant and representative of the composition of the society. That is not the focus of this chapter though. The episodes selected for analysis here are in Cameroon English (see Appendix).

## 3. Collective Face, Cultures and Postcolonial Pragmatics

One of the major aims of the postcolonial pragmatics framework is to account for the impact of the collectivist, multicultural, multilingual and multiethnic nature of postcolonial societies on social interaction. These aspects have generally been overlooked in most previous research that relies on Western monocultural and monolingual frameworks. In the Western-based studies, overarching attention is paid to the atomistic needs of the individual and his or her face wants. Taking this position as universal, the collectivist and group-based faces of most African cultures have often been misrepresented. In these cultures, Kasanga (2011: 45) signals, an individual's "loss of face through a shameful act [not just in speech] is akin to letting others down more than oneself down." So, there are other forces at work beyond individual volition that compel group members to show allegiance to the group; defend and protect its social esteem vis-a-vis other groups. Some of these have been addressed by Nwoye (1992), de Kadt (1994, 1998), Kasanga (2006), and Anchimbe (2008), among others.

The complex nature of the collectivist society's expectations, members' expectations of each other through, for instance, the onlooker response (see Anchimbe 2011, 2018), as well as respect for the society's social norms must be incorporated into any analysis that aims to appropriately explain the communicative choices in these societies. Earlier studies about pragmatic phenomena in African societies have accentuated the importance of this complex web of interconnectedness. For instance, Nwoye (1992: 317) narrates a personal experience in which he asked for help from a man and his son, both strangers to him, with pushing his car that had suddenly broken down. Without using any hedges or politeness markers, his request for assistance was immediately met with prompt action. For the father and son who helped him, what mattered was not the way they were addressed but rather the public self-esteem of their group, i.e., the village in which the car had broken down. They knew if they did not help—help being a default social expectation of their society—the stranger would think badly of their village and may recount his negative experience to others hence leading to a negative appraisal of their group. Postcolonial pragmatics looks beyond the verbalized discourse into non-verbalized sociocultural norms and expectations in its approach to postcolonial social interactions.

The strong collectivist impetus of these societies is not only implied in behavior patterns and choices in speech, but are often also clearly verbalized. This could be through positive judgements of their society and culture or identity alignments with it. In a study of collective identity construction by students at the University of KwaZulu-Natal, South Africa, Ige (2010) finds out that male Zulu students, who refer to themselves as *Zulu-bradas* (brothers—in plural, meaning 'group'), portray themselves "in ways that would maintain and reinforce their cultural identity, generally as members of a group" (Ige 2010: 3050). As students living in a multicultural and multilingual context, i.e., the city, where group boundaries are blurred by the presence of people from many other ethnic and linguistic groups, the question arises of how this group cultural identity influences their self-image as individuals? To this, Ige (2010: 3050) illustrates that, among the *Zulu-bradas*, the "collective identity tends to supersede their individual identity and may result in suppression of the individual self." However, this individual self also exists (cf., Lienhardt 1985) but is often the marked counterpart of the group self (Kasanga 2006, 2011) which is generally unmarked or is the default.

The reason why projecting the collectivist self is considered default behavior is because people grow up in such an environment and socialize into it. Like language, the norms of a society are acquired in childhood and consolidated as one grows up in the society. On a personal note, Kasanga (2011: 47–8), taking his collectivist culture as point of reference, explains how sharing or generosity is a default social norm:

> In my own culture, I learnt quite early that almost anything could be shared with siblings, relatives, neighbours, and even passers-by out of norm-based generosity. A gift received called for a favour in return either to the same benefactor or, through circular generosity, to a third party.
>
> Kasanga 2011: 47–8

The cultural expectation of circular generosity mentioned above seems to have coalesced in postcolonial societies with the Christian canons of kindness and generosity. There is potentially a blend of pre-colonial cultural expectations, as signalled by Kasanga (2011) and Christianity expectations, as can be seen in the excerpt below from Anchimbe (2018: 264). In an interview about the refusal of offers, a 25-30 year-old female Cameroonian was asked if she was disappointed when her offer was refused by a friend of hers:

> I was not disappointed. I was not surprised, but I told her, I said "you are refusing me blessings" because when you give something to somebody, the heavens bless you. So, I told her "you have refused me receiving my blessings from above."
> 
> Anchimbe 2018: 264

Even though circular generosity seems to be replaced here by "blessings from above," the underlying meaning remains the same. The only difference is the register. God uses other humans to bless people, the respondent added later in the interview. The default behavior of generosity binds Christians in this example at two collectivist or group levels: they are members of the society (clan, village, etc.) and the church. Postcolonial pragmatics treats religion as a central analytical component since it affects the lives and discourses of people in postcolonial societies.

The exemplification of the functioning of the collectivist face and culture in postcolonial societies above lays the foundation for the analysis in this study. Having shown how the individual self is submerged into the collective self, I then applied a postcolonial pragmatics perspective to the data, illustrating that individual face, even in the public space of the radio and in an indigenized ex-colonial language, is submerged in the group face when the need for that arises. Utterances, which in Western pragmatics theories would be considered utterly face threatening, are not at all face threats in this context in as much as they serve to preserve the group's face.

## 4. Individual Lives in Collectivist Faces

Although the interactions in the excerpts below are in Cameroon English, some of the cultural facets embedded in them stem from indigenous social norms that have coalesced with colonially-introduced norms, or have hybridized with them into a new complex system of social interaction. What stands out as the underlying societal construct in the excerpts is the collectivist basis that permeates speakers' intentions and speech. Both the verbal and non-verbal elements of the interactions indicate, implicitly and explicitly, that members want to defend the collectivist group by playing the roles expected of them or by fitting themselves into the appropriate social stratum. Social stratification in this case is at the level of age, social status, kinship and gender.

A significant dimension of the collectivist base in the interactions is the fact that members of the society consider themselves as being related almost on a kinship level. This relationship can be captured using the conceptual metaphor COMMUNITY IS FAMILY. As illustrated below, this is not only limited to the use of kinship terms for non-kin interlocutors. It extends to social commitments, kinship-like tasks, etc. which members perform for each other. In performing these commitments and tasks, the individual (both their face and status) is only relevant in as much as s/he can relate and fit into the larger societal structure, governed by postcolonial pragmatic components like age, social status, gender, religion, history, sociocultural norms of respect, generosity, deference, alignment, etc. These components usually play dominant roles in interpersonal communication irrespective of the context in which the interaction takes place.

Members of the society feel obliged to perform any of these group-based social roles whenever the situation warrants it. For instance, the host of the "Happy Birthday" program flouts her duty as journalist by adopting the position of a mother or aunt to reproach a young girl for getting pregnant while still in school and while she is not yet married (see excerpt 3). Accepting this shift to family space on radio, the young mother apologizes for her mistake, accepts the consequences and issues advice to other girls like her who may make the same mistake.

So, clearly individual faces or statuses cease to matter when the expectations of the COMMUNITY IS FAMILY understanding are not met. In the analysis below, five ways are identified in which this happens in the data. First, the underlying need to live up to social norms and expectations is identified (4.1). Second, the obligation members have to reproach those who do not live up to these expectations is shown (4.2). Third, the duty members have to advise those who flout social norms is described (4.3). Fourth, the rationale members have for informing others of their respect for social norms in a bid to claim societal recognition is explained (4.4). Fifth, the importance of respect behavior in these asymmetrical interactions is expounded on (4.5).

## 4.1 Living up to Social Expectations

Every society has expectations of how members should behave both verbally and physically or non-verbally. What makes collectivist societies different is the extent to which these expectations or norms often supersede members' individualism and how they are enforced. Often unwritten and acquired in childhood, social norms and expectations in these societies are enforced by members' reliance on a collective repertoire they all share and protect. Aware of these norms, they serve as checks and judges of each other's behavior in their different capacities, i.e., in accordance with societal roles attached to age, parenting, gender, social status, etc.

In the research literature, three concepts have been proposed to explain this. Kasanga (2011) uses the notion of circular generosity to justify why people in the collectivist context of The Congo generously give to others. They know that when they give, others would also give to them. Anchimbe (2011, 2018) introduces the concept of the onlooker response to underscore how the impact of onlookers in a communicative situation forces interlocutors to abide by social norms for fear of being accused of letting down the group's values. At the level of speech, the concept of attitudinal filtration (Anchimbe 2006, 2014), illustrates how members, through their negative attitudes, force other speakers to abandon foreign speech forms and to use only speech forms from the community or the language variety they speak. Using their community's speech forms helps them keep their linguistic identity and belonging to the community.

One of the social norms or expectations recurrent in the radio program is that women are expected to get married before having kids. Where this is not the case, any member of the society old enough to be a parent would normally feel called upon by social duty to reproach and then advise the young mother. As excerpts 1 and 2 below show, asking about the age and marital status of the mothers is a common thing on the program. Without hesitations or objections to this apparent prying into their private space or life, the mothers answer the questions. The answers to these two questions set the tone for the rest of the interaction. If the mother is married, the conversation continues in a relaxed and supportive manner (excerpt 2)—proof that the mother has lived up to the expectations of the society. But if the mother is not married, she is reproached, chastised, reprimanded, advised and corrected (excerpt 1)—proof that she has not lived up to the expectations.

Excerpt 1. M.E. 23-year old, unmarried, student (22–12–2007)
Host: Good morning.
Lady: Good morning Madam. I am called M.E.
Host: How old are you?
Lady: 23 years.
Host: Is this your first delivery?
Lady: Yes.
Host: Are you married?
Lady: No.
Host: (Pause) Are you in school?
Lady: Yes
...
Host: And how comes? You know it is not easy to start breeding children when you are going to school, not so?
Lady: Yes.

The two interlocutors in excerpt 1 above are bound by the social norms and expectations of their society. The host observes a brief pause after the answer to the question about marriage is negative. This gives her the time to switch from the role of a radio host to that of a mother. The mother role grants her the social responsibility to reproach and advice the young mother. On her part, the young unmarried mother continues to be cooperative, sharing even more information about herself when she knows implicitly that she would be reproached. She accepts the reproach respectfully since it comes from an older member of the society with a mother-like or aunt-like status.

In excerpt 2, when the marriage question is answered positively, the host does not pause. She continues with questions related to building a family, i.e., the number of children she has, their sexes, and whether the young mother is happy with two daughters. The question about having only daughters is an implicit reference to the strong patriarchal hereditary culture of the society where only male children have inheritance rights. In excerpt 2, the host does not need to switch roles because the society's expectation for having kids has been met. She joins the mother in celebrating the birth of the child in a normal and smooth manner.

Excerpt 2. A.E. 23-year old, married, teacher-trainee (17–11–2007)
Host: Good morning Madam.
Lady: Good morning Aunty

| | |
|---|---|
| Host: | What is your name? |
| Lady: | My name is A.E. |
| Host: | How old are you? |
| Lady: | 23 years old. |
| Host: | Are you married? |
| Lady: | Yes |
| Host: | Is this your first delivery? |
| Lady: | No. Second. |
| Host: | Was the first a baby girl too? |
| Lady: | Yes. |
| Host: | So you have two daughters. |
| Lady: | Yes, I do. |
| Host: | Are you happy? |
| Lady: | Very very happy. |

The two young mothers in excerpts 1 and 2, both 23 years old, receive starkly different treatments from the host only because of their marital status at the time they give birth. Even though the interactions take place on radio, a public utility, and the young mothers are not anonymous since they introduce themselves by their real names, they discuss their private lives as though they were in their homes. With the information they provide, listeners could easily trace them and identify them. They may, thereafter, also be exposed to more reproach from their neighbors, extended family, or the rest of the community. Sharing the information on radio and accepting potential consequences is proof of the power of social norms and members' respect for them. Neither the host nor the mothers lose (individual) face because they have played the roles expected of them by society. The host asks the questions so as to determine her next action while the mothers answer honestly so as not to lose their place as honest members of the society—even if this earns them reproach as in excerpt 3.

## 4.2 Reproaching for Breaking Social Norms

It is normal for members of any society to be reproached, reprimanded, corrected and even punished when they violate norms of their society. In some societies, members are summoned to family or community judicial or customary circles where the reproach or punishment is performed. In such a case, the act of reproaching is routinized since it is performed in the presence of a specific group of people and in a given location. However, in excerpt 3 (a continuation of excerpt 1), the reproach is performed in public, on the radio, and is broadcast to everyone who is listening. The location is physically the hospital ward but then the reproach act is felt beyond this physical location.

As established above (4.1), having a child out of wedlock and while still in school is against the social norms and expectations of the Cameroonian society within which the program is set. Before performing the reproach in excerpt 3, the host asks several questions to ascertain that the young mother clearly fell short of social expectations. She is not married and she is still in school. The host even asks for the name of the school and the class, both of which the young mother provides. This further removes any possibility of anonymity that she could otherwise enjoy. The first reproach turn "And how comes? You know it is not easy to start breeding children when you are going to school, not so?" ends with the tag question, "not so?" which leaves the interviewee little room for contradiction. She, therefore, timidly and remorsefully says "Yes." This acknowledgement is followed by a series of three very pointy questions, "How? Are you happy about this? Was it a mistake?," which are not really intended to be answered but indicate the extent to which the host, now taking on a mother-like role, is dissatisfied with the young mother's behavior. As in the typical family context where authority lies with parents and is consolidated by their age superiority, the young mother knows it is expected of her to be humble and to accept the reproach. She, therefore, confesses that "It was a mistake" and makes it clear that she has accepted the situation, "But I just take it as it comes," and whatever consequences it might expose her to.

Excerpt 3. M.E. 23-year old, unmarried, student (22-12-2007). *Continued from excerpt 1*

| | |
|---|---|
| Host: | Where do you school?[2] |
| Lady: | Step by Step Secondary School |
| Host: | Step by Step. What form? |
| Lady: | Form five. |
| Host: | <u>And how comes? You know it is not easy to start breeding children when you are going to school, not so?</u> |
| Lady: | Yes. |
| Host: | <u>How? Are you happy about this? Was it a mistake?</u> |
| Lady: | It was a mistake. But I just take it as it comes. |
| ... | |
| Host: | After this, do you intend to go back to school? |
| Lady: | Yes |
| Host: | Are you sure this is not going to be a setback to you? |
| Lady: | No. |
| Host: | The child's father, has he been here to see you? |
| Lady: | No. |
| Host: | He has not yet come. |
| Lady: | Yes. |
| Host: | Does he know that you are here? |
| Lady: | No |

Predicating the reproach with "You know it is not easy…" implies that the young mother is supposed to have been aware of the social norm, the need to respect it and the consequences if it is not respected. In other words, she must have been socialized into the society. This leaves the mother no chance to say she did not know. The only option she has is to confess that it was a mistake. She is ready for the consequences: "I just take it as it comes."

The reproach does not end with giving birth before marriage but extends to the relationship between the mother and the father of the child. Like an adult member of the society who is expected to enforce its norms, the host asks about the father of the child: "The child's father, has he been here to see you?" To drive the point home that the child was born out of an illicit, probably secret relationship, the host asks if he is aware at all: "Does he know that you are here?" In excerpt 4 below, the young mother says she will inform him later: "with time he will know," further accentuating the fact that having a child under these circumstances is against norms and expectations of the society. She does not celebrate the birth of her child in the same way as the mother in excerpt 2 (see Appendix 2) does. She subsumes her individual face into the collective group's face, accepts the reproach and promises to be a better member of the society. Perhaps to atone for letting the group down, she agrees to advice girls in her age who are at risk of making the same mistake (excerpt 4).

## 4.3 Giving Advice on Social Expectations

A feature of collectivist societies is their inclusiveness, i.e., the desire to keep every member attached to, and included within, the network of the group. It includes the readiness to help those in pain, share with those in need and assist those in difficulty (see Nwoye 1992, Kasanga 2011). This is because the esteem and public recognition of their group depends on all its members abiding by the norms and playing the roles expected of them. It, therefore, becomes logical that a reproach be followed by a piece of advice that is intended to re-grant the wayward member access to the group. It could be equated to giving them another chance to qualify as or maintain their place as a deserving member of the group. A recent study on health advice in radio phone-ins in France and Cameroon by Drescher (2012) reveals how Cameroonian callers are ready to reveal their health issues on radio in the hope of receiving advice if not from the traditional healer in the studio then from other listeners. The radio becomes an extended family space where interpersonal assistance is expected to be the norm.

The data from the "Happy Birthday" program reveals two levels of advice-giving: the asymmetrical level where the host functioning as an adult or a mother figure advises the young mother, and the peer-level advice in which the young mother advises other women of her age and standing (excerpt 4). Whereas the former is directed at the interlocutor who is in the same location as the advice-giver, the latter is directed at a group that is not present.

In excerpt 4, the peer-level advice pits education against pregnancy before marriage. The host requests for this advice, not for the young mother, who has made the mistake, but for her "friends who are, who are still in school." Both avoid addressing the issue of marriage directly but it is implied in their conversation.

Excerpt 4. M.E. 23-year old, unmarried, student (22–12–2007). *Continued from excerpt 3*
    Host:  Ok. What piece of advice do you have for your friends who are, who are still in school?
    Lady:  I want just to encourage them to work hard in school because education is the solution, is the best thing in life nowadays.
    ...
    Host:  The child's father, has he been here to see you?

| Lady: | No. |
| --- | --- |

...

| Host: | You don't want him to know? |
| --- | --- |
| Lady: | No, with time he will know. |
| Host: | With time, what does that mean? You are supposed to work hand in glove, you don't know that? Because the two of you will have to put your heads together to be able to raise this child, is it a lie? |
| Lady: | No, it is true. |

In the asymmetrical level advice, the host uses the power granted to her by her age and social status to advise the young mother. She asks very threatening questions like "With time, what does that mean?," and refutes the mother's decision not to inform her child's father of the delivery at this time. Not aware of the reasons behind this decision, the host nevertheless strongly advises her to inform him since the two have to put their "heads together to be able to raise this child." Again, like in excerpt 3, her advice ends with a tag question, "is it a lie?" which inherently leaves her no options but to agree, "No, it is true."

Age and social status stand out as unavoidable postcolonial pragmatics components in understanding not only the intentions of the speakers but also their linguistic choices. They both share a common group face that must not be lost, not even when a young member does not live up to societal expectations. They immediately switch to kinship-like roles, move the interaction into family-like space where reproach, confession, apology, and advice take place often. The public nature of the radio does not stop them, neither are they repudiated by the audience—they too are part of the collectivist entity. In the next section, I explain why the rest of the community is either enthusiastically invited to join in celebrating the birth of the child (excerpt 6) or is largely kept out probably out of shame for not living up to the society's norm (excerpt 5).

## 4.4 Involving the Group

In Ghanaian English, the traditional ceremony welcoming a newly born baby to the community is called *outdooring*. Here the baby is presented to the society as their new member. In Cameroon English, a similar celebration of birth is called *born house*. These ceremonies indicate that childbirth is a positive event that is celebrated not only by the parents and immediate family but also by the society as a whole. However, as excerpts 5 and 6 show, these ceremonies are tied to other social norms and expectations. They tend to be performed mostly when the child is born in wedlock. As discussed below, the unmarried mother feels inhibited to involve many people in the birth of her child, not even the father.

Pride in respecting social norms goes with letting others know. This frees the individual of the onlooker response and any negative attitudinal rejections s/he could be exposed to in the society. In the two excerpts below, there is a significant disparity in the number of people M.E., the unmarried student, (excerpt 5) and A.E., the married student, (excerpt 6) inform about the delivery of their children. While M.E. feels reluctant to inform many people—certainly because she knows she let them down by having a child while still in school and before getting married, A.E.'s list is unending. She is married and has just completed her training as a teacher.

Excerpt 5. M.E. 23-year old, unmarried, student (22–12–2007). *Continued from excerpt 1*

Host: Ok, you have people you like to inform that you are ahh in this hospital. This is the Christmas time. Who are these people? And what do you want to tell your people?

Lady: I want to tell my father Mr. Daniel A. at Alakuma and my step-mother Madame Esther T. and my aunt Mamy Monika at Nitop 1 and my aunty at Alachuo Mamy Esther.

Host: These are the only persons?

Lady: hmmnn

Excerpt 6. A.E. 23-year old, married, teacher-trainee (17–11–2007). *Continued from excerpt 2*

Host: You have every reason to give him all the glory. Who are the people you want to inform that you have been so blessed? Your relatives and friends?

Lady: Yes, my relatives and friends.

Host: Call their names.

Lady: My friends, I have U.V. She in Dschang. I have N.M. in Dschang. I have P.C. here in Bamenda. I have my friend in Yaounde, Elsy. I have E.P. in Yaounde. I have my relatives. I have my cousin, A.G in Yaounde. I have my in-laws, Anim. I have Frisa. They are here I n Bamenda. I have hmm.

Host: These women are sitting by you.

Lady: I have my mother.

Host: Call her name.

Lady: Madame M.C. I have my sister F.E. and the husband F.N. I have my loving husband Mr. A.R. I have my loving brother-in-law, Mr. M.H. and not forgetting my brother-in-law in Yaounde, Mr. M.C.

Host: Are those all? Madame, we thank you for talking with us. This is CRTV.

In terms of numbers, M.E., the unmarried mother, informs only four people, all of them close family members (her father, step-mother and two aunts) whereas A.E., the married mother, informs fourteen individuals and three groups, i.e., relatives, friends and in-laws. M.E. opts not to inform the father of her kid. He is not mentioned by name either. But A.E. proudly refers to her husband by name along with an endearment term, "my loving husband Mr. A.R." Because she lived up to the expectations of society, she feels morally justified to inform as many people as she wants. The host asks her up to five times either to inform people of the birth or to call the names of these people. However, the host asks M.E., the unmarried mother, only twice. The weight of the guilt in M.E. can be seen in the absence of any endearment terms in her list of names. Contrastively, A.E. uses several endearment terms, e.g., "my loving brother-in-law, Mr. M.H." (excerpt 6). That both use honorifics (i.e., Madame, Mr.) and kinship address terms (Aunt, Aunty, Uncle, Mamy, Sister, etc.) is indicative of the respect system of the society. As said above, respect is age-determined and often conceptualized according to the kinship hierarchy of COMMUNITY IS FAMILY.

## 4.5 Showing Respect in line with Social Norms

Showing respect in line with the society's social norms is central to cohesion within collectivist societies. Patterns of addressing or naming people in these societies follows respect norms, which generally function through age difference, social hierarchy, kinship hierarchy, etc. A number of studies on postcolonial societies have pointed to the importance of address forms for respect in these societies. Anchimbe (2008) and Wong (2006) describe the use of kinship terms in Cameroon English and Singapore English respectively, with focus on the respect functions they play. Mühleisen (2005) discusses the place of kinship terms in the presentation of selves and others in Caribbean English-lexicon Creoles. Mulo Farenkia (2010) illustrates how politeness is realized through kinship address forms in Cameroon French while Drescher (2012) signals the importance of address strategies in advice-giving on a radio call-in program in Cameroon. What is common in these studies is the speakers' desires to project a cohesive picture of their community, i.e., as a place where respect rules are followed judiciously. We see similar tendencies in the data analyzed in this chapter.

Two types of respect-based address strategies are used in the data. The first relies on the use of honorifics while the second relies on kinship terms. In both of them, the choice of terms signals unequal or asymmetrical relationship between the mothers and the host of the program. As excerpt 7 shows, (see also excerpts 1 and 2), the host is addressed using the honorific *Madam* by M.E. and the kinship term *Aunty* by A.E. Whereas the honorific reflects the formal context of the radio (note that it is also used by the host to refer to A.E.), the use of kinship terms relocates the interaction to family space. Within the family, interaction is less formal but more flexible because the kinship space offers speakers more freedom to talk about private issues. A.E. benefits from this especially because, in the eyes of her society, she is a deserving member who respects the norms and lives up to expectations (see Appendix 2).

The choice of the kinship term *Aunty* could also be accounted for by the way the host presents herself on the program. She is a mother herself and is viewed as mother figure since she introduces herself on air as "the mother of all children."

Excerpt 7. Both M.E. and A.E. (see excerpts 1 and 2 above)
    Host:         Good morning.
    Lady (M.E.):   Good morning Madam. I am called M.E.
    ....
    Host:         Good morning Madam.
    Lady (A.E.):   Good morning Aunty

The honorific and kinship address forms in excerpt 7 are used by interlocutors in the interview for each other. However, as excerpts 5 and 6 show, they can also be used to refer to people who are not present. Besides *Aunty*, other kinship respect terms like *Mamy* (plus name) are used. In some cases, *aunt* and *Mamy* are used together for the same person, "my aunt Mamy Monika" (excerpt 5). As said above, kinship-based respect norms are so strong in this collectivist society that they are imposed on the public space of the radio where honorifics would be expected.

## 5. Conclusion

This chapter has shown that the lines between individual and group face, public and private domains, as well as personal and societal preferences are blurred or malleable in postcolonial collectivist societies. Using Cameroon as an example, these aspects were analyzed in two interviews from the prime-time Saturday morning program "Happy Birthday" on the Bamenda regional station of the Cameroon government-owned national radio network. Bearing in mind that the interactions take place in Cameroon English, an indigenized variety of English in a postcolonial context, social norms and expectations of the society were factored in and the excerpts analyzed using tenets of postcolonial pragmatics. Several components are at work in the interactions, guiding speakers' choices as they navigate through the complex web of societal norms and expectations. Among these components, as demonstrated above, are age, kinship roles, societal norms and respect.

The need to respect the society's norms weighs equally on the host and the interviewees, i.e., the mothers who have just given birth. They cooperate to ensure the society does not lose face, even when their individual faces or prestige is sacrificed in the process. For instance, M.E, endures reproach from the host for having a child before marriage and while still in school. She does not fight back the reproach or seek to justify why she did it. She confesses that it was a mistake, accepts the consequences and promises to be a better member of the society in the future. This can only be explained using the collectivist nature of the society, which conceptualizes itself as a family. The host does not hesitate to adopt a mother-like or aunt-like role when she realizes M.E. needed to be reprimanded and advised as expected of her within the family set up. M.E. does not repudiate this but rather respectfully cooperates with the host, while accepting the role of daughter or niece suggested in the host's switch.

An approach to this data that ignores the complex hybridized structure of this postcolonial society risks misrepresenting the interactions, the speakers' motivations and choices, and the intended meanings. Postcolonial pragmatics—designed to capture the various components that speakers rely on in interactions—offers a suitable path to analyzing these discourses, whether produced in an indigenized variety of an ex-colonial language, a pidgin, a creole, an indigenous lingua franca, or an inter-ethnic indigenous language. What is important is their history of colonially-induced co-existence, multiplicity and hybridism. Although colonialism triggered several major changes, multilingualism, human and language contact, interethnic interactions, etc. were already a part of these societies even before they emerged as Western-styled nation states. Studying them requires theories that take these facets into account.

## Appendices: the Complete Exchanges Between the Host and the Mothers

### Appendix 1. M.E. 23-year old, Unmarried, Student (22–12–2007)

Introductory: Our usual rendezvous ladies and gentlemen takes us to the postnatal section of the regional hospital right here in Bamenda from where we shall be reaching

## Individual Lives in Collectivist Faces 245

you. Please don't go away. Our first mother on today's edition is on Bed 23. She is so young and she is the mother of a baby boy. Who is this young lady.

Host: Good morning.
Lady: Good morning madam. I am called M.E.
Host: How old are you?
Lady: 23 years.
Host: Is this your first delivery?
Lady: Yes.
Host: Are you married?
Lady: No.
Host: Are you in school?
Lady: Yes
Host: Where do you school?
Lady: Step by Step Secondary School
Host: Step by Step. What form?
Lady: Form five.
Host: And how comes? You know it is not easy to start breeding children when you are going to school, not so?
Lady: Yes.
Host: How?... Are you happy about this? Was it a mistake?
Lady: It was a mistake. But I just take it as it comes.
Host: Ok. What piece of advice do you have for your friends who are, who are still in school?
Lady: I want just to encourage them to work hard in school because education is the solution, is the best thing in life nowadays.
Host: After this, do you intend to go back to school?
Lady: Yes
Host: Are you sure this is not going to be a setback to you?
Lady: No.
Host: The child's father, has he been here to see you?
Lady: No
Host: He has not yet come.
Lady: Yes.
Host: Does he know that you are here?
Lady: No
Host: You don't want him to know?
Lady: No, with time he will know.
Host: With time, what does that mean? You are supposed to work hand in glove, you don't know that? Because the two of you will have to put your heads together to be able to raise this child, is it a lie?
Lady: No, it is true.
Host: Ok, you have people you like to inform that you are ahh in this hospital. This is the Christmas time. Who are these people? And what do you want to tell your people?

| | |
|---|---|
| Lady: | I want to tell my father Mr. Daniel A. at Alakuma and my step-mother Madame Esther T. and my aunt Mamy Monika at Nitop I and my aunty at Alachuo Mamy Esther. |
| Host: | These are the only persons? |
| Lady: | hmmnn |
| Host: | What are you wishing for them? |
| Lady: | I wish them happy new year and Christmas in advance. |
| Host: | And what do you wish for yourself? |
| Lady: | hmmmnn smiles. A happy…ehmm a good health |
| Host: | Good health, so that you can be able to take care of your baby, right? |
| Lady: | Yes. |
| Host: | This is CRTV, we are glad you accepted to talk with us. Bye bye |
| Lady: | Bye. |

## Appendix 2. A.E. 23-year old, Married, Teacher-trainee (17-11-2007)

| | |
|---|---|
| Host: | The second baby girl on today's edition. Her mother is on bed 2. She is young, beautiful, radiating. Who is this young lady? |
| Host: | Good morning Madame. |
| Lady: | Good morning Aunty |
| Host: | What is your name? |
| Lady: | My name is A.E. |
| Host: | How old are you? |
| Lady: | 23 years old. |
| Host: | Are you married? |
| Lady: | Yes |
| Host: | Is this your first delivery? |
| Lady: | No. Second. |
| Host: | Was the first a baby girl too? |
| Lady: | Yes. |
| Host: | So you have two daughters. |
| Lady: | Yes, I do. |
| Host: | Are you happy? |
| Lady: | Very very happy. |
| Host: | When you were pregnant, did you know you were going to give birth to a baby girl? |
| Lady: | I knew it because I doing what is known as word confession, preaching the word of God. |
| Host: | Really. |
| Lady: | Because the Bible says "God is going to fulfil my heart's desire." So I was confessing it that I was going to give birth to a baby girl. |
| Host: | And your heart's desire has come to fruition. |
| Lady: | Yes. |
| Host: | Have you thanked God? |
| Lady: | Yes, I have thanked God. |

| | |
|---|---|
| Host: | What do you do in life, if I may ask? |
| Lady: | I am a teacher. |
| Host: | Where do you teach? |
| Lady: | I just graduated with the last batch of ENS. I haven't been posted. |
| Host: | You have so many degrees. The one from ENS and now you have children. You need to thank God, don't you think so, Madame? |
| Lady: | That is very true. I have to thank God. |
| Host: | Can you sing? Do you want to sing something? |
| Lady: | Yes, I can sing (she sings a song: "I give God all the glory"). |
| Host: | You have every reason to give him all the glory. Who are the people you want to inform that you have been so blessed? Your relatives and friends? |
| Lady: | Yes, my relatives and friends. |
| Host: | Call their names. |
| Lady: | My friends, I have U.V. She in Dschang. I have N.M. in Dschang. I have P.C. here in Bamenda. I have my friend in Yaounde, Elsy. I have E.P. in Yaounde. I have my relatives. I have my cousin, A.G in Yaounde. I have my in-laws, Anim. I have Frisa. They are here I n Bamenda. I have hmm. |
| Host: | These women are sitting by you. |
| Lady: | I have my mother. |
| Host: | Call her name. |
| Lady: | Madame M.C. I have my sister F.E. and the husband F.N. I have my loving husband Mr. A.R. I have my loving brother-in-law, Mr. M.H. and not forgetting my brother-in-law in Yaounde, Mr. M.C. |
| Host: | Are those all? Madame, we thank you for talking with us. This is CRTV. |
| Lady: | Thank you very much. |
| Host: | May you stay blessed! |
| Lady: | I am blessed. |
| Host: | Bye bye. |

## Notes

1 I wish to thank Marie Oben, host of the program at the time, for making her archive of the program available to me.
2 This is a common Cameroon English expression for "Where do you attend school?" or "Which school do you attend?"

## References

Anchimbe, E. A. (2006), *Cameroon English: Authenticity, Ecology and Evolution*. Frankfurt: Peter Lang.

Anchimbe, E. A. (2008), "'Come greet Uncle Eric': Politeness through kinship terms," in B. Mulo Farenkia (ed.), *Linguistic Politeness in Cameroon*, 109–19, Frankfurt: Peter Lang.

Anchimbe, E. A. (2014), "Attitudes towards Cameroon English: A sociolinguistic survey," in E. A. Anchimbe (ed.), *Structural and Sociolinguistic Perspectives on Indigenisation: On Multilingualism and Language Evolution*, 121–44, Dordrecht: Springer.

Anchimbe, E. A. (2016), "Greetings in Cameroon English," in B. Mulo Farenkia (ed.), *Im/politesse et Rituels Interactionnels en Contextes Plurilingues et Multiculturels. Situations, Stratégies et Enjeux*, 247–68, Frankfurt: Peter Lang.

Anchimbe, E. A. (2018), *Offers and Offer Refusals: A Postcolonial Pragmatics Perspective on World Englishes*, Amsterdam: John Benjamins.

Anchimbe, E. A. and R. W. Janney (2011a), "Postcolonial pragmatics: An introduction," *Journal of Pragmatics*, 43 (6): 1451–59.

Anchimbe, E. A. and R. W. Janney, eds. (2011b). "Postcolonial Pragmatics," special issue, *Journal of Pragmatics*, 43 (6).

Anchimbe, E. A. and R. W. Janney (2017), "Postcolonial pragmatics," in A. Barron, Y. Gu and G. Steen (eds.), *Routledge Handbook of Pragmatics*, 105–20, London: Routledge.

Anderson, J. A. (2006), "Request forms in English in Ghana" *Legon Journal of the Humanities*, XVII: 75–103.

Anderson, J. A. (2009), "Polite requests in non-native varieties of English: The case of Ghanaian English," *Linguistic Atlantica*, 30: 59–86.

Austin, J. L. (1962), *How to Do Things with Words*, New York: Oxford University Press.

Blum-Kulka, S., J. House and G. Kasper, eds. (1989a), *Cross-Cultural Pragmatics: Requests and Apologies*, Norwood: Ablex Publishing.

Blum-Kulka, S., J. House and G. Kasper (1989b), "Investigating cross-cultural pragmatics: An introductory overview," in S. Blum-Kulka, J. House and G. Kasper (eds.), *Cross-Cultural Pragmatics: Requests and Apologies*, 1–34, Norwood: Ablex Publishing.

Brown, P. and S. C. Levinson (1987), *Politeness: Some Universals in Language Usage*, Cambridge University Press, Cambridge.

de Kadt, E. (1994), "Towards a model for the study of politeness in Zulu," *South African Journal of African Languages*, 14 (3): 103–12.

de Kadt, E. (1998), "The concept of face and its applicability to the Zulu language," *Journal of Pragmatics* 29: 173–91.

Drescher, M. (2012), "Crosscultural perspectives on advice: The case of French and Cameroonian radio phone ins," in S. Hauser (ed.), *Contrastive Media Analysis: Approaches to Linguistic and Cultural Aspects of Mass Media Communication*, 11–46, Amsterdam: Benjamins.

Egner, I. (2006), "Intercultural aspects of the speech act of promising: Western and African practices," *Intercultural Pragmatics*, 3–4: 443–64.

Goffman, E. (1967), *Interaction Ritual: Essays on Face-to-Face Behaviour*, New York: Pantheon Books.

Grainger, K., S. Mills and M. Sibanda, (2010), "'Just tell us what to do': Southern African face and its relevance to intercultural communication," *Journal of Pragmatics*, 42 (8): 2158–71.

Hanks, W., S. Ide and Y. Katagiri, eds. (2009), *Towards an Emancipatory Pragmatics*, special issue, *Journal of Pragmatics*, 41 (1).

Ige, B. (2010), "Identity and language choice: We equals I," *Journal of Pragmatics*, 42 (11): 3047–54.

Janney, R. W. (2009), "Toward a postcolonial pragmatics," in B. Fraser and K. Turner (eds.), *Language in Life, and a Life in Language: Jacob Mey—A Festschrift*, 203–12, Bingley: Emerald.

Kachru, Y. (1991a), "Introduction: Symposium on speech acts in World Englishes," *World Englishes*, 10 (3): 295–98.

Kachru, Y. (1991b), "Speech acts in World Englishes: Toward a framework for research," *World Englishes*, 10 (3): 299–306.

Kasanga, L. A. (2003), "'I am asking for a pen": Framing of requests in Black South African English," in K. M. Jaszczolt and K. Turner (eds.), *Meaning through Language Contrast*, Vol. 2, 213–35, Amsterdam: John Benjamins.

Kasanga, L. A. (2006), "Requests in a South African variety of English," *World Englishes*, 25 (1): 65–89.

Kasanga, L. A. (2011), "Face, politeness, and speech acts: Reflecting on the inter-cultural interaction in African languages and varieties of English," in G. Sommer and C. Vierke (eds.), *Speech Acts and Speech Events in African Languages*, 41–65, Köln: Rüdiger Köppe Verlag.

Kouega, J.-P. (2007), *A Dictionary of Cameroon English Usage*, Munich: Lincom.

Lienhardt, G. (1985), "Self: public, private: Some African representations," in M. Carrithers, S. Collins and S. Lukes (eds.), *The Category of the Person*, 141–55, Cambridge: Cambridge University Press.

Lwanga-Lumu, J. C. (1999), "Politeness and indirectness revisited," *South African Journal of African Languages*, 19 (2): 83–92.

Mühleisen, S. (2005), "Forms of Address in English-Lexicon Creoles: The Presentation of Selves and Others in the Caribbean Context," in S. Mühleisen and B. Migge (eds.), *Politeness and Face in Caribbean Creoles*, 195–223, Amsterdam: John Benjamins.

Mulo Farenkia, B. (2010), "Pragmatique de la néologie appellative en situation plurilingue: Le cas Camerounais," *Journal of Pragmatics*, 42 (2): 477–500.

Mulo Farenkia, B. (2011), "Formes de «mise à distance» de l'altérité ethnique au Cameroun," *Journal of Pragmatics*, 43 (6): 1484–97.

Mustapha, A. S. (2011), "Compliment response patterns among speakers of Nigerian English," *Journal of Pragmatics* 43 (5): 1335–48.

Nelson, C. L. (1991), "New Englishes, new discourses: New speech acts," *World Englishes*, 10 (3): 317–23.

Nwoye, O. G. (1992), "Linguistic politeness and socio-cultural variations of the notion of face," *Journal of Pragmatics*, 18: 309–28.

Ouafeu, T. S. Y. (2006), "Politeness strategies in colloquial Cameroon English: Focus on three pragmatic particles: *na*, *ya* and *eihn*," *Nordic Journal of African Studies*, 15 (4): 536–44. Available online: www.njas.helsinki.fi/pdf-files/vol15num4/sando.pdf. (accessed June 5, 2008).

Searle, J. R. (1979), *Expression and Meaning: Studies in the Theory of Speech Acts*, Cambridge: Cambridge University Press.

Simo Bobda, A. (1994), *Aspects of Cameroon English Phonology*, Bern: Peter Lang.

Tinkham, T. (1991), "Sociocultural variation in Indian English speech acts," *World Englishes*, 12 (2): 239–47.

Wong, J. (2006), "Contextualising *Aunty* in Singaporean English," *World Englishes*, 25 (3/4): 451–66.

# 12

# Teaching (About) World Englishes and English as a Lingua Franca

Andy Kirkpatrick

## 1. Introduction

The understanding that English comprises a range of varieties is of long standing. Some sixty-five years ago Halliday, McIntosh and Strevens pointed out that:

> English is no longer the possession of the British, or even the British and the Americans ... In West Africa, the West Indies and in Pakistan and India ... it is no longer accepted by the majority that the English of England with RP as its accent, are [sic] the only possible models of English ... English exists in an increasingly large number of varieties.
>
> 1964: 293, cited in Bolton 2012: 14

More than twenty-five years ago, Kachru (1992: 357 ff.), the scholar who can be considered the founder of the discipline of World Englishes (WE), presented his six fallacies associated with English and English language teaching. By way of introduction, I shall repeat these here to underline that many of the current perspectives associated with the teaching of World Englishes (WE) and English as an international language (EIL) have their inspiration in rebutting these six fallacies. The six fallacies were:

Fallacy 1
That in outer and expanding circles English is essentially learned to interact with NS.

Fallacy 2
That English is necessarily learned as a tool to understand and teach American or British cultural values, or what is generally termed the Judeo-Christian traditions.

Fallacy 3
That the goal of learning English is to adopt the native models of English.

Fallacy 4

That the international non-native varieties of English are essentially "interlanguage" striving to achieve "native-like" character.

Fallacy 5

That the native speakers of English as teachers, academic administrators and materials developers provide a serious input in the global teaching of English, in policy formation, and in determining the channels for the spread of the language.

Fallacy 6

That the diversity and variation in English is necessarily an indicator of linguistic decay and that restricting the decay is the responsibility of the native scholars of English and ESL programs.

I return to respond to these later in the chapter, but here note that World Englishes scholars and those who have argued for the adoption of an EIL, Global Englishes or ELF-approach to the teaching and learning of English would readily agree that these six points contain fallacious arguments. Nevertheless, as will be seen below, these WE and ELF approaches have proved remarkably difficult to introduce in many English language classes throughout the world. The idea that English is best represented by a native speaker variety and that this is the variety that should be the classroom model has proved remarkably resilient. In this chapter I want to explore possible reasons for this resilience and to suggest ways in which it might be overcome. To do this, I shall review recent research into the adoption of a World Englishes perspective and a lingua franca approach to the teaching of English. I am making a distinction between a World Englishes perspective—which recognizes that English does not comprise a single or solely native speaker varieties, but rather recognizes the existence and legitimacy of Outer Circle and other varieties of English which typically develop among people who share linguistic and cultural backgrounds—and an English as a lingua franca approach to English language teaching, which sees English function as a shared medium of communication, typically between people who come from different linguistic and cultural backgrounds. Before proceeding, I need to explain the terms (WE and ELF) I am using. Other terms that are in current use include English as an International Language (EIL) (e.g., Matsuda 2019) and Global Englishes (GE) (e.g., Rose and Galloway 2019). In this chapter I shall use World Englishes as a cover all term for WEs, EIL and GE, distinguishing these from an ELF-approach to the teaching of English (e.g., Kirkpatrick 2014, 2018a, b; Sifakis and Tsantila 2018)

I also want to make a distinction between teaching world Englishes and adopting an English as a lingua franca approach and teaching *about* World Englishes and an English as a lingua franca approach. Teaching world Englishes and adopting an ELF approach would mean either teaching a specific variety of English as a classroom model or teaching English in a way that recognizes its function as a lingua franca. The students in such cases would be learners of English and the teachers English language teachers. In contrast, teaching *about* World Englishes and about an ELF-approach would mean introducing these concepts either to pre-service students training to become English language teachers or to in-service English language teachers in some form of professional development course such as a Diploma or MA in TESOL. I shall argue that, while teaching about World Englishes and about an ELF approach is becoming common in professional development courses for teachers, there remains little transfer from these teacher education programs into the English language classrooms. In other words, despite professional development courses introducing trainee and trained teachers to the concepts of World Englishes and ELF, very few of these teachers actually implement these ideas in their own classroom teaching. There is a significant gap, therefore, between theory and practice. The question is why? In this chapter I also want to explore the possible reasons for this.

## 2. Teaching About WEs and About an ELF-Approach

Scholars proposing that World Englishes and/or an ELF approach should be part of the curricula of professional development courses agree on the underlying philosophy that should shape such courses. Here I summarize how a selection of scholars have expressed this philosophy. In a recent state of the art article for the journal *Language Teaching*, Rose et al. (2020) use the term "Global Englishes" as a cover term for World Englishes, English as an international language, English as a lingua franca. They explain that Global Englishes "... is an inclusive paradigm that aims to consolidate the work of WE, ELF, and EIL to explore the linguistic, sociolinguistic and sociocultural diversity and fluidity of English use and the implications of this diversity of English on multifaceted aspects of society, including TESOL curricula and English language teaching practices" (2020: 2). They note that scholars recognize the need for a paradigm shift in TESOL curricula to address the mismatch between what is taught in classrooms and how English functions outside of the classroom" (2020: 2). They summarize their philosophy in six Global Englishes Language Teaching (GELT) proposals:

1. Increasing World Englishes and ELF exposure in language curricula
2. Emphasizing respect for multilingualism in ELT
3. Raising awareness of Global Englishes in ELT
4. Raising awareness of ELF strategies in language curricula
5. Emphasizing respect for diverse cultures and identity in ELT
6. Changing English teacher-hiring practices in the ELT industry

In an earlier article, Dewey (2012) proposed what he called the post-normative approach to curriculum change, an approach that, in many ways, foreshadows these GELT proposals. This approach proposed the following strategies:

Investigate and highlight the particular environment and sociocultural context in which English(es) will be used
Increase exposure to the diverse ways in which English is used globally; presenting alternative variants as appropriate whenever highlighting linguistic form

Engage in critical classroom discussion about the globalization and growing diversity of English

Spend proportionately less time on ENL forms, especially if these are not widely used in other varieties; and thus choose not to penalize non-native-led innovative forms that are intelligible

Focus(more) on communicative strategies

Dewey 2012: 163–4

Another scholar of WEs, Marlina, has summarized the philosophy for the teaching of EIL in the following way:

Teaching EIL or EIL pedagogy means the act of professionally guiding students from all Kachruvian circles to: (i) gain knowledge and awareness of the pluricentricity of English and the plurilingual nature of today's communication; (ii) inspire students to give equal and legitimate recognition to all varieties of English; and (iii) develop the ability to negotiate and communicate respectfully across cultures and Englishes in today's communicative settings that are international, intercultural and multilingual in nature.

Marlina 2014: 7

He then acknowledges that these views do not always meet with approval from teachers. Using the acronym PESTs (2014: 9) he lists their concerns over the **p**racticality of such a course, its **e**fficiency, as teachers feel that time could be better spent, **s**tandards in that students want a standard English, and **s**implicity, as teachers feel that such an EIL course would confuse their students.

Taking Asia as their context, Widodo and Fang (2019) argue that "Global Englishes (GE) is an ecological approach that recognizes the use of language in different social and cultural domains in which different languages and cultures coexist" (2019: 194). GE perspectives should be taken into account when language teachers and teacher educators design and enact English language education (ELE). It is crucial that teaching materials reflect: (i) GE as guiding theory; (ii) authenticity of English use in the 3 circles; (iii) GE-related topics; (iv) GE knowledge and language awareness; (v) GE-oriented assessment in various contexts; and (vi) GE-awareness raising tasks and activities (2019: 197). Tellingly, however, they acknowledge that the GE philosophy has been slow to influence the field of language pedagogy and assessment with assessment being in their view, the trickiest issue. Like, Marlina above, therefore, they recognize that these ideas are not being universally embraced.

I myself (Kirkpatrick 2012, 2014, 2018a, b) have proposed an ELF-approach to English language teaching, designed primarily for the East and Southeast Asian / ASEAN context. This originally comprised six principles later reduced to these five. More detailed descriptions can be found in Kirkpatrick (2018a).

Principle 1

The native speaker of English is not the linguistic target. Mutual intelligibility is the goal. The role of English as a lingua franca in ASEAN means that English is primarily used between multilinguals whose first languages comprise a variety of Asian languages and who have learned English as an additional language. There is no need for people to approximate native speaker norms. What is important is that these users of English are able to communicate successfully with each other. Strategies for negotiating meaning are more important than adherence to native speaker norms.

Principle 2
The native speaker's culture is not the cultural target. Intercultural competence in relevant cultures is the goal.
A curriculum that adopts an ELF-approach can provide information about the cultures of the people the learners are most likely to be interacting with. In the ASEAN/Asian context, this means including information about Asian cultures and religions. Most importantly, the curriculum should show learners how to talk about their own cultures and values.

Principle 3
ELF speakers make appropriate ELF teachers.
This principal was originally formulated as "Multilinguals who are suitably trained provide the most appropriate English language teachers."
As the language learning goal is not to approximate native speaker norms, but to be able to interact successfully with fellow ELF users, it follows that a multilingual who is proficient in English and who has the relevant qualifications represents an appropriate teacher. Successful users of ELF are likely to be better equipped to adopt an ELF-approach

Principle 4
Lingua franca environments provide excellent learning environments for lingua franca speakers.
Rather than sending students whose primary goal for learning English is to communicate with fellow Asian multilinguals to Inner Circle countries such as Great Britain or the United States, consideration should be given to sending them to places where English is naturally used as a lingua franca. Within Asia, Malaysia, Singapore, Brunei and the Philippines provide examples of sites where English is regularly used as a lingua franca and as a language of inter-ethnic communication. The great advantage of such sites for Asian learners of English is, paradoxically, that the native speaker is absent. Instead, English is being *naturally* used as a lingua franca between Asian multilinguals. Students will find the linguistic environment less threatening and will feel more comfortable using English

Principle 5
Assessment must be relevant to the (ASEAN) context.
In the context of ASEAN, there is an overwhelming need for an overall ASEAN approach to these issues, particularly regarding the issues of teacher and student assessment (Dudzik and Nguyen 2015). They call for ASEAN-wide proficiency

benchmarks and ELT competency frameworks to be developed, which would include creating a "common regional proficiency assessment framework" (61) and "regional English teacher competency assessment tools" (62). They also call for the development of relevant curricula (such as SE Asian cultures) and teach English "no longer by teaching and assessing only NS varieties of English but also by introducing those spoken in neighboring countries and by other regional multilingual speakers such as Singaporeans and Malaysians" (60).

Kobayashi (2017) refined or softened these principles in order for them to become relevant for wider contexts. He reduced them to 4, namely:

Principle 1
The native speaker of English is not the only linguistic target. Mutual intelligibility is nothing less than a goal.

Principle 2
The native speaker's culture is not the only cultural target. Intercultural competence in relevant cultures is nothing less than a goal.

Principle 3
Local multilinguals who are suitably trained provide more appropriate English language teachers than English teachers lacking teacher training and empathy with English learners.

Principle 4
Lingua franca environments provide excellent learning environments for international English learners.

The philosophy and principles outlined above may all sound very sensible and useful components for a pre- or in-service English language teacher education course, but how might they be implemented in actual language classroom contexts given that their adoption seems slow? A recent volume edited by Sifakis and Tsantila (2018) includes a number of chapters which offer practical advice, and here I review the chapter by Kemaloglu-Er and Bayyurt. The authors provide lesson plans on how to adopt an ELF-aware approach to teaching and say that a major aim of their chapter is to allow its readers to be then able to develop for themselves "a teacher education model underlain by ELF-awareness" (2018: 159). They suggest that teachers go through three phases on their way to be able to deliver ELF-informed classrooms. The first phase is a theoretical phase when teachers become engaged with ELF- and WE-related theory and research literature. The second phase is the application phase when teachers develop lesson plans that exemplify their understanding of ELF; these lessons should be designed to raise their students' awareness of ELF-related issues. The third phase is the evaluation phase when teachers evaluate the lessons taught. The authors note that, operating in this way, gives teachers autonomy. This is no doubt true, but it assumes teaching contexts where teachers have the autonomy to design their own materials and courses.

This, however, is often not the case, especially in Asia, where the curriculum may be set in stone and teachers required to teach it faithfully. This is a point to which I return later in the chapter.

Hino (2018) offers an interesting take on how EIL education might flourish in the Expanding Circle, using Japan as a case study. He argues that the recent dramatic increase in the number of English Medium of Instruction (EMI) courses being taught in Asia (e.g., Fenton-Smith, Humphreys and Walkinshaw 2017) provide ideal contexts for combining an EIL approach within EMI classes. For this to be successful, Hino (2018: 130–1) lists three administrative principles and six pedagogical principles which need to be observed. The three administrative principles are:

(i) Collaboration between content teachers and EIL teachers (unless the EMI class is taught by an EIL expert)
(ii) Ready access to EMI classes for both local and international students
(iii) No discrimination against NNS in the employment or assignment of EMI teachers

It is essential, in Hino's view, that EMI classes contain both local and international students for this provides a natural context for the use of ELF and EIL. In his experience, asking Japanese students to use English with each other in the classroom when Japanese students are the only students present is not only unnatural but also leads to the development of a type of Japanese English that is likely to be unintelligible to others. Only the presence of international students allows for the creation of an authentic EIL context in which the users of English will have to negotiate meaning when interacting with each other.

The six pedagogical principles are (2018: 131–3):

(i) activities to utilize authentic EIL environments in EMI classes;
(ii) refraining from identifying EMI pedagogy with Anglo-American pedagogy;
(iii) intercultural negotiation for appropriate pedagogy in EMI classes—an intercultural pedagogy;
(iv) consideration of pedagogical tradition in each disciplinary field;
(v) care for international students when the local language is additionally used in an EMI class;
(vi) EMI teachers as role models of EIL users.

The third and fourth pedagogical principles above are worthy of further comment. Hino believes that it is important that an "intercultural pedagogy" be negotiated with students if they come from different traditions. For example, when the class contains American, Chinese and Japanese students (as many of his classes do) an intercultural pedagogy would seek "reconciliation between East Asian beliefs in harmony and American values in argumentation" (2018: 132). The fourth pedagogical principle recognizes that different disciplines may have different pedagogies and these must be respected in these EMI-EIL classes. I agree that taking into account cultural differences surrounding pedagogy is crucial. The fact that these might not have been taken into account may be a reason for teachers being hesitant in adopting a WE/EIL philosophy and/or an EFL-approach. This also bears on the amount of autonomy English language teachers may or may not have.

I shall close this section of the chapter with one more example from Asia—Musthafa, Hamied and Zein's recommendations for the adoption of an ELF-approach in Indonesia. Their four recommendations are (2018: 177–87):

(i) objectives of English Language Education in Indonesia be re-oriented from Inner Circle varieties to regional varieties and ELF;
(ii) empower teachers and students as users of ELF. To ensure this they stress that "Pre-service teacher education must prepare teachers through exposure to the varieties of English used in the ASEAN context, and show that communication can be accomplished without adherence to native speaker norms" (2018: 180);
(iii) a policy on teachers' proficiency needs to be developed;
(iv) policy innovations to support teacher education need to be developed for which they recommend the setting up of an inter-ministerial group which would harmonise teacher education throughout Indonesia.

In this section, I have reviewed several scholars' views on the need to adopt a WE philosophy and/or an ELF-approach to the teaching of English and shown that many of these scholars share similar views. As Matsuda points out "the variation and diversity in English is ... a reality that we work with in order to help our students better" (2019: 150). Matsuda envisions that the understanding of WE perspectives will become so widespread "that they become part of the shared knowledge and assumptions of the field that everyone takes for granted" (2019: 150).

The problem seems to be that, while the need to adopt WE/EIL perspectives is widespread among scholars of the field and is increasingly common in professional development courses for English language teachers, their actual implementation and adoption in English language classrooms remains relatively rare. In the next section of the chapter I want to explore why this might be the case.

## 3. Teaching WEs and Adopting an ELF-Approach

In this section of the chapter I shall review recent studies which have examined the effect of introducing the WE philosophy and/or ELF-approach into professional development programs and classrooms. I must here signal my indebtedness to the work of Rose et al. (2020) as their state-of-the-art article in the journal *Language Teaching* reviews many of the studies covered here. They used strict criteria for selecting which articles to review. These were that the studies:

must contain empirical research;

must have been published between 2010-2019;

must be about English language teaching or teacher education;

must be about one or more of our key constructs (Global Englishes, World Englishes, EIL or ELF).

They first reviewed seven studies of innovation in language teacher education. I shall not review each of these here in detail but simply summarize Rose et al.'s findings. Three of these studies were conducted in Inner Circle countries (one in the United Kingdom and two in the United States) and four in Expanding Circle countries, namely Israel, Turkey, South Korea, and Italy. Two of the studies reported on one-off interventions such as a two-hour workshop while the other five reported on longer term interventions, such as in semester-long courses; the one conducted in Italy took place over two-years and investigated the extent to which, if at all, the implementation of a WE/ELF-aware module influenced the teaching practices of pre-service teachers (Vettorel and Corrizato 2016). Rose et al. make the following general comments about these studies. First the relatively low number of them suggests that this type of action research is not yet being conducted in any great numbers. Second, they note that while some of these studies showed excellent pedagogical innovations, the lack of rigor in the methodology of some of these studies meant there is a lack of evidence to demonstrate the heightened awareness claimed (2020). With regard to the longer-term Vettorel and Corrizato study, they say that, while the participants appeared positive about the curriculum innovations, "conclusions that such innovations can broaden perspectives of English language teaching are questionable" (2020: 11). They call for more longitudinal studies which include both pre- and post-course data and which investigate if and whether the ideas presented in these courses are implemented in the teachers' own classrooms.

The second set of studies they reviewed involved curriculum innovation within classrooms. Using the same criteria outlined above they selected fourteen studies. Four of these looked at classroom activities and, here again, Rose et al. are critical in that these studies typically comprise "one-shot" explorations of impact and that "there are no measures to directly capture students' beliefs before and after the tasks, and thus there is a lack of evidence to demonstrate change" (2020: 17). Their review included a subset of these studies. The six which focused on teaching WEs and EIL and which are therefore of most relevance to this chapter are reviewed in more detail below.

Fang and Ren (2018) reported that a course teaching world Englishes to English language students over the course of two terms suggested that students did develop a tolerance of diversity and, thus, to their own English. There was, however, no follow-up study to see to what extent these attitudes were maintained.

Chang (2014) looked at how the introduction of the idea of a WE-informed English language course influenced the Taiwanese students taking the course. It was perhaps not surprising that the students, in their writing about the WE topic, indicated that they had understood more about the varieties of English, but again, there was no follow up study.

Teixeira and Pozzi (2014) showed how a WE course influenced the students, all of whom were from different language backgrounds. Again, not surprisingly, the course enabled students to recognize different varieties of English, but the small number involved (7) and the lack of any follow up study means that it is impossible to see if the course influenced the students in any long-term way.

In a small case study that involved only three students who took an EIL course at an Australian university, Marlina (2013) found that, on the one hand, the students developed a greater understanding of variation in English(es), but, on the other, found it hard to see how this knowledge might connect with the worlds in which they worked. For example, despite growing to realize that their own variety of English was appropriate, their own teaching and learning contexts presented the native speaker standard as the correct model. This potential contradiction between what they were learning and what they were expected to teach may well be a major reason why courses in WE and ELF do not necessarily result in these approaches being adopted by teachers in their own classrooms. I shall return to this issue, which is connected to teacher autonomy, below.

Ali (2015) collected data during a series of five EIL workshops given to postgraduate students of linguistics in Pakistan. Findings showed that the workshops challenged the students' position about standard English but did not alter their views that their own English was deficient. Ali suggested that this might be because the notion of a standard English as being the only correct English continued to be believed in this postcolonial context.

The final study of this subset of six was conducted by Galloway (2013). Using a control and experimental group, she investigated how Japanese learners of English were influenced by taking a Global Englishes course. Again, not surprisingly, she found that those students who had taken the Global Englishes course had a greater understanding of non-native varieties of English and a greater confidence in their own English.

In their summary of their review of these six studies, Rose et al. conclude that they "provide powerful pedagogical evidence from the language classroom of the positive benefits of innovations based on Global Englishes, World Englishes, ELF and EIL proposals for change" (2020: 22). But they also note that most of the studies did not adopt a "concrete research design" and lacked any longitudinal component, rendering their results open to question.

Rose et al. also reviewed eight articles that investigated students' and teachers' attitudes to curriculum innovation in the context of WEs and an ELF approach. Most of these studies found that participants felt more comfortable with a consistent model of English than with WEs. While students and teachers were generally open to introducing students to different varieties of English, teachers had practical concerns about how they could best be taught in the classroom.

A study that did have a longitudinal component and which had a sound methodology is the replication study of English learners' attitudes to native English teachers (NESTs) and local English teachers (LETs) in Thailand (Watson Todd and Pojanapunya 2020). Their 2020 study was a replication of their 2009 study. Eliciting data using an Implicit Association Test and questionnaires, they sought answers to the following four research questions:

what are Thai university students' explicit attitudes towards NESTs and LETs?;

what are Thai university students' implicit attitudes towards NESTs and LETs?;

is there a relationship between explicit and implicit attitudes towards NESTs and LETs?;

is there a relationship between previous learning experiences with NESTs and attitudes towards NESTs and LETs?

The replication study added an additional research question, namely: "How do these findings differ from the 2009 findings?" The only other difference between the two studies was the number of participants. The 2009 study surveyed 261 undergraduates at a well-known Thai University. The 2020 study surveyed 439 undergraduates from the same university. In both cases, the majority of the participants were engineering students.

The researchers' hypothesis was that the students' attitudes in 2020 towards NESTs and LETS would have shifted to a more favorable attitude to local teachers and to a less favorable one to native English speaking teachers. They suggested two reasons for this hypothesis: first, the significant increase in tourism in Thailand since 2009 might be expected to make students far more familiar with non-native varieties of English and the use of English as a lingua franca, especially as tourists from inner circle countries comprised less than 10 percent of the total; the second reason was connected with the implementation of the ASEAN Economic Community (AEC) in 2016. This allowed for skilled worker mobility, meaning that Thai workers would be mixing with workers from other ASEAN countries where English as a lingua franca would be the most likely medium of communication.

The results of the replication study did not support the hypothesis, however, with students indicating a greater preference for NESTs and a lower preference for LETs than the students in the 2009 study. The researchers also suggested two reasons for these unexpected findings: first, there has been a significant increase in the numbers of NESTs employed in Thailand with the result that the great majority of Thai students have now studied with a NEST; second, while the implementation of the AEC gave Thais a strong motivation to improve their English, "the social discourse around the AEC focused purely on improved English, not on who English would be used with" (2020: 9). The authors conclude that the belief in the native speaker model of English and NESTs as ideal teachers remains dominant in Thailand. As they point out, "[f]or ELF advocates, such a situation is worrying" (2020: 9). They argue that ELF advocates need to broaden their audience from a purely academic one to include wider society.

Similarly worrying results for advocates of a WE philosophy to the teaching of English were obtained by Sadeghpour and Sharifian (2019). They surveyed 56 English teachers in Australia. 32 were first language speakers of English. The remainder were L2 speakers with a wide variety of first languages. Out of those surveyed, 87 percent had also taught English outside Australia. Their results found that, while more than 50 percent of those surveyed viewed WEs as relevant to their English language teaching in Australia, this was limited to their *awareness* of WEs rather than seeing them as fundamental to the teaching of English. Opponents of the idea of including WEs in the classroom felt students had come to learn Australian English and that they would feel short-changed if taught other varieties. They also felt that the inclusion of WEs would confuse learners. Based on these results, the researchers note that, despite so many studies arguing against teaching English as a single variety, and proposals for EIL/ELF approaches "research studies in different contexts have shown that teachers are still teaching English as a monolithic language" (2019: 254). They conclude that, to enable teachers to teach EIL, the teaching curriculum should reflect the multi-varietal nature of English and educators should not rely on the native speaker-based publishing industry and native speaker-based international tests. This sounds a little despairing, as scholars have been urging these types of curriculum changes for decades, but without, it would seem, much effect.

## 4. Where Does This Leave Us?

So far, this chapter has shown how several scholars—the author included—have advocated the adoption of a World Englishes philosophy and/or an ELF approach to the teaching of English. These scholars have put forward these proposals in light of the way English has developed internationally over the past few decades. The world has seen the development of new varieties of English in many Outer Circle countries so that there is now a large family of Englishes stretching from the Indian sub-continent and across much of Africa, Asia and the Caribbean. Perhaps more unexpectedly has been the fast-paced development of the role of English as a lingua franca in many Expanding Circle countries. English has become the main international lingua franca. In the context of Asia, Bolton and Bacon-Shone note:

> Since the era of European de-colonisation in Asia, which largely took place from the late 1940s to the 1960s, there has been a massive expansion in the spread of English throughout the whole of the region, in both Outer Circle and Expanding Circle societies.
>
> 2020: 49

Tables 12.1 and 12.2 show the estimated number of English speakers in Asia's Expanding and Outer Circle countries. These tables are adapted from Bolton and Bacon-Shone 2020. They arrived at these figures using data from government censuses and language surveys.

The tables indicate both the percentages and total number of the population that speaks English.

Taken together, the numbers of Tables 12.1 and 12.2 show that there are some 800 million users of English in Asia alone. This is significantly more than the number of native speakers of English. There are even more speakers of Outer Circle varieties of English in Asia than there are native speakers of it world-wide. So the question arises as to why the belief in a native speaker model and the NEST as the ideal English teacher remains so resilient?

In Kirkpatrick (2006), I argued that the resilience of the native speaker model rested on a number of factors. These included the very powerful testing and publishing industries which had an obvious vested interest in promoting a native speaker model

Table 12.1 Knowledge of English in Expanding Circle Asian Societies

| Society | Current estimates (%) | Approx. total of English speakers (million) |
| --- | --- | --- |
| Nepal | 30 | 8.5 |
| Macau | 28 | 0.2 |
| China | 20 | 276.0 |
| Myanmar (Burma) | 10 | 5.2 |
| Japan | 10 | 12.5 |
| South Korea | 10 | 5.1 |
| Taiwan | 10 | 2.4 |
| Thailand | 10 | 6.5 |
| Vietnam | 10 | 4.6 |
| Cambodia | 5 | 0.8 |
| Indonesia | 5 | 13.0 |
| Laos | 5 | 0.3 |
| **Total** | | **335.1** |

Table 12.2 Knowledge of English in Outer Circle Asian societies

| Society | Current estimates (%) | Approx. total of English speakers (million) |
| --- | --- | --- |
| Singapore | 80 | 3.1 |
| Philippines | 65 | 66.7 |
| Brunei | 60 | 0.2 |
| Hong Kong | 53 | 3.9 |
| Malaysia | 50 | 15.5 |
| Pakistan | 25 | 50.9 |
| Sri Lanka | 25 | 5.3 |
| Bangladesh | 20 | 32.6 |
| India | 20 | 260.0 |
| **Total** | | **438.2** |

and the idea that the native English speaker represented the ideal English teacher, despite so many scholars showing how fallacious this argument was. I also noted that educational bureaucrats and politicians were likely to favor native speaker models. Politicians from Inner Circle countries would favor an inner circle variety for financial reasons. In 2008, then Prime Minister of Britain, Gordon Brown, before departing on a trade mission to China said "So today I want Britain to make a new gift to the world: a commitment to help anyone—however impoverished and however far away —to access the tools they need to learn English" (https://www.theguardian.com/politics/2008/jan/17/gordonbrown.labour; accessed March 17, 2020). The "gift" would not be free.

I also argued that a further reason why a native speaker model was favored was because these had been codified. There are grammars and dictionaries of these varieties against which the learner of English can be evaluated. It is worth underlining that this evaluation always sees the learner's goal as approximating the native speaker model. This codification allows these models to be presented as standard models and this is another reason they are favored by politicians and educational bureaucrats. By insisting on a native speaker model for the classroom, they feel reassured they are offering their students a standard model, one that is universally accepted. This is linked to the notion of familiarity. People are more comfortable with the familiar than with the unfamiliar. However fuzzy the notion of a native speaker might be (Davies 1991), it is, nevertheless, a concept with which all language teachers and, importantly, language learners, are familiar. However much we, as academics, might critique the notion of the native speaker (e.g., Braine 1999), learners and teachers accept aiming for native speaker models as self-evident. Those of us advocating the adoption of a WE philosophy or an ELF approach do not yet have slogans as catchy or attractive as "Learn to speak like a native speaker." Slogans along the lines of "Add English to your multilingual repertoire "or "Learn to be a successful user of English as a lingua franca" do not have quite the same cachet at present.

A further reason that the target of the native speaker model remains resilient is that such models are associated with power and prestige—and, of course, this allows them to be promoted by the governments and institutions where these Inner Circle varieties are spoken. These varieties also have what might be called "historical authority." The United Kingdom can call itself the "true home" of "real" English and market the language as such.

These arguments for the native speaker teacher and model all ignore the sociolinguistic reality of language use and change. It is as though Kachru's six fallacies are still believed. Here I repeat them, but present counter-arguments.

Fallacy 1
That in outer and expanding circles English is essentially learned to interact with NS.
This is demonstrably not the case. As the percentages and numbers of speakers of English noted in Tables 12.1 and 12.2 above show, there are far more so-called non-native speakers of English than native speakers of it. The majority of these speakers use English with each other more than with native speakers. An example of this is that the ten nations that comprise the Association of Southeast Asian Nations (ASEAN) have adopted English as the sole working language of the group. English is the officially designated lingua franca of ASEAN.

Fallacy 2
That English is necessarily learned as a tool to understand and teach American or British cultural values, or what is generally termed the Judeo-Christian traditions.
This is also demonstrably not the case. English has been adopted by its new users to reflect and represent their own cultural values and customs. A striking example of this is the use of "English for Islamic Purposes" currently being taught in many schools attached to mosques in Indonesia and elsewhere (Kirkpatrick 2020).

Fallacy 3
That the goal of learning English is to adopt the native models of English.
The response to this is not as clear cut as the responses to the first two. There are many learners of English whose aim is to achieve a native speaker model and, in

many contexts, this is a perfectly understandable, if not laudable, aim. The problem arises when this goal is placed before all learners of English, despite the context and their reasons for learning English. It is, for example, unclear, why the hundreds of millions of Asian primary school children have a native speaker model as their target. The great majority of Asian children will be learning to communicate in English with each other and the goals of learning English therefore need to take this into account.

Fallacy 4
That the international non-native varieties of English are essentially "interlanguage" striving to achieve "native-like" character.
This is demonstrably not the case. For several decades, linguists have been describing the features of new varieties of English. Examples from Asia include, Indian Englishes, Malaysian English, Singaporean English, Filipino English and Bruneian English; and from Africa, the Englishes of Nigeria, Ghana, Uganda. The Caribbean is a rich source of new varieties of English and include Jamaican, Bajan (Barbados) and St Lucian. Far from striving to achieve a "native-like" character, these have developed their own individual character so that they can adequately represent the lived lives of their users.

Fallacy 5
That the native speakers of English as teachers, academic administrators and materials developers provide a serious input in the global teaching of English, in policy formation, and in determining the channels for the spread of the language.
This fallacy retains elements of truth to it. There is no doubt that representatives of native speaker-ism still hold immense power over the English language teaching industry. As Watson Todd and Pojanapunya (2020) have shown, the preference for native English teachers of English by Thai students has actually increased over the past decade, despite the significant increase in the regional Asian use of English as a lingua franca and the increased contact between Asians for whom English is their lingua franca.

Fallacy 6
That the diversity and variation in English is necessarily an indicator of linguistic decay and that restricting the decay is the responsibility of the native scholars of English and ESL programs.
Far from being an indicator of linguistic decay, these new Englishes are indicators of a language blossoming with new growth. Kachru himself described these new Englishes as "liberating" leading to new canons of literatures in English.

The architects of each tradition, each strand, have moulded, reshaped, acculturated, redesigned, and—by doing so—enriched what was a Western medium. The result is a liberated English which contains vitality, innovation, linguistic mix, and cultural identity. And, it is not the creativity of the monolingual and the monocultural—this creativity has rejuvenated the medium from "exhaustion" and has "liberated" it in many ways.

Kachru 1998: 106

The metaphor of English as a language blossoming with new growth has been captured for Indian English in language that exemplifies Indian English's love of extended metaphor.

> Years ago, a slender sapling from a foreign field was grafted by "pale hands" on the mighty and many-branched Indian banyan tree. It has kept growing vigorously and now an organic part of its parent tree, it has spread its own probing roots into the brown soil below. Its young leaves rustle energetically in the strong winds that blow from the western horizon, but the sunshine that warms it and the rain that cools it are from Indian skies; and it continues to draw its vital sap from "this earth, this realm," this India.
>
> Naik and Narayan 2004: 253

It is English as a literary language and its "vernacular transformations" (Ashcroft 2016: 126) that has been a major factor in making it a language, not only in, but of Asia (Kirkpatrick 2020).

Yet, as argued and illustrated above, despite all the scholarship that has described the development of new varieties of English and which has shown how English is being increasingly used as a lingua franca throughout the world, the belief that a native speaker model of English and a native-English speaking teacher is, respectively the ideal target and most appropriate teacher, remains remarkably resilient.

## 5. Conclusion

So, what is to be done? Do researchers and applied linguists just keep advocating the adoption of a WE-informed philosophy to the teaching of English and/or an ELF-approach and hope that one day English teacher educators and English teachers—and, crucially learners—will eventually see the light and cast off the yoke of the native speaker model and the native speaker teacher? This seems unlikely. One solution, as suggested above by Watson Todd and Pojanapunya would be to address a wider range of stakeholders, not just academics. This wider range of stakeholders needs to include policy makers in Ministries of Education and those who make decisions about the English language curriculum and which model of English to adopt for the classroom. This is because, in the majority of cases, curriculum change is very unlikely to come from the bottom up. Indeed, a key reason why proposals for adopting a WE philosophy and/or and ELF approach are so little taken up in actual English language classrooms is closely connected with teacher autonomy, or rather the lack of it. In their chapter of adopting an ELF-approach reviewed above, Kemaloglu-Er and Bayyurt (2018) note that, adopting such an approach gives teachers autonomy. But how many teachers in today's English language classrooms around the world have the level of autonomy that would allow them to alter the curriculum as they saw fit? In my forty years of experience in teacher education across Asia, I cannot think of a single classroom context where the local primary or secondary school teacher had this type of autonomy. In contrast, in most cases the curriculum, the materials and the goals of English language teaching classes are fixed. These are decided top down, if not by the relevant national or regional Ministries of Education, by the school's Head Teacher. In these circumstances, it is unrealistic to expect teachers who have just completed professional development courses in which they have learned about WEs and ELF to implement changes to their school's pedagogy and philosophy on their return to their school (or employment at a new school). And, as was noted by Hino above, cultural pedagogical traditions also need to be respected. Such changes can only really be successful and long-lasting, if they are approved by the relevant Ministries, school principals and senior teachers. These are the stakeholders who now need to be addressed. At the same time, we need to be aware just how resilient the desire to sound like a native speaker remains, even though people may be aware that ELF is perfectly appropriate. As an "ELF-aware" Chinese business person recently noted.

> We have learnt ENL [English as a native language] for such a long time, probably since primary school. It is always good if someone can use English like native English speakers. It is a matter of ambivalence. ELF works well in the workplaces. I do not speak ENL and my Indian clients do not speak ENL. As long as we have high acceptance to each other's non-standard use of English, we can communicate well and get the job done. It could be very weird if both of us speak English like Britons. I want to be identified as a Chinese when I speak English. However, ENL is socially preferred. No one has it but everyone wants it.
>
> Si 2020: 229

## References

Ali, Z. (2015), "The prospect and potential challenges of teaching Englishes in Pakistan," *Asian Englishes*, 17 (2): 152–69.
Ashcroft, B. (2016), "English futures," in M. O'Sullivan, D. Hubbard and C. Lee (eds.), *The Future of English in Asia*, 111–27, London and New York: Routledge.
Bolton, K. (2012), "World Englishes and Asian Englishes: A survey of the field," in A. Kirkpatrick and R. Sussex (eds.), *English as an International Language in Asia. Implications for Language Education*, 13–26, Dordrecht: Springer.
Bolton, K. and J. Bacon-Shone (2020), "The Statistics of English across Asia," in K. Bolton, W. Botha and A. Kirkpatrick (eds.), *The Handbook of Asian Englishes*, 49–80, Hoboken, N.J: Wiley-Blackwell.
Braine, G., ed. (1999), *Non-native Educators in English Language Teaching*. Mahwah, New Jersey: Lawrence Erlbaum Associates.
Chang, Y.-J. (2014), "Learning English today: What can world Englishes teach college students in Taiwan?," *English Today*, 30 (1): 21–7.
Davies, A. (1991), *The Native Speaker in Applied Linguistics*, Edinburgh: Edinburgh University Press.
Dewey, M. (2012), "Towards a post-normative approach: Learning the pedagogy of ELF," *Journal of English as a Lingua Franca*, 1 (1): 141–70.
Dudzik, D. and Q. T. N. Nguyen (2015), "Vietnam: Building English competency in preparation for ASEAN 2015," in R. Stoupe and K. Kimura (eds.), *ASEAN Integration and the Role of English Language Teaching*, 41–70, Phnom Penh: IDP.

Fang, F. and W. Ren, (2018), "Developing students' awareness of Global Englishes," *ELT Journal: English Language Teaching Journal*, 72 (4): 384–94.

Fang, F and H. P. Widodo, eds. (2019), *Critical Perspectives on Global Englishes in Asia*, Bristol: Multilingual Matters.

Fenton-Smith, B., P. Humphreys and I. Walkinshaw, eds. (2017), *English Medium Instruction in Higher Education in Asia-Pacific: From Policy to Pedagogy*, Dordrecht: Springer.

Galloway, N. (2013), "Global Englishes and English Language Teaching (ELT)—Bridging the gap between theory and practice in a Japanese context," *System*, 41 (3): 786–803. https://doi.org/10.1016/j.system.2013.07.019

Halliday, M.A.K., A. McIntosh and P. Strevens (1964), *The Linguistic Sciences and Language Teaching*, London: Longman.

Hino, N. (2018), *EIL Education for the Expanding Circle: A Japanese model*, London and New York: Routledge.

Kachru, B. B. (1992), *The Other Tongue. English Across Cultures*, Chicago: University of Illinois Press.

Kachru, B. B. (1998), "English as an Asian language," *Links and Letters*, 5: 89–108.

Kemaloglu-Er, E. and Y. Bayyurt (2018), "ELF-awareness in teaching and teacher education: Explicit and implicit ways of integrating ELF into the English language classroom," in N. Sifakis and N. Tsantila (eds.), *English as a Lingua Franca for EFL Contexts*, 159–74, Bristol: Multilingual Matters.

Kirkpatrick, A. (2006), "Which model of English: Native speaker, nativised or lingua franca?," in M. Saraceni and R. Rubdy (eds.), *English in the World: Global Rules, Global Roles*, 71–83, London: Continuum Press.

Kirkpatrick, A. (2012), "English as an Asian lingua franca: The lingua franca approach and implications for language education policy," *Journal of English as a Lingua Franca*, 1 (1): 121–40.

Kirkpatrick, A. (2014), "Teaching English in Asia in non-Anglos cultural contexts: Principles of the lingua franca approach," in R. Marlina and R.A. Giri (eds.), *The Pedagogy of English as an International Language*, 23–34, Dordrecht: Springer.

Kirkpatrick, A. (2018a), "Concluding chapter," in N. Sifakis and N. Tsantila (eds.), *ELF for EFL Contexts*, 229–41, Clevedon: Multilingual Matters.

Kirkpatrick, A. (2018b), "From EFL to ELF: The time is right," in S. Zein (ed.) *Teacher Education for English as a Lingua Franca: Perspectives from Indonesia*, 191–203, London and New York: Routledge.

Kirkpatrick, A. (2020), *Is English an Asian Language?*, Cambridge: Cambridge University Press.

Kobayashi, Y. (2017), "ASEAN English teachers as a model for international English learners: Modified teaching principles," *International Journal of Applied Linguistics*, 27 (3): 682–96.

Marlina, R. (2013), "Learning about English as an international language in Australia from three students' perspectives," *Asian EFL Journal*, 15 (3): 201–28.

Marlina, R. (2014), "The pedagogy of English as an international language (EIL): More reflections and dialogues," in R. Marlina and R.A. Giri, *The Pedagogy of English as an International Language*, 1–19, Dordrecht: Springer.

Matsuda, A. (2019), "World Englishes in English language teaching. Kachru's 6 fallacies and the TEIL paradigm," *World Englishes*, 38: 144–54.

Musthafa, B, F. A. Hamied and S. Zein (2018), "Enhancing the quality of Indonesian teachers in the ELF era: Policy recommendations," in S. Zein (ed.), *Teacher Education for English as a Lingua Franca: Perspectives from Indonesia*, 175–90, London and New York: Routledge.

Naik, M. K. and S. A. Narayan (2004), *Indian English Literature 1980–2000: A Critical Survey*, New Delhi: Pencraft International.

Rose, H. and N. Galloway (2019), *Global Englishes for Language Teaching*, Cambridge: Cambridge University Press.

Rose, H., J. McKinley and N. Galloway (2020), "Global Englishes and language teaching: A review of pedagogical research," *Language Teaching*, doi:10.1017/S02614448200000518: 1–33.

Sadeghpour, M. and F. Sharifian (2019), "World Englishes in English language teaching," *World Englishes*, 38: 245–58.

Si, J. (2020), "Is what is taught what is needed? The practicality of ELF-informed teaching in China's Business English Program," unpublished PhD thesis, Griffith University, Brisbane.

Sifakis, N. and N. Tsantila, eds. (2018), *English as a Lingua Franca for EFL Contexts*. Bristol: Multilingual Matters.

Teixeira, A. and R. Pozzi (2014), "Introducing English as an International Language in the Inner-Circle Classroom: Exploring World Englishes," *CATESOL Journal*, 26 (1): 50–9.

Vettorel, P. and S. Corrizzato (2016), "Fostering awareness of the pedagogical implications of World Englishes and ELF in teacher education in Italy," *Studies in Second Language Learning and Teaching*, 6 (3): 487–511.

Watson Todd, R. and P. Pojanapunya (2020), "Shifting attitudes towards native speakers and local English teachers: an elaborative replication," *Journal of Multilingual and Multicultural Development* DOI 10.1080/014334632.2020.1730861

Widodo, H. P. and F. Fang (2019), "Global Englishes-oriented English language education," in F. Fang and H. P. Widodo (eds.), *Critical Perspectives on Global Englishes in Asia*, 194–200, Bristol: Multilingual Matters.

# 13

# Documenting World Englishes in the *Oxford English Dictionary*: Past Perspectives, Present Developments, and Future Directions

Danica Salazar

## 1. Introduction

In 2018, the *Oxford English Dictionary (OED)* celebrated its 90th birthday—ninety years since its ten-volume first edition (*OED1*) was published in 1928. Throughout this time, and in the forty-nine years between 1879 and 1928 when James Murray and subsequent chief editors of the dictionary led a team of editors in the gargantuan task of producing instalment after alphabetical instalment of this ambitious and unprecedented lexicographical project, the *OED* has been held up as a landmark work of linguistic scholarship, and until now it is recognized as the undisputed authority on the lexical history of the English language. The *OED* is an historical dictionary of unparalleled size and scope, showing not only the current meanings of hundreds of thousands of words, but also tracing their chronological evolution through millions of quotations taken from written examples of authentic language use.

The *OED* is presently undergoing its first thoroughgoing revision and update since it was first published in full over ninety years ago. This endeavor employs over seventy editors based in Oxford and New York. The dictionary's third and latest edition is accessible through *OED Online* (oed.com), where updates are published quarterly. This makes the *OED* a work in progress, a hybrid text which combines unrevised entries from previous editions with fully revised and newly added entries. One of the key components of the dictionary's revision project is improving and enlarging its coverage of world Englishes, particularly of those varieties used outside of the United Kingdom and the United States.

This chapter begins with a chronological overview of how the *OED* has covered world Englishes throughout its long history. It will then discuss the important steps that the *OED* is currently taking towards providing a more balanced, representative, and authentic treatment of words used in a wider range of Anglophone settings, and conclude with some remarks on the future of world Englishes in the dictionary.

It should also be clarified at this point what is meant when we talk of world Englishes in the *OED*. In the *OED*, *world Englishes* is taken to mean those localized or indigenized varieties of English spoken throughout the world by people of diverse cultural backgrounds in a wide range of sociolinguistic contexts. Although, strictly speaking, all the different varieties of English currently spoken can be considered world varieties of English, in the *OED*, the term *world Englishes* only refers to varieties other than standard British and American English, which are the two major varieties that have always been considered core English by most dictionaries. All other varieties—whether they are first-language regional varieties such as Canadian English or Australian English, or second-language regional varieties such as Nigerian English, Singapore English, or Indian English, or even British dialectal varieties such as Scottish English, Manx English, or Welsh English, or sociolectal varieties such as African American English—are within the scope of world Englishes in the *OED*. Pidgins and creoles based on English are not included, since the *OED* does not consider them varieties of English but rather as separate languages that can be a source of borrowings into English. For instance, the word *sef* is recorded in the *OED* not as a Nigerian Pidgin English word, but as a Nigerian English word that has been borrowed from Nigerian Pidgin English, though the pidgin word itself may have ultimately come from the English word *safe*.

## 2. Putting the *OED*'s Coverage of World Englishes in its Historical Context

Fishman (1995: 34) urges us to "interpret dictionaries in context and see them as both resultant of and constructive of their contexts." If we are to critique the *OED* in this way, we can examine it as a product of its very particular British origins. What has been the place of what we would now call world English vocabulary in what is, still today, considered by many people as a quintessentially British institution, and where does it figure in the dictionary's present and future?

The *OED* was born in the Victorian era, a time when the homogenization and standardization of language was viewed as the main function of a dictionary, in line with the predominant scientific thinking of the period. Benson (2001: 4) argues that the "English dictionary is a historically specific form of discourse embedded within broader discourses that represent knowledge of the world in terms of metaphors of centre and periphery," with the center generally being understood as standard British English and the periphery as everything else outside this standard. The *OED*, despite the undeniable rigor of its historical methodology, cannot wholly escape criticisms for this perceived ethnocentrism.

James Murray himself, in his *General Explanations* that prefaces the first fascicle of *A New English Dictionary on Historical Principles (NED)*, the very first incarnation of the *OED*, uses the center-periphery metaphor in describing the scope of English. He presents a diagram (Figure 13.1) in which he identifies a core of English words whose "Anglicity is unquestioned" (Murray 1884: xvii). Outside this core is what we would consider today to be the bulk of world Englishes lexis—dialectal and foreign words—words beyond what was then recognized as Standard British English.

**Figure 13.1** Murray's Model of the English lexicon (1884)

Before ascribing the apparent ethnocentrism of Murray's model to his deliberate neglect of non-British cultures, it is important to note the contemporary evidence that shows Murray having staunchly defended the place of foreign and dialectal words in the *OED* (Ogilvie 2012). His correspondence from this period shows how much resistance he faced from his subeditors and superiors at Oxford University Press, as well as from consultants and reviewers, when he decided to include words such as the Philippine *abaca*, the South African *aardvark*, and the Indian *amah* in the first fascicle. The presence of these words in the *OED* serves as proof of Murray's commitment to including this type of vocabulary in the dictionary, and it is indeed during his decades-long tenure as Chief Editor that a number of Anglo-Indian words (*bungalow, chit, dal*), Southeast Asian terms (*gong, rattan, sarong, wat*), and other lexical items of similarly foreign origin (*chop-stick, ginseng, meerkat, okra*) made their way into the *OED* (Salazar 2018a).

What is more meaningful to observe about these words is the way that these non-British items were presented entirely through the lens of Victorian Britain, as a response to the needs and interests of the British Empire. A good example is the *OED* entry for the aforementioned *abaca* (Figure 13.2), which appears on page 5 of the 1884 first fascicle.

Despite being a name for a plant from halfway across the world from Britain, *abaca* managed to enter the *OED* in the late nineteenth century because of the strong natural fiber yielded by the plant and the objects that can be made from it: paper, rope, matting, hats. It is obvious that *abaca*'s Philippine origin is peripheral to the entry, and that the word made it into the dictionary by virtue of its significance to British industry, being

> ‖ **Abaca** (æ·băkă), also **abaka**. The native name of the palm (*Musa textilis*) which furnishes what is commonly known as Manilla Hemp; occasionally applied in commerce to the fibre, whence 'the most exquisite textile fabrics, and the elegant Manilla hats are manufactured.' Lindley & Moore *Treas. Bot.*, and Yeats *Nat. Hist. Comm.*

**Figure 13.2** Entry for *Abaca*, n. in the First Fascicle of *A New English Dictionary on Historical Principles* (1884, 5)

a raw material used in making everyday objects. The selection of words of foreign origin in the *NED* fascicles, published between 1884 and 1928, and in the first edition of the *OED*, published in 1928, reflects the interests and concerns of the British of the late nineteenth and early twentieth centuries: the native flora and fauna of their colonies in Asia, Africa, and the Caribbean; exotic local terms that British travellers and settlers pick up in these overseas territories; the names of the vast array of products that they import from every corner of the globe (Salazar 2018a). These words were all welcomed into the dictionary, but their alien status was marked in the fascicles and in the complete *OED1* by two parallel lines beside the headword (‖), a symbol known by the in-house term *tramline*.

The tramline method of classification was one that even Murray admitted was inherently subjective, and it was perhaps a desire to avoid inconsistencies in the use of this symbol that the Chief Editors of the 1933 Supplement to the *OED*, Charles Talbot Onions and William Craigie, decided to stop using them altogether (Brewer 2007), as they opened the dictionary's doors to even more foreignisms (*kumquat, bushveld, impala, safari, tango*, to name a few).

It should also be considered that the editorial choices made by Murray, Craigie, Onions, and their staff were significantly limited by the chiefly British and American sources they had access to in Oxford during their time. These limitations led to a certain bias in the *OED* towards loanwords relating to flora, fauna, ethnic groups, and other items of mostly historical and anthropological interest. Bolton and Butler (2008) call this type of vocabulary "Webster words," since they observed their prevalence not only in the *OED* but also in various editions of *Webster's*.

The mid-and late twentieth century brought new ideas and new theoretical frameworks in mainstream linguistics that led to a new conception of dialectal variation in English. Linguistic variation came to be seen as a natural consequence of cultural diversity, and it came to be understood that a language such as English that had been transplanted into new environments tended to adapt to these environments and that national or regional varieties of languages served to express national or regional identities. In a post-imperialist world where the globalization of English was an accepted fact, regional Englishes spoken throughout the world began to be studied as varieties in their own right, and became known collectively as world Englishes (Kachru 1986; McArthur 1987; Görlach 1990).

The *OED* responded to this paradigm shift by looking further into the written English of Anglophone regions outside the British Isles in the four-volume Supplement edited by Robert Burchfield. The Burchfield Supplements, published in the 1970s and 80s, added to the *OED* a wider variety of words that expressed various aspects of life in their places of origin (*kebaya, gamelan, sambal, nasi goreng, satay, jeepney*). However, these Supplements also marked a return to the use of tramlines to distinguish foreign words, a policy that was once again dropped in the twenty-volume Second Edition (*OED2*) that came out in 1989.

In a 1987 article, Edmund Weiner, one of the Chief Editors of the *OED*'s 1989 Second Edition, acknowledged the ad hoc treatment of regional English items in *OED1* and its subsequent supplements, and discussed possible ways of applying a more articulated policy in *OED2*. Finally, in 2000, with the launch of the Third Edition (*OED3*), then Chief Editor John Simpson explicitly recognized the status of English as a world language, and the relegation of British English from being the only standard to being one of many to be covered by the dictionary:

> From its base in Britain, the English language has expanded over the centuries to become a world language, in which individual varieties share a common core of words but develop their own individual characteristics. [...] The English of the British Isles now becomes one (or indeed several) of these varieties, whereas previously standard British English may have been regarded as the dominant form of English.
> 
> Simpson 2000

The *Financial Times* put it succinctly in a 2016 piece when it said, "the *OED* finds itself in the curious position of being a national institution called upon, almost by default, to assume the role of a global one."

In recent years, the *OED* has undertaken targeted projects to expand its record of several Englishes, publishing particularly large batches of new entries for varieties spoken in Canada, Hong Kong, India, Malaysia, Nigeria, the Philippines, Singapore, and South Africa. The following section will explain the principles and motivations behind the dictionary's current efforts in documenting world Englishes.

## 3. Current Policies and Practices on World Englishes in the *OED*

The lexicographical documentation of world Englishes is a complex undertaking made even more challenging by the fact that most people still view dictionaries as representations in paper and ink, or in screens and pixels, of a monolithic ideal of a standard language. This conceptualization of a dictionary as the definitive arbiter on correct usage puts into question the necessity, or even the propriety, of including in it those regional, colloquial, and non-standard words that characterize world Englishes lexis (Dolezal 2006).

However, as Seargeant (2011) suggests, the very linguistic ideology which has made dictionaries a powerful tool for language standardization can itself be used in changing long-held prejudices against emerging varieties of English. Adding world Englishes words to a dictionary, especially one as well-known and respected as the *OED*, serves as a recognition of their status within the English lexicon, and gives the people who use them a sense of belonging to a distinct language community with its own idiosyncratic vocabulary (Dolezal 2006). As Butler (1997) puts it, "being able to say that your words are in a dictionary [...] in general has more effect on the public perception of the validity of a variety than many words spent in linguistic theorizing." The *OED*'s reputation as a linguistic authority can turn it into an instrument for promoting diversity; by recognizing the plurality of centers of English, it can push varieties formerly in the periphery towards the center of language scholarship (Salazar 2015).

The inclusion of lexical items from world Englishes in the *OED* also gives them their rightful place in the historical record of English and contributes significantly to World Englishes research by providing crucial documentary evidence of their chronological development. Just like all other *OED* entries, entries from world Englishes have undergone a rigorous and exhaustive research process that identifies their earliest use in written texts and distills all available information on how their meaning and usage have evolved over time. All this historical dictionary data can be used for further academic inquiry on the lexis of world Englishes, and serve as proof of the longevity and stability of these words, and of the varieties of English to which they belong (Lambert 2020).

## 3.1 More Balanced and Representative Word Selection for World Englishes

In order to fully realize the benefits of greater inclusion of world Englishes, the *OED* has been making necessary adjustments to further broaden its geographical scope and ensure that its entries that fall outside of the lexical core of English are as accurate and reflective of actual usage as possible.

One of the biggest changes in modern lexicography is in the way dictionary evidence is gathered. Unlike with their predecessors in the nineteenth century and early twentieth century, the research done by today's *OED* editors is no longer restricted to published Anglo-American texts that they have physically on hand. The Internet has given twenty-first-century lexicographers greater access to non-UK and non-US sources of linguistic evidence by making them available electronically. They can also make use of other digital tools and resources designed specifically for linguistic investigation, such as Oxford Languages' massive in-house language corpora, which contains billions of words and has variety-specific segments from which to generate frequency counts that help *OED* editors identify and prioritize emerging world Englishes words for inclusion. They can also use other corpora of world Englishes, such as the GloWbE corpus (Global Web-based English Corpus, Davies and Fuchs 2015). They can consult the increasingly large body of scholarly work on the lexis of world

Englishes, as well as collaborate with an international network of consultants working on various world Englishes. They are also able to launch crowdsourcing initiatives in order to ask for word suggestions or antedatings from the very speakers of world Englishes, as it did with a crowdsourced batch of Philippine English words it published in October 2018 (Salazar 2018b), or as it does regularly through the *OED Appeals* website (https://public.oed.com/appeals/).

All of these new research tools and resources have allowed the *OED* to focus its attention on more contemporary lexis, and mechanisms of lexical innovation beyond simple borrowing. As Dolezal (2006: 702) observes, "a language variety is not the sum of its 'exotic' parts," and the *OED* is now more able to provide coverage of world Englishes that not merely amounts to a listing of loanwords referring to native plants, animals, and cultural artefacts, but encompasses all forms of lexical innovation, including a diverse range of strategies of word creation such as semantic change, fossilization, loan translation, loan blending, conversion from one part of speech to another, affixation, clipping, initialism, and compounding (Table 13.1).

New sources and methods for collecting lexical data have also enabled the *OED* to add more words from semantic fields that are of particular interest to actual speakers of world Englishes, not just to British or American lexicographers or linguistic anthropologists looking at a variety from an outsider perspective. The dictionary has recently included more words from such culturally specific domains as food and drink, places to eat, kinship terms, and informal modes of transport (Table 13.2).

These lexical innovations illustrate how users of world Englishes, who usually speak English in addition to one or more other languages, modify English in order to express in this adopted tongue their own local traditions, values, and social norms. For instance, Asian speech etiquette is characterized by a complex system of kinship terms and forms of address in which age, gender, status, and family relationships are marked by a highly specific vocabulary with no direct equivalents in English, forming a lexical gap that is filled by borrowing such words from local languages or adapting existing English words (Salazar 2017).

Now more than before, words from world Englishes are considered for inclusion in the *OED* on the basis of their salience and currency in a particular geographical area or language community, regardless of their diffusion beyond this area or community. Lexical items that may be thought of as peripheral in Standard British or American English and form no part of the vocabulary of British or American English speakers are also given space in the dictionary and defined according to local usage. For example, the *calamansi* (Figure 13.3), known in the West by the name *calamondin* as a decorative citrus plant with orange fruits, is to Filipinos a green fruit that is as essential to their cooking as the lemon is in many other parts of the world. *Calamansi* has therefore been incorporated in the *OED*, with a small-type note acknowledging its significance in Filipino cookery. Another example is *HDB* (Figure 13.4), an initialism that is little known outside of Singapore, but is ubiquitous in the city, being the name of the government-built high-rise flats that most Singaporeans live in.

Table 13.1 Examples of world Englishes words recently added to the *OED*, created using different processes of word formation

| Word | Variety | Definition | Process of word formation | Date of publication in *OED* | Date of first quotation |
|---|---|---|---|---|---|
| sarmie, noun | South African English | A sandwich. | Affixation | 2018 | 1970 |
| agric, adjective | Nigerian English | Designating an improved or genetically modified variety of crop or breed of livestock. | Clipping | 2019 | 1992 |
| timepass, noun | Indian English | An activity or interest that serves to pass the time agreeably but unproductively; an idle distraction. | Compounding | 2017 | 1982 |
| comfort room, noun | Philippine English | A room in a public building or workplace furnished with amenities such as facilities for resting, personal hygiene, and storage of personal items (now rare); (later) a public toilet. | Fossilization | 2015 | 1886 |
| HDB, noun | Singapore English | Housing and Development Board; used chiefly attributively with reference to public housing estates built and managed by the Singapore government. | Initialism | 2016 | 1961 |
| add oil, phrase | Hong Kong English | Expressing encouragement, incitement, or support: go on! go for it! | Loan translation | 2017 | 1980 |
| chakka jam, noun | Indian English | The blocking of a road or the deliberate creation of a traffic jam as a form of civilian protest; a blockade. | Loan blending | 2017 | 1972 |
| blur, adjective | Singapore English | Slow in understanding; unaware, ignorant, confused. | Part of speech conversion | 2016 | 1977 |
| colony, noun | South Asian | A housing estate constructed by an employer or organization for its workers. In later use also: any housing estate or residential community, esp. one surrounded by a closed perimeter of fences and walls. | Semantic change | 2017 | 1886 |

Table 13.2 Examples of world Englishes words recently added to the *OED* from different culturally specific semantic fields

| Semantic field | Word | Variety | Definition | Date of publication in *OED* | Date of first quotation |
|---|---|---|---|---|---|
| Food and drink | bunny chow | South African English | A South African dish consisting of a hollowed-out loaf of bread (or part of a loaf) filled with curry, typically sold as takeaway food; a serving of this. | 2018 | 1972 |
| | char siu | Hong Kong, Singapore, Malaysian English | In Cantonese cookery: roast pork marinated in a sweet and savoury sauce, typically served sliced into thin strips. | 2016 | 1952 |
| | chilli crab | Singapore, Malaysian English | A dish originating in Singapore but also popular in Malaysia, consisting of crab cooked in a sweet and spicy gravy containing red chillies and tomato. | 2016 | 1963 |
| | laksa | Singapore, Malaysian English | In Peranakan cookery: any of various types of spicy noodle soup made with meat, vegetables, or fish. | 2019 | 1846 |
| | milk tea | Hong Kong English | Any of various drinks made with tea and milk or cream; esp. a drink originating in Hong Kong, made with black tea and evaporated or condensed milk. | 2016 | 1897 |
| | yum cha | In Chinese contexts | A meal eaten in the morning or early afternoon, typically consisting of dim sum and hot tea. | 2016 | 1936 |
| Places to eat | buka | Nigerian English | A roadside restaurant or street stall with a seating area, selling cooked food at low prices. | 2019 | 1972 |
| | carinderia | Philippine English | A food stall with a small seating area, typically in a market or at a roadside, selling cooked food at low prices. | 2018 | 1910 |
| | dai pai dong | Hong Kong English | A traditional licenced street stall, typically with a small seating area, selling cooked food at low prices; (now more generally) any food stall of this type. | 2016 | 1983 |
| | dhaba | Indian English | A roadside food stall or restaurant. | 2017 | 1886 |
| | hawker centre | Singapore, Malaysian English | A food market at which individual vendors sell cooked food from small stalls, with a shared seating area for customers. | 2016 | 1966 |

(*Continued*)

Table 13.2 Continued

| Semantic field | Word | Variety | Definition | Date of publication in OED | Date of first quotation |
|---|---|---|---|---|---|
| Kinship terms or forms of address | ate | Philippine English | An elder sister. Also used as a respectful title or form of address for an older woman. | 2016 | 1937 |
| | bapu | Indian English | One's father; a father. Often as a familiar form of address. | 2017 | 1930 |
| | cousin sister | South Asian, Australian English | (a) South Asian: a female cousin of one's own generation; (b) Australian (in Australian Aboriginal usage): a closely related female relative of one's own generation. | 2017 | 1881 |
| | lola | Philippine English | One's grandmother. Also used as a respectful title or form of address for an elderly woman. | 2016 | 1934 |
| | mamak | Malaysian English | A maternal uncle or elder brother; the male head of a household. Also used as a respectful title or form of address for an older man. | 2016 | 1884 |
| Modes of transport | danfo | Nigerian English | A yellow minibus that carries passengers for a fare as part of an informal transport system in Lagos, the most populous city in Nigeria. | 2019 | 1973 |
| | jugaad | South Asian | A makeshift automobile constructed from inexpensive materials. | 2017 | 1995 |
| | okada | Nigerian English | A motorcycle which passengers can use as a taxi service. | 2019 | 1993 |

## calamansi, n.

Frequently *attributive*. The fruit of the calamondin. Also: the tree producing this fruit.

Green, unripe calamansi are commonly used in Philippine cooking, and the tree is frequently cultivated elsewhere as an ornamental garden plant.

**Figure 13.3** *OED3* definition for *calamansi*, n., first published in 2018

## H, n.

**HDB** n. *Singapore English* Housing and Development Board; used chiefly *attributively* with reference to public housing estates built and managed by the Singapore government.

**Figure 13.4** *OED3* definition for *HDB*, n., first published in 2016

### 3.2 Pronunciation Models and Audio Pronunciations for World Englishes Entries

The *OED* has also formulated specific pronunciation models for several world Englishes (see Table 13.3 for a complete list), which can all be consulted on the *OED* website (https://public.oed.com/how-to-use-the-oed/key-to-pronunciation/pronunciations-for-world-englishes/). Each pronunciation model has a dedicated page with a discussion of the rationale for the model, along with major reference sources and potential discrepancies and compromises. These models were developed using pronunciation data drawn from varietal dictionaries, knowledgeable native speakers, and online evidence of natural language use. They form the basis of variety-specific transcriptions in the International Phonetic Alphabet (IPA) for world Englishes entries, accompanied by recorded audio pronunciations. For instance, in the *OED*'s entry for the South African English word *skedonk* (Figure 13.5), there are the IPA transcriptions and audio pronunciations in British and American English that are standard for all non-obsolete *OED* entries, but alongside these is the IPA transcription in South African English, and a blue button that, when clicked, will play a recording of the word being pronounced in a South African accent, as determined by the *OED*'s pronunciation model for South African English.

The audio pronunciations are not synthesized, but are recordings made by actor-phoneticians recruited for each variety, who came to OUP's recording facilities in

**Table 13.3** List of varieties of English for which the *OED* has a Pronunciation Model (as of July 2020)

| | | |
|---|---|---|
| Australian English | Manx English | South African English |
| Canadian English | New Zealand English | Welsh English |
| Caribbean English | Philippine English | West African English |
| Hong Kong English | Scottish English | |
| Irish English | Singapore and Malaysian English | |

# skedonk, n.

View as: Outline | Full entry

**Pronunciation:** Brit. /skəˈdɒŋk/, U.S. /ˌskəˈdɑŋk/, South African /skəˈdʊŋk/
**Forms:** 19– skdonk, 19– skedonk, 19– skiedonk.

**Figure 13.5** IPA transcriptions and audio pronunciations for the South African entry *skedonk*, n. in British English, American English, and South African English

Oxford to read each transcription aloud. The *OED's* review of pronunciations for world Englishes is a work in progress, and pronunciation models for more varieties, along with transcriptions and audio recordings for corresponding entries, will continuously be added to the dictionary by its Pronunciations team.

## 3.3 More Representative Illustrative Quotations for World Englishes

The *OED* now places utmost importance on ensuring that words from world Englishes in the dictionary are illustrated by quotations from works written by speakers of the varieties in question, and published in their place of origin. Consider this entry for *buka*, a Nigerian English word for a roadside restaurant or food stall (Figure 13.6).

It can be seen that all the quotations for this entry come from Nigerian sources, from its earliest attested use in 1972 in a historical novel written by Nigerian author Kole Omotoso, to a 1991 quotation taken from Nigerian writer Ben Okri's Booker Prize-winning novel *The Famished Road*, to messages posted by Nigerians on the social media platform Twitter.

## buka, n.

View as: Outline | Full entry

Quotations: Show all | Hide all  Keywords:

**Pronunciation:** Brit. /ˈbuːkaː/, U.S. /ˈbuˌkɑ/, West African /ˈbuka/
**Inflections:** Plural *bukas*, unchanged.
**Forms:** 19– buka, 19– bukka.
**Origin:** Of multiple origins. Partly a borrowing from Yoruba. Partly a borrowing from Hausa. **Etymons:** Yoruba *búkà*, Hausa *búkkàa*.
**Etymology:** < (i) Yoruba *búkà* hut, market stall,

and its etymon (ii) Hausa *búkkàa* grass shed, hut.

*Nigerian English.*

A roadside restaurant or street stall with a seating area, selling cooked food at low prices. Cf. BUKATERIA *n.*, MAMA PUT *n.* Frequently as a modifier, as in *buka food*.

Thesaurus »
Categories »

1972  K. Omotoso *Combat* 23 When they had finished reading the paper, they went down to a buka and had a big breakfast of eko and akara.
1991  B. Okri *Famished Road* (1992) II. viii.146 But the only thing he did..was go into a bukka, put away a great bowl of pounded yam.
2009  @bellanaija 16 Feb. in *twitter.com* (accessed 16 July 2019) Buka food was tastier than home made..at least for me.
2017  @EzendiNwanyi 15 Oct. in *twitter.com* (accessed 6 Feb. 2019) I really can't wait to take Muyiwa to Lagos and show him my former life. Take him to the joints and bukas.

**Figure 13.6** *OED* entry for *buka*, n.

Although, as previously stated, the *OED* now has access to a more geographically diverse range of research resources, it remains true that the amount of lexicographical evidence available for region-specific vocabulary is still very small compared to that for general English. This is compounded by the fact that publications in postcolonial nations continue to be edited following British or American standards, so that lexical innovations in speech may not always make it into the written texts that the *OED* regularly consults (Salazar 2014). It is for this reason that *OED* editors are increasingly turning to less mediated forms of writing, such as tweets and song lyrics, in order to find quotations that more closely approximate the way that speakers of world Englishes talk, and therefore serve as more authentic illustrations of how words from world Englishes are used in real-life contexts.

The *OED* now recognizes that in most places where English is spoken as a second language, code-switching is the dominant form of communication, a fact that is apparent even in the written register. See, for instance, the following antedating for the Philippine English adjective and noun *kilig* that was brought to the dictionary's attention via a recent *OED* Appeal for antedatings (Figure 13.7).

Previously, an *OED* editor might have dismissed this quotation as an unusable Taglish sentence, but the quotation has now been added to the entry, antedating *kilig* by over ten years, from 1994 to 1981. The *OED* considers this as an acceptable quotation written not in Taglish but in Philippine English, as the base language of this sentence is actually English, with Tagalog words inserted. These insertions are not due to the writer's lack of competence or their "non-nativeness"—they are there for discoursal/ discursive reasons. They were valid choices made by a multilingual speaker from a lexical repertoire that also happens to include words from their other languages; they were choices that the speaker deemed appropriate given their interlocutor and what they were aiming to communicate.

Moving world Englishes from the periphery to the center in the *OED* entails not just documenting their idiosyncratic lexicons. It also means using more sources written in world Englishes to illustrate general English words. Just as works of classic English literature and the most important of British and American newspapers appear regularly in the dictionary's quotation paragraphs to show the development of everyday English

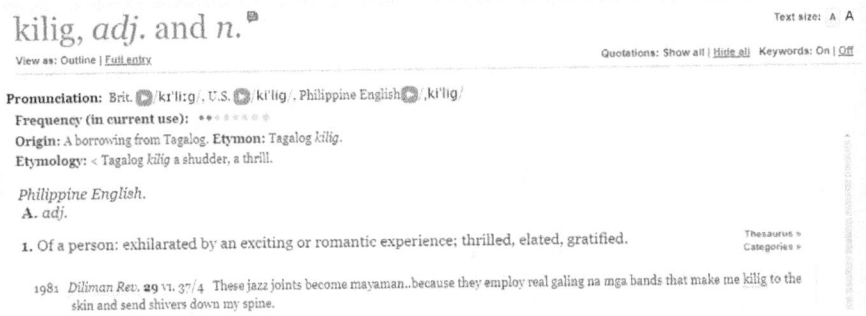

**Figure 13.7** Extract from *OED* entry for *kilig*, adj. and n.

284  Research Developments in World Englishes

words, so should works of postcolonial writers in English, and newspapers read in other parts of the English-speaking world. The OED is addressing this by including more world Englishes publications to its Reading Program, so that its team of volunteer readers can add more quotations from sources outside the United Kingdom and the United States to its digital collection of sentences or short extracts.

### 3.4 More Informative Labels and Usage Notes

The OED aims to make its system of geographical labelling clearer and more useful, and to provide more discursive information to accompany these labels. See for instance, this unrevised entry for *jeepney* (Figure 13.8), originally published in the 1976 Supplement. The entry contains really sparse information that does not tell the reader much about the jeepney's significance in Philippine transport.

Compare this to the new entry for the Filipino dish *sisig* (Figure 13.9), which includes, not just discursive metatext relating it to Filipino cuisine, but also an additional small-type note that tells the reader more about the origins of the dish, its possible variations, when it is eaten, and even cross-refers to the Filipino food custom of *pulutan*, for which the OED also has an entry (Figure 13.10).

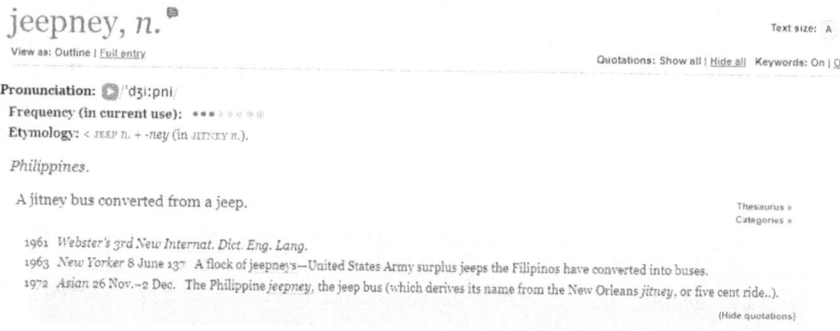

**Figure 13.8**  OED entry for *jeepney*, n.

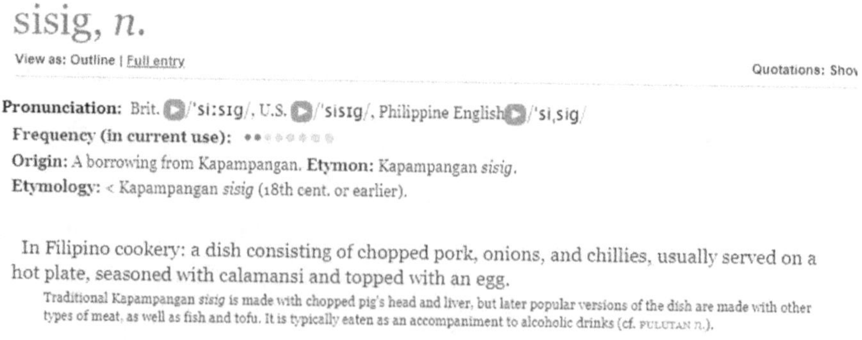

**Figure 13.9**  Extract from OED entry for *sisig*, n.

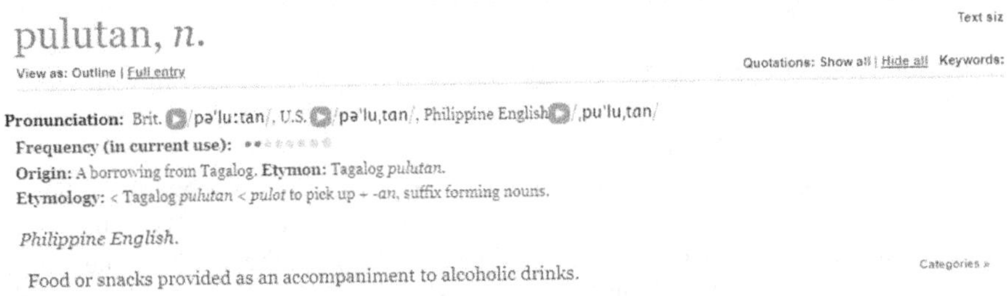

**pulutan,** *n.*

View as: Outline | Full entry

Text siz

Quotations: Show all | Hide all | Keywords:

**Pronunciation:** Brit. /pəˈluːtan/, U.S. /pəˈluˌtan/, Philippine English /ˌpuˈluˌtan/
**Frequency (in current use):** ●●●●●●●●
**Origin:** A borrowing from Tagalog. **Etymon:** Tagalog *pulutan*.
**Etymology:** < Tagalog *pulutan* < *pulot* to pick up + *-an*, suffix forming nouns.

*Philippine English.*

Food or snacks provided as an accompaniment to alcoholic drinks.

Categories »

**Figure 13.10** Extract from *OED* entry for *pulutan*, n.

## 4. Using *OED Online* to Investigate World Englishes

Lambert (2020) notes how the word "dictionary" often still brings to mind the traditional conceptualization of a heavy book containing an alphabetically ordered list of words, when in fact, a more useful and accurate way of viewing a twenty-first-century dictionary is as an online digital resource, "an amazingly versatile and highly adaptable platform for the presentation of linguistic information," and, for World Englishes scholars in particular, "a valuable avenue [...] to display research."

The same can be said specifically of the *OED*. Although the mention of its name conjures images of handsomely bound volumes on a library shelf, the *OED* has always been a pioneer in the process of digitalization that dictionaries have undergone in the past few decades. The ground-breaking computerization of the *OED* began as early as 1984, with the painstaking conversion of the decades-old print dictionary into machine-readable format so that the first edition could be electronically combined with the Burchfield supplements, along with thousands of new entries, to form the twenty-volume Second Edition published in 1989. A few years later, in 1992, the *OED* made history once again when it became available on CD-ROM, and yet again in 2000 with the launch of *OED Online*, which made the *OED* one of the first reference works of its kind to have an online presence (Gilliver 2016).

The digital transformation of the *OED* has revolutionized not only the way the dictionary is compiled, but also how it is used. It has made the *OED* fully searchable, thus freeing users from the limitations imposed by the alphabetical order and enabling them to mine the dictionary's rich trove of lexical data in ways that can be tailored to various scholarly purposes (Brewer 2004). Simpson (2013) points to how the introduction of the electronic *OED* has shifted the focus of interest from single-word lookups to more general investigations of linguistic trends.

The profound impact of digitalization on the *OED* also extends to world Englishes. There are relatively few studies on the vocabulary of world Englishes, because lexical studies require massive language corpora, which are currently unavailable for varieties other than British and American English. The *OED*, as a massive depository of diachronic linguistic data, is uniquely able to fill this research gap. The digital, online format of its vast and varied content is particularly suited for uncovering patterns of word use that can help inform investigations of linguistic and extralinguistic phenomena that are of interest to World Englishes researchers.

## 4.1 Advanced Search

Using the Advanced Search function on *OED Online*, users can apply different filters that narrow down searches for world Englishes entries matching a particular criterion or set of criteria. For example, a search for words in the *OED* that originate in Indian subcontinent languages shows that of the 1,469 entries in the dictionary that come from languages such as Bengali, Hindi, Sanskrit, Tamil, and Urdu, 261 (18%) belong to the subject category Religion and Belief (Figure 13.11a). Further limiting the search results to this subject category and examining the list that this brings up reveals the nature and significance of these South Asian words: they are words relating to principles of Buddhist and Hindu philosophy and mythology (e.g., *jiva, prajna, samsara, satya*),

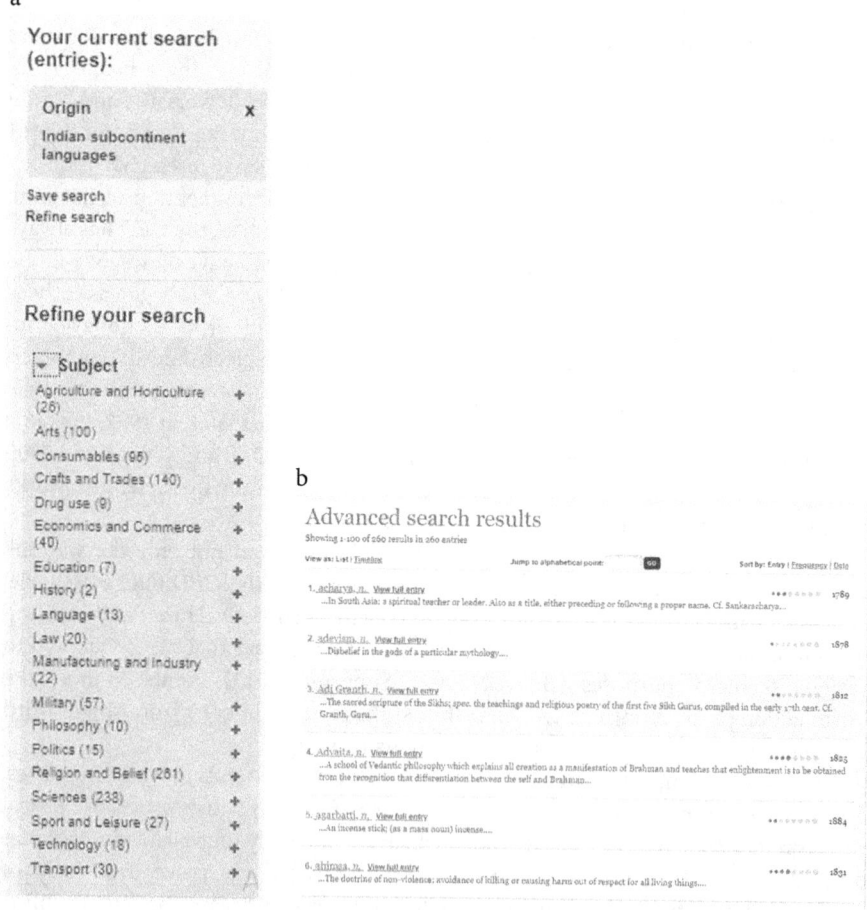

**Figure 13.11a/b** Advanced Search results for words from Indian subcontinent languages in the *OED* (11a) / Advanced Search results for words from Indian subcontinent languages in the *OED*, limited to the subject category religion and belief

or to specific practices of these religions such as yoga (e.g., *asana, ashram, ashtanga, hatha yoga, vinyasa*) and religious festivals (e.g., *Diwali, Holi, Kumbh Mela*). Many of these words have gained such currency in English that they have developed extensions of meaning and become part of everyday vocabulary (e.g., *avatar, guru, juggernaut, karma, mantra, nirvana, pundit*). It can be seen from this example how a refined *OED* search can give insight into the dominant semantic fields in a particular variety of English as recorded lexicographically.

The Advanced Search function can also identify which varieties of English have borrowed from certain substrate languages, and conversely, which substrate languages have had the most lexical influence on a particular variety. For instance, launching an advanced search for words coming from African languages (Figure 13.12a) reveals that unsurprisingly, African varieties have borrowed several words from these languages, but so have Caribbean English and North American English; a similar advanced search for words used in the Caribbean region (Figure 13.12b) shows that Caribbean vocabulary mostly comprises words of English origin and loanwords from European languages such as Spanish and Portuguese, but also includes words that have been borrowed from African languages, Indian languages, and Native American languages, as well as from Caribbean creoles.

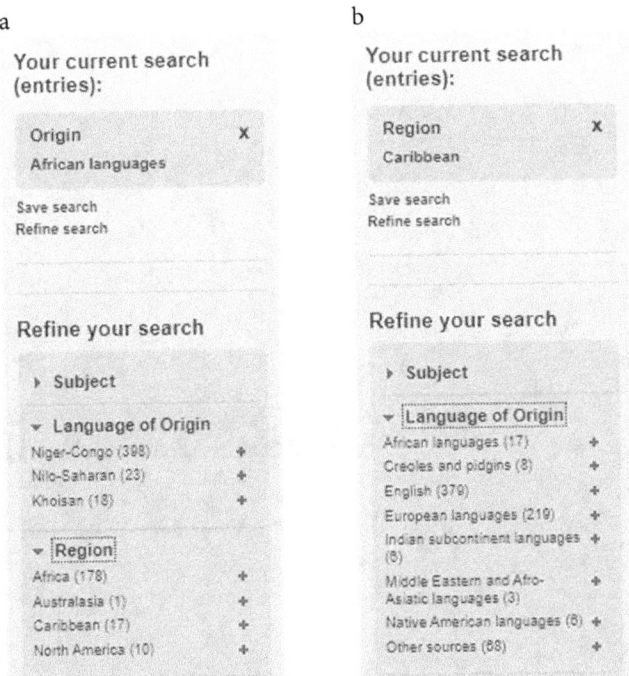

**Figure 13.12a/b** Advanced Search results for words from African languages in the *OED* (12a) / Advanced Search results for words from the Caribbean in the *OED* (12b)

## 4.2 Timelines

Another search feature of *OED Online* is Timelines, which enables a user to generate graphs that show the number of words first recorded by the *OED* within different time periods. Timeline searches can also be limited by various subject, region, and origin categories. An example is the graph in Figure 13.13 illustrating the patterns of borrowing into English from Niger-Congo languages over five centuries, which should be of interest to researchers of various African Englishes who wish to determine the points in time in which there has been the most contact between English and the Niger-Congo languages that form the substrate of many African varieties of English. It can be observed from the graph that borrowing began with the oldest Niger-Congo word recorded by the *OED*, the ethnonym *Kongo*, which is first attested in a 1597 English translation of a book written by Portuguese merchant Duarte Lopes, one of the earliest European accounts of Central Africa; peaked in the late nineteenth century, a period of accelerated British colonial expansion in Africa; and continues to today, with sustained lexical borrowing of Niger-Congo words into English by African speakers who use English alongside their native Niger-Congo languages.

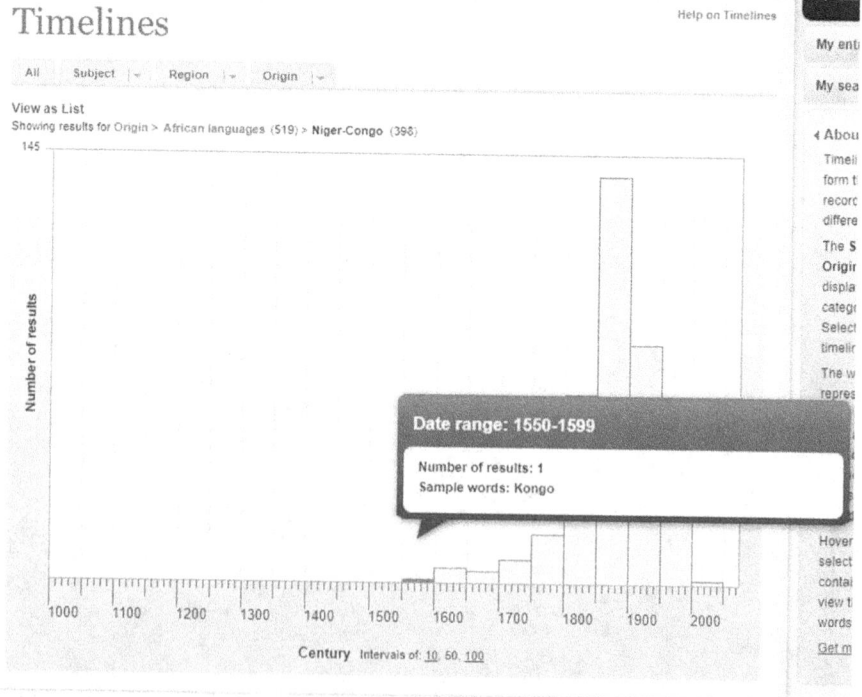

**Figure 13.13** *OED* Timeline graph for words originating in Niger-Congo languages

## 4.3 Insights from Individual *OED* Entries

Even the traditional single-word look-up can still be a source of valuable information for World Englishes research. One simple but fundamental question for lexical studies of world Englishes that can be answered by simply consulting an *OED* entry is whether a word or sense that has been found to be characteristic of a particular variety is indeed a new word or sense that developed within this variety.

Mesthrie (2003) observes that most research in World Englishes has been on the transfer from substrates to New Englishes, and is based on comparisons between contemporary world Englishes corpora and either a British or American English corpus. Mesthrie also cites a study by Davy (2000), who used the *OED* to show that several lexical and grammatical features of African English actually have a long history in British English. Both Mesthrie and Davy question whether current British and American English is always the relevant superstrate to compare to the substrate, and caution against always taking deviations from contemporary British and American English corpora as sufficient evidence for what Davy calls linguistic or normic newness.

One typical example of a word that many people consider to be unique to Philippine English is *comfort room*, which is one of the most commonly used terms in the Philippines to refer to a toilet. However, the *OED* entry for *comfort room* (Figure 13.14) contains evidence of this compound being used in the United States as early as 1886, continuing to be used by Americans during the early years of the American occupation of the Philippines, thus giving an indication of when the term may have been picked up by Filipinos, and then falling out of use in America in the mid-twentieth century and remaining in current use only in the Philippines. The *OED* provides convincing proof that *comfort room* is not a Philippine coinage but rather an archaic usage in American English preserved in contemporary Philippine English.

*OED* entries also show how spelling conventions have changed for certain words from world Englishes. This is particularly interesting for older loanwords that have been borrowed into English from other languages during a time before firm orthographic rules for such loanwords had been set. The extract from the entry for *chaudhuri*, n. (Figure 13.15) lists the nineteen different spellings that *OED* lexicographers have found for this nearly 250-year-old word.

## comfort, *n*.

**comfort room** *n.* (originally) a room in a public building or workplace furnished with amenities such as facilities for resting, personal hygiene, and storage of personal items (now rare); (later) a public toilet (now chiefly *Philippine English*); cf. RESTROOM *n.*

1886 *Santa Fe Daily New Mexican* 24 Dec. On the west side of the third floor..are the large public comfort rooms, closets, lavatories, cloak rooms, post-office, etc.
1920 *Railway Age* 2 Apr. 1087/1 The men are provided with comfort rooms, containing stoves, toilet facilities, wash basins, etc.
1929 *Decatur* (Illinois) *Herald* 7 Nov. 18/3 In the back of the retail salesroom..are women's and men's comfort rooms.
1985 F. MARCOS in *N.Y. Times* 1 Nov. A10/5 I was able to urinate as much as 3,000 c.c. in one day... If you'd seen me going to the comfort room.
2009 C. S. BOND & L. M. SIMONS *Next Front* v. 56 A pink-painted 'comfort room', said to be the first indoor flush toilet on the island.

**Figure 13.14** *OED* entry for *comfort room*, n.

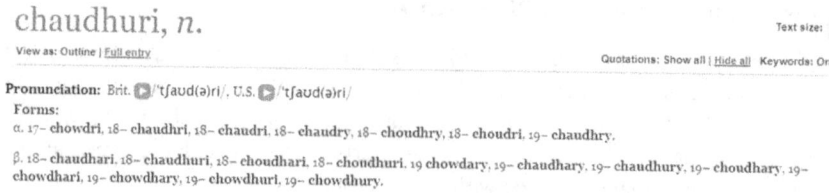

Figure 13.15  Extract from *OED* entry for *chaudhuri*, n.

### 4.4 The *OED* Text Visualizer

A new and dynamic means of exploring *OED* data is the *OED* Text Visualizer, available in beta version at the time of writing (https://oed-text-visualizer.oxfordlanguages.com/). This tool displays in a visual format the *OED*'s etymologies and first usages for words found in a piece of text provided by the user. Figure 13.16 shows an example of a Text Visualizer graph generated from an extract taken from the second chapter of the 2016 novel *Sarong Party Girls* by Singaporean author Cheryl Liu-Lien Tan.

Each bubble in the graph represents a word in the text. Hovering the mouse pointer over a bubble displays more information about the word, while clicking on it opens the *OED* entry for the word. The size of the bubble indicates the corresponding word's frequency of occurrence in the text; the color of the bubble designates the language from which the word has been either inherited or borrowed or within which it has been formed. In the case of this text, it is teal for Germanic languages, blue for English, red for Romance languages, purple for Latin, and yellow for other languages. The position of a bubble on the x-axis denotes the word's first recorded use based on the first quotation listed in the *OED*, while its position on the y-axis signifies the word's frequency in modern English, on a logarithmic scale.

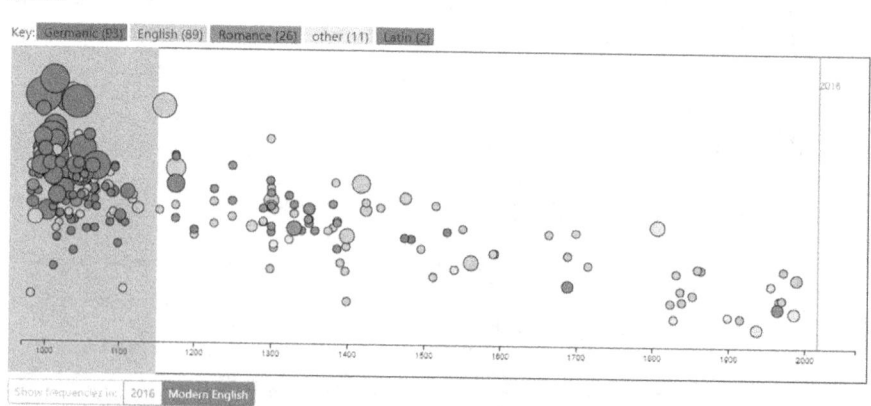

Figure 13.16  *OED* Text Visualizer graph for an excerpt from *Sarong Party Girls* (Tan 2016)

The concentration of large teal and blue bubbles in the upper left side of the graph implies that the majority of the words in this extract are very old Germanic or English words belonging to the common core of the English lexicon shared by many varieties of the language—function words such as articles, prepositions, and conjunctions, but also highly frequent content words such as *see, up, want,* and *spot*. Words that are specific to Singapore, such as *ang moh, aiyoh, Ah Beng,* and *lah*, are represented by small yellow dots in the lower right side of the graph, indicating the newness of these words and their relative infrequency in the text. Based on the lexical evidence presented in this graph, it can be argued that although *Sarong Party Girls* provoked considerable discussion upon its publication for being a novel in Singlish, it is not in fact written in Singlish but in Singapore English. The text is largely composed of high-frequency words found in most English writing, but is also characterized by a smaller set of less frequent but highly distinctive and contemporary Singapore English vocabulary that gives life to the novel's characters and places them within the milieu of twenty-first-century Singapore.

While still in beta version, the OED Text Visualizer is only optimized to annotate texts of up to five hundred words written after 1750. A fully optimized version of the tool without these limitations is currently under development, and will be made available soon. With further improvement of the Text Visualizer, it will become an even more effective means of carrying out diachronic lexical analyses of long stretches of actual discourse in world Englishes.

## 5. The Future of World Englishes in the OED

As the OED carries on with its work of documenting the lexicon of world Englishes, there remains much room for critique, for new ideas for resources and technologies, and for new ways to use the vast amounts of data stored in the dictionary. World Englishes provide particularly fertile ground for innovation in the OED, as they bring up a variety of research questions that lead to productive re-examinations of its practices and policies.

At the time of writing, the OED is preparing for the imminent publication of large batches of new words and revised entries for Bermudian English, Caribbean English, Irish English, Kenyan English, Tanzanian English, Ugandan English, and African American English, while continuing to monitor developments in other varieties of English.

Looking to the future, the OED's goal for world Englishes is to fulfil the needs of its increasingly global audience through wide-ranging, inclusive, and representative coverage of their words and usage. This can only be achieved through collaboration with local partners, and so the OED is introducing several new ways of engaging with the World Englishes research community. There is the OED Researchers Advisory Group (https://oed-group.oxfordlanguages.com/), an invitation-only group for academics who use the OED in their research, and are willing to participate in surveys, forum discussions, and other tasks within the RAG interface in order to share their ideas and expertise relating to different aspects of the dictionary's ongoing projects on world Englishes.

There is also *OED* Labs, an initiative which invites scholars of various fields to contribute to the development of new functionalities for the exploration of *OED* content (https://languages.oup.com/research/oed-labs/), such as the Text Visualizer described above, and the *OED* Researcher API, a tool that enables researchers to make use of datasets extracted from across the *OED* to support research in a wide variety of disciplines.

With every new development, the *OED* is evolving into something much more than a dictionary. It is now becoming a dynamic and flexible lexical database that can be a starting point or a regular stop in the research journey of scholars seeking to investigate world Englishes lexica. By adding new words, revising existing entries, and developing better tools and methodologies, the *OED* is increasing the quantity and further improving the quality of the lexical data it contains for world Englishes, so that it can be an even bigger, more balanced, more representative, and more reliable dataset that can help researchers answer a variety of questions on how English is used by different communities around the world.

## References

*A New English Dictionary on Historical Principles: Part 1: A-Ant*. 1884. Oxford: Oxford University Press.

Benson, P. (2001), *Ethnocentrism and the English Dictionary*, London and New York: Routledge.

Bolton, K. and S. Butler (2008), "Lexicography and the description of Philippine English vocabulary," in M. L. S. Bautista and K. Bolton (eds.), *Philippine English: Linguistic and Literary Perspectives*, 175–200, Hong Kong: Hong Kong University Press.

Brewer, C. (2004), "The electronification of the *Oxford English Dictionary*," *Dictionaries: Journal of the Dictionary Society of North America*, 25: 1–43.

Brewer, C. (2007), *Treasure-House of The Language: The Living OED*. New Haven and London: Yale University Press.

Butler, S. (1997), "Selecting South-east Asian words for an Australian dictionary: How to choose in an English not your own," in E. W. Schneider (ed.), *Englishes Around the World Vol. 2. Caribbean, Africa, Asia, Australia. Studies in Honour of Manfred Görlach*, 273–86, Amsterdam: John Benjamins.

Davies, M. and R. Fuchs (2015), "Expanding horizons in the study of World Englishes with the 1.9 billion word Global Web-based English Corpus (GloWbE)," *English World-Wide*, 36 (1): 1–28.

Davy, J. (2000), "A conservative view of the New Englishes," Paper presented at the *First International Conference on Linguistics in Southern Africa*, January 12–14, University of Cape Town.

Dolezal, F. (2006), "World Englishes and lexicography," in B. Kachru, Y. Kachru and C. Nelson (eds.), *The Handbook of World Englishes*, 694–708, Oxford: Blackwell.

Fishman, J. A. (1995), "Dictionaries as culturally constructed and culture-constructing artifacts: The reciprocity view as seen from Yiddish sources," in B. Kachru and H. Kahane (eds.), *Cultures, Ideologies, and the Dictionary: Studies in Honour of Ladislav Zgusta*, 29–34. Tübingen: Max Niemeyer Verlag.

Gilliver, P. (2016), *The Making of the Oxford English Dictionary*, Oxford: Oxford University Press.

Görlach, M. (1990), *Studies in the History of the English Language*, Heidelberg: Carl Winter.

Kachru, B. (1986), "The power and politics of English," *World Englishes*, 5 (2/3): 121–40.

Lambert, J. (2020), "Lexicography and World Englishes," in D. Schreier, M. Hundt, and E. W. Schneider (eds.), *The Cambridge Handbook of World Englishes*, 408–35, Cambridge: Cambridge University Press.

McArthur, A. (1987), "The English languages?," *English Today*, 11: 9–13.

Mesthrie, R. (2003), "The World Englishes paradigm and Contact Linguistics: Refurbishing the foundations," *World Englishes*, 22 (4): 449–61.

Murray, J. A. H. (1884), "General explanations," in *A New English Dictionary on Historical Principles: Part 1: A-Ant*, xvii–xxiv. Oxford: Oxford University Press.

Ogilvie, S. (2012), *Words of the World: A Global History of the* Oxford English Dictionary, Cambridge: Cambridge University Press.

Salazar, D. (2014), "Towards improved coverage of Southeast Asian Englishes in the *Oxford English Dictionary*," *Lexicography*, 1: 95–108.

Salazar, D. (2015), "The vocabulary of non-dominant varieties of English in the *Oxford English Dictionary*," in R. Muhr, D. Marley, A. Bissoonauth-Bedford and L. Kretzenbacher (eds.), *Pluricentric Languages Worldwide and Pluricentric Theory*, 11–27. Vienna: Peter Lang.

Salazar, D. (2017), "Release Notes: Indian English," *OED* Blog. Accessed July 26, 2020. https://public.oed.com/blog/september-2017-update-release-notes-indian-english/.

Salazar, D. (2018a), "From 'Abaca' to 'Kilig': World English and the *OED*," *OED* Blog. Accessed July 12, 2020. https://public.oed.com/blog/abaca-kilig-world-english-oed.

Salazar, D. (2018b), "Philippine English in the October 2018 Update," *OED* Blog. Accessed July 26, 2020. https://public.oed.com/blog/philippine-english-in-the-september-2018-update/.

Seargeant, P. (2011), "Lexicography as a philosophy of language," *Language Sciences*, 33: 1–10.

Simpson, J. (2000), "Preface to the Third Edition of the *OED*," Accessed July 12, 2020. http://public.oed.com/the-oed-today/preface-to-the-third-edition-of-the-oed.

Simpson, J. (2013), "Mediums of access to the *Oxford English Dictionary*," In G. Stickel and T. Varadi (eds.), *Lexical Challenges in a Multilingual Europe: Contributions to the Annual Conference 2012 of EFNIL in Budapest*, 95–110. Frankfurt am Main: Peter Lang.

Tan, C. L.-L. (2016), *Sarong Party Girls*, New York: William Morrow.

Weiner, E. (1987), "The new *OED* and World English," *English Today*, 3 (3): 31–4. (Reprinted from *English World-Wide*, 7: 259–66).

# Index

Note: Figures are indicated with an italic '*f*' following the page number, tables with an italic '*t*' and notes by '*n*'. The number following '*n*' indicates the note number if there is more than one note on the page.

*abaca, OED* entry for 273–274
abrogation, of the English language 15
accents, impact of overseas travel on accents of world Englishes-speakers 158
Achebe, Chinua 14
Afghanistan 64*t*
Africa
    Lugard's picture of African natives as CHILD metaphor 210–211
    postcolonial communities 231
    pre-colonial conceptualizations of homosexuality in 217
    research on use of English in 52
African Englishes
    features of 289
    semantics of *witch* and *witchcraft* in 221
    Timelines in *OED Online* 288
Afrikaans/Afrikaners 7, 121, 124–125, 128, 131, 138, 139
Agard, John 15
Akinola, Peter, Archbishop 219–220
American dictionaries 177, 178
American English 154, 158, 159, 164
    cultural metaphors 184
    global adoption of 150
    media and 162–163
    production of bath and trap vowels in 164
    social media and online language use of 165
    spellings 155
American University of Sharjah, United Arab Emirates 99
Americanization, of World Englishes 150, 153, 162, 165

Amin, Idi 54
Anchimbe, Eric 8
Anglicists, view towards India 205
Anglo-Indian English 77, 223, 273
anglophony 29, 30, 31, 34, 35, 37–42
Ansaldo, Umberto 7
appropriation, of English 15, 16–17, 20, 24
Arab countries, World Englishes research in 52
Arabic 96, 97
    attitudes towards Arabic in UAE study 105*t*, 107
    *khaleeji* or Gulf Arabic 98
    Modern Standard Arabic (MSA) 98
    role in Arabic-speaking nations 98
    role in South Asia 103
ASEAN *see* Association of Southeast Asian Nations (ASEAN)
Asia
    contact history of Englishes in non-settler colonies 7
    English language teaching 254–255
    evolution of Englishes in 73
    knowledge of English in Expanding Circle Asian societies 262, 263*t*
    knowledge of English in Outer Circle Asian societies 262, 263*t*
    speech etiquette 277
Asian Englishes 7, 75, 76, 81
Association of Southeast Asian Nations (ASEAN) 254, 255–256, 264
    Economic Community (AEC) 261
Australia, English teachers in 261
Australian English 261, 281*t*

Baba Malay 75
Baganda 54, 59

Bahrain 63*t*
*banglas* 223
Bantu education 125, 128
Bantu languages 136–137, 138
Bhutan, Kingdom of 64
Bioko, Equatorial Guinea 78
Black petty bourgeoisie 125
Black South African English 49, 122
Black South African English corpus 7
   analysis of English language attitudes in 121–147
   attitudes towards
      the English language 131, 140–141*t*
      English people 127, 140*t*
      language practices 133, 141*t*
      languages in education 141–142*t*
   views on skills in English in 132–133
black South Africans
   attitudes towards English 122–123
   education for 125
   repression of 124
Bokwe, John Knox, Reverend 135
Bonilla, Yarimar 22, 24
Bonnecarrere, Paul Auguste Francois 208
*born house* 241
Botswana 63*t*
Brazilian English 185
Britain *see* United Kingdom
British colonizers 8
British empire 12–13, 212, 222
   expansion of 14
British English 75, 150, 154, 155
   cultural metaphors 184
   institutional dominance of 162
   and the *OED* 272, 275, 289
   pitch 79
   production of bath and trap vowels in 164
   teaching of British English in Ugandan schools 54
British Home Office, asylum procedures of the 23
British Malaya 75
Brown, Gordon 263
Brunei 53, 64
Buganda 53
buggery 213, 214
*buka*, *OED* entry for 282

*bungalow* 222–224
Burchfield, Robert 275
Burkina Faso 217

*calamansi*, *OED* entry for 277, 281*f*
*calamondin* 277
calquing 36
*Cambridge Handbook of World Englishes* (Schreier, Hundt and Schneider) 2
Cameron, Sir Donald C. 210
Cameroon English 8, 231, 233, 235, 244
   *born house* (celebration of birth) 241
   kinship terms in 243
Cameroon *Happy Birthday* radio show 231–249
   applicability of postcolonial pragmatics to collectivist cultures 233–235
   data used in analysis of 232–233
   exchange between married teacher-trainee and host 246–247
   exchange between unmarried student and host 244–246
   giving advice on social expectations 240–241
   individual lives and faces in terms of the society's group face and social norms 235–243
   interactions 235
   living up to social expectations 236–238
   marital status 236–237
   new mothers informing people of births 242
   reproaching for breaking social norms 238–240
   social norms in 231–249
   use of English, Cameroon Pidgin English and French in 233
Cameroon Province 221
Cantonese 79, 88, 110
   particles 80
Cape Colony 128
catch phrase 184
Ceylon (now Sri Lanka) 55
*chaudhuri*, *OED* entry for 290, 290*f*
Chicano English 153
China 51, 96
Chinese languages/dialects 109

Chinese Singaporeans, English, Mandarin, and Hokkien used by 83
Christianity, notion of the "family of man" 207
Circle Model 115
Clapham Junction 177
climate
    and differences between nations 226*n*.12
    of Eastern territories 208
codes, mixed 82–84
code-switching 35, 36, 37, 58, 135, 283
Coetzee-Van Rooy, Susan 7
collectivist societies
    inclusiveness 240
    showing respect in line with social norms 243
    social norms and expectations 236–237
Colloquial Singapore English (Singlish) 109, 111, 150, 163, 166 *see also* Singapore English
colonial cultural conceptualizations 7, 199–230
    CHILD metaphor 210
    CHILD/PUPIL metaphor 210
    COLONIZED identity 200
    COLONIZERS identity 200
    COLONIZER/TEACHER role 211
    cultural–conceptual framework during colonial period 224
    FAMILY concept 212
    IDENTITY OF CULTURE IS IDENTITY OF LOCATION 208
    impact of 199
    MORAL CONTAGION concept 213
    native populations lagging behind Western civilization notion 207
    NATIVE/PUPIL concept 211
    PARENT/ADULT/TEACHER concept 201, 210
    PARENT-CHILDREN concept 210, 225*n*.1
    PHYSICAL CONTAGION concept 213
    PURE versus IMPURE/POLLUTED dichotomy 213
    STATES ARE LOCATIONS metaphor 208

    UP VERSUS DOWN schema 210, 213
    US VERSUS THEM schema 200, 201, 208
colonialism, legacies of 13
coloniality 20
    of knowledge 19
    of present modes of learning 13
colonies 50
    cultural practices in 212–221
    English-medium education in 74
    metaphors for relation between colonizer and colonized 200
colonizers, distance between colonial subjects and 207
Colston, Edward 13
*comfort room* 289
Commonwealth 50
COMMUNITY IS FAMILY metaphor 235, 236
computer-mediated communication 84–88
congee (congee houses) 77
Congo, the, circular generosity in 236
contact languages, variationist research on 152
Contagious Diseases Acts (1864–1869) 212
Cook Islands 52, 53, 64*t*
Craigie, William 274
creoles 78, 272
Crystal, David 7, 18
cultural allusions 174, 176
cultural background 173
cultural lexicon of global Englishes 173–198
cultural memories 182
cultural metaphors 183–185
Cultural Orientation Model 150, 152
cultural pedagogical traditions 267
cultural practices, in colonies 212–221
cultural references 174
cultural taxonomy 179–183

da San Bartolomeo, Paolino 77
*dancing girl* 222
Das, Kamal 15
decolonization
    "decolonizing the mind" 19

of World Englishes 6, 11–28
  limitations of 16–20
  meaning of 21–24
  methodological issues 22–23
*Decolonizing (world) Englishes* (Saraceni and Jacob) 6
Denglish 40–41
Dhivehi/Divehi language 55, 56
Dhlomo, H. I. E. 125, 126
Dhlomo, R.R.R. 126
dialects 7, 31, 34
  attitudes of communities towards 164
  as a code 32
*Dialects of English* (De Gruyter) 2
dictionaries 177, 178, 182 *see also* Oxford English Dictionary
diglossic model 150
Divehi/Dhivehi language 55, 56
domestic workers 160
double-voicing 35
*Down Second Avenue* (Mphahlele) 123
*Drum* magazine 126, 131
*Dual Mandate, The* (Lugard) 199, 206, 211
Dubai 52, 96–99, 115–116
Dynamic Model of postcolonial Englishes 50, 60, 109, 115, 149–150, 167

East Africa 53, 206
  racial segregation in educational system 226n.14
*EastEnders* 162
ecology 74, 81
*Education of the South African native* (Jabavu) 136
Edwards, Hansen 163
Egypt 51, 52, 58, 64
EIL *see* English as an International Language
*Elfstedentocht* 175–176
elite use of English 47
emojis 43
English as a foreign language (EFL) 48, 60
English as a Lingua Franca (ELF) 3, 6, 8, 161, 251–269
  teaching about World Englishes and 253–258
  teaching World Englishes and 258–262
  in Uganda 59
English as a native language 267

English as a second language (ESL) 16, 48, 60
English as an International Language 154, 254
  fallacies 251–252
  pedagogical principles 257
English language education 254
English Medium of Instruction (EMI) courses, in Asia 257
English teachers, autonomy of 266
*English Today* 3, 177
*English World-Wide* (journal) 1
English(es)
  dominance of 18
  global expansion of 18
  history and geography of 18
  in heteroglossic informal digital communication 42
  inequalities between English and other languages 19
  non-educated forms of 62
  non-postcolonial 61
  second language varieties of 224
  spread of 14
  transplantation in new places 15
English(es) at the grassroots
  feature-based analyses of 2
  and grassroots Englishes 56–57
  interaction with other languages 7
  interactions in post-protectorates and at the grassroots 47–71
  internal variation and dialect contact 7
  research on 57–58
  as social practice 29–45
  in Uganda 58–59
Equatorial Guinea 78
eSwatini 63*t*
ethical issues 22–23
Eurasians, in Singapore 76
Expanding Circle countries 50, 149, 154
  EIL education in 257
  studies of innovation in language teacher education 259
Expanding Triangles Model 150
expressions 173

Facebook 38
"family of man" notion 207, 208, 209
Farenkia, Mulo 243

Fernando Po Creole English 78
fetishism 220
figure of speech 183
Filipino English 160
Filipinos 83
*Financial Times* 275
Finzel, Anna 7
Former Protectorates, uses of English in 63–65
forms of address 277
Forth Bridge 183
French
   in Cameroon radio show 233, 243
   in United Arab Emirates 104

Gambia 52, 63t
*General Explanations* (Murray) 272
generosity 234–235
genre 31, 33, 34
German 41
Ghana
   Asante courts 217
   *outdooring* traditional newborn baby welcoming ceremony 241
   welcoming a newborn baby in 241
Giles, Douglas G. 128
Global Data Model 179–183, 186–197
Global Englishes 252, 253
   cultural lexicon of 173–198
Global Englishes Language Teaching (GELT) 253
*Global Post* 175–176
globalization 3, 19
glocalized form of learning 23
grammar 16–20, 33
Grant, Charles 203–205
grassroots Englishes 47, 56–57 *see also* English(es) at the grassroots
Gulf English 107–108, 115, 161
Gulf states 52

half-castes 210, 222
*Handbook of Varieties of English* (Kortmann and Schneider) 2
*Handbook of World Englishes* (Kachru and Kachru) 2
HDB 277, 281f
heteroglossia 34–37
Hindi, *yaar* and *na* particles 80

Hinduism 202, 204
   *Garbhadan Sanskaar* insemination ceremony 216
   SEVEN STEPS in traditional wedding ceremonies 216
Hindus 215
Hinglish 56
Hitchcock, Alfred 183
HKE *see* Hong Kong English
homosexuality 212–220, 225n.6
   in Africa 215, 217–218
   in India 203, 214, 216–217, 219, 220
   legislation for 214–215, 220
   in Nigeria 214–215, 218, 219–220
   in Yoruba tradition 218–219
Hong Kong 39, 95, 96
   British English examinations 155
   Cantonese in 79, 111, 112
   Chinese-medium schools in 110
   English-medium schools in 75, 110
   ethnic background in 109
   first spoken languages in 112
   role of English in 7, 109, 111, 116
Hong Kong English 88, 109
   as outer circle variety 115
   *shroff* in 76
Hunt, Tristram 12, 14
hybridity of English(es) 29, 30, 35

Igbo 217–218
Imidushane people 128
Imperial British East Africa Company 53
"imperial hygiene" 213
imperialism, legacies of 13
*Imvo* (newspaper) 128, 129, 130, 133–134
indexical fields 151
indexicality principle 32
Indi, homosexuality legislation 214
India 199, 202–207
   accounts of immoral practices in 203
   British attitudes towards 202
   colonial history texts in 8
   colonial metaphoric system 204
   conceptualizations of reproduction in 217
   co-presence of English with Hindi and other Indian languages 39
   decolonizing Englishes in 20
   English-medium education in 74–75

homosexuality legislation 214, 219
  Macaulay's Minute on Education 74
  pre-colonial conceptualizations of
    homosexuality in 216
  promiscuity and prostitution in 203
  use of English in 16–17
Indian English 76, 80, 266
  words in *OED* 222
Indian languages 109
Indian South African English (SAfE) 122
Indians, Grant on 209
Indomania 202
Indonesia, adoption of an ELF-approach
    in 258
Indophobia 205
Indo-Portuguese 77
Inner Circle countries 20, 22, 51, 149, 154,
    155–156
  Englishes in 24
  geographic mobility in 157
  language teacher education in 259
  migration from 160
Instagram 166, 167
interactions across Englishes 48–49
interlocutors 231–232
International Corpus of English 80, 82
International Phonetic Alphabet (IPA) for
    world Englishes 281
International Singapore English 150
Internet 276
Iraq 51, 64
isiZulu 121, 122
Issa, Ahmad Al- 7

Jabavu, D.D.T. 135–137
Jabavu, J.T. 125
Jacob, Camille 6
James, Allan 6
Japan 156
  EIL education in 257
  influence on Japanese learners of
    English by Global Englishes
    course 260
Japan Exchange and Teaching program 156
Japanese English 257
*jeepney*, *OED* entry for 284
Johnson, Boris 12
Jones, William 202
Jordan 52, 64

Kachru, Braj 1, 14, 21
  six fallacies 264–265
Kachru, Yamuna 232
*Kanthapura* (Rao) 15
Kassim, Sumaya 12
Kenyan English 155
Khontsiwe, L.S. 131–132
kinship terms 243, 277
Kipling, J. Lockwood 223
Kiribati/Tuvalu, Republic of 64
Kirkpatrick, Andy 8
Kiswahili 53, 54
Korean learners of English 159
Koza, Elliott 134, 135
Kuwait 52, 63*t*

language contact 73
  linguistic structuring as types of 36
*Language Teaching* 253, 258
language(s)
  cognitive processing of 36
  as a holistic mix 29
  perception and attitudes 151
  place of 18–20
  and power 21
  as social semiotic 31
  variationist research on contact
    languages 152
League of Nations
  Article 22 of the covenant of the 201
  on gradual civilization of native
    populations 207–208
  mandates 47, 50, 63–65
  view of half-castes 210
  on witchcraft 220, 221
lects 34, 153
Lee Kuan Yew 111
Leimgruber, Jakob R. E. 7
lexical borrowings 42
lexicogrammar 34, 37
lexicon, types of 178–179
lexicophonology 34
lexicosemantics 34, 36
lexis 165
Lim, Lisa 7
linguicism 19
linguistic codes 36
  as formal entities 31
linguistic imperialism 19

*Linguistic Imperialism* (Phillipson) 18
linguistic studies, cross-cultural 182
linguistic variation 274
local cultural references 174
local English teachers (LETs), English learners' attitudes to 260–261
Local Singapore English 150
*Longman Dictionary of English Language and Culture* 177, 178, 182
Lopes, Duarte 288
Luganda 53
Luhlongwane, Nowadi 127–128

Mabandla, Mbovane 129
Macaulay, Lord, *Minute on Education* 74, 205
Magubelu, James 128
*Mahabharata* 216
Malawi 52, 63t
Malay 108, 112
Malaysian English 39
Malaysians, picking up accents after visiting countries 158
Maldives, the 47–48, 64
    English in 7, 55–56, 59–60
Malé 55, 59
male friendship 217
Malinowski, Bronisław 206–207
Mandarin 79, 96, 108, 110, 111
mandates 50–56
marriage 213
Marshall Islands, Republic of the 52, 65
masculinity 213
Matthews, Frieda 123, 124, 130–131
Matthews, Z.K. 123, 124, 129, 138, 139
Ma'ya 79
Mazibuko, Lindiwe 158
Mbaise, woman-to-woman marriages 218
Mbelle, Isaiah Budiwana 134–135
media
    role in community language change and speakers' patterns of language use 161–162
    traditional 162–165
medium of instruction 51, 57
Meierkord, Christiane 6–7
metaphors 7, 21
    cultural 183–185

ENGLISH IS A TRAVELLER metaphor 18, 24
representations of English 18
Micronesia, Federated States of 65
Middle East Gulf states, English as the lingua franca in 161
migration 159–161
*Minute on Indian Education* (Macaulay) 74, 205
mobility 157–166
Models of world Englishes 61–62
Moffat, Robert 201, 208
monogenetic theories of the human kind 209
monolingual discourse 38
Mozambique 50, 63t
Mufwene, Salikoko 16
Muir, Dr. Thomas 136
multilectalism 35
multilingualism 34, 36
    and the role of English in Singapore 108–110
    in South Africa 135
    in the United Arab Emirates 95–119
    use of English as a co-language in 38
multimedia in English language curricula 156
Murray, James 271
    model of the English lexicon 272–273
museums, decolonization of 12

Namibia 50, 52, 63t
Narada-smriti states 217
native English teachers (NESTs), English learners' attitudes to 260–261
native speaker model 263–264
nativization, of English 20, 24, 166
Nauru 65
Ndamase, Mangala 133
neo-colonialism 19
Nepal 64
Netherlands, the 175–176
Netherlands Antilles 78
*New Account of East-India and Persia, A* 77
*New English Dictionary on Historical Principles, A (NED)* 272
New Englishes, research on pragmatics of 232

New Orientalists 202–203
New Zealand, advertising campaign for beer 174
Nicaragua & Honduras 64
Niger-Congo languages 288, 289
Nigeria 16–17
  homosexuality in 214–215, 219
  Same Sex Marriage (Prohibition) Act 220
  witchcraft in 221
  *yan daudu* (gay community) 218
Nigerian English 79
Niue 65t
*Non-Sovereign Futures: French Caribbean Politics in the Wake of Disenchantment* (Bonilla) 22

Obasanjo, Olusegun 219
*Observations on the State of Society among the Asiatic Subjects of Great Britain* (Grant) 203
OED *see* Oxford English Dictionary
OED Labs 292
OED Online 285–291
  Advanced Search function 286–288
  timelines 288–289
official languages 49
  English as official language in Uganda 54
  in former protectorates 51, 52, 61
  in Hong Kong 96
  in Singapore 79
  in South Africa 121
  in United Arab Emirates 95, 96
Okri, Ben 282f
Oman 57–58
Omotoso, Kole 282
Onions, Charles Talbot 274
online language use 165–166
Onysko, Alexander 30, 36, 73, 184
Orunmila 218
other, the 200
otherness 208
Outer Circle countries 16, 50, 57, 149, 155
ownership, of English 16
*Oxford English Dictionary* 8, 56, 177 *see also* OED Online
  Burchfield Supplements 275
  current policies and practices on world Englishes in the 275–285

documenting World Englishes in 271–293
entries from India 222
entries from sub-Saharan Africa 222
future of world Englishes in the 291–292
historical context of 272–275
illustrative quotations for world Englishes 282–284
informative labels and usage notes 284–285
insights from individual *OED* entries 289–290
pronunciation models and audio pronunciations for world Englishes entries 281–282
Research Advisory Group 292
Researcher API 292
revision of 271
Singapore English particles 81
Southeast Asian terms in the 273
text visualizer 290–291, 292
word selection for world Englishes for 276–281
words recently added to 278–280t
*Oxford Handbook of World Englishes* (Filppula, Klemola and Sharma) 2

Pacific Islands 52–53
Pakistani English 49, 260
Palau, Republic of 65
Papiamentu 78
Papua New Guinea 65
particles 80–81
Peranakan English 75
phenotype borrowing 36
phenotype transfer/interference 37
Philippine English 80, 159, 277, 283, 289
Philippines, the 159, 160
Phillipson, Robert 18–19
Pichi 78
Pidgin/Pijin 53, 79, 272
pitch 79
Plaatje, Sol 126, 132, 134
Playfair, John 202
polygamy 203, 225n.6
polygenetic theories 209
Polzenhagen, Frank 7

*Postcolonial English: Varieties Around the World* (Schneider) 16
postcolonial English(es) 224, 231, 232
    Dynamic Model of 50, 60, 109, 115, 149–150, 167
postcolonialism
    impact on the English language 221–224
    social interaction in postcolonial societies 233–235
post-protectorates 47, 50–56
Progressivism 125
promiscuity 203
pronunciation
    of BATH- and TRAP-class words 158
    of the GOOSE vowel 49
    models and audio pronunciations for world Englishes entries in OED 281–282
    in speakers of Colored South African English 62
prostitution 203, 212, 213, 225n.6
Protected States 50–56, 63–65
*pulutan*, Filipino food custom 284, 285f
*Punch* 183
Putonghua 96, 110

Qatar 63t

radio show, Cameroon *see* Cameroon *Happy Birthday* radio program
Rahbari, Sharareh 7
Rao, Raja 14, 15
*Recollections* (Matthew) 123
*Record of Rites* 77
register 31, 32–33, 34
Renge, Manyaki 135
repertoire 153
Reynolds, Umhlali 130
Rhodes, Cecil 12, 13
Rig Veda ancient text 216
Rojak 39–40
*Routledge Handbook of World Englishes* (Kirkpatrick) 2
*Routledge Studies in World Englishes* 2
Rushdie, Salman 15
Rwanda 50, 63t

Salazar, Danica 8
same sex marriage 220

same-sex friendships/relationships 216, 218
Samoa 65
Samoan English 53
Sanskrit 202, 217, 225n.2
Saraceni, Mario 6
Saramaccan 78
*Sarong Party Girls* (Tan) 290–291
Schneider, Edgar 16
Second Language Acquisition 159
semilingualism 136
Sentso, Dyke H. 131
Serbian, and English 41–42
Serblish/Anglosrpski 41–42
sexuality 212–220
*Shetland Dialect, The* 3
shopping 176
*shroff*, use in Asian Englishes 76
Siemund, Peter 7
Simpson, John 275
Singapore 75–76, 154
    American and British film and television programs in 162
    education system and standard British English in 155
    effect of UK and US travel on Singaporeans 158–159
    English and Mandarin bilingualism in 114
    English as language of instruction in 110
    ethnic distribution in 108
    expatriate children attending local schools in 156
    Filipino maids in 160
    Hokkien as the Chinese intra-ethnic lingua franca 79
    home language use of vernaculars in 111–112
    language policy in 111
    language use in different generations in 114, 150
    Malay in 114
    Mandarin in 111, 114
    media consumption habits 164–165
    migration to 160
    multilingualism in 95–96, 108–110
    postvocalic /r/ in 162, 163
    role of English in 7, 109, 111

social media and online language use in 166
South Asia immigrants and Tamil Indian community in 160
Speak Good English Movement 111
Speak Mandarin Campaign 111
Tamil in 114
Voices of Children in Singapore project 158, 160–161
Xiao Mei Mei ("younger sister") 166, 167
Singapore English 39, 109, 150, 155, 291
see also Colloquial Singapore English (Singlish)
analysis of 152
Corpus of Singapore English Messages (CoSEM) 167–168
High or acrolectal variety 150
as outer circle variety 115
tapped/trilled /r/ in 160
*toh* in 166
Singlish *see* Singapore English
Sinitic languages 7, 79
*sisig*, (Filipino dish) 284
siSwati-English bilingualism 52
*skedonk*, OED entry for 281, 282f
social communication 38
social interactions, in postcolonial societies 233–235
social media 165–166
social practice, Englishes as 6, 29–45
social practice dialect 34
social semiotic modes 31, 32
sociolinguistics 4, 21, 47, 150, 152, 167
sodomy 214
Solomon Islands 53, 65
Somalia 63t
Sotadic Zone 215
South Africa
African languages in 136–137, 138, 139
attitudes of indigenous black community towards English in 123–126
attitudes towards Afrikaans 139
decolonizing Englishes in 20
education in 129–130
English, Afrikaans and other languages in 7
English language attitudes in 121–147

German treatment of native people in 130
interactions of Englishes of 49
interpretation at events and translation of documents 134
language policy in 123
literacy in home languages 135–136
mission-educated elite 124, 125
"Rhodes Must Fall" movement in 12
role of English in the colonization of 122
use of African languages as media of instruction in 138
use of English in education in 124
varieties of English in 122
Western and African medicine in 131
South African English 281
cultural metaphors 184
South Africans Improvement Society 132
South Asia 16–17, 103
South Yemen 64
Speak Good English Movement 155
Speak Mandarin Campaign 110
spirituality 222
Spolsky, Bernard 19
spread of English language 18, 24, 74
Sri Lanka (formerly Ceylon) 55
Standard British English 155
Standard Singapore English 150
Stanford, Walter 135
Starr, Rebecca Lurie 7
stress 79
sub-Saharan Africa 199
attitudes towards traditional African belief systems 206–207
role and position of the colonizer in 206
texts of the colonial history in 8
words in *OED* from 222
Sudan 63t
Surinam 78

Tagalog 40, 83
Taglish 40–41, 83
Taiwanese students, influence of World Englishes-informed English language course on 259
Tamil 108, 112
Tamil Indian Singaporeans 160
variation of English /r/ among 153

Tamlish 56
Tan, Cheryl Liu-Lien 290–291
Tanzania (formerly Tanganyika) 52, 63*t*, 210
taxonomy 179–183
Teaching English as a Foreign Language 154, 155
teaching World Englishes 251–252
   curriculum innovation within classrooms 259
*teapoy* 224
tenor 183, 184
Thailand, English learners' attitudes to NESTs and LETs 260–261
"Third World" varieties of English 14
*39 Steps, The* (Hitchcock) 183
Three Circles of English model 1, 149
Tibet 52, 64
TOEFL 155
Togo 208
Tokelau 65
tone 78–79
Tonga 50, 53, 65
tourism
   in the Maldives 60
   in Uganda 59
tourist English 58
trade colonies 57
tramline method of classification 274
translanguaging 35
transnational dialect contact 149–172
   impact on language variation 168
   in online language use 165
   sources of 153–166
transnational mobility 157–166
Trevor-Roper, Hugh 206
tricodal/trimodal model of Englishes 6, 31–34, 36
   basic categories 31–32
   data analysis 37–42
trust territories 50–56
Tutelage 125
Tweedledum and Tweedledee 177
Twitter 165, 166
typology, research on world Englishes 77–81

UAE English 107
Uganda 7, 47–48, 53–54, 58–59, 63*t*
Ugandan English 48
Ugandan Indian English 48
UK English *see* British English
United Arab Emirates (UAE) 63*t*, 95
   attitudes towards English in 106*t*, 107
   English as medium of instruction in 97, 98, 99
   English teaching at secondary level in 97–98
   English-speaking university students in 161
   language attitudes and repertoires in 99–108
   language policy in 98–99, 110
   languages spoken in 96, 101–104
   role of English in 7, 96–97
   South Asian citizens in the 103
   use of French in 104
United Kingdom 264
   attitude towards "her colonies" 200
   media 164
United Nations 50
United Nations Trust Territories 47, 50
   English in 51–52, 63–65
   former 52–53, 60–62
universe of discourse 179
Urban Dictionary 182
US English *see* American English

Van Rooy, Bertus 7
*Varieties of English Around the World* (Benjamins) 2
Verwoerd, H.F. 125
Victoria and Albert Museum 12
vocabularies of Englishes 7
vowels
   bath and trap in American English 164
   cot-caught-court 164–165
*Voyage to the East Indies, A* 77

*Webster's Dictionary* 274
wedding ceremonies, SEVEN STEPS in traditional Hindu 216
Weiner, Edmund 275
West Africa, pre-colonial conceptualizations of homosexuality in 216
WhatsApp 166, 167

white South Africans 122, 137
Wilhelm, Das 217
witchcraft 220–221
Wolf, Hans-Georg 7
World Englishes
  contact issues in 73–74
  de-silencing Englishes users within 21–23
  English as a lingua franca and teaching about 8, 251–269
  future research 4–6
  language variation investigations 151–153
  models of 60–61, 149
  need for cultural lexicons across 176–177
  in the *OED* 271–272, 275–285
  research in 1, 2, 6–8
  and transnational dialect contact 153–166
  usage of 81–88
  and varieties of English 1–4
*World Englishes* (Hopkins, Decker and McKenny) 2
*World Englishes* (journal) 1, 53
*World Englishes* (Saraceni et al.) 2
World War I (WWI) 50
World War II (WWII) 50, 54, 55, 532
writers
  in postcolonial settings 14
  writing back to the center of the former empire 15

Xosa 135, 137

Yoruba, and homosexuality 218–219

Zambia 52, 63*t*
Zimbabwe 52, 63*t*
Zulu students 234

www.ingramcontent.com/pod-product-compliance
Lightning Source LLC
Chambersburg PA
CBHW052149300426
44115CB00011B/1585